石油教材出版基金资助项目

石油高等院校特色规划教材

Oil Well Logging

石 油 测 井
（英汉对照）

高　辉　主编

石油工业出版社

内 容 提 要

本书基于大量国内外测井教材、培训资料和论文成果编写而成。内容包括了石油测井技术领域的基本知识，以及适合于硕士、博士研究生和专业技术人员的新技术和新方法。本书涉及油气储层测井评价的基本概念、基础理论和井下环境，以定性分析和定量解释为主线将各个章节有效衔接，涵盖了目前主要的测井技术。

本书既可作为我国石油、地质类院校相关专业本科留学生的教学用书，也可供从事现场工作的科研人员参考。

图书在版编目（CIP）数据

石油测井：英汉对照 / 高辉主编．—北京：石油工业出版社，2023.6
石油高等院校特色规划教材
ISBN 978-7-5183-6049-9

Ⅰ．①石… Ⅱ．①高… Ⅲ．①油气测井 - 高等学校 - 教材 - 英、汉 Ⅳ．①TE151

中国国家版本馆 CIP 数据核字（2023）第 106811 号

出版发行：石油工业出版社
（北京市朝阳区安定门外安华里 2 区 1 号楼 100011）
网　　址：www.petropub.com
编辑部：（010）64251362
图书营销中心：（010）64523633
经　　销：全国新华书店
排　　版：三河市聚拓图文制作有限公司
印　　刷：北京中石油彩色印刷有限责任公司

2023 年 6 月第 1 版　2023 年 6 月第 1 次印刷
787 毫米 ×1092 毫米　开本：1/16　印张：15
字数：420 千字

定价：40.00 元
（如发现印装质量问题，我社图书营销中心负责调换）
版权所有，翻印必究

前　言

西安石油大学于2010年为石油工程专业本科生（留学生）首次开设石油测井（Oil Well Logging）课程，课时为36学时，后来增加到48学时。2015年石油与天然气工程学科的硕士研究生（留学生）开始学习现代测井技术（Advanced Well logging）课程，课时为36学时。至今，留学生的测井教学已经走过了十多个年头，在此期间，先后有5名教师投入到课程的教学过程中，课程组不断讨论完善教学内容和方法，发现对于留学生的测井课程教学，应该抓住如下几个要点：（1）本科生的课程内容应该浅显易懂，硕士生的课程多讲解实例分析；（2）挖掘留学生善于交流的特点，课堂讨论有利于提高讲授效果；（3）多给予留学生独立思考和查阅文献的时间与空间，让他们带着问题上课，有助于活跃课堂氛围。

同时，"一带一路"倡议让我国各大石油企业"走出去"的步伐不断加快、与国外企业合作的深度和广度不断扩大，相关从事测井服务和油气田勘探开发的专业技术人员对于中英文对照的测井读本的渴望也越来越强烈。本书正是在这两大背景下应运而生，于2017年春开始着手编写。

本书编写人员先后查阅了大量的国内外测井教材、培训资料和相关论文，在前人的基础上编写成本书。本书具备以下几个特点：

（1）内容丰富，包括了适用于本科生和一般技术人员浅显易懂的基本知识，以及适合于硕士、博士研究生和专业技术人员的新技术和新方法。

（2）从油气储层测井评价的基本概念、基础理论和井下环境入手，以定性分析和定量解释为主线，将各个章节有效衔接，成为一个有机的整体，涵盖了目前主要的测井技术。

（3）既注重理论内容学习，又在每个章节中加入了实例，使理论与实践充分结合，注重加强学生的工程训练，激发学生独立思考、自主学习的潜能，培养学生分析问题、解决实际问题的能力。

全书由西安石油大学石油测井课程组教师编写。编写人员分工如下：高辉编写第一章、第三章和第八章；王妍编写第二章和第十章；杨懿编写第四章、第五章和第六章；王琛编写第七章和第九章；屈乐编写第十一章和第十二章；李腾参与了本书英文部分的编写与修订工作；博士生何梦卿，硕士生张晓、徐润滋、宋星雷、王亚兰、张喆参与了本书的文字整理、绘图等工作。全书由高辉担任主编并统稿。

感谢本书参考文献的作者和译者，以及在本书编写过程中给予关心的石油工程学院、研究生院、国际教育学院的领导和老师。限于水平和时间，书中难免有些不妥之处，敬请各位专家和读者给予指正，以便不断改进和完善。

编者
2023年2月

目 录

1 Review of Basic Concepts — 1
基本概念回顾 — 1

- 1.1 Overview — 1
  - 概述 — 1
- 1.2 Logging Techniques — 4
  - 测井技术 — 4
- 1.3 Determination of Parameters — 8
  - 参数确定 — 8
- 1.4 Borehole Environment — 19
  - 井眼环境 — 19
- Exercises — 23
- 课后练习 — 23

2 Resistivity Basic and Spontaneous Potential — 25
电阻率基本原理与自然电位测井 — 25

- 2.1 Introduction — 25
  - 引言 — 25
- 2.2 The Concept of Bulk Resistivity — 26
  - 体积电阻率的概念 — 26
- 2.3 Electrical Properties of Sand stone and Brine — 28
  - 砂岩盐水的电学性质 — 28
- 2.4 Spontaneous Potential — 31
  - 自然电位测井 — 31
- 2.5 Log Examples of the SP — 38
  - 自然电位测井实例 — 38
- Exercises — 40
- 课后练习 — 40

3 Fundamentals of Electrical Logging Interpretation 42
电法测井解释基础 42

3.1 Introduction 42
　　引言 42

3.2 Early Electrical Logging Interpretation 43
　　早期的测井解释 43

3.3 Empirical Approaches to Interpretation 45
　　基于实验的定量解释方法 45

3.4 A Review of Electrostatics 48
　　静电场知识回顾 48

3.5 Principle of Resistivity Logging 50
　　电阻率测井原理 50

Exercises 52
课后练习 52

4 Electrode Devices 53
电极测井系列 53

4.1 Introduction 53
　　引言 53

4.2 Unfocused Devices：The Short Normal 53
　　未聚焦的普通电阻率：短电位电极系 53

4.3 Focused Devices 56
　　聚焦测井系列 56

4.4 Microelectrode Devices 70
　　微电阻率测井设备 70

Exercises 73
课后练习 73

5 Induction Devices 75
感应测井 75

5.1 Introduction 75
　　引言 75

	5.2	Review of Magnetostatics and Induction	76
		电磁感应知识回顾	76
	5.3	The Two-coil Induction Devices	82
		双线圈系感应测井	82
	5.4	Geometric Factor for the Two-coil Sonde	84
		双线圈系几何因子	84
	5.5	Focusing the Two-coil Sonde	91
		双线圈系感应测井仪聚焦特性	91
	5.6	Induction Log Example	93
		感应测井曲线实例	93
	Exercises		94
	课后练习		94

6 Sonic Log — 97
声波测井 — 97

	6.1	Acoustic Signals	98
		声音信号	98
	6.2	Acoustic Waves	99
		声波	99
	6.3	Elastic Properties of Rocks	102
		岩石的弹性性质	102
	6.4	Sound Wave Velocities	104
		声波速度	104
	6.5	Sound Wave Propagation, Reflection and Refraction	105
		声波传播、反射和折射	105
	6.6	Measurement of the Speed of Sound	107
		测量声速	107
	6.7	Applications	115
		应用	115
	Exercises		120
	课后练习		120

7 Borehole Compensated Sonic Logging
补偿声波测井 ... 121
... 121

7.1 Measuring Point ... 122
测量点 ... 122

7.2 Depth of Investigation ... 123
探测深度 ... 123

7.3 Vertical Resolution ... 124
垂向分辨率 ... 124

7.4 Units of Measurement ... 124
测量单位 ... 124

7.5 Factors Influencing the Measurement ... 125
影响测量的因素 ... 125

7.6 Interpretation ... 135
测井解释 ... 135

7.7 Environmental and Other Effects ... 141
环境及其他 ... 141

Exercises ... 147
课后练习 ... 147

8 The Gamma Ray Log
自然伽马测井 ... 149
... 149

8.1 Generalities ... 149
概述 ... 149

8.2 Principle of Gamma-ray Log ... 151
自然伽马放射性测井原理 ... 151

8.3 Simple Gamma Ray Tools ... 154
自然伽马测井仪器 ... 154

8.4 Application of Simple Gamma Ray Log ... 155
自然伽马射线测井的应用 ... 155

Exercises ... 159
课后练习 ... 159

9 The Density Log   161
密度测井   161

9.1 Generalities   161
概述   161

9.2 Principles of Measurement   163
密度测井原理   163

9.3 Density Logging Instrument   163
密度测井仪器   163

9.4 Application of Density Log   165
密度测井应用   165

Exercises   174
课后练习   174

10 The Neutron Log   176
中子测井   176

10.1 Generalities   176
概述   176

10.2 Principles of Measurement   178
中子测井测量原理   178

10.3 Neutron Logging Tools   179
中子测井仪器   179

10.4 Application of Neutron Log   181
中子测井的用途   181

Exercises   193
课后练习   193

11 The Nuclear Magnetic Resonance Log   194
核磁共振测井   194

11.1 Generalities   194
概述   194

11.2 Principle of NMR Physics   194
核磁共振的原理   194

11.3　Logging Tools of NMR　197
　　　核磁共振测井仪　197

11.4　Qualitative Uses of NMR　199
　　　核磁共振测井的定量评价　199

Exercises　205
课后练习　205

12　The Electrical Imaging Log　207
　　　电成像测井　207

12.1　Generalities　207
　　　概述　207

12.2　Electrical Imaging Tools　208
　　　电成像测井仪　208

12.3　Electrical Image Sedimentary Interpretation　211
　　　电成像测井沉积解释　211

12.4　Electrical Image Structural Interpretation　216
　　　电成像测井构造解释　216

12.5　Quantitative Uses of Electrical Images　222
　　　电成像测井的定量评价　222

Exercises　224
课后练习　224

References　226
参考文献　226

1 Review of Basic Concepts
基本概念回顾

1.1 Overview
概述

1.1.1 The Definition of Well Logging
测井的定义

Well logging in the petroleum industry refers to "an applied technology to record the changes of the physical properties of the formation with the depth by a measuring apparatus in the wellbore." The logging we shall be discussing in this book, sometimes referred to "wireline logging", are obtained by means of measuring equipment (logging tools) lowered on cable (wireline) into the well. Measurements are transmitted up the cable (which contains one or several conductors) to a surface laboratory or computer unit. The recording of this information on film or paper constitutes the well-log. Logging data may also be recorded on magnetic tape. By using these large amounts of logging data, each logging curve records a different property of the rocks penetrated by the well. Wireline logging is performed after an interruption (or the termination) of drilling activity, and parameters acquisition method is different from those obtained in "drilling-logs" (of such things as drilling-rate, mud-loss, torque, etc.) and "mud-logs"(drilling mud salinity, pH, mud-weight, etc.) during drilling operations.

石油工业中的测井是指"使用专用仪器记录井内随深度变化的岩层物理性质的一门应用技术"。本书中将要讨论的测井，有时称为电缆测井，其记录是通过用钢丝电缆（测井电缆）下放至井内的测量设备（测井工具）获得的。测量数据通过电缆（包含一根或几根导体）传输到地面实验室或计算机单元。将这些信息记录在胶片或者纸上，就构成了测井曲线。测井数据也可以记录在磁带上。通过使用这些大量的测井数据，每条测井曲线都记录了所钻岩石的不同性质。电缆测井是在钻井作业中断（或终止）后进行的，其参数获取方式不同于钻井过程中的"钻测井"（钻速、钻井液漏失、扭矩等）和"钻井液录井"（钻井液矿化度、pH 值，钻井液密度等）。

1.1.2 The Importance of Well Logging
测井的重要性

Geology is the study of the rocks making up the Earth's crust. The field of geology that is of most importance to the oil industry is sedimentology, for it is in certain sedimentary environments that hydrocarbons are formed. Finding oil reservoirs entails a precise and detailed study of the composition, texture and structure of the rocks, the colour of the constituents, and identification of any traces of animal and plant organisms. This enables the geologists: to identify the physical, chemical and biological conditions prevalent at the time of deposition; and to describe the transformations that the sedimentary series has undergone since deposition. They must also consider the organisation of the different strata into series, and their possible deformation by faulting, folding, and so on. The geologist depends on rock samples for this basic information. These rock samples usually come from three sources: on the surface, these are cut from rock outcrops; subsurface, these samples are taken from cuttings and cores which obtained while drilling.

地质学是一门研究构成地壳的岩石的学科。对石油工业最重要的地质学领域是沉积学，因为碳氢化合物是在特定沉积环境中形成的。寻找油藏就需要精确而详细地研究岩石的组成、结构和构造，成分的颜色，并识别任何动植物的痕迹。这使地质学家能够：①确定沉积时普遍存在的物理、化学和生物条件；②描述沉积序列自沉积以来发生的转变。他们还须考虑不同地层的地层序列的组合方式，以及它们可能发生的断层、褶皱等变形。地质学家通过岩石样品获取这种基本信息。这些岩石样品通常有三个来源：在地面，这些岩样取自野外露头；在地下，这些岩样取自钻井时获取的岩屑和岩心。

Cuttings (the fragments of rock flushed to surface during drilling) are the principle source of subsurface sampling. However, the reconstruction of a lithological sequence in terms of thickness and composition, from the cuttings that have undergone mixing, leaching, and general contamination, during their transportation by the drilling-mud to the surface, cannot always be performed with confidence. Where mud circulation is lost, the analysis of whole sections of formation is precluded by the total absence of cuttings. In addition, the smallness of this kind of rock sample does not allow all the desired tests to be performed. Another way to obtain rock samples underground is from cores, it obtained while drilling (using a core-barrel), by virtue of their size and continuity, can permit a thorough geological analysis over a chosen interval. However, for economical and technical reasons, this form of coring is not common practice and is restricted to certain drilling conditions and types of formation.

岩屑（在钻井过程中冲到地表的岩石碎片）是地下取样的主要来源。然而，在岩屑被钻井液携带至地表的过程中，受到混合、过滤和普遍污染的影响，根据厚度和组分来重建岩性序列并不是可靠的。在钻井液漏失的情况下，由于完全没有岩屑，无法对整个地层进行分析。此外，这种小尺寸的岩石样本并不能满足所有实验的需求。另一种获取地下岩样的方式是从岩心中获得的，是在钻井（使用岩心筒）时获得的，由于岩心尺寸合适且连续，可在选定区间内进行完整的地质分析。然而，由于经济和技术原因，这种取心形式并不常见，且仅限于特定钻井条件和地层类型。

As a result of these limitations, it is quite possible that the geologist may find rock samples with poor quality, missing or non-representative. Consequently, fundamental questions about oil exploration may not be answered:

(1) Has a potential reservoir structure been located?

(2) If so, is it oil bearing?

(3) Can it be inferred the presence of a nearby reservoir?

An alternative and very effective approach to this problem is to measure on site by running well-logs. In this way, the parameters related to porosity, lithology, hydrocarbons, and other rock properties can be obtained.

由于这些局限性，地质学家很可能会发现质量较差、缺失或不具代表性的岩石样品。因此，有关石油勘探的基本问题可能无法得到回答：

（1）是否确定了潜在的储层构造？

（2）如果有，是否含油？

（3）可否推断出附近的油藏？

解决这一问题的另一种非常有效的方法是借助测井曲线进行现场测量。通过这种方法，可以获得与孔隙度、岩性、碳氢化合物和其他岩石性质有关的参数。

The first well-log, a measurement of electrical resistivity, devised by Marcel Schlumberger and Conrad Schlumberger, was run in September 1927 in Pechelbronn (France). They called this, with great foresight, "electrical coring". Since then, the advances in science and technology have led to the development of a vast range of highly sophisticated measuring techniques and equipment. Well-log measurements have widely applications in the evaluation of the porosities, saturations of reservoir rocks and depth correlations. More recently, however, geologists have realized that logging data is very important for studying the formation and obtaining its information. Through logging it can be measured a number of physical parameters related to both the geological and petrophysical properties of the strata that have been penetrated; properties which are conventionally studied in the laboratory from rock-samples. In addition, logs can reflect the fluid properties in the pores of the reservoir rocks.

1927年9月，马塞尔·斯伦贝谢和康拉德·斯伦贝谢在佩彻布朗（法国）进行了第一次测井，即电阻率测井。他们极富远见地称之为"电取心"。从那时起，科学和技术的进步导致了一系列高度复杂的测量技术和设备的发展。测井测量在储层岩石孔隙度、饱和度和深度对比方面有着广泛的应用。然而，近年来地质学家认识到测井数据对于研究地层和获取地层信息非常重要。通过测井，可以测量与已钻透地层的地质及岩石物理性质有关的一些物性参数，这些参数通常是在实验室通过岩心样品来研究的。此外，测井曲线还可以反映储层岩石孔隙中流体的性质。

Log data constitute a "carte" of the rock; the physical characteristics they represent are the consequences of physical, chemical and biological (particularly geographical and climatic...) conditions prevalent during deposition; and its evolution during the course of geological history. The descriptions of the various logging techniques contained in this book will show that such relationships do indeed exist, and it can be assumed: a significant change in geological characteristic will generally manifest itself through rock physical parameter which can be detected by one or more logs; and change in log response indicates a change in one geological parameter.

测井数据构成了岩石的"名片",它们所代表的物理特征是沉积过程中普遍存在的物理、化学和生物(特别是地理和气候……)条件的结果,及其在地质历史过程中的演变。本书中对各种测井技术的描述将表明,这种关系确实存在,且可以假设:①地质特征的显著变化通常会通过岩石的物理参数表现出来,这些物理参数可以被一种或多种测井方法检测到;②测井响应的变化指示了地质参数的变化。

1.2 Logging Techniques
测井技术

1.2.1 Classification of Log Measurements
测井测量方法分类

In this book we are confining our interest to logs that are used for the evaluation of the rock and its fluid content. This will include both open-hole and cased-hole measurements.

在本书中,我们的关注点仅限于用于评估岩石及其流体含量的测井曲线,包括裸眼井测井和套管井测井。

These measurements grouped into two broad categories: those arising from natural (or spontaneous) phenomena, and those arising from induced phenomena. The first group simply employs a suitable detector to obtain the measurement; the second group requires an appropriate type of emitter to "excite" a particular response in the formation, in addition to a detection system.

测井测量方法可分为两大类:自然(或自发)现象对应的测量方法和诱导现象对应的测量方法。第一类仅仅使用一个合适的检测器来获得测量结果;第二类除了需要使用检测系统外,还需要一个合适类型的发射器来"激发"地层中的特定响应。

1.2.2 Natural Phenomena
自然现象

The following is a list of logging techniques corresponding to natural phenomena:

(1) Natural gamma radioactivity, which can be measured as a total gamma-ray count-rate, as in the classical gamma-ray log; and as count-rates corresponding to selected energy bands, as in the natural gamma-ray spectrometry log (NGS).

(2) Spontaneous potential: the S.P. log.

(3) Formation temperature: the temperature log.

(4) Hole-diameter: the caliper log, which in fact is a measurement strongly related to the mechanical or chemical properties of the rock.

(5) Inclination of the hole: the deviation log, which measures both the angle of the hole from the vertical, and its direction (or azimuth).

以下是与自然现象相对应的测井技术列表：

（1）自然伽马放射性：在自然伽马测井中可以测量总伽马射线计数率，在自然伽马能谱测井（NGS）中可以测量与所选定能带对应的计数率。

（2）自然电位：自然电位测井。

（3）地层温度：温度测井。

（4）井径：井径测井，实际上是一种与岩石力学或化学性质密切相关的测量方法。

（5）井眼倾斜度：井斜测井，可以测量井眼的井斜角度和方位（或方位角）。

1.2.3 Physical Properties Measured by Inducing Responses from the Formation
通过诱导地层响应测量的物理特性

1.2.3.1 Electrical Measurements
电法测量

Electrical measuring systems include the use of electronic systems and the use of induction coils. Each system can run different logging methods, as listed below:

Using electrode system: electrical survey (ES), laterolog (LL), micro-log (ML), micro-laterolog (MLL), spherically focused log (SFL), micro-spherically focused log (MSFL), high-resolution dipmeter (HDT).

Using inductive coils: induction log (IL).

电法测量系统包括电子系统和感应线圈。每种系统可以运行不同的测井方法，如下所列：

采用电极系统：普通电阻率测井（ES）、侧向测井（LL）、微电极系测井（ML）、微侧向测井（MLL）、球形聚焦测井（SFL）、微球形聚焦测井（MSFL），以及高分辨率地层倾角测井（HDT）。

采用感应线圈：感应测井（IL）。

1.2.3.2 Nuclear Measurements
核法测量

By the irradiation of the formation with gamma rays or neutrons, the density, photoelectric absorption coefficient, and the hydrogen index of the layer are measured.

1) Density

Gamma rays are emitted from a source. The Compton scattered gamma rays returning from the formation are detected: formation density (FDC).

2) Photoelectric absorption coefficient (related to average atomic number)

A low-energy gamma ray phenomenon, the lithology-density log (LDT) is an improvement and extension of the density log. In addition to recording the density of the rock, it also measures the photoelectric absorption coefficient of the formation, which is related to the lithology. During logging, the downhole instrument records the higher and lower energy parts of the scattered gamma rays. The intensity of scattered gamma rays in the high energy part depends on the density. The low energy part is mainly related to lithology, but also related to density. Photoelectric absorption coefficient can be obtained after processing.

3) Hydrogen index

The formation is continuously bombarded by high energy neutrons, which are slowed by successive elastic collisions with atomic nuclei, particularly those of hydrogen. There are several techniques in use, involving the detection of: neutron-thermal neutron logging (CNL, NT) (thermal neutrons have been slowed down to thermal energy), neutron-gamma logging (N) (Gamma rays emitted when these thermal neutrons are captured by atomic nuclei), neutron-epithermal neutron logging (NE, SNP, and CNL) (epithermal neutrons, i.e. those neutrons not yet slowed down to thermal energy).

4) Macroscopic thermal neutron capture cross-section (Z)

High-energy neutrons are emitted in short bursts. The rate of decay of the thermal neutron population in the formation is measured between bursts. This is a neutron capture phenomenon [thermal neutron decay time (TDT) or neutron lifetime logging (NLL)].

5) Elemental composition

Gamma rays emitted from interactions between high energy neutrons and certain atomic nuclei are analyzed spectroscopically. There are three types of interaction important for induced gamma ray spectroscopy.

Fast neutron or inelastic interaction: fast neutron refers to the free neutron produced in the nuclear fission reaction. The kinetic energy of fast neutron decreases under the inelastic action, and the degree of action can be reflected by secondary gamma logging, secondary gamma spectrum logging (IGT, GST) and carbon-oxygen ratio logging.

Neutron capture: a nuclear reaction in which a nucleus collides with one or more neutrons to form a heavy nucleus. Because neutrons have no electric charge, they can enter the nucleus more easily than protons with a positive charge, which can be measured using captured gamma ray spectroscopy (GST, IGT), chlorine logs.

Activation logging (activation and subsequent decay of radioactive isotopes): Formation characteristics are determined by detecting activated gamma rays. Depending on the source of radiation used, activated neutrons can be determined by high-resolution spectroscopy (HRS).

6) Proton spin relaxation time

A pulsed DC magnetic field momentarily aligns the nuclear magnetic moments of the protons. After the pulse, the time required for the protons of the formation to stop processing about the Earth's magnetic field is measured. This spin relaxation time which can be measured by nuclear magnetic resonance log (NML) can be used to evaluate residual oil.

通过伽马射线或中子辐射地层，可测量地层的密度、光电吸收系数和氢指数。

1) 密度

伽马源放出伽马射线，经过地层返回的康普顿散射伽马射线被检测到，即：密度测井

（FDC）。

2）光电吸收系数（与平均原子序数有关）

岩性—密度测井（LDT）是密度测井的改进和推广，是一种低能伽马射线现象。除了记录岩石的密度，它还测量地层的光电吸收系数，而光电吸收系数和岩性有关。测井时，井下仪器记录散射伽马射线的高能部分和低能部分。高能部分的散射伽马射线强度取决于密度。低能部分主要与岩性有关，同时与密度有关。经处理后可得到光电吸收系数。

3）氢指数

地层被高能中子连续轰击，高能中子通过与原子核，特别是氢原子原子核的连续弹性碰撞而减速。在用的几种技术，包括：中子—热中子测井（CNL，NT）（热中子慢化到热能）、中子—伽马测井（N）（热中子被原子核俘获时放射出伽马射线）、中子—超热中子测井（NE，SNP，CNL）（超热中子还没有慢化到热中子）。

4）宏观热中子俘获截面（Z）

高能中子在短暴中释放。地层中热中子群的衰减速率是在爆发之间测量的，这是一种中子俘获现象［热中子衰减时间（TDT）或中子寿命测井（NLL）］。

5）元素组成

用能谱法分析高能中子与某些原子核相互作用发射出的伽马射线。有三种类型的相互作用对诱导伽马射线能谱很重要。

快中子或非弹性相互作用：快中子指在核裂变反应中产生的自由中子。在非弹性作用下，快中子动能降低，作用程度可以通过二次伽马测井、二次伽马能谱测井（IGT，GST）、碳氧比测井来反映。

中子俘获：一个原子核与一个或多个中子碰撞，形成重核的核反应。由于中子不带电荷，它们比带正电荷的质子更容易进入原子核，这可以通过俘获伽马射线光谱（GST，IGT）、氯测井测量。

活化测井（放射性同位素的活化和随后的衰变）：通过探测活化伽马射线来确定地层特征。根据所利用的射线源不同，可以用高分辨率能谱（HRS）确定活化的中子。

6）质子自旋弛豫时间

脉冲直流磁场对质子的核磁矩瞬时校准。脉冲之后，测量地层质子停止绕地球磁场运转所需的时间。核磁共振测井（NML）测量的自旋弛豫时间可用于评价剩余油。

1.2.3.3 Acoustic Measurements
声学测量

An acoustic signal is sent into the formation. We may measure:

(1) The velocity of the compressional wave and the shear wave (acoustic logging).

(2) The transit time from a surface gun to a downhole geophone (well shooting).

(3) The amplitude of a selected peak or trough in the acoustic wave-train arriving at a receiver. The compressional or shear-wave arrivals may be of interest (amplitude logging).

(4) The relative amplitudes of the various components of the wave-train, the configuration

of the wave-train [variable density logging (VDL), sonic waveform photography, well seismic (WST), borehole televiewer (BHTV)].

声波信号被发送到地层中，我们可以测量：
(1) 纵波速度和横波速度（声波测井，AC）。
(2) 从地面射孔枪到井下检波器的传输时间（地震测井，WST）。
(3) 到达接收器的声波列中选定的波峰或波谷的振幅（可能感兴趣的是纵波或横波的波至）（振幅测井，A）。
(4) 波列各分量的相对振幅，波列的构型［变密度测井（VDL）、声波波形测井、地震测井（WST）、声波井下电视（BHTV）］。

1.3　Determination of Parameters
　　　参数确定

1.3.1　Fluids
　　　　流体

The arrangement of the grains usually leaves spaces (pores and channels) which are filled with fluids: water, air, gas, oil, tar, etc. (Fig.1.1). Just how much fluid is contained in a rock depends on the space or porosity available.

颗粒的排列通常会留下空隙（孔隙和喉道），这些空隙被水、空气、天然气、油、沥青等流体充填（图1.1）。岩石中究竟含有多少流体，取决于可用的空间或孔隙度。

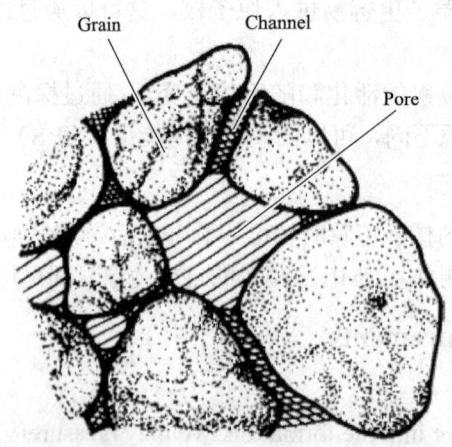

Fig.1.1　Interstitial spaces in a clastic rock (from Oberto et al.,1984)
图1.1　碎屑岩内颗粒间隙（据 Oberto 等，1984）

With the exception of water, these pore-fluids have one important property in common with the large majority of matrix minerals, they are poor electrical conductors. Water, on the other hand, conducts electricity by virtue of dissolved salts.

除了水以外，这些孔隙流体与大多数岩石骨架矿物有一个重要的共同性质，即它们都是弱导电体。另一方面，水通过溶解的盐来导电。

Therefore, the electrical properties of rocks are greatly affected by their water saturation. The quantity of water in the rock is a function of the porosity, and the extent to which that porosity is filled with water (as opposed to hydrocarbons). This explains why the resistivity of a formation is such an important log measurement. From the resistivity we can determine the percentage of water in the rock (provided we know the resistivity of the water itself). If we also know the porosity, we may deduce the percentage of hydrocarbons present (the hydrocarbon saturation).

因此，岩石的电性受其含水饱和度的影响较大。岩石中的含水量是孔隙度以及这些孔隙中充满水（而不是碳氢化合物）的程度的函数。这解释了为什么地层电阻率是测井测量中如此重要的一项。根据电阻率，我们可以确定岩石中水的百分比（前提是我们知道水本身的电阻率）。如果还知道孔隙度，我们就可以推断出碳氢化合物的百分比（烃饱和度）。

1.3.2 Porosity
孔隙度

Porosity is the fraction of the total volume of a rock that is not occupied by the solid constituents. There are several kinds of porosity:

孔隙度是岩石总体积中不被固体成分占据的部分。孔隙度分为以下几种：

1.3.2.1 Total Porosity ϕ_t
总孔隙度 ϕ_t

ϕ_t, affected by all the void spaces (pores, channels, fissures, vugs) between the solid components, The calculation formula is

总孔隙度 ϕ_t 受固体组分之间所有空隙空间（孔隙、喉道、裂缝、孔洞）的影响。计算公式为

$$\phi_t = \frac{V_t - V_s}{V_t} = \frac{V_p}{V_t} \tag{1.1}$$

Where, V_p is volume of all the empty spaces (generally occupied by oil, gas or water), m^3; V_s is volume of the solid materials, m^3; V_t is total volume of the rock, m^3.

式中，V_p 为空隙的总体积（通常由油、气或水充填），m^3；V_s 为固体物质的体积，m^3；V_t 为岩石的总体积，m^3。

We distinguish two components in the total porosity:
我们将总孔隙度分为两部分：

$$\phi_t = \phi_1 + \phi_2 \tag{1.2}$$

ϕ_1 is the primary porosity, which is intergranular pore or intercrystalline pore. It depends on the shape, size and arrangement of the solids, and it is the type of porosity encountered in clastic rocks. ϕ_2 is the secondary porosity, made up of vugs caused by dissolution of the matrix, and fissures or cracks caused by mechanical forces. It is a common feature of rocks of chemical or organic (biochemical) origin.

ϕ_1 是原生孔隙，是粒间孔或晶间孔。它取决于固体的形状、大小和排列，是碎屑岩中常见的孔隙类型。ϕ_2 是次生孔隙，由岩石骨架溶蚀所形成的孔洞和由机械作用形成的裂纹或裂缝组成。这是化学或有机（生物化学）成因岩石的共同特征。

1.3.2.2　Interconnected Porosity $\phi_{connect}$
　　　　连通孔隙度 $\phi_{connect}$

$\phi_{connect}$ is made up only of those spaces which are in communication. This may be considerably less than the total porosity. Consider pumice-stone for instance, where ϕ_t is of the order of 50%, but $\phi_{connect}$ is zero, because each pore-space is isolated from the others, there are no interconnecting channels.

连通孔隙由相互连通的孔隙空间构成。这可能比总孔隙度小得多。以浮石为例，其总孔隙度为50%，但其连通孔隙度为零，因为各个孔隙空间都是彼此孤立的，没有相互连接的通道。

1.3.2.3　Potential Porosity ϕ_{pot}
　　　　流动孔隙度 ϕ_{pot}

ϕ_{pot} is that part of the interconnected porosity in which the diameter of the connecting channels is large enough to permit fluid to flow (greater than 50μm for oil, 5μm for gas). ϕ_{pot} may in some cases be considerably smaller than $\phi_{connect}$. Clays or shales, for instance, have a very high connected porosity (40% ～ 50% when compacted, and as much as 90% for newly deposited muds). However, owing to their very small pores and channels, molecular attraction prevents fluid circulation.

流动孔隙度是指连通通道的直径足以允许流体流动（油大于50μm，气大于5μm）的连通孔隙的部分。在某些情况下，流动孔隙度通常小于连通孔隙度。例如，黏土或泥岩具有非常高的连通孔隙度（压实时为40%～50%，在新沉积的泥质中达到90%）。然而，由于其孔喉直径非常小，分子间的吸引力阻碍了流体流动。

1.3.2.4　Effective Porosity ϕ_e
　　　　有效孔隙度 ϕ_e

ϕ_e is a term used specifically in log analysis. It is the porosity that is accessible to free fluids, and excludes, therefore, non-connected porosity and the volume occupied by the clay-bound water or clay-hydration water (adsorbed water, hydration water of the exchange cations) surrounding the clay particles.

有效孔隙度（ϕ_e）是一个专门用于测井分析的术语。它是自由流体可以进入的孔隙度，因此不包括非连通孔隙度和黏土颗粒周围的黏土结合水或黏土矿物化合水（吸附水、交换阳离子的化合水）的体积。

N.B. Porosity is a dimensionless quantity, by definition a fraction or ratio. It is expressed either as a percentage (e.g.,30%), as a decimal (e.g.,0.30) or in porosity units (e.g.,30p.u.).

注：孔隙度是无量纲的量，根据定义孔隙度是一个分数或比例。它可以表示为百分数（如30%），也可以表示为十进制数（如0.30）或孔隙度单位（如30p.u.）。

The geological and sedimentological factors influencing the porosity of a rock will be discussed later in this book.

影响岩石孔隙度的地质因素和沉积因素将在本书后面讨论。

1.3.3 Resistivity and Conductivity 电阻率和电导率

The resistivity (R) of a substance is the measure of its opposition to the passage of electrical current. It is expressed in units of $\Omega \cdot m$. If a cube of material of sides measuring 1 meter, with a resistivity $R = 1\Omega \cdot m$ would have a resistance of 1Ω between opposite faces.

物质的电阻率（R）是其对电流通过的阻力的量度，单位是欧姆（$\Omega \cdot m$）。若一个边长为1m的立方体材料的电阻率$R = 1\Omega \cdot m$，则其相对面之间的电阻为1Ω。

The electrical conductivity (C) is the measure of the material's ability to conduct electricity. It is the inverse of the resistivity, and is usually expressed in units of milliohm/m (mΩ/m) or mS/m (millisiemens per meter).

电导率（C）是衡量材料导电能力的量度，为电阻率的倒数，通常以毫欧姆/米（mΩ/m）或毫西门子/米（mS/m）为单位。

$$C = 1000/R \tag{1.3}$$

There are two types of conductivity:

(1) Electronic conductivity is a property of solids such as graphite, metals (copper, silver, etc.), hematite, metal sulfides (pyrite, galena) etc.

(2) Electrolytic conductivity is a property of electrolyte solution. For instance, Dry rocks have extremely high resistivity. The conductivity of sedimentary rocks is produced by the electrolysis of water or a mixture of water and hydrocarbons which exists in the pores, and the water phase must be continuous to improve conductivity.

电导率可分为两种类型：

（1）电子电导率是固体如石墨、金属（铜、银等）、赤铁矿、金属硫化物（黄铁矿、方铅矿）等的一种特性。

（2）离子电导率是电解质溶液的一种特性。例如，干燥岩石电阻率极高。沉积岩的导电性是由孔隙中存在的水或水和碳氢化合物的混合物电解产生的，其中水相必须是连续的才能够提高导电性。

The resistivity of a rock depends on the following properties.

(1) The resistivity of the water in the pores: this will vary with the nature and concentration

of its dissolved salts.

(2) The quantity of water present: that is, the porosity and the saturation.

(3) Lithology: i.e. the nature and percentage of clays present, and traces of conductive minerals.

(4) The texture of the rock: i.e. distribution of pores, clays and conductive minerals.

(5) The temperature: it is a physical quantity that expresses hot and cold.

岩石的电阻率取决于以下几种性质。

（1）孔隙中水的电阻率：这将随其溶解盐的性质和浓度而变化。

（2）存在的水的含量：即孔隙度和饱和度。

（3）岩性：即存在的黏土的性质和比例，以及导电矿物的痕迹。

（4）岩石的结构：即孔隙、黏土和导电矿物的分布。

（5）温度：表示冷热程度的物理量。

Resistivity may be anisotropic by virtue of stratification (layering) in the rock, caused, for instance, by deposition of elongated or flat particles, oriented in the direction of a prevailing current. This creates preferential paths for current flow and fluid movement and electrical conductivity is not the same in all directions.

电阻率可能是各向异性的，这是由岩石的层理（分层）导致的，例如，是由细长或扁平颗粒在流体流动的主流方向上沉积造成的。这就形成了电流和流体运动的优先路径，而导电率在所有方向上都是不一样的。

Defined horizontal resistivity (R_H) in the direction of layering, and vertical resistivity (R_V) perpendicular to this.

定义地层成层方向的电阻率为水平电阻率（R_H），垂直于地层成层方向的电阻率为垂直电阻率（R_V）。

The anisotropy coefficient, λ, is:

各向异性系数 λ 为：

$$\lambda = (R_V / R_H)^{1/2} \tag{1.4}$$

This can vary between 1.0 and 2.5, with R_V generally larger than R_H. It is R_H that we measure the lateral logging and other resistivity tools (induction), whereas the classical electrical survey reads somewhere between R_H and R_V.

各向异性系数 λ 在 1.0～2.5 之间变化，R_V 一般大于 R_H。用侧向测井和其他电阻率工具（感应）测量 R_H，而传统电法测量读数在 R_H 和 R_V 之间。

The mean resistivity of an anisotropic formation is:

各向异性地层的平均电阻率为：

$$R = \sqrt{R_H R_V} \tag{1.5}$$

The anisotropy of a single uniform layer is microscopic anisotropy. When we talk of the overall characteristic of a sequence of thin resistive layers, this is heterogeneous anisotropy. In such a series, the current tends to flow more easily along the layers than across them, and this anisotropy will affect any tool reading resistivity over a volume of formation containing these fine layers.

单一均匀层的各向异性是微观各向异性。当我们讨论一系列薄层电阻层的整体特征时，这就是非均匀的各向异性。在这种序列中，电流更容易沿着层面流动，而不是穿过地层，这种各向异性会影响任何工具在包含这些薄地层的地层系列上读取电阻率。

Microscopic anisotropy occurs in clays, and mud cakes. In the second case, the resistivity measured through the mud cake perpendicular to the wall of the hole is higher than that parallel to the axis. This has an effect on the focused micro-resistivity tools (MLL, PML) which must be taken into account in their interpretation. The λ, and thickness, h_{mc} of anisotropy mud-cake is electrically equivalent to the λ, thickness, and h_{mc} of an isotropic mud-cake whose resistivity is equal to the average value.

微观各向异性出现于黏土和滤饼中。在第二种情况下，通过垂直于井壁的滤饼所测得的电阻率要高于平行于井眼轴线的电阻率。这对聚焦微电阻率工具（MLL，PML）有影响，在测井解释时必须加以考虑。各向异性滤饼的 λ、厚度 h_{mc} 依照电学特性可以等效为一个电阻率等于平均值的各向同性滤饼的 λ 和 h_{mc}。

Summarizing, what we call the true resistivity (R_t) of a formation is a resistivity dependent on the fluid content and the nature and configuration of the solid matrix.

总之，我们所说的地层真电阻率（R_t）是一个与流体含量、固体的岩石骨架的性质和结构有关的电阻率。

1.3.4 The Relationship between Resistivity and Salinity
电阻率与矿化度之间的关系

We have mentioned that the resistivity of an electrolyte depends on the concentration and type of dissolved salts. Referring to Fig.1.2, notice that the resistivity decreases as concentration increases, up to a certain maximum beyond which undissolved, and therefore non-conducting salts impede the passage of current-carrying ions.

我们已经提到电解质的电阻率主要取决于溶解盐的浓度和类型。如图 1.2 所示，电阻率随着浓度的增加而降低，当浓度达到某个最大值时，未溶解的非导电盐会阻止载流离子的通过。

The salinity is a measure of the concentration of dissolved salts. It can be expressed in several ways: μg/g of solution; g/liter of solvent; and g/liter of solution. The chart of Fig.1.3 permits easy conversion between these units. Sodium chloride (NaCl) is the most common salt contained in formation waters and drilling muds. It is customary to express the concentrations of other dissolved salts in terms of equivalent NaCl for evaluation of the resistivity of a solution. Fig.1.4 shows the multipliers (Dunlap coefficients) for conversion of some ionic concentrations to their NaCl equivalents. For a solution of mixed salts simply take the sum of the equivalent concentrations of each type of ion present.

矿化度是溶解盐浓度的量度，可以用以下几种方式表示：μg/g（溶液）；g/L（溶剂）；

g /L（溶液）。通过图 1.3 可将这些单位轻松转换。氯化钠（NaCl）是地层水和钻井液中最常见的盐。为了评价溶液的电阻率，通常用等效 NaCl 来表示其他溶解盐的浓度。图 1.4 显示了某些离子浓度转换为 NaCl 当量时的换算系数（邓拉普系数）。对于混合盐溶液，只需简单地将各类型离子的当量浓度相加即可。

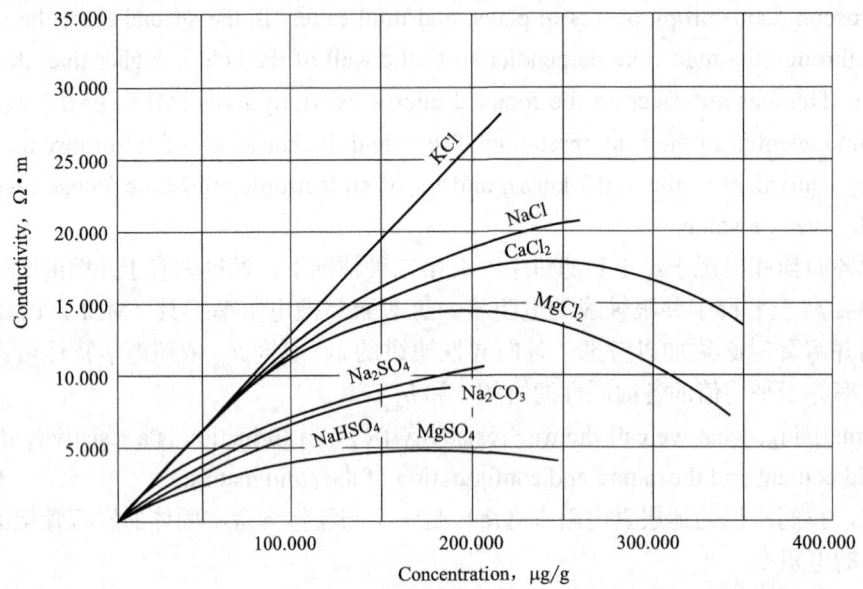

Fig.1.2　The correlation between conductivity and electrolyte concentration (from Oberto et al., 1984)

图 1.2　电导率与电解质浓度的关系（据 Oberto 等，1984）

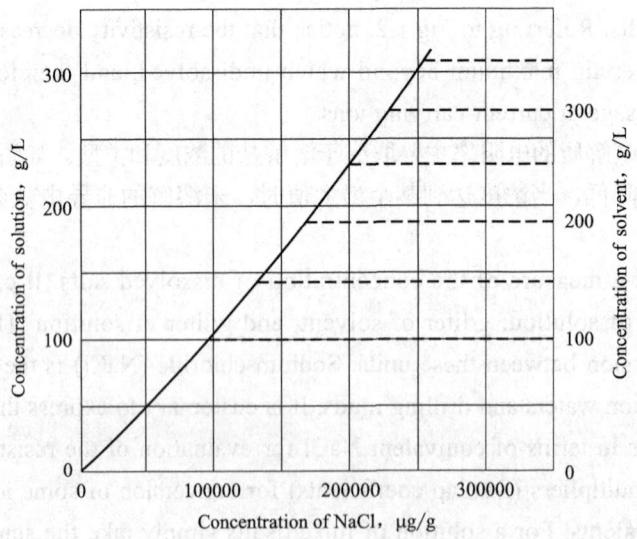

Fig.1.3　The equivalence between the various units of concentration. (from Oberto et al.,1984)

图 1.3　各浓度单位之间的等价关系（据 Oberto 等，1984）

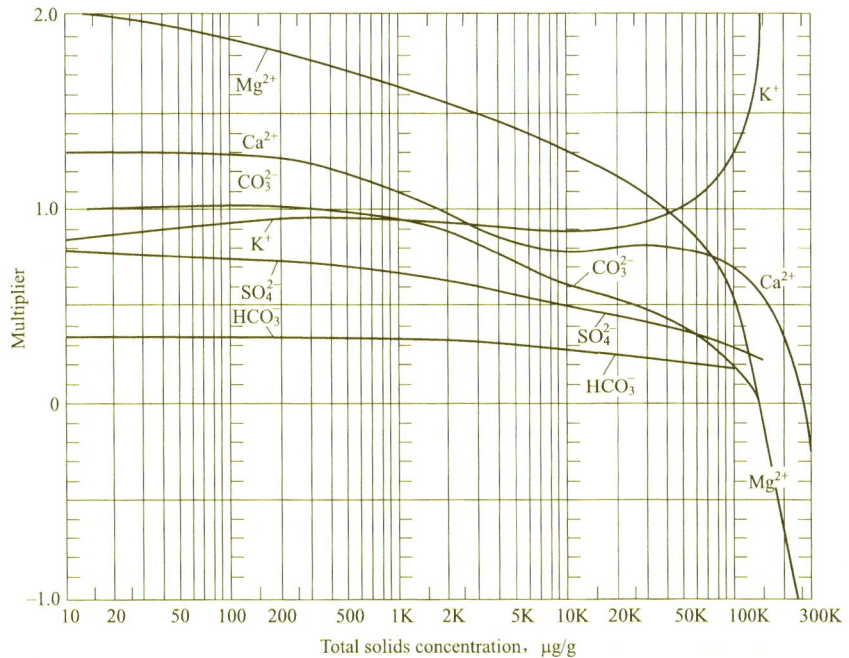

Fig.1.4 The multipliers to convert ionic concentration to equivalent NaCl concentration (courtesy of Schlumberger, 1987)

图 1.4 不同离子浓度转换为等效 NaCl 浓度的换算系数（据 Schlumberger，1987）

1.3.5 Relationship between Resistivity and Temperature
电阻率与温度之间的关系

The resistivity of a solution decreases as the temperature increases. Fig.1.5 can be used to convert the resistivity at a given temperature to that at any other temperature. Arps' formula approximates this relationship by the following formula:

随着温度升高，溶液的电阻率降低。图 1.5 可以将给定温度下的电阻率转换为任意温度下的电阻率，Arps 公式可以将其近似为：

$$R_{wT°F} = R_{75°F}\left(\frac{75°F + 6.77}{wT°F + 6.77}\right) \tag{1.6}$$

Where R_{wT} is the solution resistivity at formation temperature $T(°F)$. 75°F is a commonly used reference temperature. More generally：

其中 R_{wT} 是指在地层温度 T（°F）时溶液的电阻率，75°F 是常用参考温度，一般来说：

$$R_{wT_2} = R_{wT_1}\left[\frac{T_1 + 6.77}{T_2 + 6.77}\right] \quad (°F) \tag{1.7a}$$

$$R_{wT_2} = R_{wT_1}\left[\frac{T_1 + 21.5}{T_2 + 21.5}\right] \quad (°C) \tag{1.7b}$$

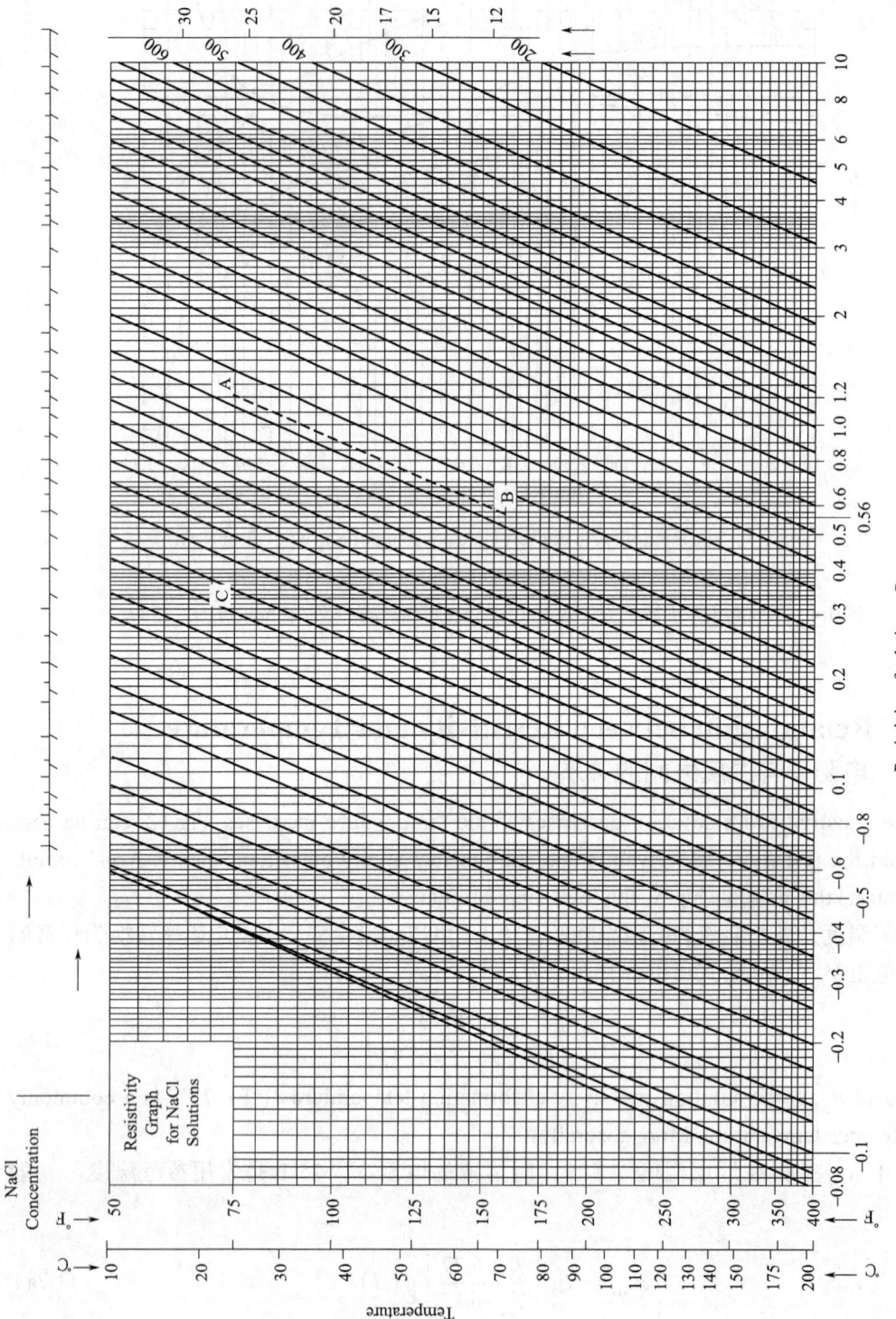

Fig.1.5　The relationship between resistivity, salinity, and temperature (courtesy of Schlumberger, 1987).

图 1.5　电阻率、矿化度和温度之间的关系（据 Schlumberger, 1987）

For example, R_m is 1.2Ω·m at 75°F (point A on chart), Follow trend of slanting lines (constant salinities) to find R_m at other temperatures; for example, at Formation Temperature (FT)=160°F (point B) read R_m=0.56Ω·m. The conversion shown in this picture is approximated by Arps formula.

例如，电阻率 R_m 在温度 75°F 时为 1.2Ω·m（图中的 A 点），可顺斜线趋势（恒定矿化度）得到其他温度下的电阻率 R_m；例如，在地层温度（FT）=160°F（B 点）时，电阻率 R_m=0.56Ω·m。由 Arps 公式可近似表示此图中所示的关系。

1.3.6 The Resistivity of Clays
黏土的电阻率

With the exception of pyrite, hematite, graphite and a few others, the dry minerals have infinite resistivity.

无水矿物除了黄铁矿、赤铁矿、石墨等少数矿物外，电阻率为无穷大。

Certain minerals do exist that appear to be solid conductors. Clay minerals are an example. According to Waxman and Smith (1967), a clayey sediment behaves like a clean formation of the same porosity, tortuosity and fluid saturation, except that the water appears to be more conductive than expected from its bulk salinity [Fig.1.6(a)].

确实存在某些似乎是固体导体的矿物，例如黏土矿物。据 Waxman 和 Smith（1967）的研究，黏土沉积物表现为孔隙度、曲度和流体饱和度相同的纯地层，只是水的导电性似乎比其预期的整体矿化度更高［图 1.6（a）］。

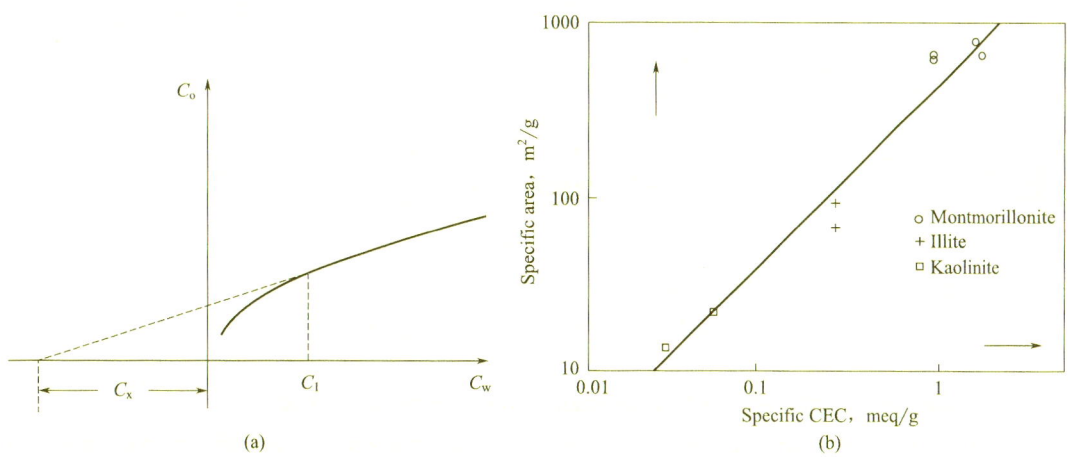

Fig.1.6　The conductivity C_o of a shaly water-saturated formation as a function of the conductivity C_w of the water (a) and the relation between specific CEC and specific area for API standard clays (b) (from Patchett, 1975).

图 1.6　页岩水饱和地层的电导率 C_o 与水的电导率 C_w 的函数关系（a）以及 API 标准黏土的阳离子交换量比与比表面积的关系（b）（据 Patchett，1975）

Clays are sheet-like particles, very thin (a few angstroms), but have a large surface area depending on the clay mineral type. There is a deficiency of positive electrical charge within the clay sheet. This creates a strong negative electrical field perpendicular to the surface of the clay sheet which attracts positive ions (Na^+, K^+, Ca^{2+}, ...) and repels the negative ions (Cl^-, ...) present in the water (Clavier et al., 1977). The amounts of these compensating ions constitute the Cation Exchange Capacity which is commonly referred to as the CEC (meq /g) or Q, (meq/cm³).CEC is related to the specific area of clay and so depends on the clay mineral type. It has its lowest value in kaolinite and its highest values in montmorillonite and vermiculite (Table 1.2).

黏土是非常小的薄片状颗粒（几埃），但表面积很大，具体取决于黏土矿物的类型。黏土薄片内正电荷较少，因此产生了一个垂直于黏土颗粒表面的强负电场，吸引阳离子（Na^+、K^+、Ca^{2+}、…）并排斥水中的阴离子（Cl^-，…）（Clavier 等，1977）。补偿离子的数量构成了阳离子交换量，通常被称为 CEC（meq/g）或 Q（meq/cm³）。CEC 与黏土的比表面积有关，因此取决于黏土矿物类型。高岭石 CEC 值最低，蒙脱石和蛭石 CEC 值最高（表 1.2）。

The excess of conductivity observed within clays is due to these additional cations are held loosely captive diffuse-layer surrounding the clay particles (Fig.1.7).

在黏土中观察到的电导率过高的现象是由于这些额外的阳离子松散地吸附在黏土颗粒周围的扩散层上（图 1.7）。

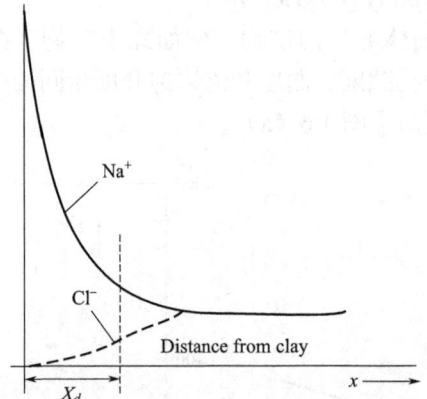

Fig.1.7　Schematic of diffuse-layer concentrations (Gouv model) (from Clavier et al., 1977).
图 1.7　扩散层浓度示意图（Gouv 模型）（据 Clavier 等，1977）

Thus the conductivity of a clayey sediment is the sum of two terms:

(1) One associated with free water or the water-filled porosity (indeed this type of sediment has porosity as high as 80% at the time of deposition. Subsequently, as they become compacted, some of the free water is expelled. However, this porosity is never reduced to zero in sedimentary rocks which have not yet reached the metamorphic phase).

(2) The other associated with the CEC. This can be expressed in another way. A clayey sediment has a conductivity which depends on its porosity on one hand, and on the effective conductivity, C_{we} of the water it contains on the other hand.

因此，黏土沉积物的电导率是以下两项电导率之和：
（1）与自由水或充满水的孔隙度有关的电导率（实际上这种类型的沉积物在沉积时孔

隙度高达80%，随后被压实时，一些自由水被排出。然而，在未到变质阶段的沉积岩中，孔隙度永远不会降到零）。

（2）与阳离子交换量CEC有关的电导率。这可以用另一种方式来表达，黏土沉积物的电导率一方面取决于其孔隙度，另一方面取决于它所含水的有效电导率C_{we}。

Clays are widely encountered not only in discrete layers but in mixtures with other rocks such as sands, limes tones.

黏土矿物不仅广泛地存在于不连续的地层中，而且会与其他岩石（如砂岩、石灰岩）混合在一起。

When dealing with formations containing clays, therefore, we can no longer consider the solid matrix to be non-conductive. Formation factor, porosity, saturation must be taken into account in calculations based on resistivity measurements. The influence of the clay will depend on the percentage present, its physical properties and the manner in which it is distributed in the formation.

因此，在评价含有黏土矿物的地层时，不能认为固体的岩石骨架不导电。根据电阻率测量结果进行计算时，必须考虑到地层因素、孔隙度、饱和度等因素。黏土矿物的影响取决于黏土矿物的相对含量、物理性质及在地层中的分布情况。

1.4　Borehole Environment 井眼环境

Where a hole is drilled into a formation, the rock plus the fluids in it (rock-fluid system) are altered in the vicinity of the borehole. A well's borehole and the rock surrounding it are contaminated by the drilling mud, which affects logging measurements. Fig.1.8 is a schematic illustration of a porous and permeable formation which is penetrated by a borehole filled with drilling mud.

当地层被钻开时，在钻孔附近的岩石及其流体（岩石—流体系统）会发生改变。井眼及其周围会被钻井液污染，从而影响测井的测量结果。图1.8是由充满钻井液的钻孔穿透的多孔渗透性地层的示意图。

This schematic diagram illustrates an idealized version of what happens when fluids from the borehole invade the surrounding rock. Dotted lines indicate the cylindrical nature of the invasion.

该示意图说明了当井眼流体侵入周围岩石时发生的理想情况。虚线表示侵入呈圆柱形。

The definitions of each of the symbols used in Fig.1.8 are listed as follows:

d_h——hole diameter;

d_i——diameter of flushed zone (inner boundary; flushed zone);

d_j——diameter of invaded zone (outer boundary; invaded zone);

Δr_j——radius of invaded zone (outer boundary);

h_{mc}——thickness of mud cake;

R_m—resistivity of the drilling mud;
R_{mc}—resistivity of the mud cake;
R_{mf}—resistivity of mud filtrate;
R_s—resistivity of shale;
R_t—resistivity of univaded zone (true resistivity);
R_w—resistivity of formation water;
R_{xo}—resistivity of flushed zone;
S_w—water saturation of uninvaded zone;
S_{xo}—water saturation of flushed zone;

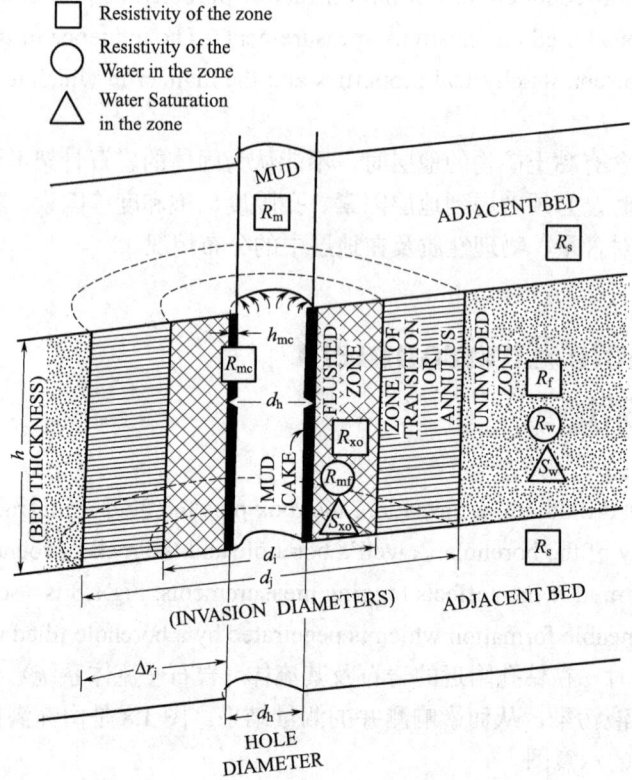

Fig.1.8 The borehole environment and symbols used in log interpretation (courtesy of Schlumberger)
图 1.8 井眼环境和测井解释中使用的符号（据斯伦贝谢）

图 1.8 中各个符号的定义如下：
d_h——孔径；
d_i——冲洗带直径（内边界，冲洗带）；
d_j——侵入带直径（外边界，侵入带）；
Δr_j——侵入带半径（外边界）；
h_{mc}——滤饼厚度；
R_m——钻井液电阻率；
R_{mc}——滤饼电阻率；

R_{mf}——钻井液滤液电阻率;

R_s——泥岩电阻率;

R_t——原状地层电阻率(真电阻率);

R_w——地层水电阻率;

R_{xo}——冲洗带电阻率;

S_w——原状地层含水饱和度;

S_{xo}——冲洗带含水饱和度。

Hole Diameter (d_h)—A well's borehole size is described by the outside diameter of the drill bit. But, the diameter of the borehole may be larger or smaller than the bit diameter because of wash out and/or collapse of shale and poorly cemented porous rocks. Or build-up of mud cake on porous and permeable formations (Fig.1.8). Borehole sizes normally vary from 7⅞ inches to 12 inches, and modern logging tools are designed to operate within these size ranges. The size of the borehole is measured by a caliper log.

孔径(d_h)——井眼尺寸由钻头外径来描述。但是,井眼直径可能大于或者小于钻头直径,这是由于泥岩和胶结不良的多孔介质被冲刷和/或坍塌,或在多孔渗透性地层上形成滤饼(图1.8)。井眼尺寸通常在7.875英寸到12英寸之间,现代测井工具可以在这些尺寸范围内工作。井眼的尺寸可以用井径测井测量。

Mud—Today, most wells are drilled with rotary bits and use special mud as a circulating fluid. The mud helps remove cuttings from the well bore, lubricate and cool the drill bit, and maintain an excess of borehole pressure over formation pressure. The excess of borehole pressure over formation pressure prevents blow-outs. The density of the mud is kept high enough so that hydrostatic pressure in the mud column is always greater than formation pressure. This pressure difference forces some of the drilling fluid to invade porous and permeable formations. As invasion occurs, many of the solid particles (i.e. clay minerals from the drilling mud) are trapped on the side of the borehole and form mud cake (Fig.1.8). Fluid that filters into the formation during invasion is called mud filtrate (Fig.1.8). The resistivity values for drilling mud, mud cake, and mud filtrate are recorded on a log's header.

钻井液——如今大部分井都采用旋转钻头钻井,并用特殊的钻井液作为循环流体。钻井液有助于从井筒中清除岩屑,润滑和冷却钻头,并保持井眼压力高于地层压力。井眼压力高于地层压力可防止井喷。钻井液密度保持足够高,因此钻井液柱中的静水压力总是大于地层压力。这种压差将迫使一些钻井液侵入多孔、渗透性的地层。侵入发生时,许多固体颗粒(即来自钻井液的黏土矿物)滞留在钻孔一侧,形成滤饼(图1.8)。侵入过程中渗滤到地层中的流体称为钻井液滤液(图1.8)。钻井液、滤饼和钻井液滤液的电阻率值均被记录下来。

Invaded zone—the zone which is invaded by mud filtrate is called the invaded zone. It consists of a flushed zone and a transition or annulus zone. The flushed zone occurs close to the borehole (Fig.1.8) where the mud filtrate has almost completely flushed out a formation's hydrocarbons and/or water. The transition or annulus zone, where a formation's fluids and mud filtrate are mixed. Occurs between the flushed zone and the uninvaded zone. The uninvaded zone is defined as the area beyond the invaded zone where a formation's fluids are uncontaminated by mud filtrate.

侵入带——被钻井液滤液侵入的区域称为侵入带。侵入带包括冲洗带和过渡带（或环空区）。冲洗带在井眼附近（图1.8），此时钻井液滤液几乎完全冲刷出地层中的碳氢化合物和水。过渡带（或环空区）中，地层流体和钻井液滤液在此混合。发生在冲洗带和未侵入带之间原状地层定义为侵入带以外的区域，即地层流体未被钻井液滤液污染的区域。

The depth of mud filtrate invasion into the invaded zone is referred to as the diameter of invasion (Fig.1.8). The diameter of invasion is measured in inches or expressed as a ratio: d_j/d_h (where d_h represents the borehole diameter). The amount of invasion which takes place is dependent upon the permeability of the mud cake and not upon the porosity of the rock. In general, an equal volume of mud filtrate can invade low porosity and high porosity rocks if the drilling muds have equal amounts of solid particles. The solid particles in the drilling muds coalesce and form an impermeable mud cake. The mud cake then acts as a barrier to further invasion. Because an equal volume of fluid can be invaded before an impermeable mud cake barrier forms, the diameter of invasion will be greatest in low porosity rocks. This occurs because low porosity rocks have less storage capacity or pore volume to fill with the invading fluid, and as a result, pores throughout a greater volume of rock will be affected. General invasion diameters ratio are:

钻井液滤液进入侵入带的深度被定义为侵入直径（图1.8）。侵入直径以英寸为单位或用比例表示：d_j/d_h（其中 d_h 表示井眼直径）。侵入量取决于滤饼的渗透率，而与孔隙度无关。通常情况下，若钻井液中的固体颗粒含量相等，那么等体积的钻井液滤液可以侵入低孔隙度和高孔隙度的岩石。钻井液中的固体颗粒结合并形成不渗透的滤饼。然后滤饼就成了进一步侵入的屏障。由于在不渗透滤饼阻屏障形成之前，可以侵入等量的流体，所以在低孔隙度岩石中侵入的直径最大。这是因为低孔隙度岩石的储集能力或孔隙体积较小，难以填充侵入流体，因此，更大体积的岩石孔隙将受到影响。一般侵入直径比为：

d_j/d_h = 2 (for high porosity rocks);
d_j/d_h = 5 (for intermediate porosity rocks);
d_j/d_h = 10 (for low porosity rocks);
d_j/d_h = 2 （高孔隙度岩石）；
d_j/d_h = 5 （中孔隙度岩石）；
d_j/d_h = 10 （低孔隙度岩石）。

Flushed zone- The flushed zone extends only a few inches from the wellbore and is part of the invaded zone. If invasion is deep or moderate, most often the flushed zone is completely cleared of its formation water by mud filtrate. When oil is present in the flushed zone, you can determine the degree of the flushing by mud filtrate from the difference between water saturations (S_w) in the flushed zone and the uninvaded zone (Fig.1.8). Usually, about 70% to 95% of the oil is flushed out; the remaining oil is called residual oil [S_{ro}= 1.0−S_{xo}, where S_{ro} equals residual oil saturation (The amount of hydrocarbon trapped within the rock pores is termed Residual Oil Saturations, ROS)].

冲洗带——冲洗带距离井筒只有几英寸，是侵入带的一部分。如果侵入较深或中等深度，通常冲洗带中地层水会被钻井液滤液完全清除。当冲洗带中有油存在时，可以通过冲洗带和原状地层的含水饱和度（S_w）的差值来确定钻井液滤液的冲洗的程度（图1.8）。通常，约 70%～95%的油被冲出，剩下的油被称为剩余油 [$S_{ro} = 1.0 - S_{xo}$，其中 S_{ro} 为剩余油饱和度（ROS）]。

Uninvaded zone–the uninvaded zone is located beyond the invaded zone (Fig.1.8). Pores in the uninvaded zone are uncontaminated by mud filtrate; instead, they are saturated with formation water, oil or gas.

原状地层——原状地层位于侵入带之外（图1.8）。原状地层的岩石孔隙未受到钻井液滤液污染；相反，它们被地层水、油或气饱和。

Even in hydrocarbon-bearing reservoirs, there is always a layer of formation water on grain surfaces. Water saturation (S_w) of the uninvaded zone is an important factor in reservoir evaluation (Fig.1.8). By using water saturation data, a geologist can determine a reservoir's hydrocarbon saturation. The formula for calculating hydrocarbon saturation is:

即使在含油气的储层中，岩石颗粒表面也始终存在一层地层水。原状地层的含水饱和度（S_w）是储层评价的一个重要参数（图1.8）。利用含水饱和度数据，地质学家可以确定储层的含油饱和度。计算含油气饱和度的公式为：

$$S_h = 1.0 - S_w \qquad (1.8)$$

Where: S_h——hydrocarbon saturation (i.e. the fraction of pore volume filled with hydrocarbons), %;

S_w——water saturation in the uninvaded zone (i.e. fraction of pore volume filled with water), %.

式中　S_h——含烃饱和度（即孔隙体积中含烃的比例），%；

S_w——原状地层含水饱和度（即孔隙体积充满水的比例），%。

The ratio between the uninvaded zone's water saturation (S_w) and the flushed zone's water saturation (S_{xo}) is an index of hydrocarbon move ability.

原状地层的含水饱和度（S_w）与冲洗带的含水饱和度（S_{xo}）之比是碳氢化合物的可动性指数。

Exercises
课后练习

1.1　State the definition of well logging.

1.2　State the objective of well logging.

1.3　State the classification of well logging.

1.4　State classification of Porosity.

1.5　What is porosity, permeability, resistivity, water saturation?

1.6　Compute the porosity of a formation composed of uniform spherical grains of radius r arranged in the most "open" cubic packing. (The unit cube with side of length $2r$ spans eight grains, see Fig.1.9)

1.7　What is the porosity (or liquid volume fraction) of an 11 lb/gal mud, assuming that it consists of water and clay particles of density 2.65 g/cm^3? The density of water is 8.3 lb/gal (1.00 g/cm^3).

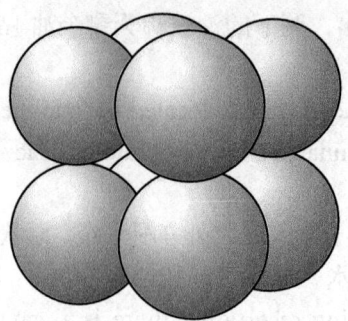

Fig.1.9 The most "open" cubic packing structure

图 1.9 最"开放"立方体组成结构

1.8 Do resistivity measurements tend to reflect secondary porosity (vugs and fractures), inter-granular porosity, or both?

1.9 What would you recommend for a logging suite to determine water/oil saturation in a shaly sand sequence? Explain your choice of tools.

1.10 What does the symbol S_w, S_{xo}, S_h, R_t, R_i, R_{xo}, R_m, R_{mc}, R_{mf} represent respectively?

1.11 What is mud? State the uses of the mud.

1.12 What is open hole log?

1.13 What is invaded zone?

1.14 What is flushed zone?

1.15 What is transition zone?

1.16 What is uninvaded zone?

2 Resistivity Basic and Spontaneous Potential
电阻率基本原理与自然电位测井

2.1 Introduction
引言

Electrical logging is the earliest logging method developed. It is mainly used to measure the resistivity of the rock around the borehole and the size of the natural electric field downhole. Historically, the first logging measurements were electrical in nature. In the early resistivity logging process, people often found that when the power supply electrode of the downhole tool is not powered, the potential change can still be measured in the well. Studies have shown that this potential change is related to the permeability of the rock formation, which is different from the artificial electric field. It is called the natural electric field. The spontaneous potential method is simple and highly practical, and it is still one of the necessary logging methods to classify lithology and study reservoir properties.

电法测井是发展最早的测井方法，主要用于测量井眼周围岩石的电阻率及井下自然电场大小。历史上首次测井的本质上就是电法测井。在早期电阻率测井过程中，人们经常发现，当井下仪器的供电电极未供电时，仍可在井内测量到电位变化。研究表明，这种电位变化与岩层渗透性有关，与人工电场不同。它被称为自然电场。自然电位方法简便实用，至今仍是岩性划分和储层物性研究必不可少的测井方法之一。

Also, in this chapter the concept of a bulk property of materials, known as resistivity, is examined. It is a quantity related to the more familiar resistance. The contrasting resistivity between relatively insulating hydrocarbons and the conductive formation brines is the basis for hydrocarbon detection. The quantitative relationships between resistivity and hydrocarbon saturation are taken up in the next chapter. Here, the electrical characteristics of rocks and brines are reviewed, including the temperature and salinity dependence of electrolytic conduction, which is of great importance in hydrocarbon saturation determination. The final section of the chapter is an elementary presentation of the physical mechanisms responsible for the generation of the spontaneous potential observed in boreholes.

此外，在本章中还研究了材料的一种体积特性，即电阻率的概念。这是一个与我们更为熟悉的电阻有关的概念。绝缘的油气与导电的地层卤水在电阻率的差异是识别油气层的基本依据。电阻率与含油饱和度之间的定量关系将在下一章讨论。本章综述了岩石和地层卤水的电性特征，包括电解传导的温度及矿化度依赖性，这对确定烃类饱和度有重要的意义。本章的最后部分是对在井筒中观察到的自然电位产生的物理机制的基本介绍。

2.2 The Concept of Bulk Resistivity
体积电阻率的概念

In order to understand the basic resistivity measurements used in standard logging procedures, the notion of resistivity is reviewed. It is a general property of materials, as opposed to resistance, which is associated with the geometric form of the material.

为了理解在标准测井程序中使用的基本电阻率测量方法，对电阻率的概念进行了回顾。它是材料的一般性质，与电阻相反，电阻与其几何形态有关。

The familiar expression of Ohm's law:

欧姆定律表达式为：

$$V = IR \quad (2.1)$$

It indicates that a current I flowing through a material with resistance R is associated with a voltage drop V. The more general form of this equation, used as an additional relationship in Maxwell's equations, is

该式表明流过具有电阻 R 的材料的电流与电压 V 有关。该式更加普遍的形式是作为麦克斯韦方程的一个附加关系，即：

$$\overline{J} = \sigma \overline{E} \quad (2.2)$$

where $\overline{J}$ is the current density, a vector quantity; $\overline{E}$, is the electric field and the constant of proportionality, σ is the conductivity of the material, Resistivity, a commonly measured formation parameter, is defined as the inverse of conductivity: and is an inherent property of the material.

式中，$\overline{J}$ 为电流密度，矢量；$\overline{E}$ 为电场强度，比例常数 σ 为材料的电导率，电阻率是常用的地层参数，定义为电导率的倒数，是材料的固有属性。

$$R = \frac{1}{\sigma} \quad (2.3)$$

As the illustration of Fig.2.1 indicates, a material of resistivity 1 Ω•m with dimensions of 1 m on each side will have a total resistance, face-to-face, of 1 Ω. Thus a system to measure resistivity would consist of a sample of the material to be measured contained in a simple fixed geometry. If the resistance of the sample is measured, the resistivity can be obtained from the relation:

如图 2.1 所示，电阻率为 1Ω•m，边长 1m 的材料，其两个对应面间的总电阻率为 1Ω。因此，一个测量电阻率的系统将由一个包含在简单固定几何中的被测材料样品组成。

如果样品的电阻被测量，电阻率可以通过以下关系得到：

$$R = \rho \times \frac{l}{A} \tag{2.4}$$

Where l is the separation of the two plates; A is the surface area of the electrode; and ρ is resistivity.

The expression of ρ is:

式中，l 为两个对应面之间的距离；A 为电极表面积；ρ 为电阻率。

ρ 其表达式为：

$$\rho = R \times \frac{A}{l} \tag{2.5}$$

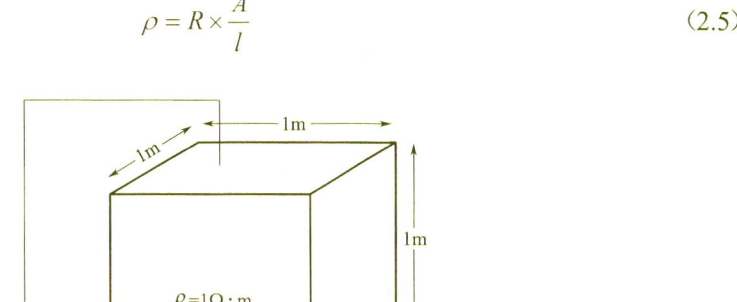

Fig.2.1　A 1m cube of characteristics resistivity 1 Ω•m has a resistance of 1Ω face to face（from Darwin V.Ellis,2008）

图 2.1　特性电阻率为 1Ω•m 的边长为 1m 的立方体的对应面间的总电阻为 1Ω（据 Darwin V.Ellis，2008）

A current, I, is passed through the sample and the corresponding voltage, V, is measured. Which becomes using Ohm's law:

一个电流 I 通过样品可得到相对应的电压 V。利用欧姆定律，将会变成：

$$\rho = \frac{V}{I}\frac{A}{l} = k\frac{V}{I} \tag{2.6}$$

This constant k, referred to as the system constant, converts the measurement of a voltage drop V, for a given current I, into the resistivity of the material.

这个常数 k 被称为系统常数，它将给定电流 I 时电压降 V 的测量值转换为材料的电阻率。

The practical exploitation of such a system is shown in Fig.2.2, which shows the so-called mud cup into which a sample of drilling fluid can be placed for the determination of its resistivity. From the dimensions given in the figure, the system constant can be calculated to be 0.012m. The resistivity, ρ, in Ω, is then obtained from the measured resistance R.

这种系统的实际开发图如图 2.2 所示，图 2.2 展示了可以将钻井液放入所谓的钻井液杯中，以测定其电阻率。根据图中给出的尺寸，可计算出系统常数为 0.012m。单位为 Ω 的电阻率 ρ 可根据测量到的电阻 R 得到。

$$\rho = R\frac{A}{l} = R \times 0.012 \tag{2.7}$$

For this particular measuring device, a sample of salt water with a resistivity of 2 Ω•m in the chamber would yield a total resistance of 166Ω.

对于这种特殊的测量设备，腔室内电阻率为 2Ω•m 的盐水样品将产生 166Ω 的总电阻。

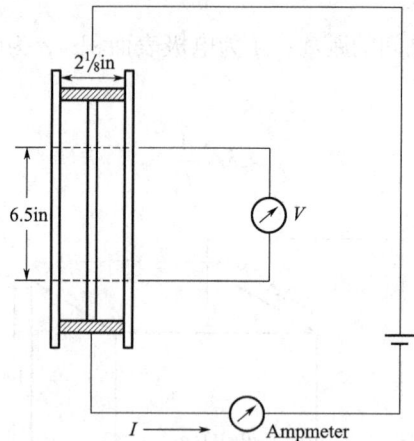

Fig.2.2 A schematic diagram of a mud cup, used for determining the resistivity of a mud sample（from Darwin V.Ellis,2008）

图 2.2 用于测量泥浆电阻率的钻井液杯的示意图（据 Darwin V.Ellis，2008）

2.3 Electrical Properties of Sand stone and Brine 砂岩盐水的电学性质

There are two general types of conduction: electrolytic and electronic. In electrolytic conduction, the mechanism is dependent upon the presence of dissolved salts in a liquid such as water. Examples of electronic conduction are provided by metals, which are not covered here.

一般有两种传导类型：离子导电型和电子导电型。离子导电机制依赖于诸如水等液体中溶解的盐类的存在。电子导电型的例子是由金属提供的，这里没有涉及。

Table 2.1 illustrates the resistivity of some typical materials. Notice the range of resistivity variation for salt water, which depends on the concentration of NaCl. Typical rock materials are in essence insulators. The fact that reservoir rocks have any detectable conductivity is usually the result of the presence of electrolytic conductors in the pore space. The conductivity of clay minerals is also greatly increased by the presence of an electrolyte. In some cases, the resistivity of a rock may result from presence of metal, graphite, or metal sulfides. The table shows that the resistivity of formations of interest may range from 0.5 to 10^3 Ω•m, nearly four orders of magnitude.

一些常见材料的电阻率列于表 2.1 中。注意盐水的电阻率变化范围，它取决于 NaCl

的浓度。典型的岩石材料本质上是绝缘体。事实上，任何可检测到电导率的储层岩石通常是由于孔隙空间中存在电解质导体。由于电解质的存在，黏土矿物的导电性也大大增加。在某些情况下，岩石的电阻率可能是由于金属、石墨或金属硫化物的存在造成的。表格显示，常见目的层的电阻率在 $0.5\Omega \cdot m$ 到 $10^3 \Omega \cdot m$ 之间变化，近四个数量级。

Table 2.1 Resistivity values (from Tittman,1986)

		Resistivity, $\Omega \cdot m$
Material	Marble	$5 \times 10^7 \sim 1 \times 10^9$
	Quartz	$1 \times 10^{11} \sim 3 \times 10^{14}$
	Petroleum	2×10^{14}
	Distilled	2×10^{14}
	saltwater (15℃, 2000μg/g)	3.4
	saltwater (15℃, 10μg/g)	0.72
	saltwater (15℃, 20μg/g)	0.38
	saltwater (15℃, 100μg/g)	0.09
	saltwater (15℃, 200μg/g)	0.06
Typical formations	Clay/shale	2~10
	Saltwater sand	0.5~10
	Oil sand	$5 \sim 10^3$
	"Tight" limestone	10^3

表 2.1 常见的电阻率值（据 Tittman，1986）

		电阻率, $\Omega \cdot m$
材料	大理石	$5 \times 10^7 \sim 1 \times 10^9$
	石英	$1 \times 10^{11} \sim 3 \times 10^{14}$
	石油	2×10^{14}
	蒸馏水	2×10^{14}
	盐水（15℃，2000μg/g）	3.4
	盐水（15℃，10μg/g）	0.72
	盐水（15℃，20μg/g）	0.38
	盐水（15℃，100μg/g）	0.09
	盐水（15℃，200μg/g）	0.06
常见地层	黏土/泥岩	2~10
	含水砂岩	0.5~10
	含油砂岩	$5 \sim 10^3$
	致密石灰岩	10^3

The conductivity of sedimentary rocks is primarily of electrolytic origin. It is the result of the presence of water or a combination of water and hydrocarbons in the pore space as a continuous phase. The actual conductivity will depend on the resistivity of the water in the pores and the quantity of water present. To a lesser extent, it will depend on the lithology of the rock matrix, its clay content, and its texture (grain size and the distribution of pores, clay, and conductive minerals). Finally, the conductivity of a sedimentary formation will depend strongly on temperature.

沉积岩的导电性主要取决于沉积岩内的电解质。它是水或者油水组合作为一个连续相存在于孔隙空间的结果。实际的电导率将取决于孔隙中水的电阻率以及水的数量。在较小程度上，它取决于岩石骨架的岩性、黏土含量以及结构（粒度和孔隙、黏土以及导电矿物的分布）。最后，沉积地层的导电性很大程度上取决于温度。

Fig.2.3 graphically presents the resistivity of saltwater (NaCl) solutions as a function of the electrolyte concentration and temperature. Look at the figure to determine resistivity for concentrations of 4,000μg/g and 40,000μg/g. At a temperature of 100°F, the resistivities are 0.12Ω·m and 1.0Ω·m, or nearly in the ratio expected. It can also be seen from the figure that the resistivity of the solution decreases when the temperature rises.

图2.3 生动地展示了盐水（NaCl）溶液的电阻率随电解质浓度和温度的变化而变化。查看图表确定浓度4000μg/g 和40000μg/g 时的电阻率。在100°F 的温度下，电阻率为0.12Ω·m 和1Ω·m，或接近预期的比例。从图中也可看出，随着温度的升高，溶液的电阻率下降。

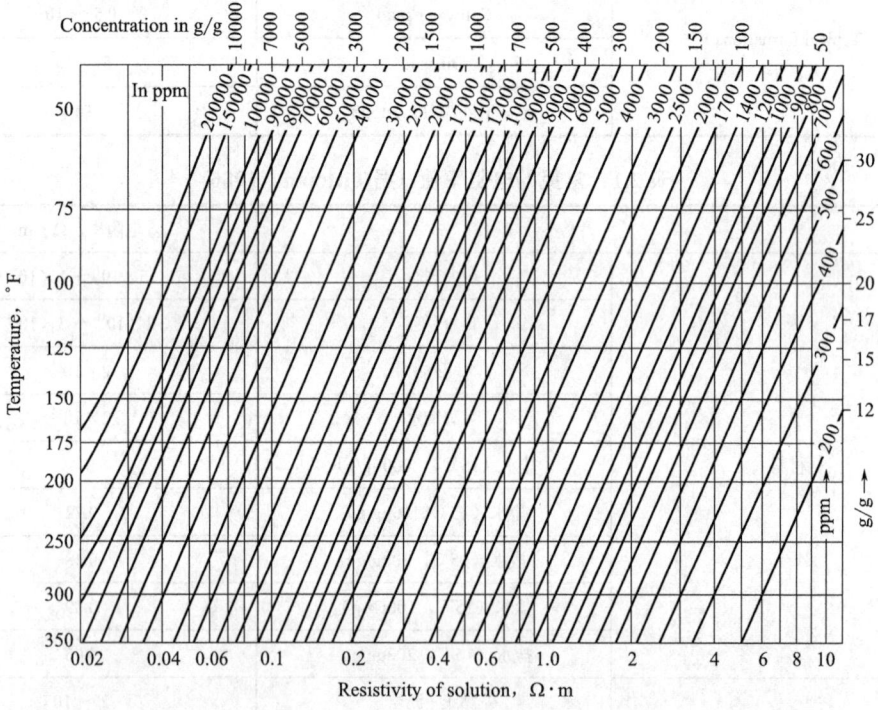

Fig.2.3 A nomogram for determining the resistivity of an NaCl solution as a function of the NaCl concentration and temperature. (g/g is grains/gallon)(from Schlumberger, 2005)

图2.3 确定NaCl溶液电阻率随浓度、温度变化的列线图（据斯伦贝谢，2005）

2.4 Spontaneous Potential
自然电位测井

Spontaneous potential was shown in the last section to be of considerable practical use in the identification of permeable zones. The origins of the spontaneous potential in wellbores involve both electrochemical potentials and the cation selectivity of shales. However, the underlying basis for the spontaneous potential is the fundamental process of diffusion-the self-diffusion of the dissolved ions in the fluids in the borehole and in the formation.

本章最后，讨论在渗透层识别方面具有相当实用价值的自然电位测井。井筒内自然电位的产生与电化学电动势和泥岩阳离子的选择性有关。然而，自然电位的根本基础是扩散的基本过程——井筒和地层内流体中的溶解离子的自我扩散。

Electrochemical potentials of interest to the generation of the spontaneous potential are the liquid junction potential and the membrane potential. Fig.2.4 schematically illustrates the situation for the generation of the liquid-junction potential. To the left is a saline solution of low NaCl concentration. To the right is one of a higher ionic concentration, as indicated by the sketch of electrolyte number densities $n_+(x)$ and $n_-(x)$ as a function of position. To add a note of realism, imagine the borehole, filled with a fluid of low salinity, to the far left of the figure. The first zone will then correspond to a permeable invaded zone, and the second region, to the undisturbed formation with water of greater salinity.

产生自然电位的电化学电动势主要有液接电动势（扩散电动势，译者注）和膜电动势（扩散吸附电动势，译者注）。图 2.4 示意性地说明了扩散电动势的产生。图左为低 NaCl 浓度的盐水溶液。图右为一较高离子浓度的液体，如图所示，电解质数密度 $n_+(x)$ 及 $n_-(x)$ 可作为位置的函数。为了更加真实，假设在图的最左边，是一个充满低矿化度液体的井筒。第一个区域对应的是渗透性的侵入带，第二个区域对应的是未扰动的矿化度较高的地层。

A concentration gradient, as indicated in the upper panel, results in diffusion. The higher mobility of Cl^- causes a charge separation as indicated by the sketch of the Cl^- and Na^+ concentrations。

如图 2.4 所示，浓度差导致扩散现象。如 Cl^- 和 Na^+ 浓度示意图所示，Cl^- 迁移率较高，导致电荷分离。

Because of the particle concentration gradient, dn/dx, where $n=n_+ +n_-$, there will be a diffusion of both Na^+ and Cl^- ions from the region of higher concentration to that of lower concentration. An approximation of the diffusion process, known as Fick's law, is given by:

由于粒子浓度梯度 dn/dx，其中 $n=n_+ +n_-$，Na^+ 和 Cl^- 都会由高浓度区扩散至低浓度区。扩散过程近似，被称为菲克定律，即：

$$J_{\text{diff}} = -D\frac{dn}{dx} \tag{2.8}$$

Where the current density of diffusing particles is J_{diff}. The diffusion constant D can be shown to be related to the mobility of the ions and the temperature, so that one can write:

式中，J_{diff} 为扩散离子的电流密度，$\dfrac{dn}{dx}$ 为离子浓度梯度，扩散常数 D 与离子迁移率和温度有关，故上式可写为：

$$J_{diff} = -\mu kT \dfrac{dn}{dx} \tag{2.9}$$

This connection between mobility and diffusion is called the Nernst-Einstein relation.
这种移动性和扩散之间的联系被称为能斯特—爱因斯坦关系。

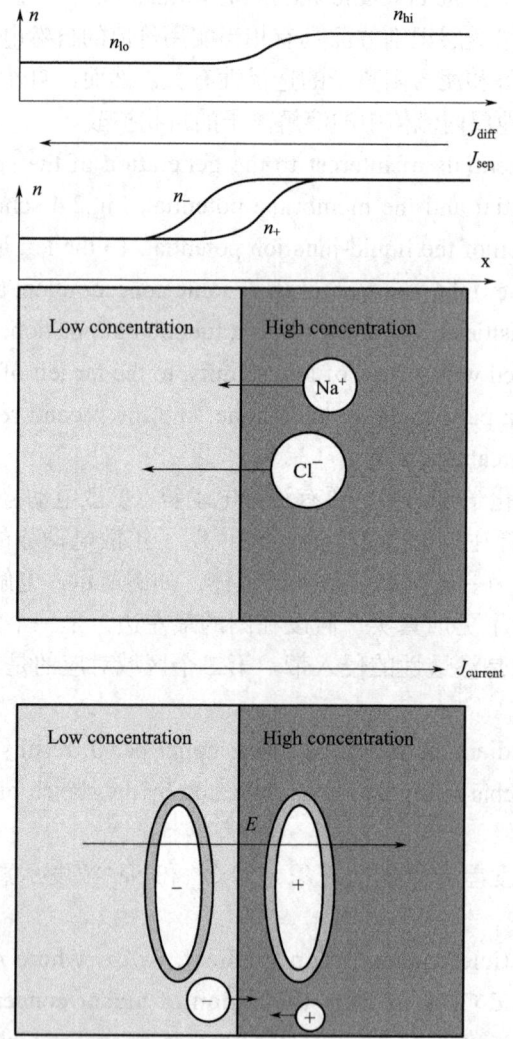

Fig.2.4　Schematic representation of the mechanism responsible for the generation of the liquid-junction potential (from Darwin V.Ellis, 2008)

图 2.4　扩散电动势产生机理示意图（据 Darwin V.Ellis，2008）

Because the Na$^+$ and Cl$^-$ ions have different mobilities, with $\mu_{Cl^-} > \mu_{Na^+}$, the diffusion will tend to produce a charge separation. The higher mobility Cl$^-$ ions will more readily migrate to the region of lower concentration and tend to create an excess negative charge to the left and a net excess positive charge to the right, as indicated in the lower half of Fig.2.4. The diffusion ionic current that produces this charge separation with the excess negative charge on the left of the figure can be written as:

由于 Na⁺ 和 Cl⁻ 具有不同的迁移率，且 Cl⁻ 迁移速率大于 Na⁺，因此，扩散使得电荷分离。如图 2.4 下方所示，较高迁移率的 Cl⁻ 更容易迁移到较低浓度的区域，并倾向于在左侧富集较多的负电荷，在右侧富集正电荷。产生这种电荷分离的扩散离子电流与图中左边的多余负电荷之间的关系可以表述为：

$$J_{sep} = -(\mu_{Cl} - \mu_{Na})kT\frac{dn}{dx} \quad (2.10)$$

The diffusion current, by itself would continue to accumulate excess negative charge in the region of low ionic concentration and positive charge in the region of high concentration were not for the electric field that results from the charge separation. With accumulating charge separation, an electric field, $\overline{E}$, grows with the orientation shown in the lower panel of the figure. The effect of the electric field is to impose a drift velocity on the ions, speeding up cations to the left and slowing down anions diffusing to the left. The magnitude of the electric field will increase until the diffusion of the anions and cations is the same, resulting in an equilibrium consisting of a constant electric field and no additional charge separation. However diffusion, although modified, continues. The liquid junction potential E_d is the expressed as:

扩散电流不是由电荷分离产生的电场造成的。扩散电流本身会在离子浓度低的区域继续积累过量的负电荷，在离子浓度高的区域继续积累正电荷。随着电荷分离的积累，电场 $\overline{E}$ 随着图 2.4 下方所示的方向增大。电场的作用是加强离子的迁移速度，从而使阳离子向左侧扩散加快，使阴离子向右侧扩散减慢。电场强度将持续增强，直至阴离子和阳离子的扩散相同，从而形成一个由恒定电场且没有电荷分离组成的平衡。然而，扩散虽然有所改善，但仍在持续。扩散电动势表示为：

$$E_d = K_d \lg \frac{R_{mf}}{R_w} \quad (2.11)$$

Fig.2.5 is a schematic representation of the circuit producing the SP. The cell marked E_d corresponds to the liquid junction potential just discussed and is sketched with the polarity corresponding to a higher electrolyte concentration in the formation water than in the mud filtrate. As can be seen from the figure, an additional source of the spontaneous potential is associated with the shale. This second component of the SP is the result of the membrane potential generated in the presence of the shale that contains clay minerals which have large negative surface charge.

图 2.5 是 SP 曲线电路示意图。所有标记的单元 E_d 对应刚刚讨论过的扩散吸附电动势，其极性与地层水中电解质浓度高于钻井液滤液浓度相对应。从图中可以看出，自然电位的另一部分与泥岩有关。自然电位的这第二个组分是在含有黏土矿物的泥岩中产生扩散吸附电动势的结果，而黏土矿物具有大量的负表面电荷。

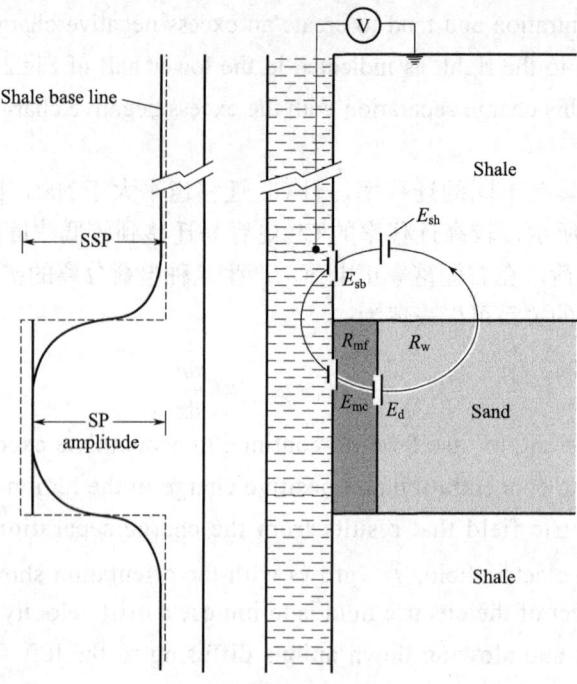

Fig 2.5 A schematic representation of the development of the spontaneous potential in a borehole (from Dewen,1983)

图 2.5 井中自然电位产生机理示意图（据 Dewen，1983）

Now what does that mean? First we define shale to be a conglomeration of fine grained particles, many of which are clay minerals. We will assume that it is nearly impermeable to fluid flow, but that it is still capable of ionic transport, although considerably altered by the presence of clay minerals. The shale acts like a cation-selective membrane. This property is related to the sheet-like structure of the alumino-silicates that form the basic structure of clay minerals. At the surface of the clay minerals there is a strong negative charge related to unpaired Si and O bonds. When the clay mineral particles are exposed to an ionic solution, one containing Na^+ and Cl^- for example, the anions will be repulsed by their surfaces while the cations will be attracted to the surface charge. Forming the so-called electrical double layer as shown in the right-hand portion of Fig. 2.6. Close to the clay layers, the fluid will be dominated by cations since the anions are excluded by electrostatic repulsion. In this manner, in a complex mixture of clay minerals and other small mineral particles, with pore spaces even too small to permit the hydraulic flow of water, the cations will be able to diffuse along the charged surfaces. From high concentration to low concentration while the negative Cl^- ions will tend to be excluded. Such a diffusion process will tend to accumulate a positive charge on the low ionic concentration side of the shale barrier producing an attendant electric field. In the practical situation of Fig.2.5, the cations from the fluid saturating the porous sand zone diffuse through the shale to the borehole with the lower cation concentration.

那这代表什么呢？首先，我们将泥岩定义为细粒颗粒的集合体，其中许多是黏土矿物。我们假设泥岩几乎不能渗流流体，但离子可以迁移，尽管由于黏土矿物的存在而发生了很大的变化。泥岩就像一层阳离子选择性膜。这种性质与形成黏土矿物基本结构的铝硅酸盐的片状结构有关。在黏土矿物表面有一个与未配对的 Si—O 键有关的强负电荷。当黏土矿物颗粒暴露在离子溶液中，例如含有 Na$^+$ 和 Cl$^-$ 的溶液，阴离子会被它们的表面电荷排斥，而阳离子会被表面电荷吸附，形成如图 2.6（b）所示的所谓的双电层。近黏土层表面的离子以阳离子为主，因为静电排斥阴离子。通过这种方式，在黏土矿物和其他小矿物颗粒的复杂混合物中，其孔隙空间小到不允许水流动，阳离子能够沿着带电表面从高浓度扩散到低浓度中，而带负电荷的 Cl$^-$ 将会排斥在外。这种扩散将使正电荷在泥岩层中低离子浓度侧积累，并产生伴随电场。在图 2.5 的实际情况中，饱和多孔砂岩层带流体中的阳离子通过泥岩向井眼扩散，砂岩层中阳离子浓度较低。

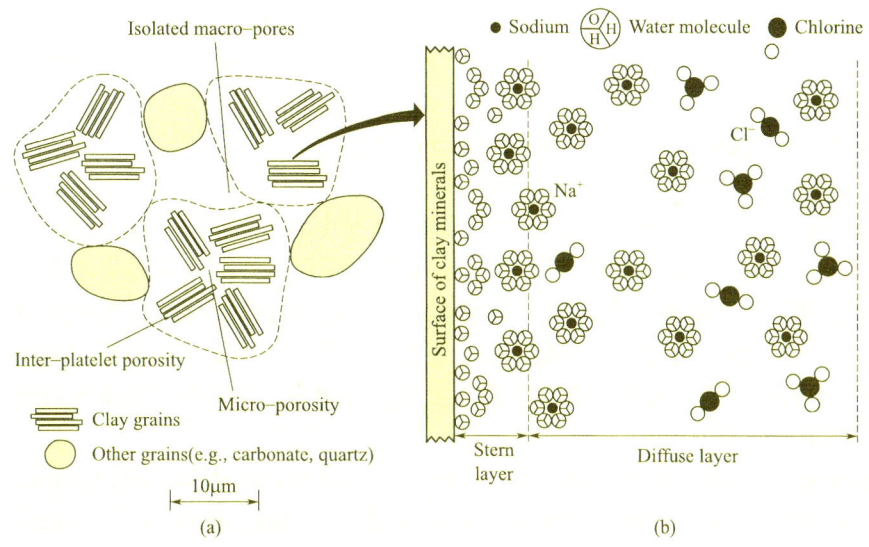

Fig.2.6 A representation of a shale on the left, consisting of rock mineral grains and small platy clay particles (a). On the right the distributions of ions close to the face of one of the clay minerals is shown, which illustrates the so-called electrical double-layer (b). (from Reviland Leroy,1997)

图 2.6 泥岩微观结构示意（由岩石矿物颗粒和片状黏土颗粒组成）（a）和靠近其中一种黏土矿物表面的离子分布（即所谓的双电层）（b）（据 Reviland 和 Leroy，1997）

To aid a quantitative description, Fig.2.7 shows a simplified setup for evaluating the membrane potential when a semipermeable shale barrier separates the solutions of two different salinities. The natural diffusion process is impeded because of the negative surface charge of the shale. The Cl$^-$ ions which otherwise would diffuse more readily are prevented from traversing the shale membrane, whereas the less mobile Na$^+$ ions can pass through it readily. The result is that the effective mobility of the Cl$^-$ in this case is reduced to nearly zero.

为了便于定量描述，图 2.7 显示了由泥岩半透膜分隔出的两种不同矿化度溶液的用于评估扩散吸附电动势的简化装置。由于泥岩表面负电荷的影响，离子扩散作用受到影响。迁移速率较快的 Cl$^-$ 不能穿过泥岩膜，而迁移速率较低的 Na$^+$ 则较易地通过泥岩膜。最终 Cl$^-$ 的有效迁移速率在这种情况下减少到几乎为零。

The magnitude of the membrane potential E_{da} can thus be expressed as:

因此，扩散吸附电动势的大小可表示为：

$$E_{da} = K_{dd} \lg \frac{R_{mf}}{R_w} \tag{2.12}$$

Fig.2.5 also shows how the SP is measured, between an electrode in the borehole and a distant reference. The shale baseline represents the natural potential between the two electrodes, without electrochemical effects, and is ideally a straight line from top to bottom. The static spontaneous potential (SSP), is the ideal SP generated by electrochemical effects when passing from the shale to a thick porous clean (shale-free) sand if no current flowed. In practice, the electrode can only measure the potential change in the borehole. Although the mud is usually less resistive than the formation, the area for current flow is much smaller in the borehole than in the formation, so that the borehole resistance is usually much higher than the formation resistance. Most of the potential drop therefore takes place in the borehole with the result that the measured SP amplitude in the center of the bed is close to the SSP.

图 2.5 还显示了如何测量井中电极和远处参考点间的自然电位 SP。泥岩基线代表两个电极之间的自然电位，不存在电化学效应，理想情况下从上到下是一条直线。静自然电位（SSP）是在没有电流流动的情况下，从泥岩传递到厚层多孔纯含水砂岩时因电化学效应产生的理想 SP。在实际测量中，电极只能测量井筒内的电位变化。虽然钻井液的电阻通常比地层小，但井眼中的电流流动截面积要比地层小得多，因此串联回路中井眼电阻通常远高于地层电阻。因此，大部分电位下降仅发生在井眼中，使得厚层含水砂岩地层中心测得的 SP 幅度接近 SSP。

In the best of cases, the measurement of the SP allows the identification of permeable zones and the determination of formation water resistivity. A deflection indicates that a zone is porous and permeable and has water with a different ionic concentration than the mud. Since the mud filtrate resistivity can be measured, the formation water resistivity can be calculated using factors that are well known for NaCl solutions. In practice the electrochemical potential is often written in terms of effective water resistivities R_{mfe} and R_{we} rather than actual resistivities. These are equal to R_{mf} and R_w except for concentrated or dilute solutions. In concentrated solutions, below about $0.1\Omega \cdot m$ at 75°F, the conductivity is no longer proportional to the number, density of charge carriers and their mobilities. At high concentrations the proximity of the ions to one another is increased; their mutual attractions begin to compete with the solvation to reduce their mobilities. In dilute solutions of most oilfield waters, other ions than Na^+ and Cl^- become increasingly important. Numerous charts exist for the determination of R_w from the SP, knowing R_{mf} and temperature.

最佳情况下，自然电位可用来识别渗透层及确定地层水电阻率。曲线异常表明该井段为多孔的渗透层段，且地层水中离子浓度与钻井液不同。由于可以测量钻井液滤液电阻率，因此可以使用众所周知的 NaCl 溶液系数来计算地层水电阻率。在实际应用中，电动势势通常用有效电阻率 R_{mfe} 和 R_{we} 来表示，而不是实际电阻率。除浓溶液或稀溶液外，它们等同于 R_{mf} 和 R_w。在浓溶液中，在 75°F 时低于 $0.1\Omega \cdot m$，电导率不再与载流子的数量、密度和迁移率成正比。在高浓度时，离子彼此之间互相接近，它们之间的相互引力开始与减少它们流动性的溶解作用竞争。在大多数油田水的稀溶液中，除 Na^+ 和 Cl^- 之外的其他离子变得越来越重要。在已知 R_{mf} 和温度的情况下，可应用图版通过 SP 曲线来求取地层水电阻率 R_w。

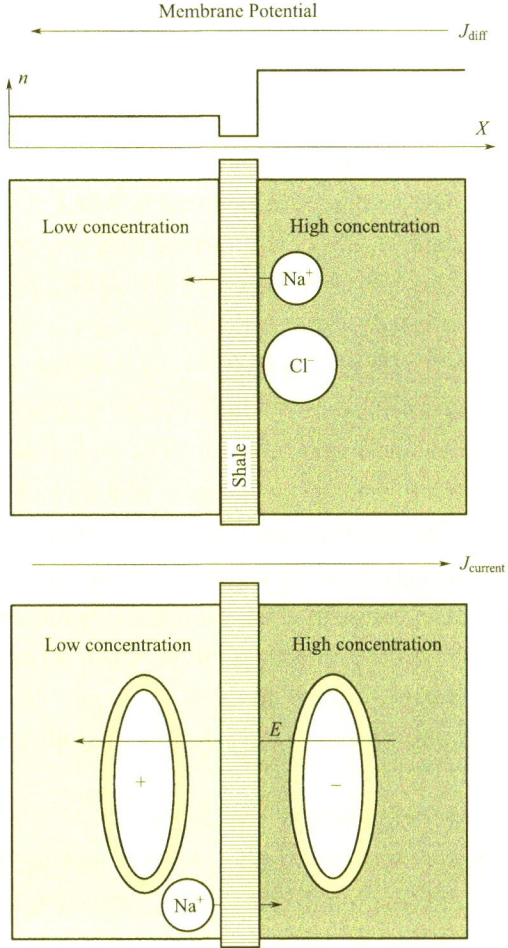

Fig.2.7 A schematic representation of the mechanism responsible for the generation of the membrane potential (from Darwin V.Ellis, 2008)

The diffusion process is altered by the selective passage of Na^+ through the shale membrane

图 2.7 扩散吸附电动势产生机理示意图（据 Darwin V.Ellis，2008）

Na^+ 的选择性通过改变了泥岩膜的扩散过程

The SP is also used to indicate the amount of clay in a reservoir. When the shale contained in the sandstone is distributed in layers to form a sandy shale interaction layer, and the resistivity of the layered shale and the sandy layer is not much different, the shale content of the formation can be calculated by the following formula:

SP 曲线还用于指示储层泥质含量。当砂岩中所含泥质呈层状分布形成砂泥质交互层，且层状泥质和砂质层的电阻率差别不大时，地层的泥质含量可用下式计算：

$$V_{sh} = 1 - \frac{PSP}{SSP} \tag{2.13}$$

2.5 Log Examples of the SP
自然电位测井实例

The measurement of the SP is probably the antithesis of the high-tech image of many of the logging techniques to be considered in subsequent chapters. The sensor is simply an electrode (often mounted on an insulated cable, known as the "bridle," some tens of feet above any other measurement sondes) which is referenced to ground at the surface, as indicated in Fig.2.8. The measurement is essentially a DC voltage measurement in which it is assumed that unwanted sources of DC voltage are constant or only slowly varying with time and depth.

自然电位测井可能与后续章节中介绍的许多应用到高科技技术的测井方法有所不同。如图 2.8 所示，传感器只是一个电极（通常安装在绝缘电缆上，称为"电缆"，比任何其他测量探头高出约几十英尺），它与地面接地有关。该测量本质上是一种直流电压测量，其中假定不需要的直流电压源是恒定的，或者只是随时间和深度缓慢变化。

To illustrate some of the characteristic behavior to be anticipated by the SP measurement on logs, refer to Fig.2.8. In the left panel of this figure, a sequence of shale and clean sand beds is represented, along with the idealized response. The shale baseline is indicated, and deflections to the left correspond to increasingly negative values. From the top, in the first sand zone, there is no SP deflection since this case represents equal salinity in the formation water and in the mud filtrate. The next two zones show a development of the SP which is largest for the largest contrast in mud filtrate and formation water resistivity. In the last zone, the deflection is seen to be to the right of the shale baseline and corresponds to the case of a mud filtrate which is saltier than the original formation fluid.

图 2.8 可用来说明自然电位曲线的特点。在图 2.8（a）中显示了一系列泥岩、纯砂岩以及理想的自然电位曲线响应。其中泥岩基线已经标出，向左偏转表示负异常增加。在自上而下的第一个砂岩层中，自然电位曲线无异常幅度，此种情况表明地层水和钻井液矿化度相同。接下来的两个砂岩层自然电位曲线异常幅度增加，当钻井液滤液和地层水电阻率差异程度最大时，自然电位异常幅度最大。在最后一个砂岩层中，可以看到曲线偏转至泥岩基线的右侧，代表该砂岩中钻井液滤液的矿化度高于钻井液。

The second panel of Fig.2.8 illustrates several cases, for a given contrast in mud filtrate salinity and formation water salinity, where the SP deflection will not attain the full value seen in a thick, clean sand. The first point is that the deflection will be reduced if the sand bed is not thick enough because not enough of the potential drop occurs in the borehole. The transition at the bed boundary is much slower for the same reason. Depending mainly on the depth of invasion and the contrast between invaded zone and mud resistivity, the bed thickness needs to be more than 20 times the borehole diameter to attain its full value.

在图 2.8（b）中展示了如下几种情况。在给定钻井液滤液与地层水矿化度对比关系的情况下，SP 曲线的偏转无法达到厚层完全含水砂岩的异常幅度最大值。第一点，如果砂岩层不够厚，由于井筒内的势能下降不够大，曲线异常幅度会减小。同样的原因，层间的转变要慢得多。由于侵入深度、侵入带与钻井液电阻率的关系，通常认为当层厚大于 20

倍井径时，在含水纯砂岩中异常幅度才可能达到最大。

The second point is the effect of clay in reducing the SP, as already discussed. The third point is the effect of oil or gas. In a clean sand, the electrochemical potentials are not affected by oil or gas, but the formation resistivities are higher so that the transition at bed boundaries may be slower and a thicker bed may be needed for full SP development. However, the effect of oil or gas is stronger in shaley sand. The electrochemical potentials are reduced compared to a water-bearing sand because there is less water in the pore space, so that the effect of the surface-charged clay particles is proportionately higher.

第二点如前文所述，是黏土的作用降低了 SP 曲线的幅度。第三点是储层含油或含气时对自然电位曲线的影响。在纯砂岩中，电动势不受油气的影响，但当地层电阻率较高时，地层边界的转换会变慢，需要较厚的地层才能使曲线异常幅度达到最大值。油气对泥质砂岩的影响更强。与含水砂岩相比，由于孔隙中水分较少，电动势减小，因此表面带电的黏土颗粒的影响更大。

The baseline often drifts slowly with time and depth. Sharper shifts occur when the membrane potential at the top of sand is different to that at the bottom. This happens when the top and bottom shales have different cation selection properties, and also when the formation water or hydrocarbon saturation changes within the sand.

泥岩基线常常随着时间和深度慢慢漂移。当砂岩顶部以上泥岩的扩散吸附电动势与底部之下泥岩不同时，变化会更加明显。这是由于砂岩上下围岩具有不同的阳离子选择性吸附作用导致的。当地层水或油气的饱和度发生变化时，泥岩基线也将发生变化。

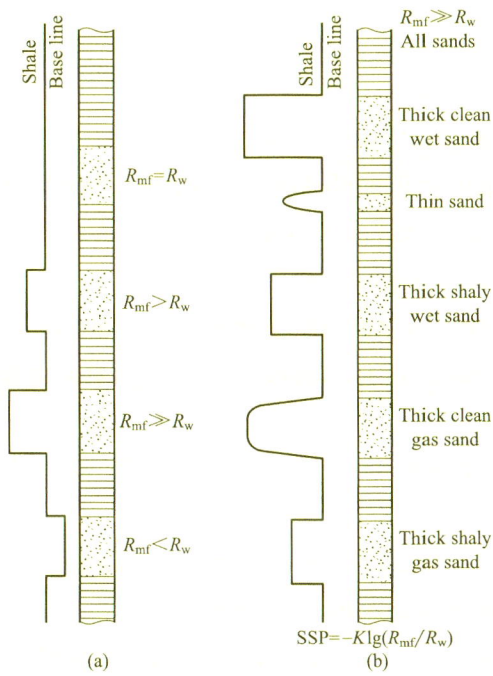

Fig.2.8　Schematic summary SP curve behavior under a variety of different logging circumstances commonly encountered（from Asquith,1982）

图 2.8　不同条件下自然电位曲线形态示意图（据 Asquith，1982）

Exercises
课后练习

2.1 What are the uses of SP log?

2.2 What influences SP measurement?

2.3 Circle two of the following which can cause the resistivity of a rock to increase:

(A) An increase in connate water resistivity

(B) A decrease in tortuosity

(C) A decrease in formation porosity

(D) An increase in water saturation

2.4 An SP log run across a porous and permeable formation in a well in which the salinity of the mud is greater than the salinity of the formation water will show:

(A) A deflection to the left of the shale baseline

(B) No deflection

(C) A deflection to the right of the shale baseline

2.5 On an SP log, all things being equal, the greater the SP deflection the greater the value of R_w (formation water resistivity), True of False?

2.6 The response of the Spontaneous Potential Tool is unaffected by the presence of hydrocarbon. True of False?

(A) True

(B) False

(C) It depends on the depth of invasion

2.7 In the log example of figure below, indicate the shale baseline and zone the log into three major units; label the shale and the two reservoir units. Assuming that the lower reservoir is water-filled, answer the following questions.

(a) Is the mud filtrate more or less saline than the formation water?

(b) Is the average porosity of the upper reservoir greater or less than that of the lower reservoir?

(c) In the upper reservoir, which curve(s) indicate(s) why the neutron porosity is greater than the density porosity?

(d) On the basis of the resistivity curves alone, the upper reservoir may be split into two portions. Do they both contain hydrocarbons? Why?

(e) Which of the two zones do you expect to be more permeable?

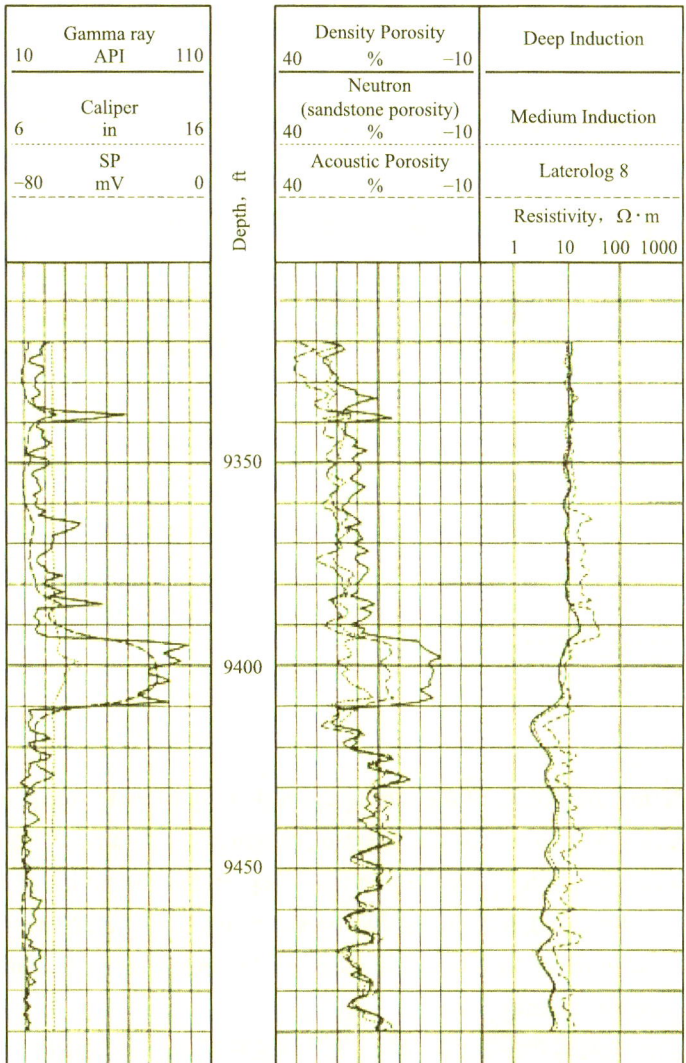

Fig.2.9 Logging curve

图 2.9 测井曲线

3 Fundamentals of Electrical Logging Interpretation
电法测井解释基础

3.1 Introduction
引言

Before considering the details of measuring the resistivity of earth formations, let us look at the usefulness of such a measurement. The desired petrophysical parameter from resistivity measurement is the water saturation S_w. In the previous chapter, the resistivity of various materials, including brines, was discussed. The focus was on the resistivity of a porous rock sample filled with conductive brine in order to relate this measurable parameter to formation properties of interest for hydrocarbon evaluation.

在详细介绍岩石电阻率测量之前,我们先探讨这种测量方法的用途。通过电阻率测量可得到含水饱和度 S_w 这一岩石物理参数。在前一章中讨论了包括盐水在内的各种材料的电阻率。研究的重点是充满导电盐水的多孔岩样的电阻率,以便将这一可测量参数与油气评价中感兴趣的地层性质联系起来。

In this chapter the empirical basis for the interpretation of resistivity measurements is reviewed. (The word "empirical" should be taken in its best sense here, meaning based on observation and experiment, and without implying that principles or theory have been disregarded.) For many years, at the outset of well logging, it was not possible to address the water saturation question any more precisely than whether the resistivity of a formation was high or low. It was through the work of Archie that it became possible to be more quantitative about the interpretation of a formation resistivity measurement and to link resistivity to formation water resistivity, porosity, and water saturation.

本章回顾了电阻率测井的经验基础("经验主义"一词在这里应该得到最好的理解,即基于观察和实验,而不是意味着原则或理论被忽视)。多年来,在测井刚开始的时候,除了地层电阻率是高还是低之外,不可能更精确地解决含水饱和度的问题。正是通过

Archie 的工作，人们才能够定量解释地层电阻率的测量结果，将地层电阻率、地层水电阻率和地层含水饱和度之间的关系定量确定下来。

The chapter ends by presenting the principle of the simplest electrical logging measurements. For this application, a review of some basic notions of electrostatics is made to indicate how, in a very idealized situation, the measurement of isotropic formation resistivity might be made.

本章最后介绍了最简单的普通电阻率的测量原理。针对这一应用，本章回顾了一些基本概念，以说明在非常理想的情况下如何进行各向同性地层电阻率的测量。

3.2 Early Electrical Logging Interpretation 早期的测井解释

Fig.3.1 shows a log of spontaneous potential and formation resistivity made prior to 1935. The notations on the figure make clear which zones are oil-bearing and which are water-bearing. It seems possible, noting the higher resistivity, that zone *a-A* contains more oil (has a lower S_w) than zone *B-b*. But how can this be verified?

图 3.1 为 1935 年测量的自然电位和地层电阻率曲线。图中标注了油层和水层。考虑到油层段 *a—A* 的电阻率较高，似乎比水层段 *B—b* 含有更多的油（但油层段 S_w 较低）。但是如何验证呢？

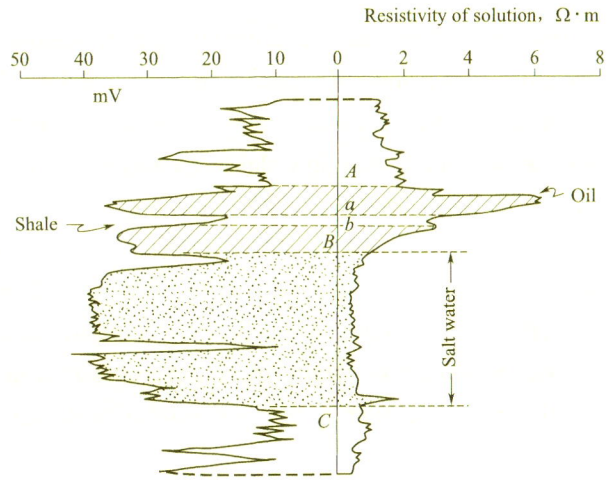

Fig.3.1　An early resistivity-SP log (from Martin et al., 1938)

图 3.1　早期自然电位—电阻率组合测井（据 Martin 等，1938）

The "standard" procedure at the time was to take a core sample, representative of the zones in question, and to make laboratory measurements of its resistivity under different conditions of water saturation. Fig.3.2 is an example of two such core sample measurements. Presumably the core was saturated with water of the same resistivity as the undisturbed formation water for the resistivity determination. In the laboratory, the water was progressively displaced by hydrocarbon, and the measured resistivity of the sample was plotted as a function of the water saturation.

当时的"标准"程序是取一个具有代表性的岩心样品,并在不同含水饱和度条件下对其电阻率进行实验室测量。图 3.2 所示为两个岩心测量实例。假定岩心饱和地层水与原状地层所含地层水具有相同的电阻率。实验过程中,地层水逐渐被烃取代,测量得到的电阻率可被绘制为含水饱和度的函数曲线。

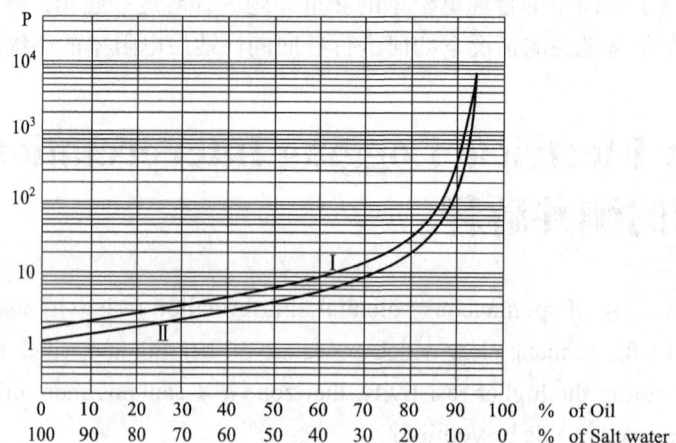

Fig.3.2 Resistivity measurements of two core samples as a function of water saturation for use in electric log interpretation (from Martin et al., 1938)

图 3-2 两个岩心电阻率与含水饱和度函数关系图版(据 Martin 等,1938)

At about the same time, M.C. Leverett was conducting experiments with unconsolidated sands, to determine the relative permeability of oil and water as a function of the water saturation. As a by-product of his research, he measured the conductivity of the material in a sample chamber, after a calibration of the system constant, in order to conveniently determine the fraction of kerosene and water in his permeable samples. Fig.3.3 is a summary of his calibration data. The fractional water saturation (S_w) is plotted versus the normalized conductivity. The normalizing point for this latter scale was taken to be the conductivity of the sample in the chamber when it was completely saturated with salt water. Appropriately normalized points from the core measurements of Fig.3.2 can be shown to clearly track Leverett's measurements and indicate the possibility of a general method for relating the resistivity of a porous sample to the water saturation.

与此同时,M.C. Leverett 在对未固结砂岩进行实验,以确定油水的相对渗透率与含水饱和度之间的关系。作为他研究的副产品,在校准了系统常数后,他测量了取样室中材料的导电性,以便更为方便地确定渗透性样品中煤油和水的比例。图 3.3 是对他校准数据的汇总。绘制了含水饱和度与归一化电导率的关系。后者是取样室样品被盐水完全饱和时的电导率。进行适当归一化后,从图 3.2 可以清楚地看出 Leverett 的测量结果,同时指出多孔岩样的电阻率与含水饱和度具有某种关联的可能性。

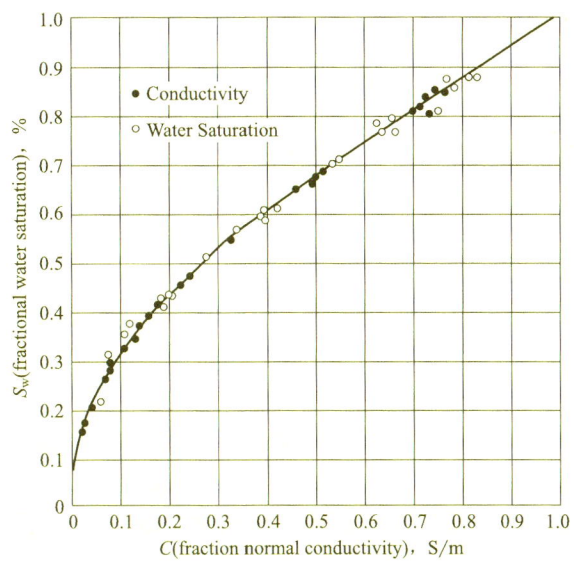

Fig.3.3 Relationship between core conductivity and water saturation (from Leverett,1939)
Calibration curve of Leverett's core holder with sand pack, showing variation of relative
conductivity as a function of water saturation

图 3.3 岩心电导率与含水饱和度关系曲线（据 Leverett，1939）
莱弗里特岩心夹砂器的校准曲线，其显示了相对电导率随含水饱和度的变化

3.3 Empirical Approaches to Interpretation
基于实验的定量解释方法

3.3.1 Formation Factor
地层因素

Shortly after the publication of Leverett's work, G.E. Archie of Shell was making electrical measurements on core samples, with the aim of relating them to permeability. His measurements consisted of completely saturating core samples with saltwater of known resistivity R_w and relating the measured resistivity R_o of the fully saturated core to the resistivity of the water. He found that, regardless of the resistivity of the saturating water, the resultant resistivity of a given core sample was always related to the water resistivity by a constant factor F. He called this the formation factor, and his experiments are summarized by the following relation:

在 Leverett 成果发表后不久，壳牌公司工程师 Archie 对岩心样品进行了电阻率测量，希望找到其与岩石渗透性之间的关系。用已知电阻率 R_w 的盐水完全饱和岩心样品，测量到的完全饱和岩心的电阻率 R_o 与水的电阻率 R_w 具有一定的关系。他发现，无论饱和水的电阻率是多少，由此而产生的给定岩心样品的电阻率总是与水的电阻率有一个常数因子 F

的关系。他将其称为地层因素。他的实验总结出以下关系：

$$R_{\text{sample}} \equiv R_0 = FR_w \tag{3.1}$$

Fig.3.4 is an example of his work on cores from two different locations, where the formation factor F is plotted as a function of permeability and, almost as an after thought, porosity (on a much compressed scale). Although he was searching for a correlation with permeability, he finally admitted that a generalized relationship between formation factor and permeability did not exist, although one seemed to exist for porosity. That is the formation factor is a function of porosity and can be expressed as a power law of the form:

图 3.4 所示为 Archie 对两个不同位置岩心的研究实例，其中，地层因素 F 被绘制为渗透率的函数，几乎是事后才想到的，也被绘制为孔隙度（在压缩的尺度上）的函数。尽管 Archie 一直努力寻找渗透率与地层因素的相关性，但他最终承认，地层因素与渗透率之间的相关性并不存在，而是与孔隙度存在这种关系函数，即地层因素是孔隙度的函数，可以表示为：

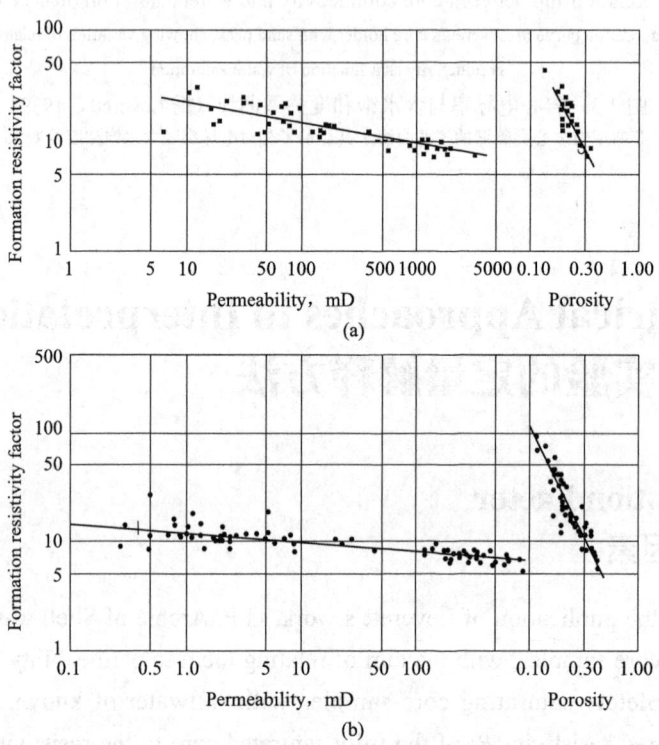

Fig.3.4 Examples of the attempts to correlate the electrical formation factor with permeability and porosity for water-saturated rock samples from two regions (from Archie,1942)

图 3.4 两个不同含水岩石样品的地层因素与渗透率、孔隙度之间的关系（据 Archie，1942）

$$F \approx \frac{1}{\phi^m} \tag{3.2}$$

Where the exponent m is very nearly 2 for the data considered. The exponent m was named the cementation exponent, as it was observed to increase with the cementation of the grains. In general, it was recognized that *m* increased with the tortuosity of the electric path through the pore space.

式中指数 *m* 非常接近 2。该指数被称为胶结指数，随颗粒胶结程度增加而增加。一般来说，胶结指数随孔隙空间的电路径的迂曲度而增加。

3.3.2 Archie's Synthesis
阿尔奇公式

The practical application of resistivity measurements is for the determination of water saturation. This was made possible by another observation of Archie. He noticed that the data of Leverett and others could be conveniently parameterized after having plotted the data in the form shown in Fig.3.5. On log–log paper, the data of water saturation versus relative resistivity plotted as a straight line, suggesting a relationship of the form:

电阻率测量的实际应用是确定含水饱和度。这是阿尔奇通过另一次观察而实现的。他注意到以图 3.5 所示的形式绘制数据后，可以方便地对 Leverett 等人的数据进行参数化。在双对数坐标下，含水饱和度与电阻率的关系呈直线型，其关系如下：

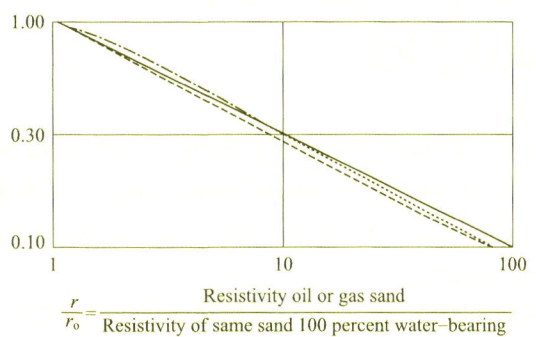

Curve	Investigator	Type sand	Salinity of Water. Grams NaCl per Liter	Oil or Gas	Porosity Fraction
—·—·—	Wyckoff	Various Uncons. Cores		CO_2	Various 0.40
————	Leverett		8 approx.	Oil	0.20 and
------	Martin		130	Oil	0.45(?)
··········	Jakosky	Friable	29 approx.	Oil	0.23

Fig.3.5 A synthesis of various resistivity/saturation experiments, indicating a general power-law relationship (from Archie,1942)

图 3.5 不同岩心电阻率与饱和度关系拟合图（据 Archie，1942）

$$S_w = \left[\frac{R_t}{R_o}\right]^{\frac{1}{n}} \tag{3.3}$$

The exponent *n*, called the saturation exponent, is very nearly 2 for the data considered. From this, an approximate expression for the water saturation is:

式中，指数 *n* 称为饱和指数，一般接近于 2。由此，含水饱和度的近似表达式为：

$$S_w \approx \sqrt{R_o/R_t} \tag{3.4}$$

However, the fully saturated resistivity R_o (which is not usually accessible in formation evaluation), can be related to the water resistivity using the previously discovered Archie relationship. So the expression becomes:

然而，使用之前的阿尔奇公式可将完全饱和的电阻率 R_o（在地层评价中通常不可获得）与水的电阻率建立相关性，故表达式就可变为：

$$S_w^n = \frac{a}{\phi^m} \frac{R_w}{R_t} \tag{3.5}$$

Where the constants *a*, *m*, and *n* need to be determined for the particular field or formation evaluated.

不同油田或不同层位的常数 *a*、*m* 和 *n* 都不同。

3.4　A Review of Electrostatics
　　　静电场知识回顾

Now that the fundamental ideas of resistivity interpretation have been explored, it is appropriate to consider the question of how resistivity measurements of sedimentary formations are made in situ. First, we make a rapid review of some basic notions of electrostatics, which forms the basis for resistivity measurements.

关于电阻率解释的基本原理已做讨论，现在就考虑如何测量原地沉积地层的电阻率是合适的。首先，我们快速回顾了静电学的一些基本概念，这些概念是电阻率测量的基础。

One concept of considerable use is that of the electrostatic potential, which follows directly from Coulomb's law. To arrive at an understanding of the electrostatic potential and to derive a simple expression for it, consider the case (Fig.3.6) of two charges (q_1 and q_2) at a distance r from one another. Coulomb's law states that the force of repulsion between the two charges is inversely proportional to the square of the separation and varies directly with the product of the magnitudes of the charges. This can be expressed as:

一个非常有用的概念是静电势，它遵循库仑定律。为了理解静电势并推导静电势的简单表达式，考虑一下两个电荷（q_1 和 q_2）彼此距离为 *r* 的情况（图 3.6）。库仑定律指出，两个电荷之间的排斥力与距离的平方成反比，与电荷大小的乘积成正比，用公式可表示为：

$$F = \frac{1}{4\pi\varepsilon_0} \frac{q_1 q_2}{r^2} \tag{3.6}$$

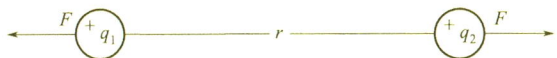

Fig.3.6 Two charged particles separated by a distance r, exhibiting a repulsive force F

图 3.6 间隔距离为 r 的两个带电粒子间的斥力为 F

This leads directly to an expression for the electric field vector $\bar{E}$, which is defined as the force per unit charge, from which it follows:

上式可得到矢量电场强度的系数 $\bar{E}$，即单位电荷所受的力，可表示为：

$$\bar{E} = \frac{1}{4\pi\varepsilon_0} \frac{q}{r^2} \hat{r} \tag{3.7}$$

Here $\hat{r}$ is the unit vector in the direction from the charge producing the field to the point of observation. Eq.3.7 gives the electric field strength at any point r from a charge of magnitude q.

式中 $\hat{r}$ 为产生场的电荷到测量点方向的单位向量。式（3.7）给出了电荷 q 在静电场中任一点 r 处的电场强度。

From the definition of work W, which is the integral of the opposing force over the distance traveled, one can be expressed as:

根据功 W 的定义，它是反作用力对移动距离的积分，可以写成：

$$W = -\int_a^b \bar{F} \cdot d\hat{s} \tag{3.8}$$

For a unit of charge in an electric field, is:

对于电场中的单位电荷，上式可改写为：

$$W = -\int_a^b \bar{E} \cdot d\hat{s} = -\frac{q}{4\pi\varepsilon_0} \int_a^b \frac{dr}{r^2} = -\frac{q}{4\pi\varepsilon_0} \left[\frac{1}{r_a} - \frac{1}{r_b} \right] \tag{3.9}$$

It is to be noted that the amount of work done in moving from point a to point b is independent of the path taken. It depends only on the value of the two end points. Thus in analogy with the notion of potential energy, the electrostatic potential $\phi(P)$ is defined as:

需要注意的是，从点 a 到点 b 所做的功与路径无关，只与始末位置有关。因此，根据势能的概念，定义静电势 $\phi(P)$ 为：

$$\phi(P) = -\int_{P_0}^{P} \bar{E} \cdot d\hat{s} \tag{3.10}$$

Or:

或：

$$\bar{E} = -\nabla \phi \tag{3.11}$$

The reference point P_0 is usually taken to be at a distance infinitely removed from the charge producing the potential, and $\phi(P_0)$ is set to zero. In this case $\phi(P_0)$ is also called the voltage V. For a point charge, this results in:

参考电势 P_0 通常被认为与产生电位的电荷距离无限远，故 $\phi(P_0)$ 为 0。在这种情况下，$\phi(P_0)$ 也被称为电压 V。对于点电荷，其计算式为：

$$\phi(r) = \frac{q}{4\pi\varepsilon_0}\frac{1}{r} = V(r) \tag{3.12}$$

3.5 Principle of Resistivity Logging 电阻率测井原理

Fig.3.6 shows the setup for measuring the resistivity of a homogeneous formation whose conductivity σ (or its inverse, the resistivity) is isotropic. It consists of a current source of intensity I and a voltage-measurement electrode M at some distance r from the current emission at point A. The resistivity of the homogeneous medium is R_t, so its conductivity σ is given by $\sigma = 1/R_t$. (Conductivity is usually written as σ in measurement physics, and as C in log interpretation.)

图 3.6 为测量电导率（或其倒数——电阻率）为各向同性的均匀地层的电阻率的测量装置示意图。它由一个位于 A 点的电流强度为 I 的点电源和一个距离点电源 r 的电压测量电极 M 组成。均匀介质的电阻率为 R_t，因此其电导率 $\sigma = 1/R_t$。（注意电导率通常在实验物理用 σ 表示，测井解释中常把电导率记为 C）。

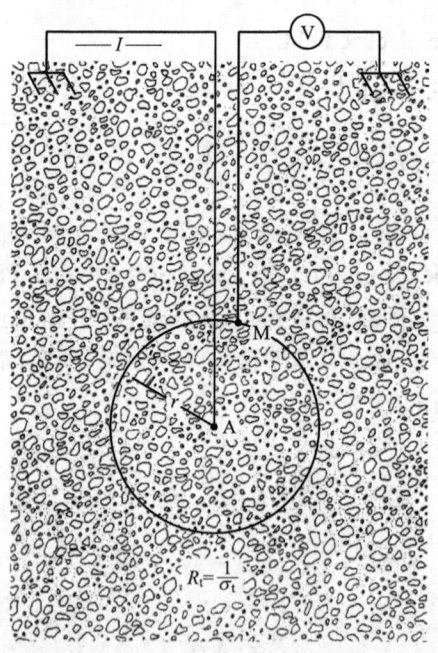

Fig.3.6　Idealized experiment for determination of the resistivity of an infinite uniform medium of conductivity σ (= $1/R_t$) (from Darwin V. Ellis, 2008)

It consists of the injection of a current at point A, and measurement of the potential at point M at a distance r from the current electrode

图 3.6　测定电导率 σ (= $1/R_t$) 的均匀介质电导率的理想装置（据 Darwin V. Ellis，2008）

它包括位于 A 点的注入电流，以及位于点电源外 r 处的 M 点的电动势测量

One way to determine the relationship between the potential at M and the current I is to use some of the relationships from electrostatics. The current I, being a continuous source of charge, can be thought of as producing a potential V, just as would be expected from some equivalent point charge q:

确定 M 处电势和电流 I 之间关系的一种方法是使用静电学理论。作为一个持续的电荷源，可以认为电流 I 产生了电势 V，就像从一些等价的点电荷 q 中预期的那样：

$$V(r) = \frac{1}{4\pi\varepsilon_0} \frac{q}{r} \tag{3.13}$$

The problem is to relate the equivalent charge q to the current I.
问题是将点电荷 q 与电流 I 联系起来。

At any point in the system there will be a current density $\bar{J}$ given by:
静电场内任一点的电流密度 $\bar{J}$ 可用下式表示：

$$\bar{J} = \sigma\bar{E} = -\sigma\frac{\partial}{\partial r}V(r) = \frac{\sigma}{4\pi\varepsilon_0}\frac{q}{r^2}\hat{r} \tag{3.14}$$

Where $\hat{r}$, the unit vector is directed radially outward from the current source. In order to put the expression for potential in terms of the total current, I, the current density is integrated over the surface of a sphere enclosing the current source:

式中，$\hat{r}$ 为点电源向外指向的单位向量。为了用电势来表达总电流 I，电流密度在包含电流源的球面上进行积分，有

$$I = \int \bar{J} \cdot dS = \frac{\sigma q}{4\pi\varepsilon_0 r^2} 4\pi r^2 = \frac{\sigma q}{\varepsilon_0} \tag{3.15}$$

And q is solved for in terms of I:
故 q 可以用 I 表示为：

$$q = \frac{\varepsilon_0 I}{\varepsilon} = IR_t \tag{3.16}$$

This expression for q is now put back into the potential for a single-point charge, Eq (3.12), to obtain the voltage at a distance r from the current source:
为了获得距离电流源 r 处的电压，将 q 代入式（3.12）中，可得：

$$V(r) = \frac{\varepsilon_0 IR_t}{4\pi\varepsilon_0 r} \tag{3.17}$$

A less tortuous determination of the potential is obtained from Ohm's law in spherical geometry. For the source of current I, the current density on the surface of a sphere of radius r centered on the source is:

从球面几何的欧姆定律中可以得到一种比较简单的电势确定方法。对于电源 I，以源为中心的半径为 r 的球面上的电流密度为：

$$J = \frac{I}{4\pi r^2} \tag{3.18}$$

The relation between current density and electric field implies that:
电场强度与电流密度的关系可表示为：

$$E = \frac{R_t I}{4\pi r^2} \qquad (3.19)$$

From this expression, the voltage at a distance r from the current source is obtained from:
据此表达式，可知距离点电源 r 处电压为：

$$V(r) = \phi(r) = -\int_{\infty}^{r} \frac{R_t I}{4\pi r^2} \, dr = \frac{R_t I}{4\pi r} \qquad (3.20)$$

Thus the value of R_t is found to be:
故，电阻率 R_t 应为：

$$R_t = 4\pi r \frac{V}{I} = k \frac{V}{I} \qquad (3.21)$$

The setup of Fig.3.6 can be considered as a rudimentary monoelectrode measurement device for determining formation resistivity. For this device the tool constant k is seen to be $4\pi r$, where r is the spacing between the current electrode and the measurement point. Knowing the injected current and the resultant voltage, the resistivity of the homogeneous medium R_t may then be found.

图 3.6 可以看作是测量地层电阻率的基本单电极测量装置。对于这个装置，常数 k 等于 $4\pi r$，其中 r 为点电源到测量点 M 之间的距离。只要测出电流强度和电压，即可求出均匀介质的电阻率 R_t。

Exercises
课后练习

3.1 State the differences between resistivity and resistance.

3.2 State the factor affecting resistivity.

3.3 What is the Archie's First Equation?

3.4 What is the Archie's Second Equation?

3.5 What is the Formation Factor?

3.6 The resistivity of a water-bearing sand was found to be 0.8Ω•m. If the formation water resistivity is 0.10Ω•m and for the formation the relationship between the formation factor F and porosity has been established as $F = \dfrac{0.81}{\phi^2}$, What is the porosity of the formation?

4 Electrode Devices
电极测井系列

4.1 Introduction
引言

We have seen the utility of knowing formation resistivity and an idealized approach to making the measurement. This chapter focuses on the evolution of one type of electrical logging tool: electrode devices, so named because the measurement elements are simply metallic electrodes. These devices utilize low-frequency current sources, in most cases below 1,000 Hz. The historical progression from the normal device to traditional focused dual laterologs will be traced. An indication of the measurement limitations for each of these types of tools will be given and related to their design. The methods used for the prediction and interpretation of their response will be discussed.

我们已经了解了地层电阻率的实用性以及测量地层电阻率的理想方法。本章重点介绍电极系测井装置的演变过程。之所以称其为电极系测井，是由于此类仪器的测量元件都是金属电极。这类仪器通常使用低频电流源，频率一般低于1000Hz。我们将了解从最基础的普通电阻率测井到双侧向测井的演变过程，以及每种仪器的与其设计相关的测量限制。本章将详细介绍应用于预测及解释其响应的各类测井方法。

4.2 Unfocused Devices: The Short Normal
未聚焦的普通电阻率：短电位电极系

The earliest commercial device, the short normal, is illustrated in Fig.4.1. It bears a strong resemblance to the thought experiment of the preceding chapter. The differences include the presence of a borehole and a sonde (on which the current electrode A and measure electrode M are located). As indicated in the figure, the spacing between the current electrode and voltage electrode was 16in, and thus the designation "short."

早期商业化的普通电阻率测井仪为短电位电极系，其电极系结构如图 4.1 所示，这与前一章的理想实验非常相似。不同点在于存在井眼和探头（供电电极 A 与测量电极 M 所在的位置）。如图所示，供电电极 A 到测量电极 M 间的距离仅为 16 英寸，故称为短电位电极。

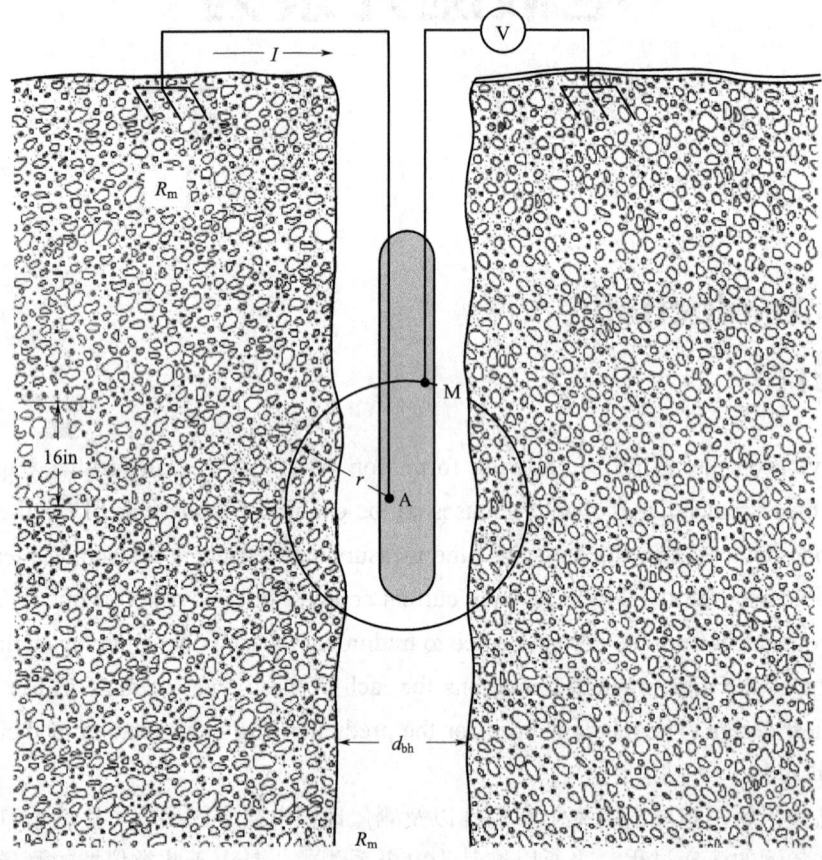

Fig.4.1　A schematic representation of the short normal (from Darwin V.Ellis, 2008)
A 16in spacing is indicated between current electrode A and measure electrode M
图 4.1　短电位电极系示意图（据 Darwin V.Ellis，2008）
电流电极 A 和测量电极 M 之间的间距为 16in

Two basic problems are associated with the short normal, both related to the presence of the borehole, which is normally filled with a conductive fluid. There is a sensitivity of the measurement to the mud resistivity and hole size, as indicated in Fig.4.2. In a borehole filled with very conductive mud, the current tends to flow in the mud rather than the formation. In this case, the apparent resistivity as deduced from the injected current and resultant voltage will not reflect the formation resistivity very accurately.

普通电阻率测井有两个问题无法解决，这两个问题都与充满钻井液的井眼环境有关。该测量方法对于钻井液电阻率和井眼尺寸敏感，如图 4.2 所示，当井眼中充满易于导电的钻井液时，电流趋向于在钻井液中传导，而非在地层中。在这种情况下，由注入电流和电压推导出的视电阻率不能很准确地反映地层电阻率。

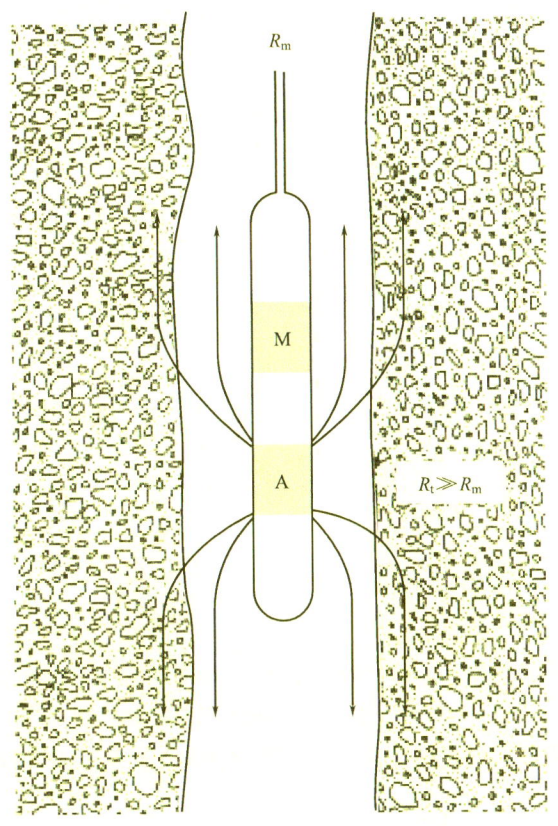

Fig.4.2 Idealized current paths for the short normal in a very conductive borehole mud (from Darwin V.Ellis, 2008)

图 4.2 电阻率极低的盐水钻井液中井中电流线的理论分布（据 Darwin V. Ellis，2008）

The second difficulty with this measuring technique is illustrated in Fig.4.3. Once again, the conductive borehole fluid provides an easy current path for the measure current into adjacent shoulder beds of much lower resistivity (R_s) than the formation (R_t) directly opposite the current electrode. In this case, the apparent resistivity (from the measurement of the voltage of electrode M and the current I, in combination with the tool constant) will again be representative not of the resistive bed, but, more likely, of the less resistive shoulder bed.

这种测量技术的第二个难点如图 4.3 所示。相对于正对着电极的地层的电阻率（R_t），围岩电阻率（R_s）要小得多，而井眼内导电的流体使得测量电流更容易进入围岩。因此，视电阻率（由测量通过电极 M 的电压和电流 I，结合工具常数所得）仍旧不能反映地层电阻率，测得的电阻率更多反映的是电阻率较低的围岩的电阻率。

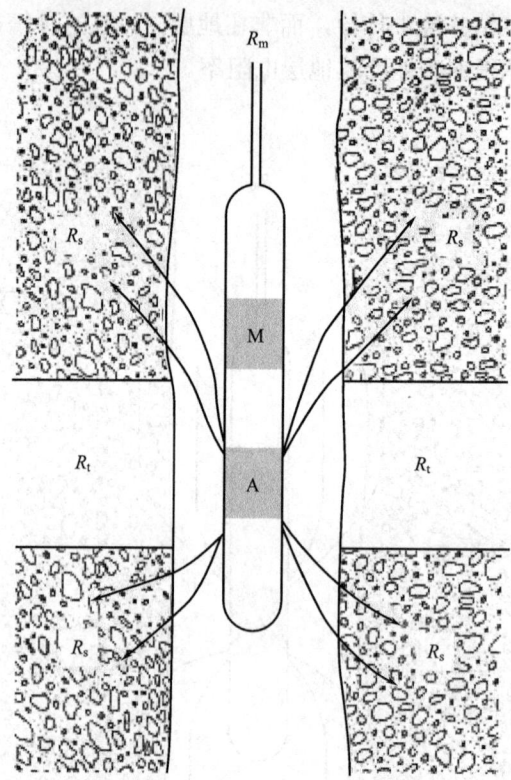

Fig.4.3　Idealized current paths for the short normal in front of a thin resistive bed ($R_t \gg R_s$) (from Darwin V.Ellis,2008)

图 4.3　目的层为薄层时理论上电流路径（$R_t \gg R_s$）(据 Darwin V. Ellis，2008)

4.3　Focused Devices
聚焦测井系列

4.3.1　Laterolog Principle
　　　侧向测井原理

The next step in the evolution of electrical tools was the implementation of current focusing. Fig.4.4 illustrates, on the left half of the diagram, the current paths for the normal device in the case of a resistive central bed. The current tends to flow around it, through the mud, into the less resistive shoulders. The desired current path is shown on the right half of the figure, where the measure current is somehow forced through the zone of interest.

电法测井经改进后的一大发展是实现了电流聚焦。如图 4.4 所示，就高电阻夹层来说，左图为未聚焦的普通电阻率测井的电流路径。电流倾向于绕过目的层、穿过钻井液，流入阻力较小的围岩中。预期的电流路径如右图所示，由于采取了适当的聚焦措施，电流线被聚焦进入了目的层。

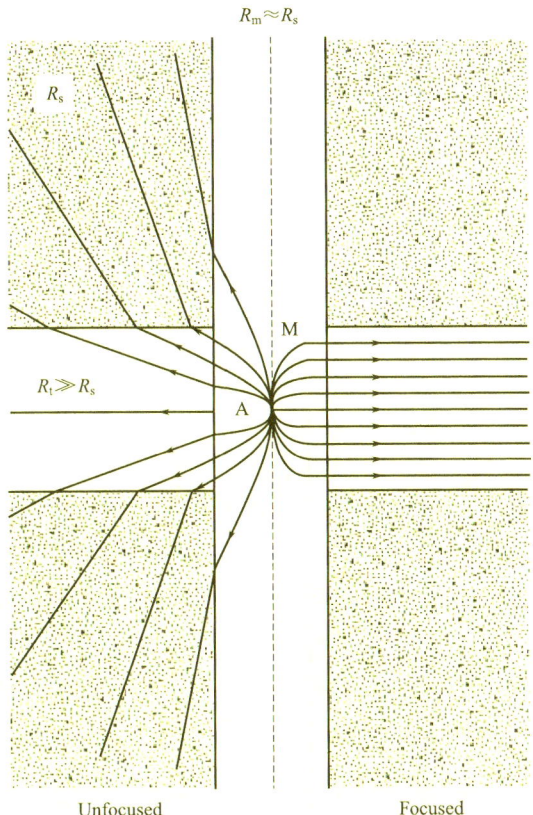

Fig.4.4 Idealized patterns of current flow in the borehole and formation from a central electrode(from Schlumberger, 2005)

On the left the pattern is altered from the expected radial pattern because of the presence of a highly resistive bed.

On the right is the desired flow, so that the resistivity of the bed of interest is sampled properly

图 4.4 井眼及地层中电流线的理想分布模式（据斯伦贝谢，2005）

左侧由于高阻层的存在，电流线分布模式与预想模式不同；

右侧是预期的电流线分布，这样就可以测量目标层电阻率

The principle of focusing is shown in Fig.4.5, where there are now three current emitting electrodes, A_0, A_1, and A_1'. This type of array is known as a guard focusing device and is commonly referred to as a Laterolog-3 (LL3) device. The potential of electrodes A_1 and A_1' is held constant and at the same potential as the central electrode A_0. Since current flows only if a potential difference exists, there should, in principle, be no current flow in the vertical direction. The sheath of current therefore emanates horizontally from the central measurement electrode. The current emitted from the focusing, or "guard" electrodes is often referred to as the "bucking" current, as its function is to impede the measure current from flowing in the borehole mud. It is the continuous adjustment of the bucking current which keeps A_1 and A_1' at the same potential as A_0. Since the electrodes A_1 and A_1' are elongated, the current lines at their inner ends are nearly horizontal, which forces the current sheath from A_0 to remain horizontally focused deep into the formation.

聚焦原理如图4-5所示，有3个供电电极A_0、A_1和A_1'，这类配置为聚焦测井，通常被称为三侧向测井（LL3）设备。电极A_1和A_1'的电势保持恒定，且与主电极A_0电势相同。因为电流只有在存在电位差的情况下流动，所以原则上讲，垂向上应该没有电流。因此，电流从主测量电极水平发出。从聚焦（或屏蔽）电极中发出的电流通常被称为屏蔽电流，因为它的功能是阻止测量电流在井眼钻井液中流动。在测量过程中不断调整屏蔽电流，保证A_1和A_1'主电极A_0电势一致。由于电极A_1和A_1'被拉长，它们内端的电流线几乎是水平的，这就使得主电极A_0发出的电流保持水平，聚焦地流入地层深处。

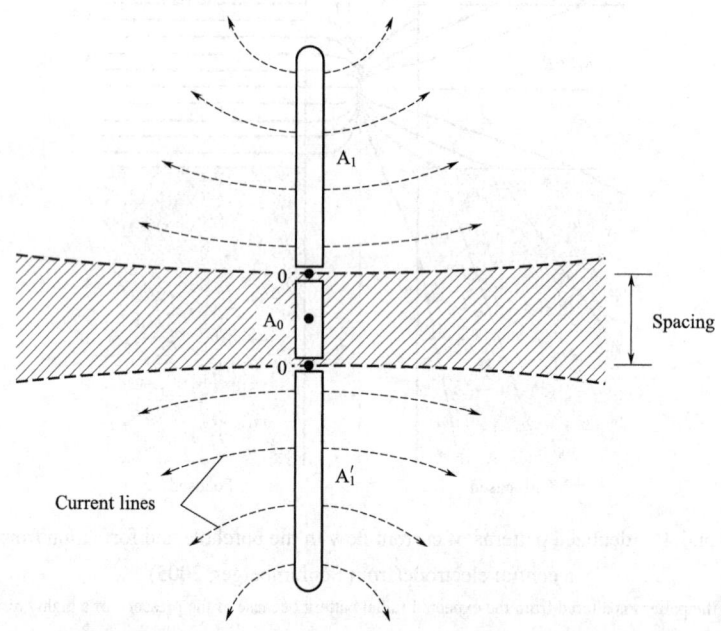

Fig.4.5　Idealized current distribution from the Laterolog-3 device in a homogeneous formation, with current focused into the formation（from Serra，1984）

图4.5　理想化各向同性地层中三侧向电流分布示意图（据Serra，1984）

Despite these good intentions, the LL3 device still showed some difficulty with bed boundaries. This is illustrated in Fig.4.6, which shows cases of large contrast between the shoulder bed resistivity R_s and the value of R_t. For the thick resistive bed in the upper portion of the figure, $R_t > R_s$ the principal measure current is seen to be escaping through the mud and into the shoulder. In the lower example, for a thin conductive streak, $R_t < R_s$, current is seen to seek it out sooner than expected, giving a broader apparent bed thickness than in the previous case.

尽管与普通电阻率测井仪器相比，三侧向有明显的优势，但在地层界面处缺陷也比较明显。如图4.6所示，地层电阻率R_t与围岩电阻率R_s差异明显。在图4.6上半部分的厚电阻层，地层电阻率R_t大于围岩电阻率R_s，主电流自主电极发出后，通过钻井液流入了围岩。在图4.6下半部分的薄层，地层电阻率R_t小于围岩电阻率R_s，主电流比预期更快地流入电阻率较低的薄层，说明三侧向聚焦能力有限，纵向分层能力较差。

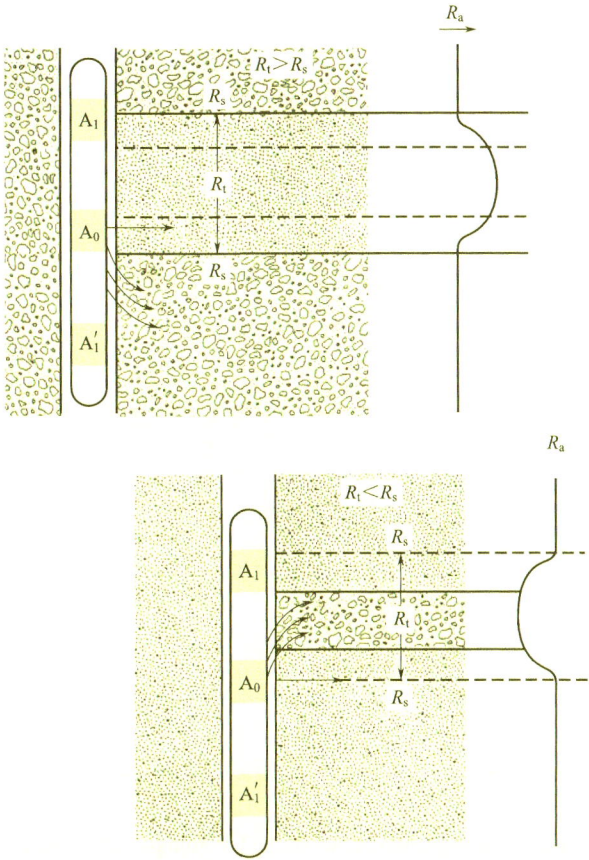

Fig.4.6 The effects of shoulder bed resistivity on the behavior of an LL3 device(from Darwin V. Ellis, 2008)
The top sketch indicates current passing through the mud into a highly conductive shoulder. The bottom sketch indicates the effect of a thin conductive bed

图 4.6　围岩电阻率对三侧向测井测量影响（据 Darwin V. Ellis，2008）
顶部示意图说明电流线经过钻井液进入高电导率围岩中，底部示意图说明目的传导层为薄层时电流线分布情况

Another approach to focusing the measure current is the seven electrode device, or LL7. The electrode configuration of one such device is sketched in Fig.4.7. The guard electrodes A_1 and A_1' are no longer elongated: instead, additional monitoring electrodes have been introduced in order to impede the flow of current parallel to the sonde though the borehole mud. This is achieved by varying the bucking current of the guard electrodes so that the potential drop between the pairs of monitor electrodes (i.e., $M_1 - M_1'$ and $M_2 - M_2'$) is zero. Since the potential drop is zero along this vertical direction, the current will be focused into the formation.

另一种聚焦测量电流的方法是七电极装置，或称七侧向测井（LL7）。其电极系结构如图 4.7 所示，屏蔽电极 A_1 和 A_1' 长度不再延长，取而代之的是在屏蔽电极旁增加了两对监督电极，以阻止与电极系平行的电流流过井眼钻井液。通过调整屏蔽电极的屏蔽电流，使得两对监督电极（$M_1 - M_1'$ 和 $M_2 - M_2'$）之间的电位降为零。由于沿井眼垂直方向的电位降为零，电流被聚焦到地层中。

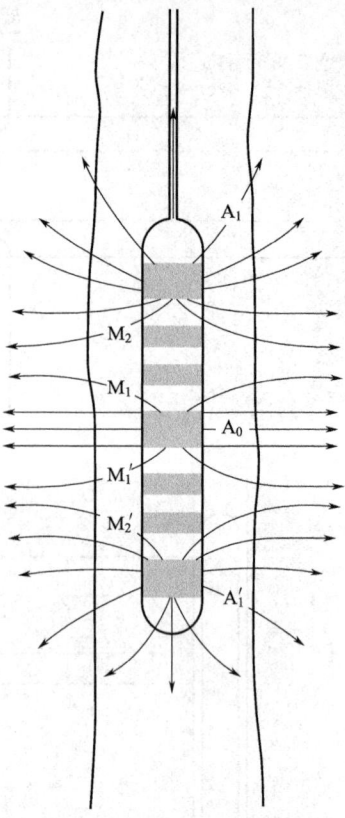

Fig.4.7 The electrode configuration of the Laterolog-7 (from Serra, 1984)
Monitor electrodes drive the bucking current in the guard electrode to maintain a differential voltage of zero. The array is symmetric with A_0 in the center

图 4.7 七侧向电极系结构示意图（据 Serra，1984）

主电极 A_0 位于中心，监督电极位于主电极两侧，测量时保持监督电极电压降为 0

4.3.2 Spherical Focusing
球形聚焦测井

Another approach to compensating for the effect of the borehole is the concept of spherical focusing. In this technique, which has been adopted for medium and shallow resistivity measurements, bucking currents attempt to establish the spherical equipotential surfaces that would exist if no borehole were present. Fig.4.8 is a rough sketch of the equipotential surfaces which surround the current electrode in a normal device, as a result of the presence of the conductive mud in the borehole. Instead of spherical surfaces, they are of elongated shape. The objective of the spherical focusing is to provide a bucking current to force the equipotential lines to become spherical once again. Then the potential difference at two points along the sonde will be determined by the resistivity of a slice of formation in a spherical shell with radii equal to the two spacings. The depth of investigation can be controlled by the size of the shell. The idea is more clearly presented in Fig.4.9.

另一种补偿井眼钻井液影响的聚焦测井为球形聚焦测井。该方法常用于测量中、浅地层电阻率。如果没有井眼影响，屏蔽电流就可以建立一个球形等势面。图 4.8 所示为由于钻孔中导电钻井液的存在，普通电阻率测井装置中围绕供电电极形成电位等势面。该等势面不是球面，而是细长的椭圆形。球形聚焦测井的目的是提供屏蔽电流以迫使等势面再次变为球形，然后记录测量电极两点的电位差进而确定地层电阻率，其探测深度可由球形的半径大小来控制。图 4.9 为球形聚焦测井电流线示意图。

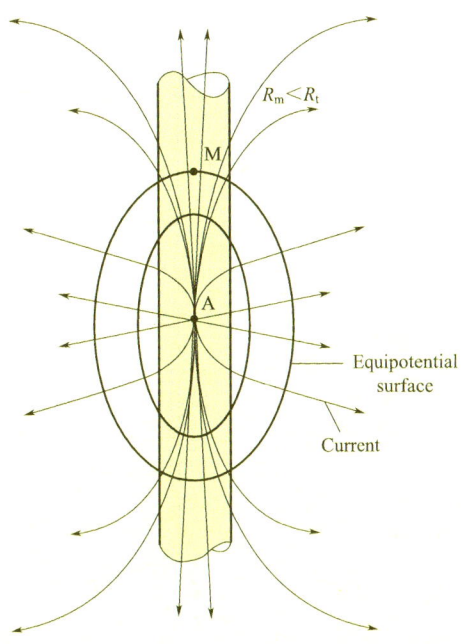

Fig.4.8 Approximate current lines and equipotential surfaces for the short normal in a borehole (from Darwin V. Ellis, 2008)

图 4.8 井筒中短电极电位的近似电流线及等势面分布示意图（据 Darwin V. Ellis，2008）

The electrode A_0 furnishes two sources of current; the measure current, which is returned to a distant electrode, and the bucking current. The bucking current, also called auxiliary current, returned to the electrodes A_1 and A_1' is varied so that the potential difference between two sets of monitor electrodes (M_1–M_2 and M_2' – M_2') is zero. The measure current is adjusted to maintain a constant potential between M_0 and the two sets of monitor electrodes. The dashed lines in Fig.4.9 then trace out approximately two surfaces of constant potential. These cause the measure current injected by the central electrode to flow radially outward, at least until the outer potential surface is reached. The volume of formation investigated will be nearly the space between the two equipotential surfaces, with the exclusion of the region close to the borehole interface, which is "plugged" by the bucking current. The bucking current can be viewed either as setting up the equipotential surface or providing the current through the mud so that the actual measure current is forced into the formation.

球形聚焦中主电极 A_0 提供两个同极性的电流源，分别为返回到远处电极的测量电流和屏蔽电流。测量过程屏蔽电流又称为辅助电流，返回至回路电极 A_1 和 A_1'，该电流为变化的电流，通过调节补偿电流使得两组监督电极（M_1–M_2 和 M_2' – M_2'）之间的电位差为 0，同时调节测量电流以保持电极 M_0 和两组监督电极之间的电位为恒定电位。图 4-9 中虚线绘出了恒定电位的等势面。这样使得主电极发出的测量电流向外流动，至少到达外部电位表面。球形聚焦所探测到的地层体积几乎为两个等势面之间的空间，同时又不包括靠近井眼附近介质的区域，这主要是由于该区域被补偿电流所"堵住"（屏蔽）。屏蔽电流不仅建立了等势面，而且仅在钻井液中流动，将同极性的测量电流聚焦进入地层。

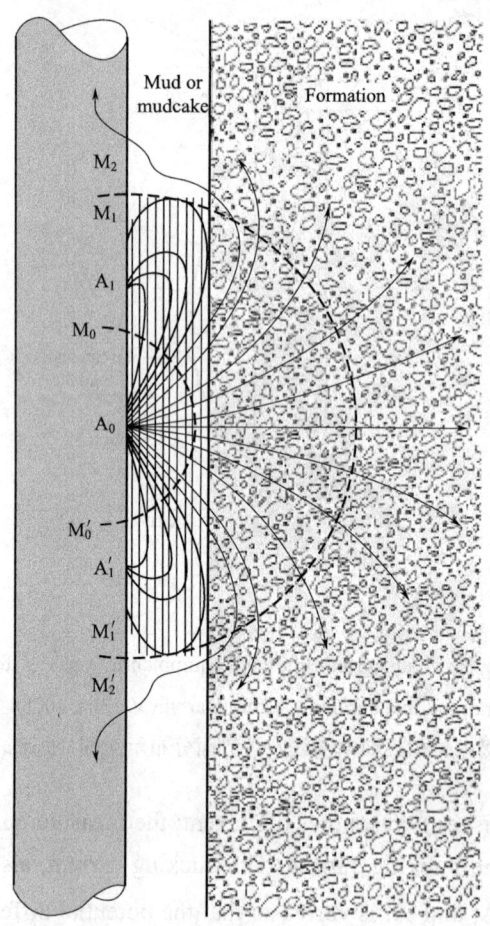

Fig.4.9　The electrode configuration of the spherically focused array (Courtesy of Schlumberger, 2008)
图 4.9　球形聚焦测井电极系结构及电流线分布示意图（据斯伦贝谢，2008）

4.3.3　The Dual Laterolog
双侧向测井

　　The most common traditional electrode devices use a dual focusing system. Those known as dual laterologs combine the features of the LL3 and LL7 arrays, in an alternating sequence of measurements. By rapidly changing the role of various electrodes, a simultaneous measurement of deep and shallow resistivity is achieved. Fig.4.10 shows the current paths computed for such a device. On the left side of the figure, the electrodes are in the deep configuration. The length of the guard electrodes, which use parts of the sonde, is about 28 ft to achieve deep penetration of a current beam of 2 ft nominal thickness. On the right side, they are in the shallow configuration.

目前最常见的聚焦测井仪为双侧向测井系统。双侧向在交替测量序列中，结合了三侧向和七侧向测井仪各自的优点，通过快速改变各种电极的作用，实现了深、浅电阻率的同时测量。图 4-10 为双侧向测井设备的电流线路径图。图左侧为深侧向电流分布，探测器中屏蔽电极间距离为 28 英尺，电流层厚度为 2 英尺，图右侧为浅侧向电流分布图。

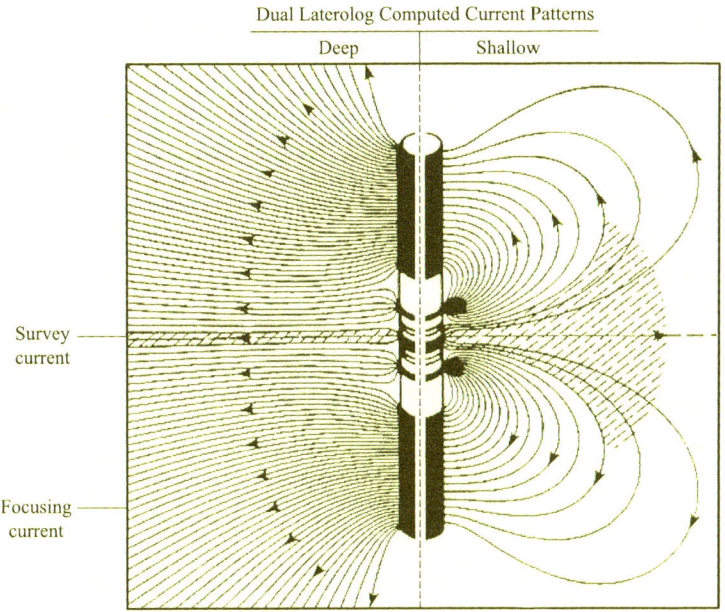

Fig.4.10 The electrode configuration and current distribution from the dual laterolog (from Chemali R, 1983)
The central electrode is the source of measure current for both shallow and deep modes. In the deep mode, both the two long electrodes and the smaller electrodes next to them are sources of bucking current. In the shallow mode, the bucking current is sent from the small to the long electrodes to provide a type of spherical focusing

图 4.10 双侧向测井仪电极系结构及电流线分布（据 Chemali R，1983）
中心电极是深、浅侧向测量电流的来源。在深模式下，两个长电极和它们旁边的小电极都是屏蔽电流的来源。在浅模式下，屏蔽电流从小电极流入长电极，以提供一种球形聚焦

For purposes of comparison of the different electrical measuring devices, it is convenient to think of the signal measured as being the result of the influence of three distinct regions of the measuring environment, as shown earlier in Fig.1.8: the borehole, the invaded zone, and the undisturbed formation. Each of these zones is attributed its own characteristic resistivity: R_m, R_{xo}, and R_t. Generally, the mud resistivity R_m is much less than either R_{xo} or R_t.

为比较不同电阻率测井探测特性，可将测量信号视为在井眼周围三个不同区带不同测量环境影响下的结果，如图 1.8 所示：自井轴中心依次向外的测量环境可划分为井眼、侵入带和原状地层，这些区域的电阻率分别记为 R_m，R_{xo}，和 R_t，通常情况下，钻井液电阻率 R_m 远小于 R_{xo} 或 R_t。

In this model, the response of an electrode device can be conveniently thought of as an approximately linear combination of the invaded zone and the true resistivity. This is expressed as:

在该函数模型中，电阻率的测量值可被认为是侵入带和地层真电阻率的线性函数，其表达式为：

$$R_a = J(d_i)R_{xo} + (1 - J(d_i))R_t \tag{4.1}$$

Where R_a is the apparent resistivity. The pseudogeometric factor J is a normalized weighting factor which gives the relative contributions of the invaded zone (of diameter, d_i) and virgin zone, to the final answer. It is referred to as the pseudogeometric factor (as opposed to a pure geometric factor) since the weighting function will actually be influenced by the contrast between R_{xo} and R_t. Fig.4.11 illustrates the pseudo geometric factor for several of the devices discussed, for the case of invaded zone resistivity that is greater than that of the virgin zone as well as the case of an invaded zone that is one tenth the resistivity of the virgin formation.

式中 R_a 是视电阻率。伪几何因子 J 是归一化的加权因子，它给出了侵入带（直径 d_i）和原状地层对测量值的相对贡献。它被称为伪几何因子（与纯几何因子相反），因为加权函数实际上会受到侵入带电阻率 R_{xo} 和原状地层电阻率 R_t 的影响。图 4.11 为侵入带电阻率大于原状地层电阻率（实线）和侵入带电阻率为原状地层电阻率十分之一（虚线）两种情况下，不同侧向测井仪器的伪几何因子 J 解释图版。

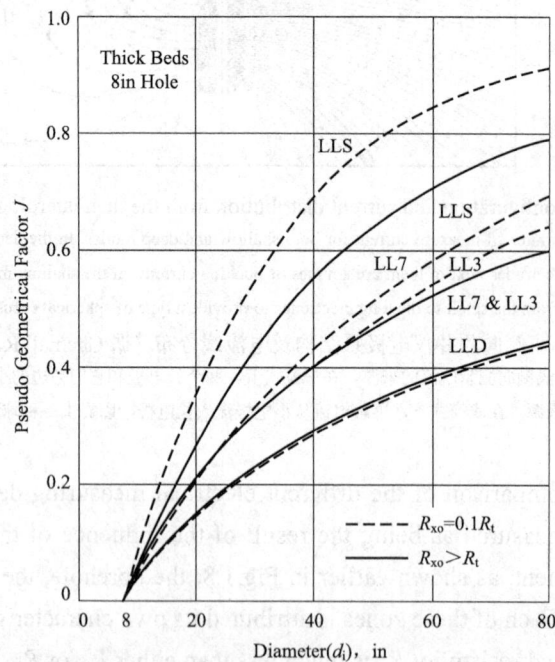

Fig.4.11 The comparison of calculated pseudo geometric factors for a number of common Laterolog devices. LLD and LLS refer respectively to the deep and shallow arrays of a dual laterolog device (Courtesy of Schlumberger, 2005)

图 4.11 常见侧向测井伪几何因子值的比较，LLD 和 LLS 分别指双侧向的深侧向和浅侧向（据斯伦贝谢，2005）

The pseudo geometric factors can be used to estimate the influence of the invaded zone on the measurement of resistivity when there is a contrast between R_t and R_{xo}. The shallow curve (marked LLS) rises steeply and indicates that in the case of a more conductive invasion zone ($R_{xo} = 0.1R_t$), half of the shallow response comes from the first 8 inch of invasion and 90% comes from within a diameter of about 80 inch. The deep measurement (marked LLD) shows less sensitivity to the invaded zone since only about 15% of its response comes from a diameter of 20 inch. (or the first 6 inch of invasion in this calculation for an 8 inch borehole). The actual signal from the invaded zone depends not only on the responses shown in Fig.4.11 but also the resistivity. Thus if $R_{xo} = R_t$, 15% of the total signal will come from the invaded zone for d_i =20in., whereas if $R_{xo} = 0.1R_t$ only 1.5% will.

当 R_t 和 R_{xo} 存在对比时，伪几何因子可用于评价侵入带对电阻率测量值的影响。在侵入带电阻率小于原状地层电阻率（$R_{xo} = 0.1R_t$）的情况下，浅侧向曲线（标记为 LLS）急剧上升，测量值的一半影响来自于侵入的前 8 英寸，当侵入直径到 80 英寸时，对应伪几何因子值为 0.9，说明测量值的 90% 贡献来自于侵入带。与浅侧向相比，深侧向对侵入带的影响敏感性较低，当侵入直径为 20 英寸（或 8 英寸井眼情况下开始侵入的前 6 英寸）时，深侧向对测量值的贡献为 15%。侵入对测量值的影响不仅取决于图 4.11 所示的侵入直径，还取决于电阻率。因此，如果 $R_{xo} = R_t$，侵入半径 d_i =20 英寸，则测量值的 15% 贡献来自侵入带，而如果 $R_{xo} = 0.1R_t$，则只有 1.5% 贡献来自侵入带。

It is important to note the laterolog's sensitivity to the borehole. Fig.4.12 shows the correction charts for the deep and shallow measurement of a particular dual laterolog device. This chart is for a centered tool. Other charts are available for an eccentered tool, the eccentricity being characterized by the standoff between tool and borehole wall. It is seen that the deep reading is rarely in error by more than 10%, for a variety of borehole sizes and resistivity contrasts. The shallow measurement, however, may differ by as much as 30% from the value of R_t in large boreholes and for resistivity contrasts in excess of 1000.

需要值得注意的是侧向测井对井眼大小非常敏感。图 4.12 为双侧向测井的深、浅侧向测量的校正图版，适用仪器居中的情况。当仪器不居中时，可采用偏心距由仪器与井壁之间的距离来表征的其他图版。从图版中可以看出，对于不同的井眼尺寸和 R_{LLD}/R_m 比值，深侧向测井读数误差很少超过 10%。而浅侧向在大井眼且当 R_{LLS}/R_m 比值大于 1000 的情况下，相对 R_t 的误差可超过 30%。

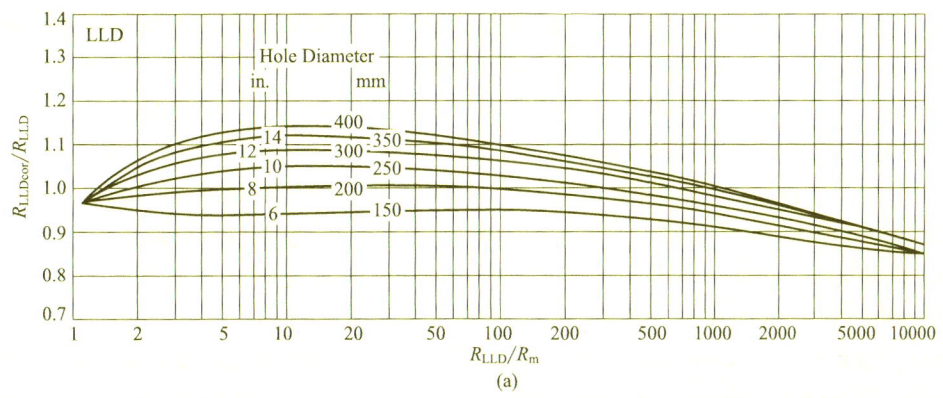

Fig.4.12 A borehole correction chart for the deep and shallow laterolog measurements （from Schlumberger, 2005）

图 4.12 双侧向井眼校正图版（据斯伦贝谢，2005）

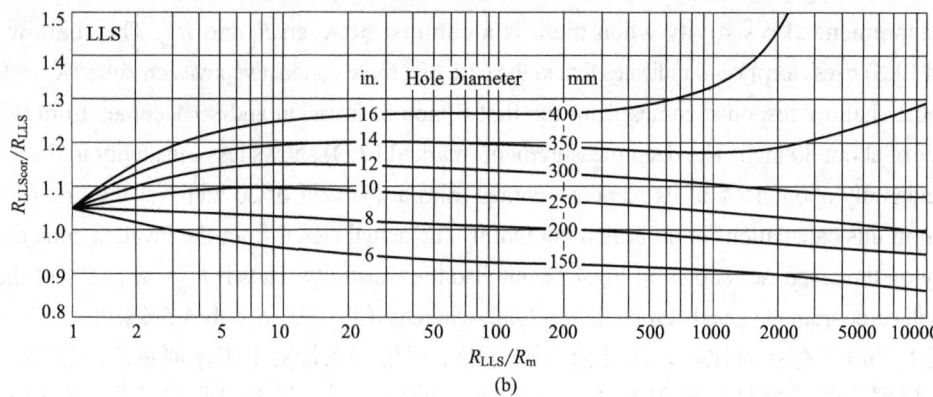

Fig.4.12 A borehole correction chart for the deep and shallow laterolog measurements （from Schlumberger, 2005）

图 4.12 双侧向井眼校正图版（据斯伦贝谢，2005）(续)

4.3.4 Dual Laterolog Example
双侧向曲线实例

Fig.4.13 shows a typical dual laterolog presentation for a hypothetical reservoir. The reservoir consists of a water zone and a hydrocarbon zone of moderate porosity. Only two of the curves shown on the log are uniquely associated with the dual laterolog, coded LLS and LLD. The additional resistivity curve, denoted by MSFL, is produced by a micro resistivity device (indicating shallow depth of investigation, because of small electrode spacings), discussed in later. The curve in track 1 is a gamma ray, which can be taken to indicate clean zones.

图 4.13 为一个假定油藏的典型双侧向测井表现。储层由中等孔隙度的水层和油气层组成。测井曲线中只有两条曲线与双侧向测井相关，分别为 LLS 和 LLD。另外一条电阻率曲线为微球形聚焦曲线 MSFL，由微电阻率测井装置（电极距小，测量半径短）产生，后面章节讨论。左侧 1# 道对应自然伽马曲线，用于判断岩性。

The water zone at the bottom is characterized, in this case, by rather low-resistivity readings and the lack of separation between the deep and shallow laterolog readings. The hydrocarbon zone is indicated by the high-resistivity readings above 12,470 ft. For 20 ft below this zone the readings are higher than in the water zone. This could indicate a small amount of hydrocarbons or a change in porosity. Any further quantification of the contents of this formation will depend on further measurements or knowledge. One of the most important pieces of information will be an estimate of the porosity. If the logs are to be used for a qualitative decision, for example on whether or not to continue drilling, further processing is probably not necessary. For an accurate quantified interpretation, it will be necessary to apply corrections to the resistivity readings. Although the corrections are normally applied by software, they are most easily understood in the form of published correction charts. Most of the corrections are made in terms of the mud resistivity (R_m) and mud filtrate (R_{mf}) resistivity, which can be obtained from the log heading. The first step is to convert these two resistivity readings to the values they would have at formation temperature. This can be estimated from a recorded bottom hole temperature or from typical geothermal gradients for the region. The next step, for zones of interest, is to correct the resistivity readings for the influence of the borehole, as in Fig.4.12.

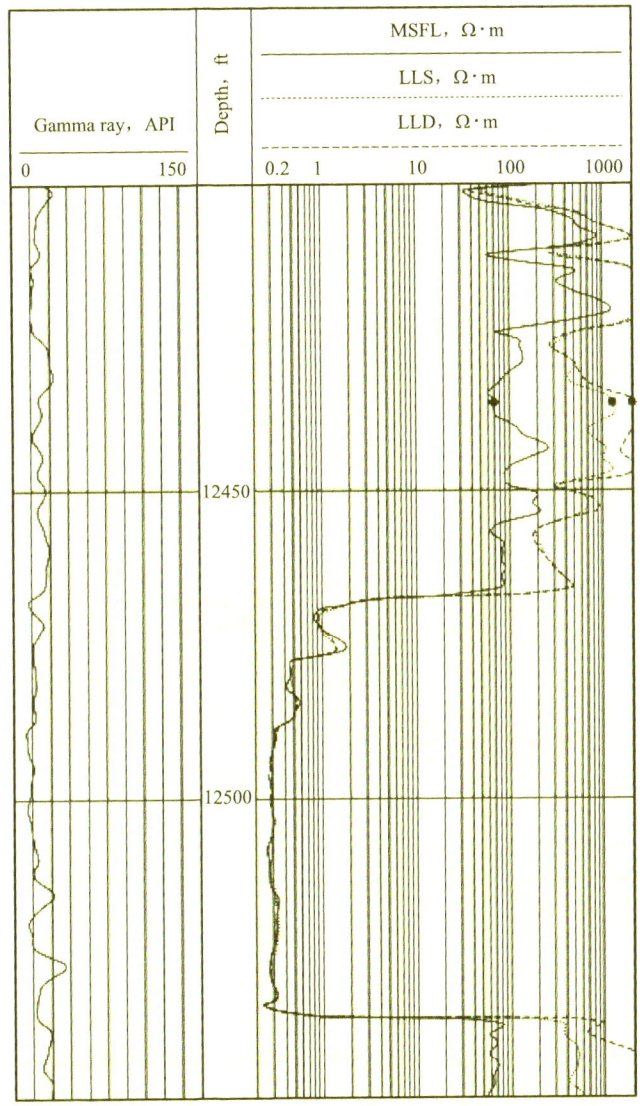

Fig.4.13 The response of a laterolog in an simulated and idealized reservoir (The marked section shows need of invasion corrections) (from Darwin V.Ellis,2008)

图 4.13 双侧向测井曲线实例（图中标记部分说明需做侵入校正）（据 Darwin V. Ellis，2008）

如图 4.13 所示，剖面底部水层因具极低电阻率，深、浅侧向读数差别不大（两条曲线分开程度较小）而被识别。12470 英尺以上井段具有高电阻率的油气层，12470 英尺之下的 20 英尺地层，读数高于水层，可能是少量油气的显示，也可能是孔隙度变化造成的结果，需要进一步补充其他测井曲线信息，对孔隙度的估算是最重要的信息之一。如果要将测井数据用于定性决策，例如是否继续钻探，则可能不需要对数据进一步处理。如果要利用上述侧向曲线资料进行准确的定量解释，则有必要对电阻率曲线读数进行校正。尽管这些校正工作通常可由计算机软件来完成，但它们最容易被理解的形式是已发布的校正图版。大多数校正是根据从井头文件读出的钻井液电阻率（R_m）和钻井液滤液电阻率（R_{mf}）来进行的。工作第一步是将这两个电阻率的读数转换为地层温度下的数值。这可以通过已经记录的井底温度或该地区典型地温梯度来估计。第二步是校正目标区域中井眼对测量值的影响，如图 4.12 所示。

The third step is to correct for the remaining effect of shoulder beds that has not been handled by the focused arrays. The cause of this effect is the alteration of the current lines near high-contrast boundaries (Fig.4.14). High-resistivity shoulders squeeze the current into the low-resistivity bed, altering the tool constant computed for a homogeneous formation and raising the apparent resistivity. Low-resistivity shoulders cause the opposite. The effect is only significant for the LLS when bed thicknesses are less than 10 ft, but can be seen on the LLD for beds up to 100 ft thick with strong contrasts.

第三步为校正未被聚焦电极系处理的围岩的剩余效应。造成剩余效应的原因是在层界面附近由于电阻率相差过大，致使电流线分布发生改变（图 4.14）。高电阻率的围岩将电流线挤入低电阻率的目的层，改变了用于计算均匀地层的工具常数，从而造成目的层测量电阻率（视电阻率）升高。右图为相反的情况。只有当目的层厚度小于 10 英尺时，围岩对浅侧向（LLS）测量电阻率影响才显著。当目的层厚度大于 100 英尺时，围岩对深侧向（LLD）测量电阻率影响才显著。

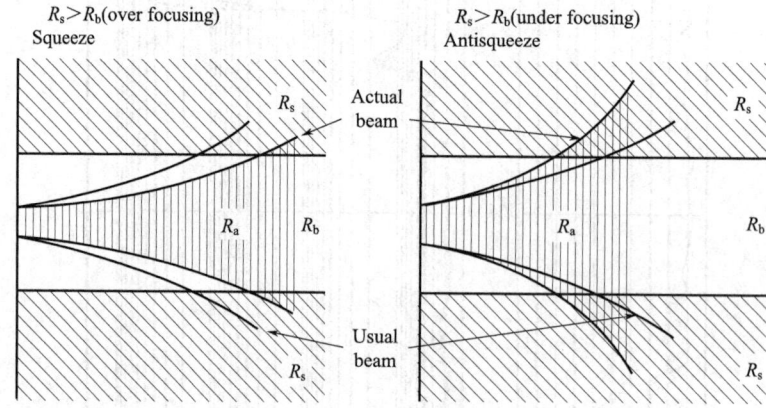

Fig.4.14　Comparison of the current beams from a laterolog when (left) the shoulder beds are more resistive than the central bed and (right) when they are less resistive （from Crary and Smith，1990）

图 4.14　围岩对侧向测井电流线分布影响比较（左侧围岩电阻率大于目的层电阻率，右侧围岩电阻率小于目的层电阻率）（据 Crary 和 Smith，1990）

The final step is the correction for invasion. Chartbook-based invasion corrections assume a step profile model with three unknowns (R_{xo}, R_t, and d_i) that can be solved with three measurements (LLS, LLD, and micro resistivity). It is assumed that the micro resistivity curve reads R_{xo}. The charts are parameterized in terms of resistivity ratios: R_{xo} compared to the deep resistivity, and the medium resistivity to the deep. In Fig.4.15, at 12,435 ft, the separation between deep and medium resistivity is a factor of 2, while the deep and micro resistivity are separated by a factor of 30. This indicates moderate invasion. Deep invasion would be signaled by a larger separation between deep and medium.

最后是对侵入的校正。基于图版的侵入校正假设剖面模型里有三个参数（R_{xo}、R_t 和 d_i），这三个参数可由三个测量值——LLS（浅侧向）、LLD（深侧向）和微电阻率来求解。假设微电阻率曲线读数为 R_{xo}。图版根据电阻率比值（深电阻率与 R_{xo} 的比值，深电阻率与中电阻率比值）来确定侵入深度和 R_t 的值。如图 4.15 中，在 12435 英尺处，深电阻率约为中电阻率 2 倍，却是微电阻率读数约 30 倍，代表侵入中等，如果侵入深度进一步加深，将造成深电阻率和中电阻率曲线读数相差悬殊。

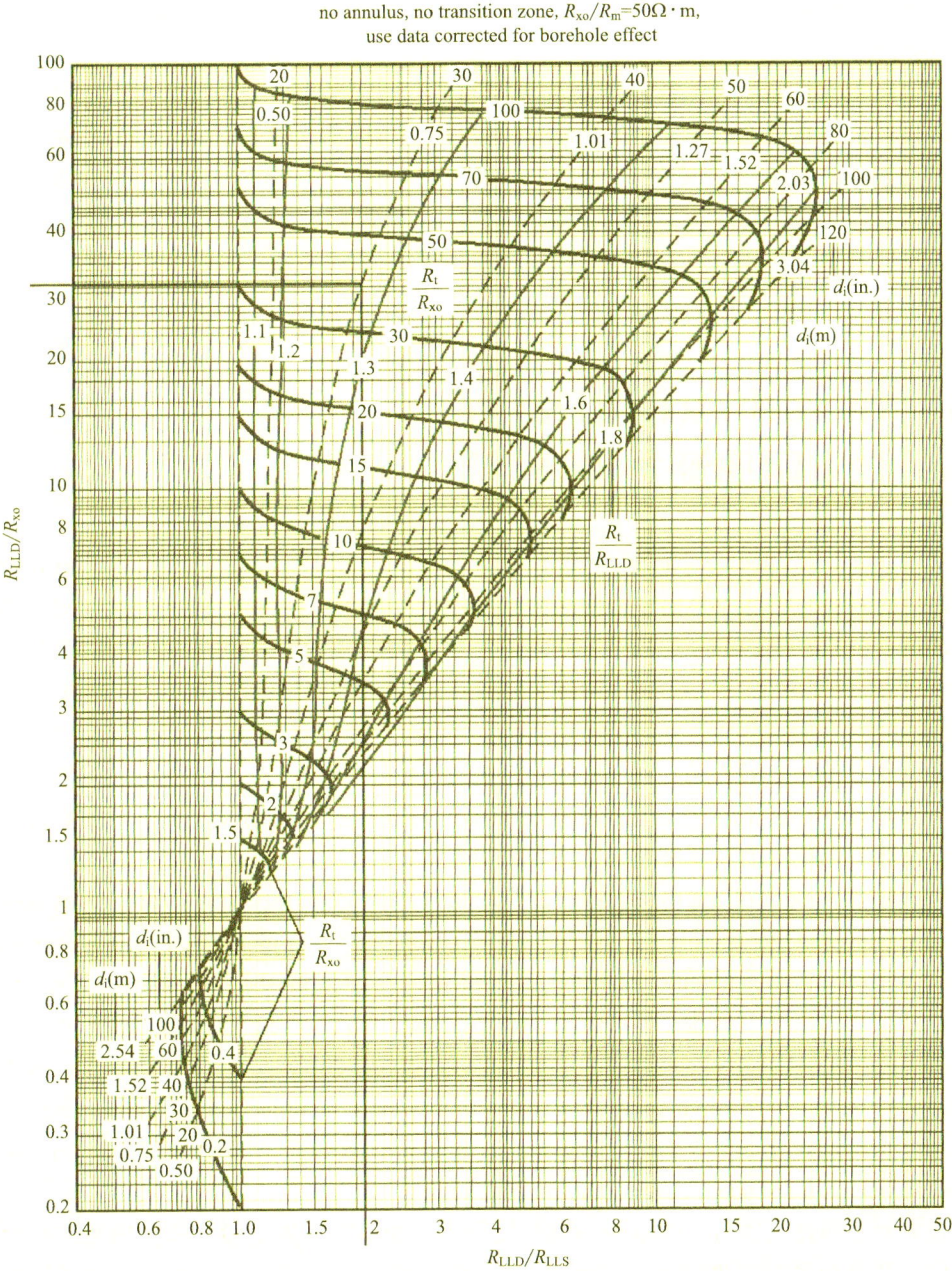

Fig.4.15　A dual laterolog invasion correction chart (Courtesy of Schlumberger)

图 4.15　双侧向测井侵入校正图版（据斯伦贝谢）

The resistivity ratios are entered into the appropriate chart, often referred to as a "tornado" or "butterfly" chart (Fig.4.15). Despite the clutter of curves, there is a wealth of information. First, the intersection of the two ratios indicates that R_t / R_{LLD} is about 1.28. This means that the deep measurement is about 28% in error from the value of R_t because of invasion effects; R_t is 1.28 times the value of R_{LLD}. Other parameterized sets of curves indicate a diameter of invasion of about 30 inch and that the value of R_t is about 40 times the value of R_{xo}. In the zone below, 12,455–12,466 ft, the shallow and the deep laterolog readings overlay. This indicates, as can be confirmed from the correction chart, that there is little invasion and that the deep resistivity needs no correction.

含有电阻率比值的侵入校正图通常被称为"旋风图"或"蝴蝶图"（图4.15）。尽管曲线错综复杂，但依然含有丰富的信息。首先，两个比值的交点表明 R_t / R_{LLD} 约为1.28。这意味着受侵入影响，测量误差约为 R_t 值的28%；R_t 是 R_{LLD} 值的1.28倍。其他曲线表明侵入直径约为30英寸，且 R_t 约为 R_{xo} 值的40倍。在图4.16中12455～12466英尺深度段内，浅侧向和深侧向读数重合。这表明，如校正图证实的那样，几乎没有入侵，深电阻率不需要校正。

4.4 Microelectrode Devices
微电阻率测井设备

Microelectrode devices, as their name implies, are electrical logging tools with electrode spacings on a much-reduced scale compared to the mandrel tools previously considered. A further distinction, a result of the smaller spacings, is that their depth of investigation is also much reduced. The electrodes are mounted on special devices, called pads, which are kept in contact with the borehole wall while ascending the well.

微电极设备，顾名思义，是一种相较于前述介绍的测井工具，电极距大为减小的电子测井工具。此外，由于缩小了电极之间的距离，其探测的深度也大大减小。测量时电极被安装在特殊的电极板上，在测量过程中紧贴井壁。

The development of microelectrode devices has undergone the same evolution as electrode tools. The first was the microlog device (Fig.4.16), which was an unfocused measurement based on the principle of a normal and a lateral. Current is emitted from the button marked A_0, and the potentials of the two electrodes M_1 and M_2 are measured. To ensure a shallow depth of investigation, the spacing between electrodes is 1 inch. The difference in potential between electrodes M_1 and M_2 forms a lateral, or inverse, measurement that is mostly influenced by the presence of mud cake. The potential on electrode M_2 forms a normal measurement which, being farther from the current source, is influenced more by the flushed zone.

微电阻率测井仪器与前述电极系测井仪经历了相似的发展阶段。首先出现的是微电极测井仪，其电极系结构如图4.16所示，是一种基于普通电阻率测量原理的未聚焦测井仪器。点电源 A_0 发出电流，电极 M_1 和 M_2 为测量电极。为保证较小的探测深度，电极之间的间距为 1in。A_0、M_1 和 M_2 组成微梯度电极系，所测视电阻率主要反映滤饼电阻率，A_0、M_2 组成微电位电极，由于其距离电流源较远所测视电阻率主要反映渗透层井段的冲洗带电阻率。

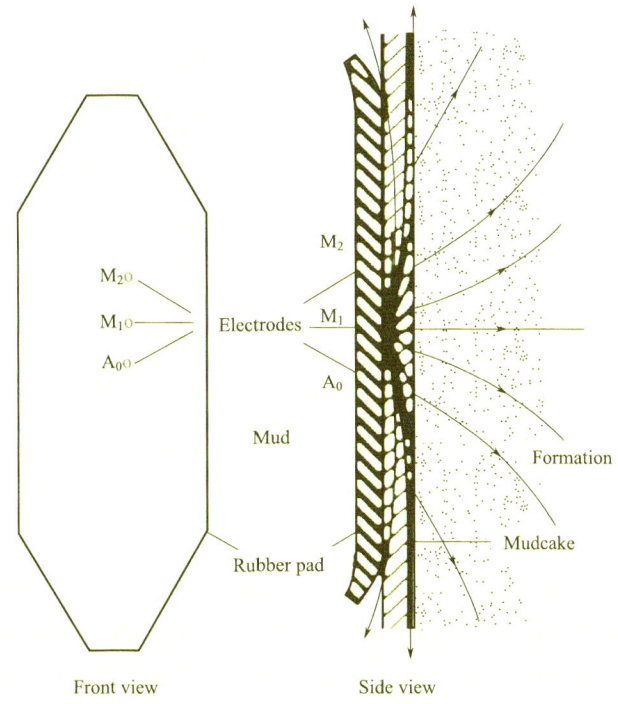

Fig.4.16　A microlog device: a pad version of the short normal and the lateral（from Serra,1984）

图 4.16　微电极测井仪电极板结构示意图（据 Serra，1984）

The influence of mud cake, especially in the case of a resistive formation and a very conductive and thick mud cake, was a major disadvantage for the purpose of determining R_{xo}, but meant that the two curves separated when there was invasion. This separation proved to be a reliable indicator of permeable zones.

滤饼对确定冲洗带电阻率 R_{xo} 有极大的影响，尤其是在地层不导电而滤饼较厚且导电的情况下。这也是微电极测井的主要不足。但同时，两条曲线在侵入时分离，因此可利用微电极曲线分开与否划分渗透层。

In order to improve the determination of R_{xo}, a focused or microlaterolog device was the next innovation. Fig.4.17 is a schematic of this device, which shares many features of the laterolog, except for dimensions. As indicated in Fig.4.17, the bucking current from electrode A_1 focuses the measure current to penetrate the mud cake. Depending on the contrast between R_{xo} and R_t, 90% of the measured signal comes from the first 2–4 in. of formation.

为改进微电极求取冲洗带电阻率 R_{xo} 时的不足，人们又提出了具有聚焦功能的微侧向测井。图 4.17 是微侧向测井仪的示意图，除尺寸不同外，该设备具备双侧向测井仪的多种特征。如图 4.17 所示，自屏蔽电极 A_1 发出的屏蔽电流迫使主电流聚焦到滤饼并进入到地层。通过对比 R_{xo} 和 R_t 可知，90% 的测量信号来自最初的 2～4 英寸地层。

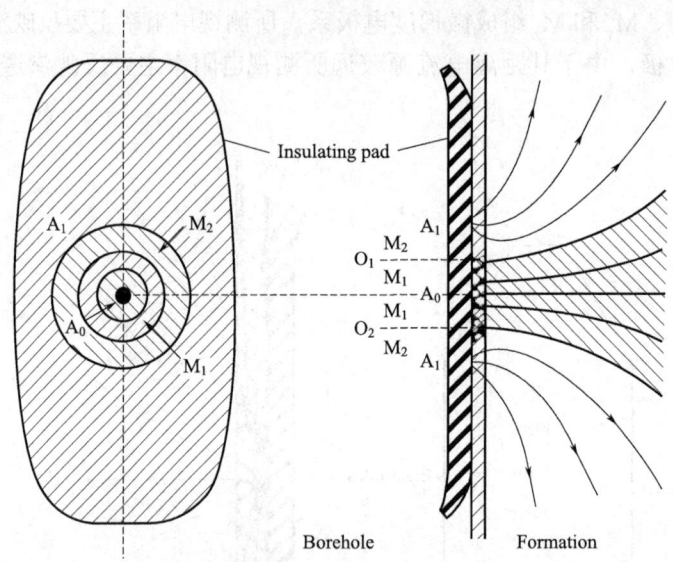

Fig.4.17　A microlaterolog device: a reduced scale and pad version of the laterolog（From Serra, 1984）
图 4.17　微侧向电极系测井装置示意图（据 Serra，1984）

Various other microelectrode devices followed the microlaterolog, each trying to minimize the effect of mud cake while not reading too deep into the formation. The two mud cake-correction charts in Fig.4.18 allow comparison between two types of devices – the microspherical log and the microlaterolog. The microspherical device is based on the same principle as the spherical log described in Section 4.3.2. The spherical focusing, as well as a larger pad, causes it to be much less sensitive to the presence of mud cake.

继微侧向后又有各种微电阻率测井方法问世，每种方法都试图最大限度降低滤饼对测量值影响，同时探测深度不能太深。图 4.18 是两种微电阻率侧向（微侧向和微球聚焦）的滤饼校正图版的比较，微球聚焦的探测原理与前述 4.3.2 节中球形聚焦测井原理相同，球形聚焦以及更大的电极板，使得测井受滤饼影响程度更小。

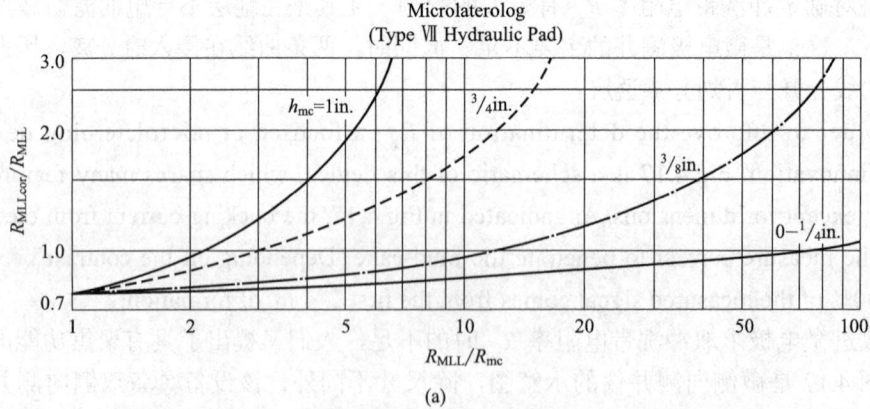

Fig.4.18　Mud cake corrections for two types of microresistivity device（Courtesy of Schlumberger, 2005）
图 4.18　两种微电阻率测井仪滤饼校正图版（据斯伦贝谢，2005）

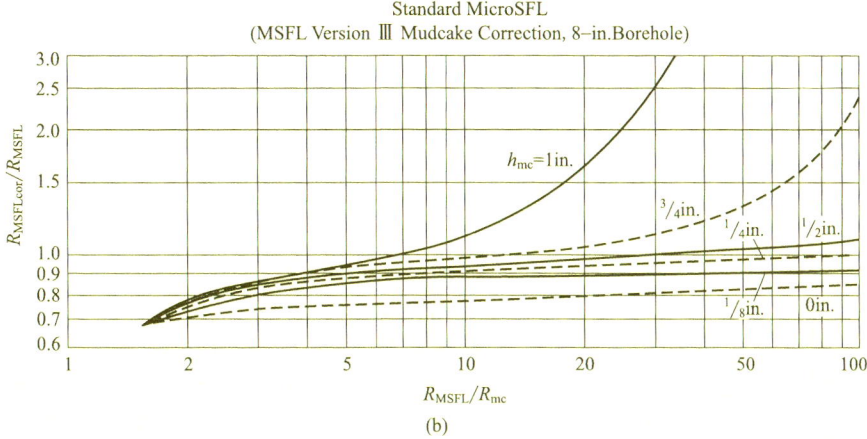

Fig.4.18 Mud cake corrections for two types of microresistivity device (Courtesy of Schlumberger, 2005)

图 4.18 两种微电阻率测井仪滤饼校正图版（据斯伦贝谢，2005）(续)

Exercises
课后练习

4.1 Which of the following resistivity logging tools will provide the best estimate of R_{xo}?
(A) LLD (B) LLS (C) MSFL

4.2 Generally with resistivity tools the greater the spacing between the measuring electrodes the greater the depth of investigation. True or False?

4.3 Fig.4.19 shows part of the log sequence pertaining to this question. Given that $a=1$, $m=2$ and $n=2$ for this sequence.

(a) What is the value of the resistivity of the connate water, R_w?

(b) Determine the water saturation for any hydrocarbon areas present.

(c) For this hydrocarbon area, determine the formation factor and the porosity.

4.4 A well is drilled through a hydrocarbon-bearing formation which is at its irreducible water saturation and it has a porosity of 28%. Rock core data indicates that $a=0.81$, $m=2$, and $n=2$. The mud used for drilling is water-base, with a salt concentration (NaCl) of 50,000μg/g. The connate water has a salt concentration (NaCl) of 20,000 ppm. The shallow and deep resistivity logs readings are 12Ω•m and 50Ω•m respectively. You should assume that the deep resistivity tool will be sensing the virgin zone, which does not experience any mud-filtrate invasion, and that the shallow resistivity tool will be sensing the flushed zone. The formation temperature is 145°F. What is the hydrocarbon saturation of the formation and what is the water saturation in the flushed zone?

4.5 Fig.4.20 is taken in an interval which consists almost entirely of sandstone reservoir of uniform porosity of 0.29. A thin shale streak and a shale bed within the sand show up on the GR.

(a) Why do the MFSL, the LLS and the LLD overlay across the shale bed?

(b) Part of the reservoir is oil bearing. At which depth would you put the OWC?

(c) What can you conclude from the fact that the MSFL and the LLD read the same resistivity in the water bearing interval?

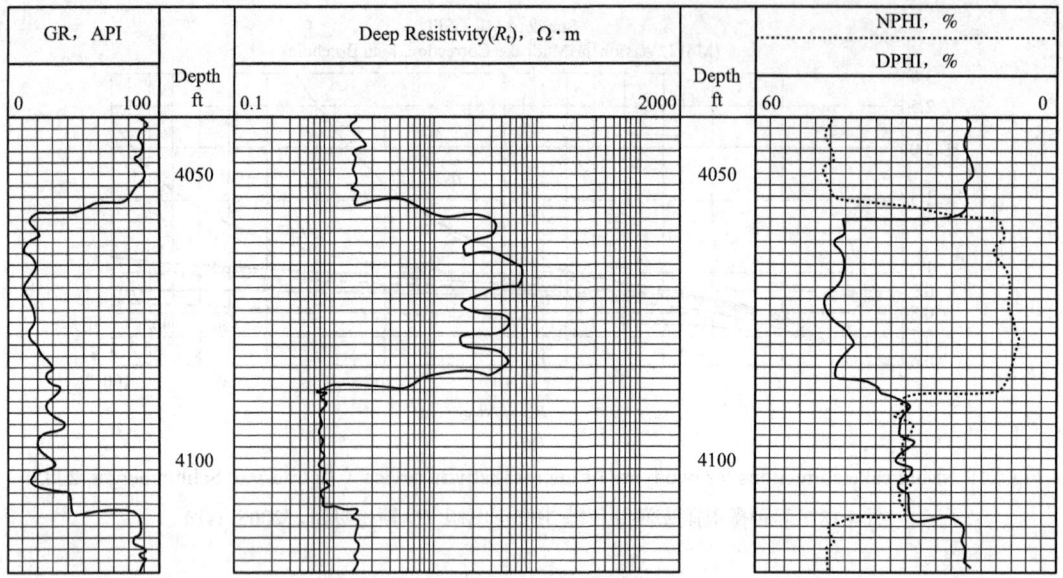

Fig.4.19 The log sequence

图 4.19 测井序列

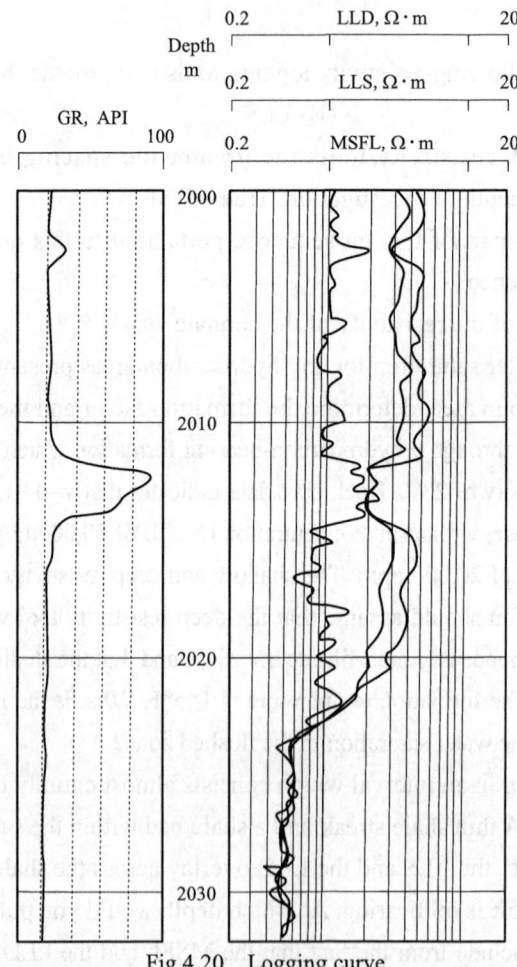

Fig.4.20 Logging curve

图 4.20 测井曲线

5 Induction Devices
感应测井

5.1 Introduction
引言

The presence of a conductive mud in the borehole is somewhat of a nuisance for electrode devices, as was illustrated in the last chapter. Many improvements have been made in electrode tool design to compensate for the problems. However, conductive borehole mud does provide one advantage: it effectively places the current and voltage measurement electrodes into electrical contact with the formation whose resistivity is to be measured.

如上一章所述,井筒中的导电钻井液会对电阻率测量造成影响。为了补偿这种影响,在电极系设计上进行了许多改进。然而,导电的井筒钻井液也有自身优点,那就是它可使电流和测量电极与待测电阻率的地层进行有效的电接触。

What about those cases in which the mud is nonconductive (oil-base mud) or nonexistent (air-filled hole)? It is for these cases that the induction tool was designed originally, although it has since found widespread use in conductive muds. Induction devices use medium frequency (several 10s of kHz) alternating current to energize transmitter coils in the sonde; they, in turn, induce eddy currents in the formation whose strength is proportional to the formation conductivity. The magnitude of the induced currents is measured by receiver coils in the tool that sense the magnetic field generated by the induced currents.

如果钻井液不导电(油基钻井液)或缺失(井筒钻井液气侵),会是什么情况呢?感应测井应运而生,尽管它也已经在导电钻井液中得到了广泛的应用。感应测井仪器发射线圈使用中频交流电(几十千赫兹),在地层中引起涡流,其强度与地层导电性成正比。继而感应电流产生磁场,其接收线圈可测量感应电流的大小。

Before discussing the principles involved in the design and operation of induction tools, this chapter reviews some of the basics of electromagnetic theory. This review will serve as the basis for analyzing the characteristics of a two-coil device in detail. The analysis will develop the notion of the geometric factor, which is used to predict the radial and vertical tool response. The development of traditional multi-coil focused devices follows directly from geometric factor theory. The chapter concludes with discussion of the preferred conditions for choosing induction or electrode devices.

本章在讨论感应测井仪的设计和操作原理之前,首先回顾电磁感应理论的基础知识,以此作为感应测井双线圈装置的基础,然后提出了几何因子概念,用于分析感应测井径向和垂向上的探测特性。传统多线圈感应聚焦设备的出现是与几何因子理论直接相关的。本章还讨论了感应测井或电极系测井的适应条件。

5.2 Review of Magnetostatics and Induction 电磁感应知识回顾

Induction devices employ alternating currents in transmitter coils to set up an alternating magnetic field in the surrounding conductive formation. This changing magnetic field induces current loops in the formation that are detectable by a receiver coil in the sonde. The details of the relationships between electric currents and magnetic fields, both steady-state and time-varying, are reviewed in this section to provide the basis for the geometric factor theory.

感应测井装置在发射线圈内通以交流电,在周围介质中建立交变磁场。这种不断变化的磁场会在地层中感应出电流环,该回路可由探头中的接收线圈检测到。本节回顾了电场和磁场之间的稳态和时变关系,为分析几何因子理论提供了基础。

5.2.1 Magnetic Field from a Current Loop 电流环的磁场

Ampere's law states that a magnetic field will be associated with the flow of an electric current and directed at right angles to it. The strength of the magnetic field B is related to the current I. In particular the integral of the tangential component of B around any closed path Γ is proportional to the current piercing the area enclosed by Γ. This is expressed as:

安培定律表明:磁场与电流的流动相关联,并与电流成直角。磁感应强度 B 与电流强度 I 有关,B 在任何闭合回路 Γ 上的切向分量的积分与穿过封闭区域的电流成正比。其数学表达式为:

$$\int_{\Gamma} \boldsymbol{B} \cdot \mathrm{d}\boldsymbol{l} = \frac{I}{\varepsilon_0 c^2} \tag{5.1}$$

Where $\mathrm{d}\boldsymbol{l}$ is a unit vector directed along the path Γ, ε_0 is the permittivity of free space and c the speed of light. Through the use of a vector identity, this is often written as:

式中,$\mathrm{d}\boldsymbol{l}$ 为沿闭合回路 Γ 指向的单位矢量;ε_0 为自由空间的介电常数;c 为光速。使用向量恒等式,上式常被写为:

$$\nabla \times \boldsymbol{B} = \frac{\boldsymbol{j}}{\varepsilon_0 c^2} \tag{5.2}$$

Where *j* is the current density, or the normal component of the current *I* divided by the surface area enclosed by *Γ*.

式中，*j* 为电流密度，即电流 *I* 的正常分流除以闭合回路 *Γ* 的面积。

One simple application of this relation is the calculation of the magnetic field associated with the current flowing in a long wire, shown in Fig.5.1. At a radial distance *r* from the wire, the path integral is just $B \cdot 2\pi r$, since the magnetic field *B* is in the form of closed circles around the current-carrying wire, and since *B* and *I* are known to be at right angles to one another. Thus the magnetic field strength relation may be determined from:

这种关系可用于计算通以电流的长导线所产生的磁场强度，如图 5.1 所示，在距离导线的径向距离 *r* 处，路径积分为 $B \cdot 2\pi r$，因为磁场 *B* 是围绕载流导线的封闭环，因此，磁场强度可用以下公式确定：

$$B \cdot 2\pi r = \frac{I}{\varepsilon_0 c^2} \tag{5.3}$$

$$B = \frac{1}{4\pi\varepsilon_0 c^2} \frac{2I}{r} \tag{5.4}$$

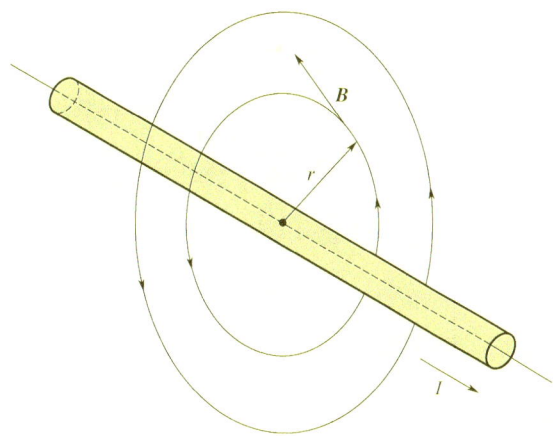

Fig.5.1 Schematic diagram of magnetic flux produced by a straight wire at current intensity *I* (from Feynman et al, 1965)

Circular lines of magnetic flux **B**, surrounding a very long straight wire carrying a current

图 5.1 电流强度 *I* 的直导线产生的磁通量示意图（据 Feynman 等，1965）

围绕着一根带电流的长直导线产生的磁通量 **B** 的圆形线

The generalized expression for calculating the magnetic field from a current element is called the law of Biot–Savart and resembles the preceding expression:

类似于前面的表达式，用于计算电流元所产生的磁场强度的广义表达式称为毕奥—萨伐尔定律，即：

$$\boldsymbol{B} = -\frac{1}{4\pi\varepsilon_0 c^2} \int \frac{I d\boldsymbol{r} \times d\boldsymbol{l}}{r^2} \tag{5.5}$$

Where d*l* is an elemental length along the current path Γ and d*r* is the unit vector in the direction of the observation point from the current element.

式中，d*l* 为沿电流路径 Γ 的电流元长度；d*r* 为电流元观察方向上的单位矢量。

A simple application of the law of Biot–Savart which will be useful in the discussion of the induction device is the calculation of the component of the magnetic field perpendicular to the plane of a circular loop of current (such as that observed in the receiver coil). As shown in Fig.5.2, the application is simple for reasons of symmetry. The vertical component B_z is to be calculated on the axis of the current loop. The sketch shows that the component dB is the result of one element of the current loop; it is oriented at right angles to the current element. The magnitude of this contribution to the magnetic field at a distance z above the loop of radius a is given from the law of Biot–Savart by:

毕奥—萨伐尔定律的一个简单应用是计算垂直圆形电流环平面的磁场分量（例如在接收线圈中观察到的分量）。如图 5.2 所示，由于对称，应用简单。可在电流环的轴上计算磁场 B 的垂直分量 B_z。如图所示，磁场 B 的垂直分量 B_z 是电流环的一个电流元作用的结果，其方向与电流元垂直。根据毕奥—萨伐尔定律，可通过下式计算半径为 a 电流环上方距离为 z 处磁场的贡献大小：

$$dB \propto \frac{I_0 a d\phi}{a^2 + z^2} \tag{5.6}$$

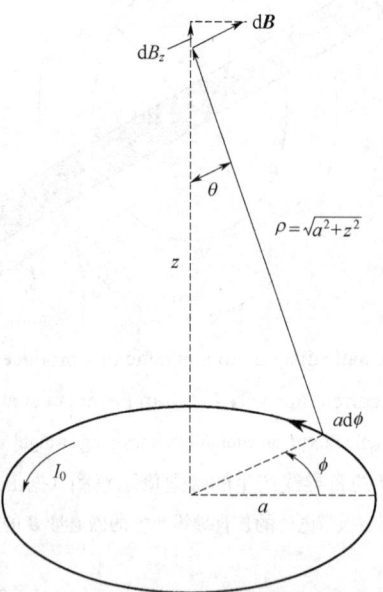

Fig.5.2　Geometry for the calculation of the vertical component of the magnetic field on the axis of a current-carrying circular loop of radius a (from Darwin V.Ellis,2008)

图 5.2　半径为 a 的闭合环路所产生的磁场的垂直分流计算示意图（据 Darwin V. Ellis，2008）

It is clear that all but the z-component of the B field will be canceled when the whole current loop is considered. The component dB_z is seen to be:

很明显地看出，当考虑整个回路电流时，除了磁场 ***B*** 的 z 分量外，其余分量均被抵消。磁场 ***B*** 在 z 方向可表示为：

$$dB_z = dB \frac{a}{\sqrt{a^2 + z^2}} \tag{5.7}$$

The total contribution to the z-component is given by the integral of all the elements of current around the loop. Merging the above two equations gives:

对 z 分量的总贡献由电流环上所有电流元的积分给出，合并上述两等式可得：

$$B_z = \int_0^{2\pi} \frac{I_0 a^2}{(a^2 + z^2)^{3/2}} d\phi = \frac{2\pi I_0 a^2}{\rho^3} \tag{5.8}$$

5.2.2 Vertical Magnetic Field from a Small Current Loop 小电流环的垂向磁场

Another relation for which there will be a need is that of the vertical component of the magnetic field away from the axis of a small current loop. For this problem, recourse is made to the magnetic vector potential ***A***, which is defined by:

另一个需要确定的是磁场垂直分量与小电流环轴之间的关系，该关系可用磁矢势 ***A*** 来描述：

$$\boldsymbol{B} = \nabla \times \boldsymbol{A} \tag{5.9}$$

And can be related to a current distribution in a fashion analogous to the relation between the electrostatic potential and a charge distribution:

与静电势与电荷分布类似，磁矢势 ***A*** 与电流分布间关系可表示为：

$$A = \frac{1}{4\pi\varepsilon_0 c^2} \int \frac{j dV}{r} \tag{5.10}$$

Here, the current density distribution must be integrated over the volume (d*V*) which contains it. Once the vector potential is obtained, then the z-component of the magnetic field is simply obtained from:

此处电流密度矢量必须对包含它的整个电流路径进行积分。一旦求得磁矢势，那么磁场的 z 分量则可表示为：

$$B_z = (\nabla \times \boldsymbol{A})_z = \frac{\partial A_y}{\partial x} - \frac{\partial A_x}{\partial y} \tag{5.11}$$

The vector potential of a small current loop can be written in analogy with the electrostatic potential at a distance *r* from a dipole which is given by:

小电流环的矢量电位可以用距离偶极子 *r* 处的静电电位类推，该偶极子由下式给出：

$$\phi(r) = \frac{1}{4\pi\varepsilon_0} \frac{p\cos\theta}{r^2} \tag{5.12}$$

Where *p* is the dipole moment (the charge times separation distance) and θ is the angle between the orientation of the dipole and the observation point. For the current loop in the *x–y* plane shown in Fig.5.3, we will write an expression for the vector potential at the point P indicated. It will consist of only two components, A_x and A_y, since there is no current distribution in the *z*-direction. To find the *x*-component of *A*, only the current in the *x*-direction is considered, as shown in Fig.5.3. The two parallel current paths are equivalent to the concept of an electric dipole. By analogy with two charged rods, each with charge per unit length λ, the dipole moment would be the total charge times the separation or:

其中 *p* 为偶极矩（电荷乘以分离距离）；θ 为偶极子的方向与观察点之间的角度。对于图 5.3 所示的 *x-y* 平面中的电流环，我们将在所示 P 点处写出磁矢势的表达式。磁矢势仅由 A_x 和 A_y 两个分量组成，因为在 *z* 方向上没有电流分布。要找到 *A* 的 *x* 分量，只考虑 *x* 方向的电流，如图 5.3 所示。两个并联电流路径等价于电偶极子的概念。通过类比两个带电杆，每个带电杆的单位长度的电荷为 λ，偶极矩将是总电荷乘以距离：

$$p = \lambda ab \tag{5.13}$$

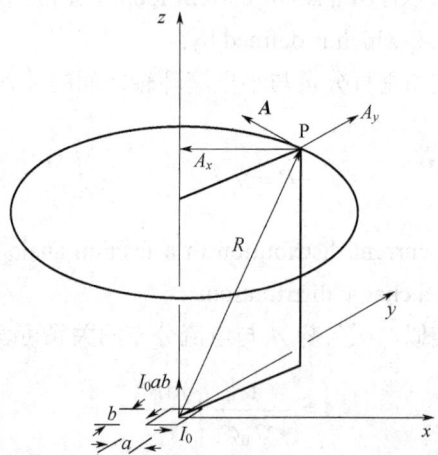

Fig.5.3 The vector potential *A*, from a small current-carrying loop of rectangular cross-section (adapted from Feynman et al)

图 5.3 矩形电流环所产生的磁矢量示意图（据 Feynman 等）

And the cosine of the angle between the point P and the dipole moment is $-\dfrac{y}{R}$. Combining the above two equations gives:

而 P 点和偶极矩夹角的余弦值为 $-\dfrac{y}{R}$，类似地，根据上两式可得：

$$A_x = -\frac{I_0 ab}{4 r \varepsilon_0 c^2} \frac{y}{R^3} \tag{5.14}$$

The *y*-component can be found in the same manner to be:

y 轴方向的分量可以同样的方式求出：

$$A_y = -\frac{I_0 ab}{4r\varepsilon_0 c^2}\frac{x}{R^3} \tag{5.15}$$

From the two components of the vector potential, the spatial dependence of the vertical component of the magnetic field can be determined:

根据磁矢量的两个分量，可以确定磁场垂向分量的空间依赖：

$$B_z \propto \frac{\partial}{\partial x}\left(\frac{x}{R^3}\right) - \frac{\partial}{\partial_y}\left(\frac{-y}{R^3}\right) \tag{5.16}$$

$$B_z \propto \frac{1}{R^3} - \frac{3z^2}{R^5} \tag{5.17}$$

5.2.3　Voltage Induced in a Coil by a Magnetic Field
　　　 线圈磁场下的感应电动势

The final review item is that of Faraday's law of induction. From experimental observations, Faraday deduced that a changing magnetic field would set up a current in a loop of conductor present in the field. He also demonstrated that a changing current in one loop of wire could induce a current in another loop of wire, as illustrated in Fig.5.4. The induced electromotive force associated with the induced current was found to be proportional to the rate of change of magnetic flux linking the circuit. This is most compactly expressed as:

最后一个复习的内容是法拉第电磁感应定律。法拉第通过实验观察，推导出一个不断变化的磁场会造成该场内的闭合回路导体产生电流，除此之外，他还发现在一个导线回路中改变电流，可以在另一个环路中感生出电流，如图 5.4 所示。法拉第发现与感应电流相关的感应电动势与通过导体回路的磁通量变化率成正比，常被表示为：

$$\nabla \times \boldsymbol{E} = -\frac{\partial \boldsymbol{B}}{\partial t} \tag{5.18}$$

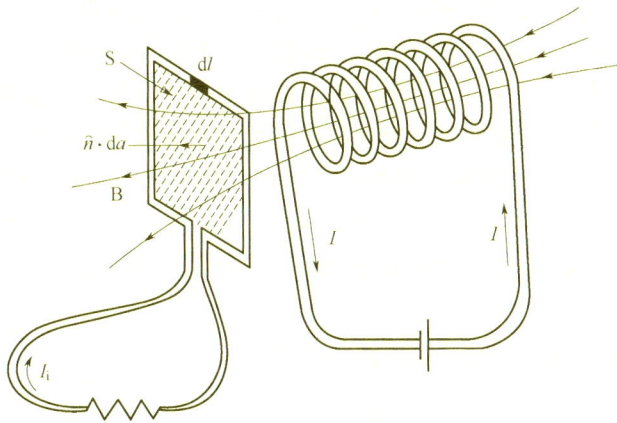

Fig.5.4　One aspect of Faraday's law of induction (from Darwin V.Ellis, 2008)
图 5.4　法拉第电磁感应定律示意图（据 Darwin V. Ellis，2008）

By Stokes's theorem the integral of $\nabla \times \boldsymbol{E}$ over the surface S of the receiver loop is equal to the line integral of $\boldsymbol{E}$ around the loop Γ so that:

根据斯托克斯定理，$\nabla \times \boldsymbol{E}$ 在接收器环路曲面 S 的积分等于场强 $\boldsymbol{E}$ 在环路 Γ 的线积分，则：

$$\oint_\Gamma \boldsymbol{E} \cdot \mathrm{d}\boldsymbol{l} = \int_S (\nabla \times \boldsymbol{E}) \cdot \boldsymbol{n} \mathrm{d}a = -\int_S \frac{\partial \boldsymbol{B}}{\partial t} \cdot \boldsymbol{n} \mathrm{d}a \tag{5.19}$$

This last expression is seen to be the time rate of change of the normal component of magnetic flux through a surface S. The integral on the left gives the voltage seen at the terminals of the receiver.

最后一个表达式被看作是磁通量的法向分量通过曲面 S 的时间变化率。左边的积分给出了在接收器端处测到的电压。

5.3 The Two-coil Induction Devices
　　双线圈系感应测井

Fig.5.5 shows the essential features of an induction logging device. It consists of a transmitter coil, excited by an alternating current of medium frequency (≈20kHz) and a receiver coil. The two coils, contained in a nonconductive housing, are presumed to be surrounded by a formation of conductivity σ. One axially symmetric ring of current-bearing formation is indicated in the figure. Before analyzing the geometric sensitivity of such a device, it is worth while to step through the sequence of physical interactions which produce, finally, a signal at the receiver. In this way we will be able to see the dependence of the detected signal on excitation frequency and formation conductivity, as well as the phase relation between received and transmitted signal. The so-called skin effect is ignored for the time being, so that the results in the next three sections are only strictly valid at low conductivity.

感应测井仪的基本特征如图 5.5 所示。它由一个发射线圈和一个接收线圈组成，向发射线圈输入一个中频（≈20kHz）交流电。假设包裹在不导电外壳内的两个线圈被电导率为 σ 的地层所包围。图中显示了一个轴对称的载流地层环。在分析这种装置的几何灵敏度之前，有必要逐步分析最终在接收线圈处产生信号的物理作用的序列。这样我们就可以看到探测信号与激发频率和地层电导率的相关性，以及接收信号和发射信号之间的相位关系。所谓的趋肤效应暂不考虑，因此下面三节的讨论限定在低电导率地层介质环境中。

The first step to consider is the excitation of the transmitter coil by the transmitter current I_t:

测井时首先通过振荡器使发射线圈激发交变电流 I_t：

$$I_t = I_0 e^{-i\omega t} \tag{5.20}$$

The transmitter coil, which can be considered as an oscillating magnetic dipole, sets up through out the formation a magnetic field B_t. The vertical component will have a time dependence given by:

发射线圈可视为一个振荡磁偶极子，建立了一个转过地层的磁场 B_t，其垂直分量的时间依赖关系为：

$$(B_t)_z \propto I_0 e^{-i\omega t} \tag{5.21}$$

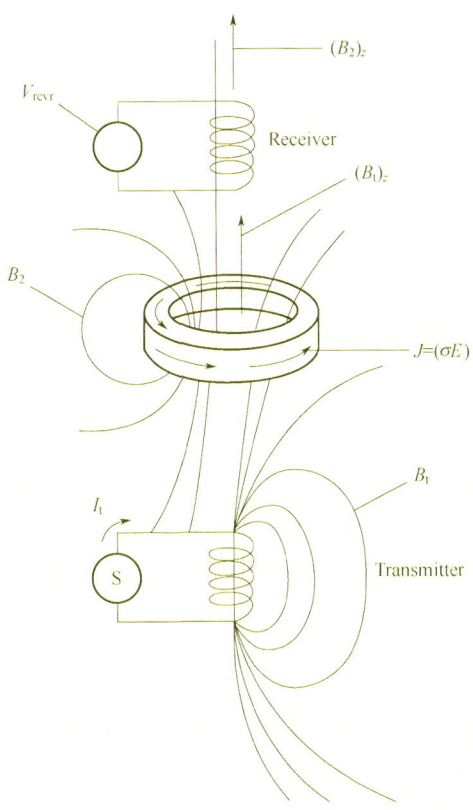

Fig.5.5 The principle of the induction tool (from Darwin V.Ellis, 2008).
The vertical component of the magnetic field from the transmitting coil induces ground loop currents. The current loops in the conductive formation produce an alternating magnetic field detected by the receiver coil

图 5-5 感应测井仪原理示意图（据 Darwin V. Ellis，2008）
发射线圈产生交变磁场，其垂直分量在导电的地层单元环中激发交变电流，在地层单元环的二次磁场作用下，接收线圈产生感生电动势和感生电流

A ring of formation material that is axially symmetric with the tool axis forms the perimeter of a surface through which passes the time-varying magnetic field. From Faraday's law, an electric field E will be set up that is proportional to the time derivative of the vertical component:

地层单元环与仪器轴轴对称，交变磁场磁力线穿过地层的单元环，根据法拉第定律，在地层单元环内将产生一个电场 E，其强度与 B_t 垂直分量的时间导数成正比：

$$E \propto -\frac{\partial (B_t)_z}{\partial t} \propto i\omega I_0 e^{-i\omega t} \tag{5.22}$$

This electric field, which curls around the vertical axis, will induce a current density in the loop of formation sketched. It will be proportional to the formation conductivity:

这些围绕井轴（垂向）弯曲的电场将在地层单元环内产生电流密度，其电流密度大小与地层电导率成正比：

$$J \propto \sigma E \propto i\omega\sigma I_0 e^{-i\omega t} \tag{5.23}$$

The current in the ground loop considered will behave like the transmitter coil; that is, it will set up its own magnetic field B_2. The vertical component of the secondary magnetic field $(B_2)_z$ has the same time dependence as the current density in the loop:

环形电流可被看作发射线圈，也就是说，它将建立自己的磁场 B_2。二次磁场（B_2）的垂直分量与环路电流密度具有同样的时间依赖性，即：

$$(B_2)_z \propto i\omega I_0 e^{-i\omega t} \tag{5.24}$$

And its time dependence will induce a voltage V_{rcvr} at the receiver coil:

它的时间依赖性使得二次磁场在接收线圈处产生感应电动势：

$$V_{rcvr} \propto -\frac{\partial (B_2)_z}{\partial t} \propto -\omega^2 \sigma I_0 e^{-i\omega t} \tag{5.25}$$

This final result indicates that the voltage detected at the receiver coil will vary directly with the conductivity of the formation and with the square of the excitation frequency.

这一最终结果表明，在接收线圈上检测到的电压随地层电导率及交变电流频率的平方而变化。

5.4 Geometric Factor for the Two-coil Sonde 双线圈系几何因子

In order to determine the geometric sensitivity of the two-coil induction sonde, we now make use of the relations derived in the review of magnetostatics. The first expression to be derived is the component of the driving magnetic field, which sets up the ground current indicated in Fig.5.6. The driving coil is considered to be a magnetic dipole source which produces a vertical component of magnetic field at a distance z above the transmitter. In this case, the dipole moment of the transmitter is given by the product of the current I_0, the winding area A_t, and the number of transmitter winding turns n_t. At any position identified by the coordinates (ρ_t, z), the vertical component, from Eq.5.16, is given by:

为了确定双线圈系探测的几何灵敏度，根据静磁学理论推导关系式。导出的第一个表达式是驱动磁场分量，它建立了如图5.6所示的接地电流。发射线圈为磁偶极子源，在其上方距离 z 处产生磁场的垂直分量。发射器的偶极矩基于电流 I_0，线圈截面积 A_t 和发射器缠绕匝数 n_t。根据式（5.16），柱坐标系（ρ_t, z）内的任何位置，其磁场强度垂直分量可由下式给出：

$$(B_t)_z \propto I_0 e^{-i\omega t} A_t n_t \left(\frac{1}{\rho_t^3} - \frac{3z^2}{\rho_t^5} \right) \tag{5.26}$$

The left side of Fig.5.6 shows the geometry factor to be considered for determining the magnitude of the current density set up in the indicated ground loop. Dropping, for convenience, the time-dependent terms and other constants, the relation for the induced electric field, from Eq.5.19 is:

图 5.6 左侧给出在图中所示的接地回路中确定电流密度大小时要考虑的几何因子。为方便起见，将随时间变化的项及其他常数去掉，式（5.19）中感应电场的关系为：

$$\oint_\Gamma E \cdot l = -\frac{\partial}{\partial t} \int_S B_n dS \tag{5.27}$$

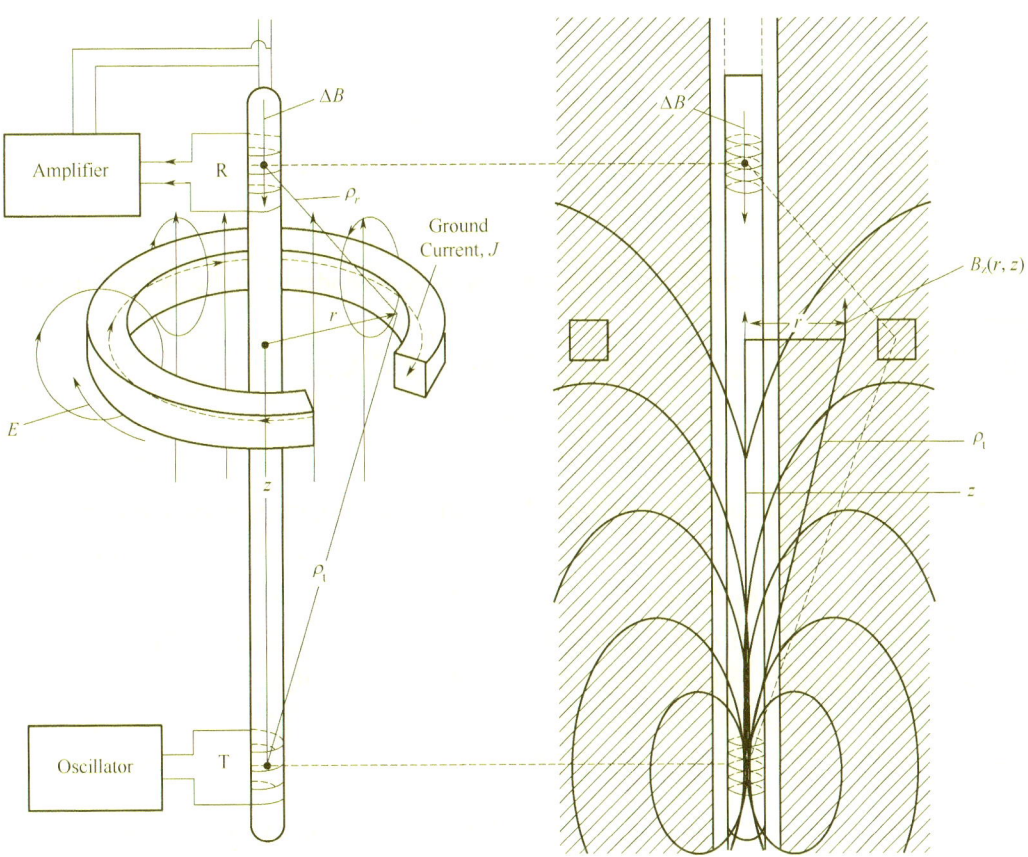

Fig.5.6 Geometry for the development of the geometric factor for a two-coil induction Sonde (from Doll, 1949)

图 5.6 双线圈系测井仪几何因子示意图（据 Doll，1949）

Where the line integral is around the loop Γ whose length is $2\pi r$ and where the surface integral is over the element whose area $S = \pi r^2$ so that $dS = 2\pi r dr$. Since the normal component of the magnetic field, B_n, is B_z, the result is:

对周长为 $2\pi r$ 的回路 Γ 线积分，对面积为 $S=\pi r^2$ 的电流元面积分，使得 $dS=2\pi dr$。因为磁场法向上的分量 B_n 为 B_z，故结果可表示为：

$$\oint_\Gamma E \cdot l = E \cdot 2\pi r \propto \int_0^r \left(\frac{1}{\rho_t^3} - \frac{3z^2}{\rho_t^5} \right) r dr \tag{5.28}$$

In the right-hand integral, ρ_t is a function of r so that the integral must be evaluated through a change of variable to give by:

右侧积分是 r 的函数，因此必须通过变量变换来求值，以此得出：

$$E \cdot 2\pi r \propto \frac{r^2}{\rho_t^3} \tag{5.29}$$

Or:

或：

$$E \propto \frac{r}{\rho_t^3} \tag{5.30}$$

This electric field then causes a current density J which is given by:

此电场可产生电流密度 J，计算式为：

$$J = E\sigma \tag{5.31}$$

Where σ is the formation conductivity. Thus the geometric dependence of the induced formation current is given by:

式中 σ 为地层电导率，因此感应电流的几何特性可由下式表示：

$$J \propto \frac{\sigma r}{\rho_t^3} \tag{5.32}$$

As in Eq.5.25, but without the time dependence, the induced voltage in the receiver coil will be proportional to the vertical component of the secondary magnetic field which passes through the receiver coil, indicated by ΔB in Fig.5.6. From Eq.5.32, it is seen to be:

如式（5.25），省略随时间变化的量的影响接收线圈中感应电动势与通过接收线圈的二次磁场的垂直分量成正比，如图 5.6 中 ΔB 所示，据式（5.32）可知：

$$V_{rcvr} \propto \Delta B \propto J \frac{r^2}{\rho_r^3} \tag{5.33}$$

Where J is the current density in the ground loop in question of radius r, and ρ_r is the distance from any point along the current loop to the receiver coil.

式中 J 是半径 r 的单元环的电流密度，ρ_r 是沿电流回路的任一点到接收线圈的距离。

Inserting Eq.5.33 and separating out those factors that depend on the geometrical position of the loop, the measured voltage is given by:

结合式（5.33），分离出单元环空间位置的因素，测量电压即为：

$$V_{rcvr} \propto g(r,z) = \frac{L}{2} \frac{r}{\rho_t^3} \frac{r^2}{\rho_r^3} \tag{5.34}$$

The above expression for g (r, z) is known as the differential geometric factor (or Doll geometric factor), since it gives, the contribution of a single ground loop of unit cross-section at position z and radius r to the final receiver output. The factor L/2 is a normalization factor so that when g (r, z) is integrated over all r and z the result is 1. The geometric factors around a single transmitter and receiver are shown in Fig.5.6.

上述 $g(r, z)$ 的表达式称为微分几何因子（又称道尔几何因子），它给出了位置为 z、半径为 r 的单元环对最终测量值的相对贡献。$L/2$ 为归一化因子，因此当 $g(r, z)$ 对所有 r 和 z 积分时，结果为 1。双线圈系测井仪的几何因子如图 5.6 所示。

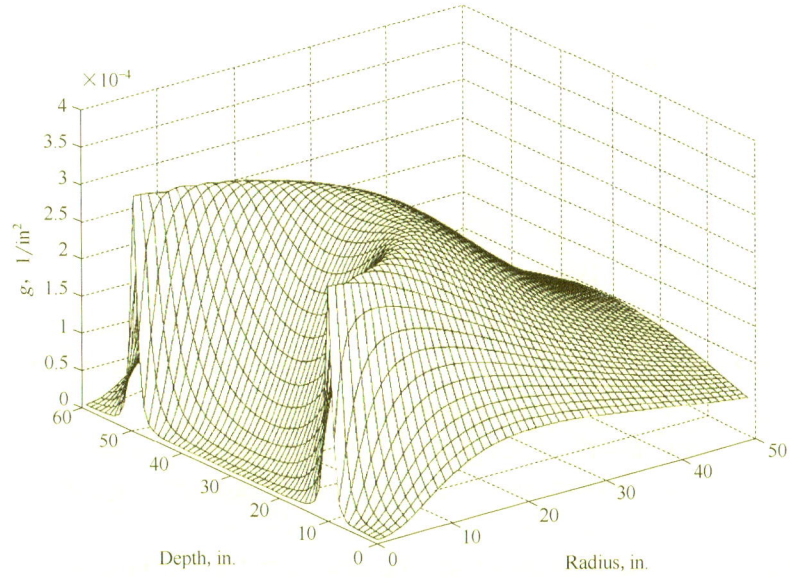

Fig.5.7 Two-dimensional plot of the geometrical factors of loops around a two-coil sonde
(from Darwin V.Ellis, 2008)

Homogeneous formations, no skin effect. The spikes near the z axis occur at the locations
of the transmitter and receiver

图 5.7 双线圈系感应测井几何因子二维图（据 Darwin V. Ellis，2008）

均匀地层，无趋肤效应，z 轴的尖峰值出现在反射器和接收器之间

It is convenient to define two other geometric factors which give information on the tool response after cumulating the response in one dimension. The first is the differential radial geometric factor, which is defined to be:

对一个维度积分后可以很方便地定义能给出仪器响应信息的另外两个几何因子。首先讨论差异化横向微分几何因子，它的定义如下：

$$g(r,z) = \int_{-\infty}^{\infty} g(r,z) \mathrm{d}z \tag{5.35}$$

It predicts the relative importance of each of the cylindrical shells of radius r to the overall response. This factor and a sketch of its radial dependence are shown in Fig.5.8. The peak in relative importance occurs at a radius somewhat less than the dimension of the coil separation.

横向微分几何因子可用来描述半径为 r，纵向上无限延伸的圆柱形壳体对测量值的贡献。该几何因子及其径向关系如图 5.8 所示。由图可知，横向微分几何因子峰值出现在壳体半径 r 略小于两线圈距离 L 时。

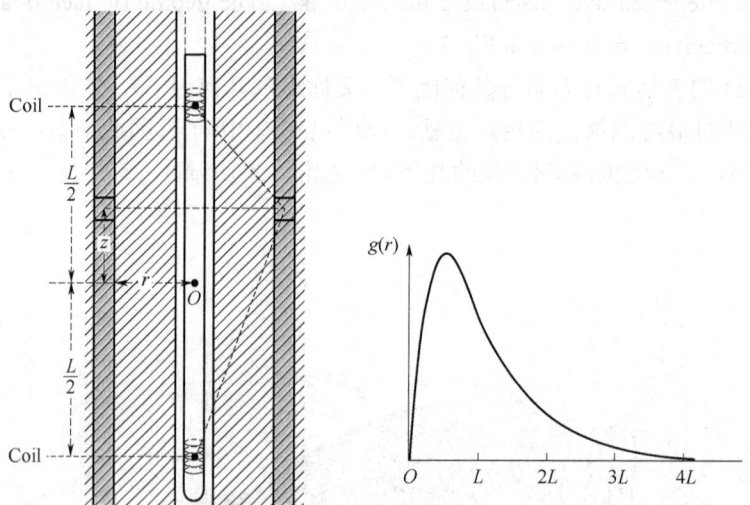

Fig.5.8 Relationship between lateral differential geometric factor and r (from Darwin V. Ellis, 2008)
Integration of the geometric factor with respect to z at a constant radial value r produces the differential radial geometric factor (homogeneous formations, no skin effect)

图 5.8 横向微分几何因子与 r 关系图（据 Darwin V. Eilis，2008）
半径为 r 的几何因子对 z 积分，产生径向微分几何因子（均匀地层，无趋肤效应）

In a similar fashion, the differential vertical geometric factor is defined as:
类似地，差异化纵向微分几何因子可定义为：

$$g(r,z) = \int_0^\infty g(r,z)\mathrm{d}r \qquad (5.36)$$

And it gives the response of a unit-thickness slice of formation, located at position z, to the overall tool response. The geometry corresponding to the integration and the response curve are shown in Fig.5.9. A fairly flat response is obtained from a slice of formation contained between the two coils, but the tapering-off of the response above and below the coils will produce signals at distances that are far above and below the coils. This is known as shoulder effect.

其物理意义为位于 z 位置的单位厚度无线延伸的薄板地层对测量值的贡献。纵向微分几何因子与位置 z 的关系曲线如图 5.9 所示。两线圈系之间的地层的测井响应曲线较为平坦，而在两个线圈之外上下两侧的响应逐渐减小，且在距离圈上下方有相当距离的位置产生信号。这就是所谓的围岩效应。

In order to get an idea of the bed boundary response, we can make an integration of the differential vertical geometric factor. Fig.5.10 shows an example of the integrated vertical factor G_v for a two-coil device with a 40 inch coil separation. A sharp transition of formation resistivity is seen by the tool as a gradual change over distance which is roughly 80 in., or two times the coil spacing. It is obvious that the conductivity readings in thin beds will be considerably affected by this type of coil arrangement.

为了了解层界面效应对测量值的影响，可以将纵向微分几何因子对 z 积分，得到纵向积分几何因子。图 5.10 为 40in 双线圈系纵向积分几何因子 G_v 示例。图中可看到地层电阻率随着距离的逐渐变化而急剧转变，而当围岩距目的层的距离约 80in，或是线圈间距的两倍时，围岩对测量值影响较小。显而易见的是，当围岩与目的层距离过近，即目的层为薄层时，围岩对电导率具有明显的影响。

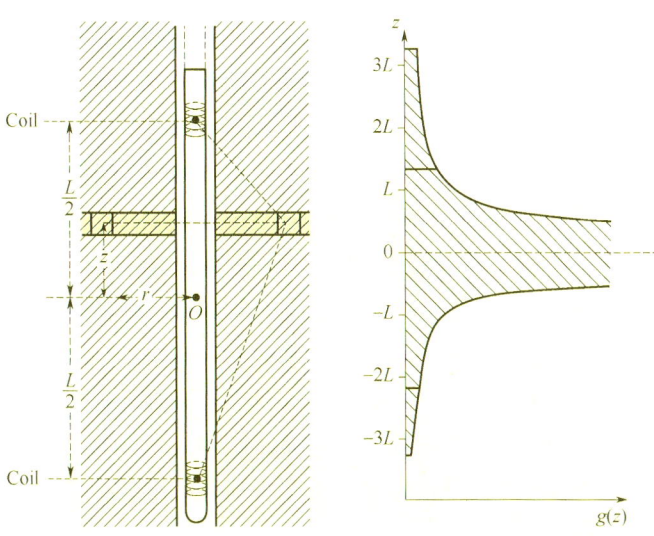

Fig.5.9 Relationship between vertical differential geometric factor and z (from Darwin V. Ellis, 2008).
The differential vertical geometric factor produced by integration with respect to r, at fixed z
(homogeneous formations, no skin effect)
图 5.9 纵向微分几何因子与 z 关系图（据 Darwin V. Eilis，2008）
在位置 z 对半径 r 积分，产生纵向微分几何因子（均质地层，无趋肤效应）

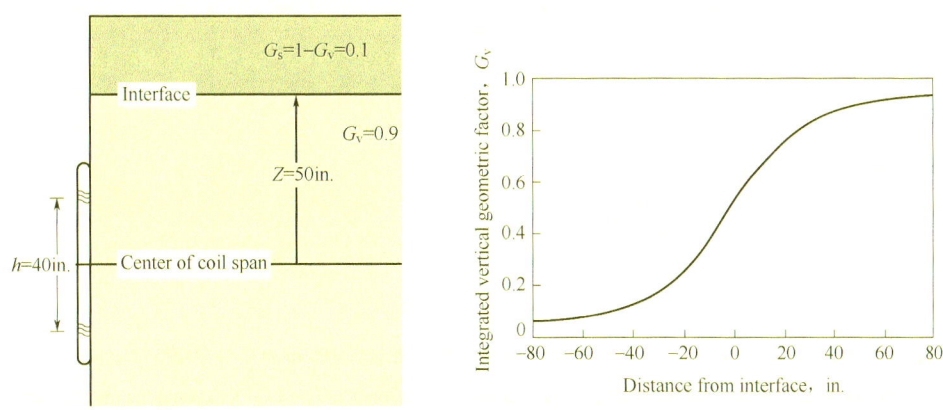

Fig.5.10 Integrated vertical geometric factor (from Dresser,1983)
At left, G_v and G_s in the shoulder bed with the coil center 50 in. from the interface; At right, the integrated vertical geometric factor, G_v, for estimating the influence of shoulder beds (homogeneous formations, no skin effect)
图 5.10 纵向积分几何因子（据 Dresser，1983）
左侧，线圈中心距层界面 50 英寸时的 G_v（目的层的纵向积分几何因子）和 G_s（围岩的纵向积分几何因子）；右侧，纵向积分几何因子 G_v，用于评价层厚的影响（均质地层，无趋肤效应）

The integrated radial geometric factor G_r for the two-coil device is shown in Fig.5.11. Approximately half the contribution comes from within 45 in. of the device. There is therefore some sensitivity to the region nearest the borehole. It would be desirable to eliminate this sensitivity to a presumed invaded zone and to put more weight on the region farther from the borehole, where the true resistivity could be measured.

双线圈系的横向积分径向几何因子 G_r 如图 5.11 所示。大约一半的贡献来自设备的 45 英寸范围内。因此，对井眼附近介质具有一定敏感性。人们期望消除假设的侵入带影响，重点关注远离井筒的区域，以便测量真实的地层电阻率。

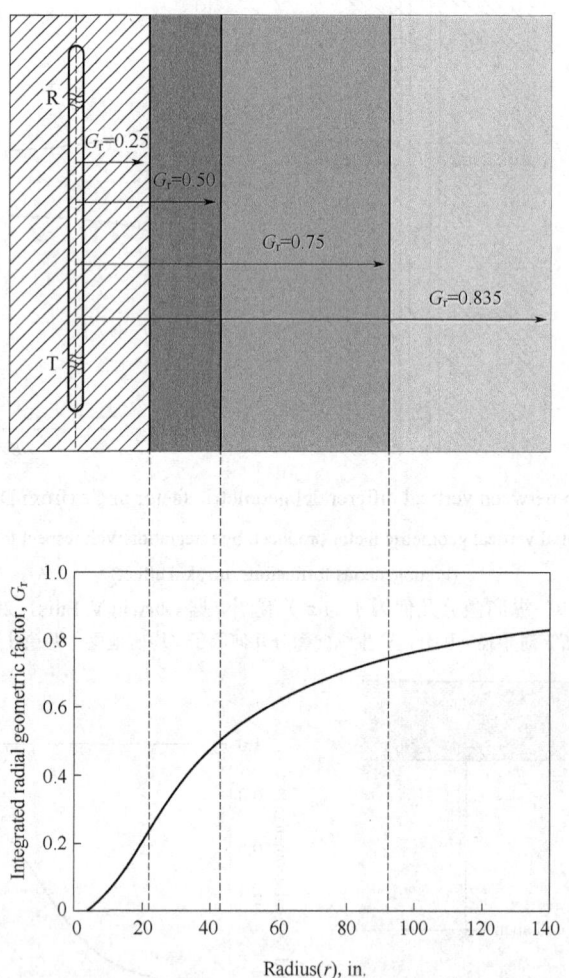

Fig.5.11　Graph of relation between integrated radial geometric factor and r （from Dresser，1983）
Above, illustration of different regions. Below, the integrated radial geometric factor, G_r, for estimating the importance of invasion (homogeneous formations, no skin effect)

图 5.11　横向积分几何因子与 r 关系图（据 Dresser，1983）
上图，关于不同地区的说明；下图，横向积分几何因子，
G_r，用以评估侵入的重要性（均匀地层，无趋肤效应）

5.5 Focusing the Two-coil Sonde 双线圈系感应测井仪聚焦特性

The response of the two-coil device examined above can be altered to minimize the "tail" of sensitivity to beds above and below the measurement coils or to decrease the sensitivity to layers closest to the borehole. For an illustration of how the response is altered or focused, we examine the technique for changing the depth of investigation of the two-coil sonde. The idea is simply to add a second receiver coil which is a bit closer to the transmitter and to use its response, which will be somewhat shallower than the original receiver, to subtract from the response of the original. By placing the receivers suitably and selecting the proper number of turns, this subtraction should eliminate much of the signal from regions close to the borehole. This principle is shown schematically in Fig.5.12. A similar procedure is used to sharpen the vertical are solution of the tool. This will change the sensitivity of the tool measurement to layers of different conductivity above and below the measurement coils.

可以调整上述双线圈设备的输出信号，以使得测量线圈上下地层的灵敏度曲线"尾部"趋近于0，或者降低对靠近井眼的地层的灵敏度。为了说明响应信号是如何聚焦或改变的，我们阐述了改变双线圈系测井仪探测深度的技术。简单说来，就是在双线圈系感应测井仪上额外增加一个靠近发射线圈的接收线圈，并用原始接收线圈的输出信号减掉新增接收线圈的输出信号。第二个接收线圈的信号比主接收线圈的输出信号微弱得多。通过将其放置在合适的位置并选择适当的匝数，可以消除大部分来自井眼附近介质的信号。该原理如图5.12所示。可用类似的步骤提高仪器垂向灵敏度。这将改变测量线圈上下不同电导率岩层的测量灵敏度。

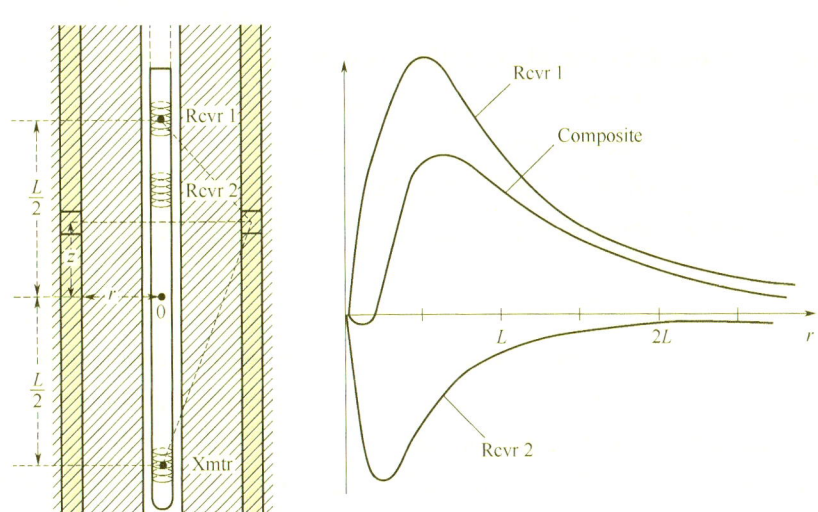

Fig.5.12　The principle of three-coil focusing (from Doll, 1949)

A second coil, wound with reverse polarity, produces a signal which cancels some of the signal from close to the borehole

图5.12　三线圈系感应测井聚焦原理（据Doll, 1949）

第二个接收线圈通以与发射线圈极性相反的电流，用来补偿井眼介质对测量值的影响

Traditional induction devices employ focused arrays of coils, usually providing two measurements of conductivity (resistivity) at different depths of investigation. The improvement of the depth of investigation of one such device can be seen by comparing the integrated radial response functions of the two-coil device in Fig.5.11 with the six-coil device in Fig.5.13. Most of the response closer than about 30 inch has been eliminated.

传统的感应测井装置采用线圈系来实现聚焦功能，通常提供在不同探测深度下两种不同的电导率（电阻率）测量值。通过比较图 5.11 中双线圈系与图 5.13 中六线圈系装置的横向积分几何因子的响应函数，可看出六线圈系装置的探测效果有显著提高。距离井轴中心 30 英寸内的介质对测量值的影响已基本消除掉。

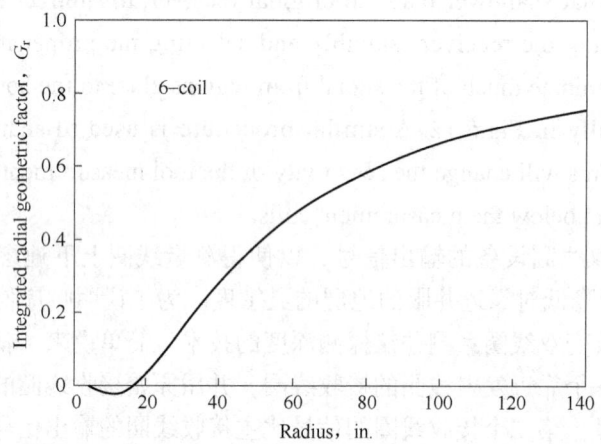

Fig.5.13 The radial depth of investigation of a six-coil induction device
(homogeneous formations, no skin effect) (from Dresse, 1983)

图 5.13 六线圈系感应测井的横向探测特性（均匀地层，无趋肤效应）（据 Dresse,1983）

Tailoring the response by the addition of coils may sound too good to be true. Of course there are limitations: the addition of focusing coils leaves some residual features in the geometric response that can cause problems in some in logging situations.

通过增加线圈来增强感应测井装置探测特性的方式效果很好，但是这种方式也具有一定的局限性：增加聚焦线圈的同时会对部分几何响应造成影响，可能在某些特定测井下引起问题。

In the preceding discussion, we have considered only homogeneous formations. In reality, layered formations of differing conductivity will be the rule, not to mention radial conductivity profiles which are far from uniform because of invasion or the presence of dipping beds. How will these affect the response of the induction tool?

在前面的讨论中，我们假设地层是各向同性的均匀介质。而在实际中，不同地层具有不同的导电性，除此之外还应考虑到由于钻井液侵入或倾斜层的存在，径向导电率千差万别。这将怎样影响测量结果呢？

An idea can be obtained from a closer examination of the composite radial geometric factor of Fig.5.13. Note the small undershoot. The impact of this imbalance is that the conductivity of the initial portion of the formation near the borehole will make a negative contribution to the total signal. This is no problem in a homogeneous formation. However, suppose there is a conductive anomaly near the borehole: taken to the extreme, this can cause a negative reading.

仔细观察图 5.13 的复合横向几何因子，可以得出这样一种观点。请注意前端这个小的反向超调，曲线左下角对应的几何因子是负值，这个现象被称为"过聚焦"，说明井眼附近介质对测量总信号贡献为负值。在均匀介质中这没有问题，但如果井眼附近介质导电异常，在极限条件下可能使得测量值为负。

5.6 Induction Log Example
感应测井曲线实例

For the sample induction log, another simulated reservoir is used. Two thick clean zones are indicated as A and B. Two much thinner clean streaks are shown as C and D. These four zones can be easily identified on the sample log presentation of Fig.5.14. For the identification of the clean zones, the SP is shown in track 1 along with a gamma ray. The ILD, ILM, and SFLU logs are displayed in tracks 3. These three resistivity curves come from a typical dual induction–shallow resistivity tool of the 1970s and 1980s. The SFL curve is an unaveraged spherically focused log. In typical induction conditions ($R_{xo} > R_t$) the SFLU provides reasonable information on R_{xo} and, not being pad-based, does not have the sensitivity to rugosity of microdevices.

为介绍感应测井，引入一模拟储层，剖面内有两个较厚储层 A 和 B，两个薄层 C 和 D。剖面图图 5.14 中可以很容易地识别出这四个储层。为划分储层，在第一道放置着 SP 和 GR 曲线。在第三道分别放置 ILD，ILM 和 SFLU 曲线，这三条曲线来自 20 世纪 70 年代至 80 年代的典型的双感应—微球聚焦测井组合。其中 ILD 为深感应曲线，用于探测原状地层电阻率；ILM 为中感应曲线，用于探测侵入较深的侵入带电阻率；SFLU 为微球聚焦曲线。在典型的感应测井条件下（$R_{xo} > R_t$），SFLU 读数可作为冲洗带电阻率值 R_{xo}，且该读数并非基于弹簧片，对微电极粗糙度并不敏感。

As in the case of the laterolog curves, the induction curves must be checked for any necessary corrections before attempting quantitative interpretation. In addition to the same general types of borehole corrections, the induction may also require correction for bed thickness and shoulder effect. The magnitude of this correction will depend on an estimate of the bed thickness and the resistivity of the shoulder beds. This type of correction will certainly be necessary for the two thin streaks of zones C and D.

与侧向测井一样，在定量解释前，必须对感应测井进行校正。除进行一般的井眼校正外，感应测井还须进行围岩—层厚校正，特别是对如图中所示的 C 层和 D 层这样的两个薄层而言，校正幅度取决于层厚及围岩电阻率。

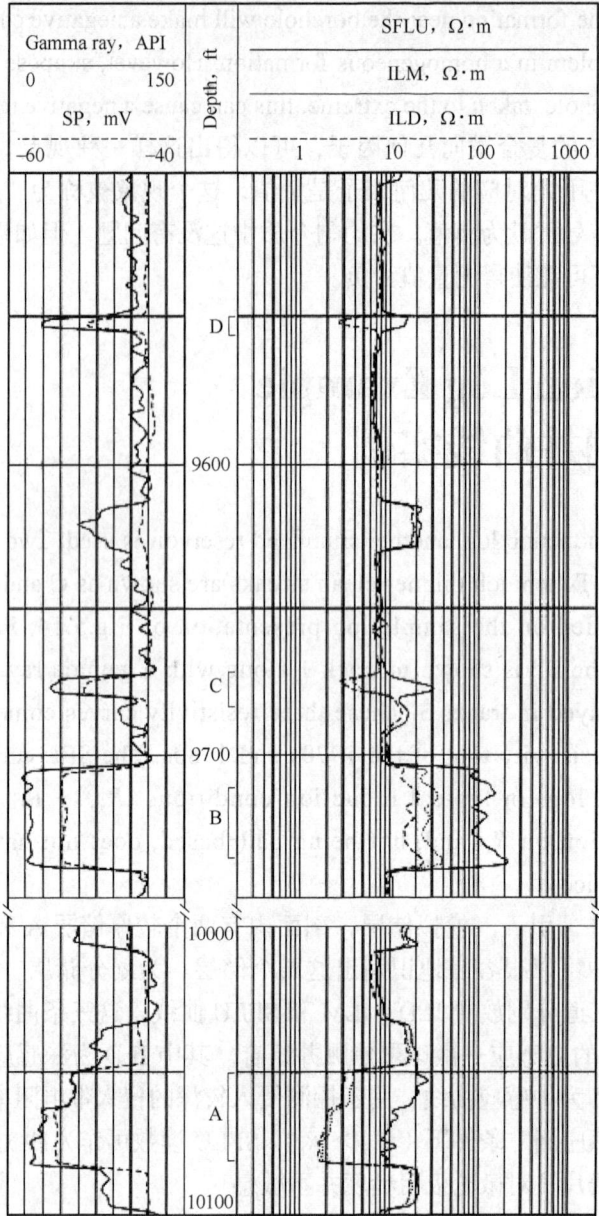

Fig.5.14 A sample of induction log(from Darwin V. Ellis, 2008)

图 5.14 感应测井曲线实例（据 Darwin V.Ellis，2008）

Exercises

课后练习

5.1 Which type of resistivity tool can be used in a well which has been drilled with oil-base mud?

(A) Laterolog　　(B) Induction　　(C) Either Laterolog of Induction

5.2 Using illustrations where applicable, briefly describe the principle of operation of the induction tool.

5.3 In what kinds of drilling fluids is the induction tool preferred over the laterolog tool?

5.4 Fig.6.15 shows part of the log sequence pertaining to this question. The resistivity of the connate water for this well has been obtained from chemical analysis of a produced water sample and was found to be $0.055\ \Omega \cdot m$. The sand shown in the logs has a formation resistivity factor given by $\dfrac{0.62}{\phi^{2.15}}$, The well has been drilled with a salt based mud which has a salt concentration of 250000 ppm.

(a) What is the height and depth range for the hydrocarbon zone in this log?

(b) What kind of fluid do you think is contained within this zone and why?

(c) Calculate the water saturation, S_w.

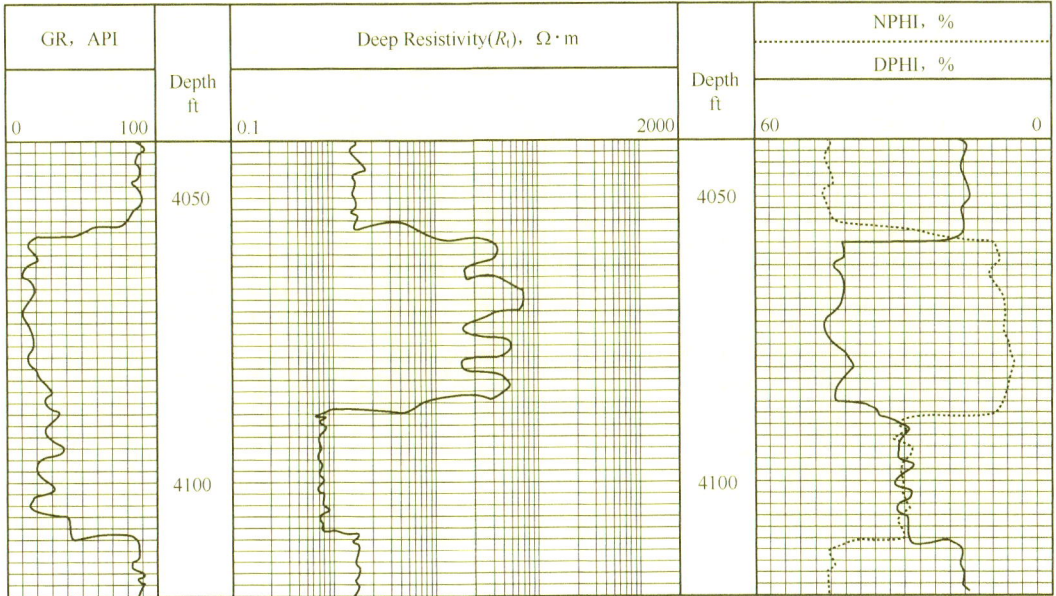

Fig.5.15 The log sequence

5.5 Given that the following sands are sandwiched between two layers of shale, draw sketches to show the log response for a resistivity log in:

(a) A salt water sand.

(b) A hydrocarbon bearing sand.

(c) A fresh water sand.

5.6 Interpretation

(a) Draw a shale baseline and find the permeable formation.

(b) Indicate the type of fluid in the permeable formation(the drilling mud is freshwater based).

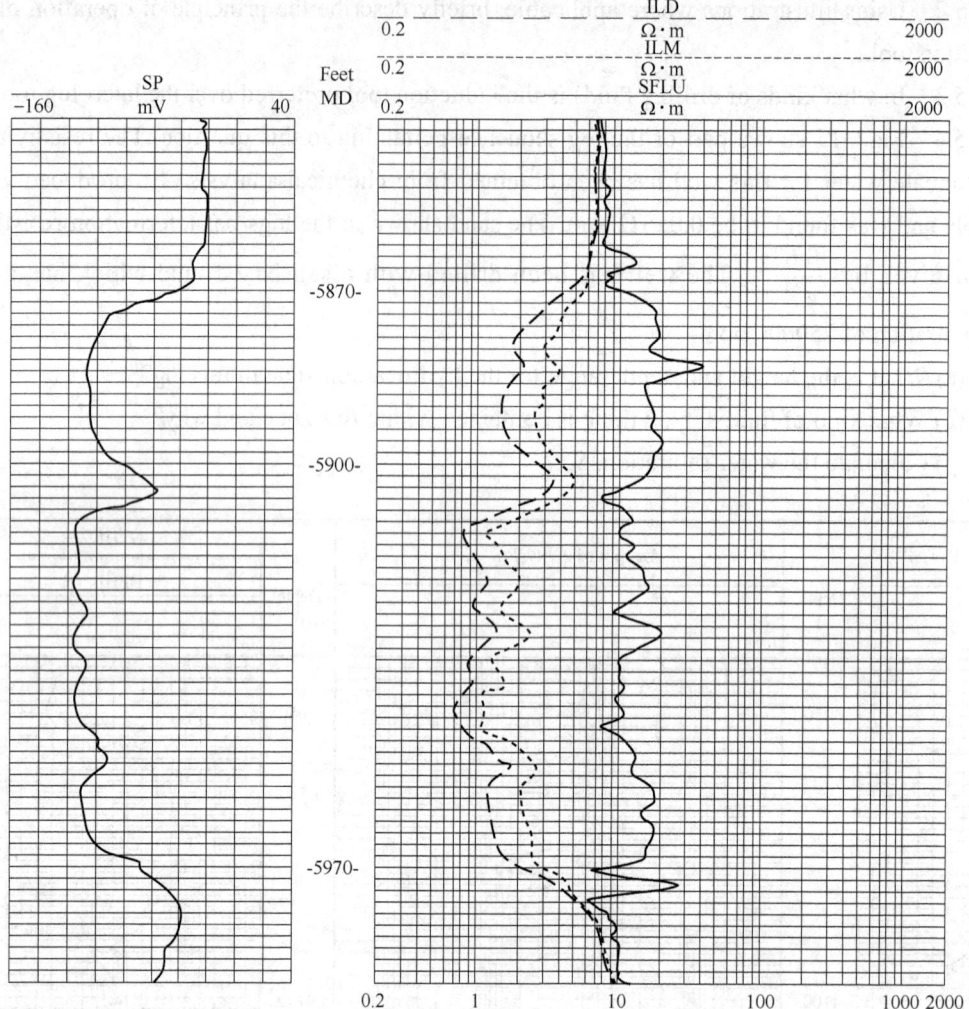

Fig.5.16 Logging curve

6 Sonic Log
声波测井

We can group together as acoustic logs those that involve recording a parameter linked with the transmission of sound waves in the formation. These parameters are mainly:

(1) The propagation speed of a wave in the formation calculated from the time taken to travel through a certain thickness of formation. This is the sonic log.

(2) The amplitude at the receiver of the first or second wave in the signal, either on arrival of the compressional wave or the shear wave. This is the sonic amplitude log which has an important application as the Cement Bond Log (CBL).

(3) The amplitude and position of the positive sections of the received signal. This is the variable density log (VDL).

我们可以将那些记录地层中声波传播的参数整理在一起，归类为声波测井。这些参数主要有：

（1）声波在地层中的传播速度，根据穿过一定厚度地层所需的时间计算得出——对应声波速度测井。

（2）信号中第一列或第二列在接收端处的振幅，或横波或纵波的波至——对应声波振幅测井，在水泥胶结测井（CBL）中有重要的应用。

（3）接收到的信号正极部分的幅度和位置——对应声波变密度测井（VDL）。

The sonic log is a porosity log that measures interval transit time (Δt) of a compressional sound wave traveling through one foot of formation. The sonic log device consists of one or more sound transmitters, and two or more receivers. Modern sonic logs are borehole compensated devices (BHC). These devices greatly reduce the spurious effects of borehole size variations, as well as errors due to tilt of the sonic tool.

声波测井是一种孔隙度测井，用于测量声波穿过一英尺地层的时差（Δt）。声波测井装置由一个或多个声音发射器和两个或多个接收器组成。现代声波测井多采用补偿声波测井仪（BHC），大大降低了井眼尺寸变化引起的杂散响应，并降低了由声波测井仪倾斜引起的误差。

Interval transit time (Δt) is the reciprocal of the velocity of a compressional sound wave. Interval transit time (Δt) is recorded in tracks #2 and #3. A sonic derived porosity curve is sometimes recorded in tracks #2 and #3, along with the Δt curve. Track #1 normally contains a caliper log and a gamma ray log or an SP log.

时差（Δt）是声波纵波速度的倒数。将时差（Δt）记录在第2号和第3号道中。有时也将声波测井衍生的孔隙度曲线记录在第 2 号、第 3 号道，同 Δt 曲线在一起。第 1 号道通常包含井径测井、伽马测井或自然电位测井。

The interval transit time (Δt) is dependent upon both lithology and porosity. Therefore, a formation's matrix velocity must be known to derive sonic porosity.

时差（Δt）取决于岩石岩性和孔隙度。因此，已知地层岩石骨架速度是推导声波孔隙度的必要条件。

6.1 Acoustic Signals
声音信号

An acoustic signal is the sound wave resulting from the release of acoustic energy (Fig.6.1).
声信号是声能释放时产生的声波（图 6.1）。

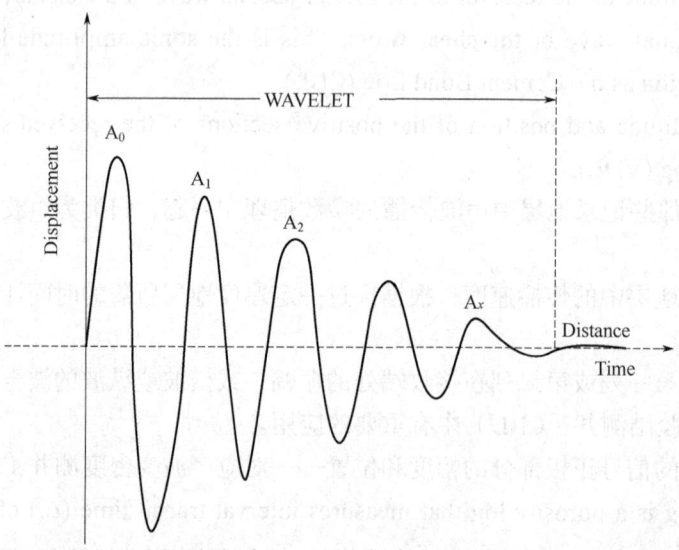

Fig.6.1. Example of acoustic signal (from Oberto et al., 1984)
图 6.1　声信号示例（据 Oberto 等, 1984）

6.1.1 Period, T
周期 T

The period of the wave is defined as the duration of one cycle, and is generally measured in microseconds. It corresponds to the time separating two successive positive wave peaks (or negative peaks), measuring the same amplitude value in the same direction each time.

波的周期定义为经过一个周期所持续时间，通常以微秒为单位。周期是两个连续正波峰（或负波峰）的间隔时间。在同一方向的任一次周期中测得的振幅相同。

6.1.2 Frequency, f
频率 f

Frequency corresponds to the number of complete cycles per second and is measured in Hertz (Hz).1Hertz=1cycle/second. Frequency is the inverse of the period, hence:

频率是一秒内完整周期重复出现的次数，以赫兹（Hz）为单位，1 赫兹 = 1 周期 / 秒。频率是周期的倒数，因此有：

$$f = \frac{1}{T} \tag{6.1}$$

Definition of the terms used in acoustics were shown in Fig.6.2.
声学中各术语的定义见图 6.2。

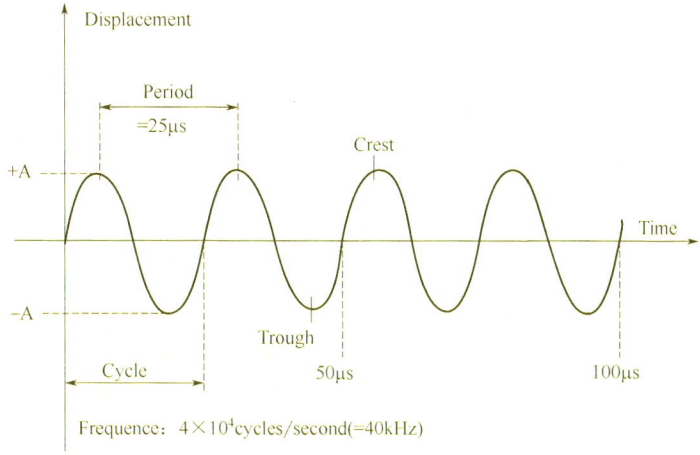

Fig.6.2　Definition of the terms used in acoustics (from Oberto et al., 1984)
图 6.2　声学中各术语定义（据 Oberto 等, 1984）

6.1.3 Wavelength, λ
波长 λ

Wavelengh is the distance travelled in one cycle by a wave front. It is equal to the ratio of the propagation speed (v) and the frequency(f):

波长是一个波前在一个周期内传播的距离。它是传播速度（v）和频率（f）之比：

$$\lambda = \frac{v}{f} \tag{6.2}$$

6.2　Acoustic Waves
声波

There are several types of sound waves, each one characterized by the particular kind of particle movement.

声波有多种类型，每种都以特定类型的粒子运动为特征。

6.2.1 Compressional or Longitudinal Waves (P-wave)
压缩波或纵波（P 波）

In Compressional wave, the particles move in a direction parallel to the direction of propagation (Fig.6.3). The speed of propagation is largest for this kind of wave compared to others and so it arrives first. It is the only wave propagated in liquids.

在这种波中，质点沿与传播方向平行的方向运动（图 6.3）。与其他波相比，这种波的传播速度最大，总是最先到达，是唯一能够在液体中传播的波。

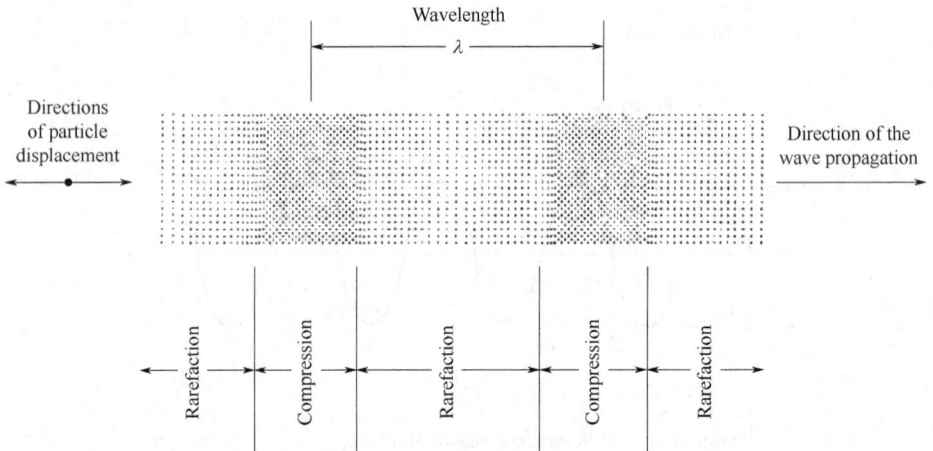

Fig.6.3　Compressional wave (from Oberto et al., 1984)

图 6.3　压缩波（据 Oberto 等, 1984）

6.2.2 Transverse or Shear Waves(S-wave)
横波或剪切波（S 波）

In transverse wave, particle movement is in a direction perpendicular to the wave direction (Fig.6.4). As mentioned, the speed of propagation is less than the P-wave with a ratio of about 1.6 to 2. No shear waves are transmitted in liquids.

在横波中质点运动方向垂直于波的方向（图 6-4）。如前所述，它的传播速度小于 P 波，其比值约为 1.6～2.0。横波在液体中不能传播。

In the formation, sound energy is transmitted by both compressional and shear wave. In the mud, energy is transmitted solely by compressional waves.

在地层中，声能同时通过纵波和横波传播。在钻井液中，声能仅通过纵波传播。

The energy transmitted by the slower shear wave is much higher than that of the compressional wave which is first to arrive. In the wave pattern received we can identify the shear wave by this feature. The ratio of amplitudes is of the order of between 15 and 20 to 1 (Fig.6.5). As shales are less rigid structurally they do not transmit transverse waves very well.

较慢的横波所传递的能量远高于最先到达的纵波。在接收到的波形中,可以通过这个特征来识别横波。声波振幅之比在 15 ∶ 1~20 ∶ 1 之间(图 6.5)。由于泥岩硬度较低,因此不能很好地传播横波。

N.B. Transverse waves may he polarized and so can he subdivided into horizontal and vertical components.

注意:横波可能会极化,因此可以细分为水平分量和垂直分量。

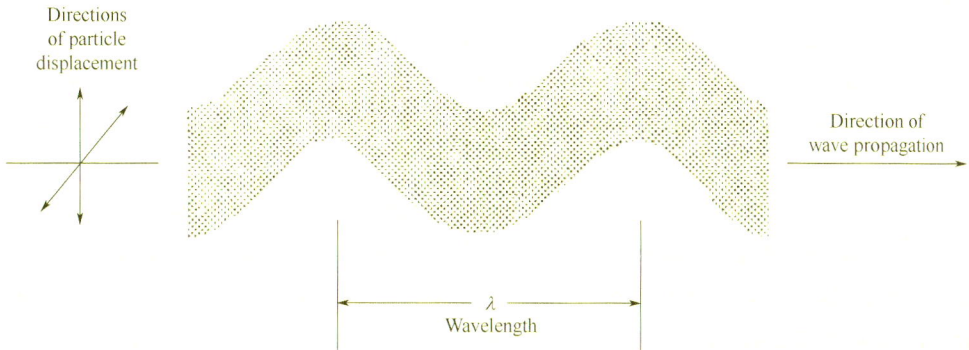

Fig.6.4　Shear wave (from Oberto et al ., 1984)

图 6.4　剪切波(据 Oberto 等, 1984)

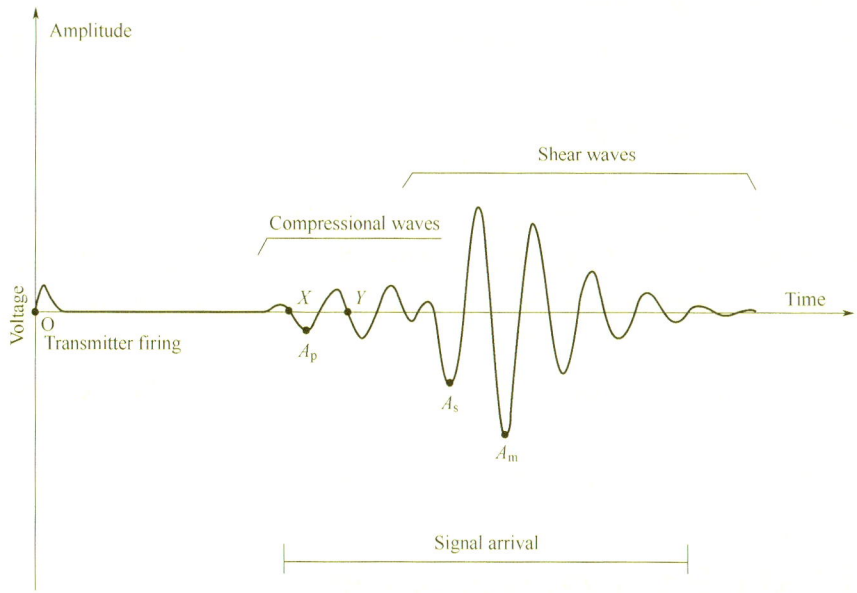

Fig.6.5　Separation of compressional and shear waves from their transit travel time and amplitude (from Oberto et al ., 1984)

图 6.5　根据传播时间和振幅分离出的压缩波和剪切波(据 Oberto 等, 1984)

6.2.3 Surface Waves
面波

Surface waves are waves transmitted on the surface within a layer whose thickness is about equal to the wave-length. They are divided as follows:

面波是在厚度约等于波长的层面上传播的波,可分为以下几种:

(1) Rayleigh waves, in which the particle motion is elliptical, and retrograde with respect to the direction of propagation. These waves are not transmitted in liquids and their velocity is around 90% of that of transverse waves.

(2) Love waves, in which particle motion is transverse to the direction of propagation but without any vertical movement. They are faster than Rayleigh waves.

(3) Coupled waves, in which the movement is diagonal. These are the fastest surface wave.

(4) Hydrodynamic waves, in which movement is elliptical but symmetrical to Rayleigh waves.

(5) Stoneley waves, that are boundary acoustic waves at a liquid-solid interface resulting from the interaction of the compressional wave in the liquid and the shear wave in the solid. By definition, the Stoneley wave must have a wavelength smaller than the borehole diameter. Particle motion in the solid will be elliptical and retrograde similar to a Rayleigh wave. The velocity of the Stoneley wave will be less than that of the compressional wave in the fluid or the shear wave in the solid.

(1) 瑞利波:质点呈椭圆形振动,并随波传播的方向逆向移动。这些波不能在液体中传播,其速度大约是横波的90%。

(2) 勒夫波:质点运动方向平行于波的传播方向,无垂直方向的运动。传播速度比瑞利波快。

(3) 耦合波:沿对角线传播,是最快的面波。

(4) 水力波:质点也呈椭圆形振动,与瑞利波对称。

(5) 斯通利波:由液体中的纵波和固体中的横波相互作用而产生的液固界面上的边界声波。根据定义,斯通利波的波长必须小于井眼直径。质点在固体中的运动是椭圆形的,并且类似于瑞利波的逆行运动。斯通利波的速度小于流体中的纵波或固体中的横波。

N.B. Sound waves transfer energy step by step by the movement of particles under elastic forces.

注意:声波通过质点在弹性力作用下的运动来逐步传递能量。

6.3 Elastic Properties of Rocks
岩石的弹性性质

Elastic Properties are the properties that define the ability of a body or rock to resist permanent deformation when deformed slightly. All solids, including rocks, follow Hooke's law which gives the proportional relation between the tension and the constraint (force).

弹性是指一个物体或岩石在轻微变形时抵抗永久变形的能力。所有固体，包括岩石，都遵循胡克定律，该定律给出了张力与约束力之间的关系。

(1) The ratio of constraint to tension in a simple linear compression or dilation is known as Young's modulus.

（1）在单一线性压缩或膨胀中，约束力与张力之比称为杨氏模量。

$$E = \frac{F/S}{dL/L} \tag{6.3}$$

Where F/S is the constraint or force applied per surface area and dL/L is the stretch or compression per unit length under the effect of the force.

式中，F/S 是施加在单位表面上的约束力（应力），dL/L 是在力的作用下每单位长度的拉伸或压缩量（应变）。

(2) The ratio of force to tension under hydrostatic compression or dilatation corresponds to the elastic bulk modulus.

（2）在外力作用下，应力与体积应变之比为体积形变弹性模量。

$$k = \frac{F/S}{dV/V} \tag{6.4}$$

Where dV/V is the change per unit volume under the effect of the force.

式中，dV/V 是在力的作用下单位体积的变化（体积应变）。

(3) The ratio of force to tension under a shear force or one that is applied tangential to the displaced surface is known as the shear modulus, μ:

（3）在剪切力或向表面沿位移方向施加的切向力作用下，切应力与切应变之比称为切变模量 μ：

$$\mu = \frac{F/S}{dL/L} \tag{6.5}$$

Where F/S is the shear force and dL/L is the shear tension or the deformation without a change in total volume.

式中，F/S 是切应力，dL/L 是总体积不变时的剪切形变量（切应变）。

To these elastic moduli we should add:

对于这些弹性系数，应该增加下列参数：

The compressibility, c (or β), which is the inverse of the elastic modulus K.

压缩系数 $c(\beta)$：体积形变弹性模量 K 的倒数。

Poisson's ratio, σ, which is a measure of the change in shape, or ratio of the lateral contraction to the longitudinal dilation.

泊松比 σ：描述形状变化的量度，是横向相对缩减与纵向相对伸长之比。

$$\sigma = \frac{\mathrm{d}l/l}{\mathrm{d}L/L} \tag{6.6}$$

Where dl/l is the transverse or lateral change.

式中，dl/l 是横向相对变化。

N.B. We also talk about the space modulus, M, which is given by：

注意：我们还讨论了空间模量 M，可由下式计算得出：

$$M = K + \frac{4}{3}\mu \tag{6.7}$$

It is a measurement of the resistance to deformation from compressional and shear force in an elastic medium.

它是弹性介质中压缩和剪切力对变形阻力的度量。

The relationship between the various elasticity coefficients: the above coefficients can all be expressed in terms of any two. If for example we use μ and K we have:

各种弹性参数之间的关系：以上系数都可以用两个其他任意参数表示。例如，对于 μ 和 K，有：

$$E = \frac{9K\mu}{3K + \mu} \tag{6.8}$$

$$\sigma = \frac{3K - 2\mu}{6K + 2\mu} \tag{6.9}$$

6.4 Sound Wave Velocities
声波速度

The velocity of sound in elastic media can be expressed using the elastic modulus. The longitudinal wave velocity, v_L is given by：

声速在弹性介质中可以用弹性模量来表示，纵波速度 v_L 和横波速度 v_T 由下式计算得出：

$$v_L = \left(\frac{K + \frac{4}{3}\mu}{\rho_b}\right)^{1/2} = \left(\frac{E}{\rho_b}\frac{1-\sigma}{(1+\sigma)(1-2\sigma)}\right)^{1/2} \tag{6.10}$$

$$v_T = \left(\frac{\mu}{\rho_b}\right)^{1/2} = \left(\frac{E}{\rho_b}\frac{1}{2(1+\sigma)}\right)^{1/2} \tag{6.11}$$

6.5 Sound Wave Propagation, Reflection and Refraction
声波传播、反射和折射

Huyghens' principle states that each point reached by a wave oscillation acts as a new source of oscillation radiating spherical waves (Fig.6.6).

惠更斯原理指出，波形振动所到达的每个点都是辐射球形波的新振源（图 6.6）。

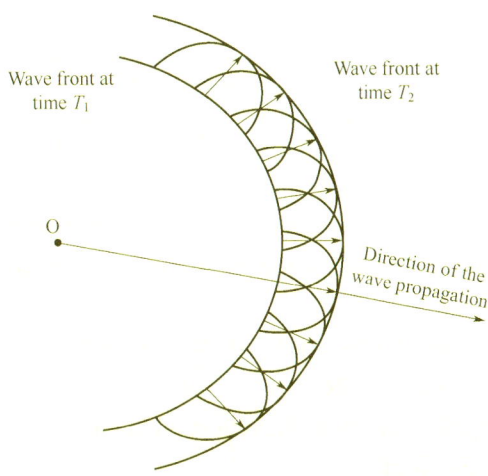

Fig.6.6 Wave propagation(from Oberto et al ., 1984)
图 6.6 波的传播（据 Oberto 等，1984）

The surface described by the in-phase oscillation at any given time is known as the wave front. The surface of separation between the set of points not in motion and those that are (or were) makes up a particular wave front called the wave surface.

任意给定时间内由同相振动所描述的表面称为波前。未在运动中的点集与那些正在（或曾经）运动的点之间的分离面构成了一个特殊的波阵面，称为波面。

Sound waves follow Descartes' law. Suppose we have two homogeneous media, isotropic and infinite with velocities v_{L_1}, v_{T_1}, and v_{L_2}, v_{T_2}, separated by a plane surface.

声波运动遵循笛卡儿法则。假设有两个各向同性、无限大的均匀介质，具有速度 v_{L_1}、v_{T_1} 和 v_{L_2}、v_{T_2}，介质被平面分隔。

Every wave L, even those purely longitudinal or transverse, incident at a point I on the separating surface at an angle i_1, gives rise to four new waves. Two of these are reflected waves, one compressional L_r at an angle r_1, one transverse T_r at an angle r_2, and the other two are refracted waves, one longitudinal L_R at an angle R_1 and the other transverse T_R at angle R_2 (Fig.6.7).

每一个波（L）以角度 i_1 在分隔面上点 I 入射，即使是纯粹的纵波或横波，也会产生四个新的波。其中两个是反射波，分别为角度为 r_1 的纵波 L_r 和为角度为 r_2 的横波 T_r；另外两个是折射波，分别为角度为 R_1 的纵波 L_R 和角度为 R_2 的横波 T_R（图 6.7）。

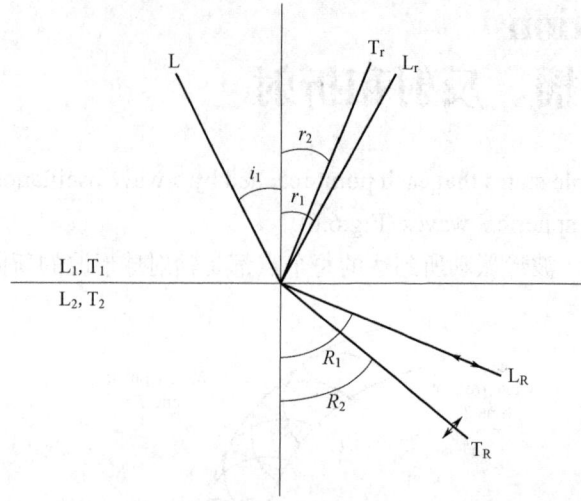

Fig.6.7 Reflection and refraction of an acoustic wave (from Oberto et al., 1984)
图 6.7 声波的反射和折射（据 Oberto 等，1984）

Other sound waves may appear due to diffraction or dispersion.
由于衍射或散射可能出现其他声波。
If we only consider longitudinal waves the reflection law is:
如果只考虑纵波，则反射定律是：

$$i_1 = r_1 \tag{6.12}$$

and the refraction law is:
折射定律是：

$$\sin i_1 / v_{L_1} = \sin R_1 / v_{L_2} \tag{6.13}$$

If $v_{L_2} > v_{L_1}$, the angle of total refraction or the critical angle of incidence, l, ($R_1=90°$) is given by the equation:

如果 $v_{L_2} > v_{L_1}$，则总折射角或临界入射角 l（$R_1 = 90°$）可由下式给出：

$$\sin l = v_{L_1} / v_{L_2} \tag{6.14}$$

We can define two critical angles of incidence, one for longitudinal and the other for transverse waves.
我们可以定义两个临界入射角，一个用于纵波，另一个用于横波。
If we consider the reflected and refracted waves given by a transverse wave, we have:
如果我们考虑由横波给出的反射波和折射波，有：

$$\frac{\sin i_1}{v_{L_1}} = \frac{\sin r_2}{v_{T_1}} \tag{6.15}$$

$$\frac{\sin i_1}{v_{L_1}} = \frac{\sin R_2}{v_{T_2}} \tag{6.16}$$

N.B. In the case of a wellbore where medium *l* is a fluid the reflected transverse wave does not exist.

注意：在介质 *l* 是流体的井筒中，反射横波不存在。

6.6 Measurement of the Speed of Sound
测量声速

A magneto astrictive transducer, excited from the surface by a signal, emits a sound wave (Fig.6.8) whose average frequency is of the order of 20 to 40kHz. The duration of the emission is short but it is repeated several times per second (10 to 60 times depending on the tool). The wave spreads in all directions from the transmitter, so producing spherical wavefronts. The wavefront passing through the mud is incident upon the borehole wall with increasing time and increasing angle of incidence as the distance from the transmitter increases (Fig.6.9).

磁致伸缩换能器从表面激发信号，发出声波（图 6.8），其平均频率约为 20~40 kHz。发射的持续时间很短，但每秒重复几次（取决于不同工具，次数介于 10 ~ 60 次）。波从发射器向各个方向传播，因此产生球面波前。穿过钻井液的波前入射到井壁上，随着与发射器距离的增加，入射时间增加，入射角增大（图 6-9）。

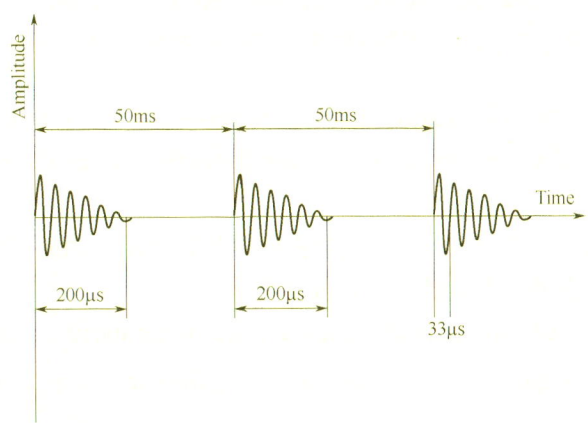

Fig.6.8 Schematic representation of the signal emitted by the transducer (from Oberto et al., 1984)

图 6.8 传感器发出信号示意图（据 Oberto 等，1984）

We can consider several cases:

(1) If the angle of incidence is less than the critical angle each incident longitudinal wave gives rise to: ① two longitudinal waves, one reflected, one refracted; and ② one refracted transverse wave (the reflected transverse wave cannot propagate in the mud).

(2) If the angle of incidence is larger than the critical angle, the incident longitudinal wave

produces a single reflected longitudinal wave.

我们可以考虑以下几种情况：

（1）如果入射角小于临界角，则每个入射纵波会产生：①两个纵波，一个为反射波，一个为折射波；②一个折射横波（反射的横波不能在钻井液中传播）。

（2）如果入射角大于入射纵波产生的临界角，则产生一个反射的纵波。

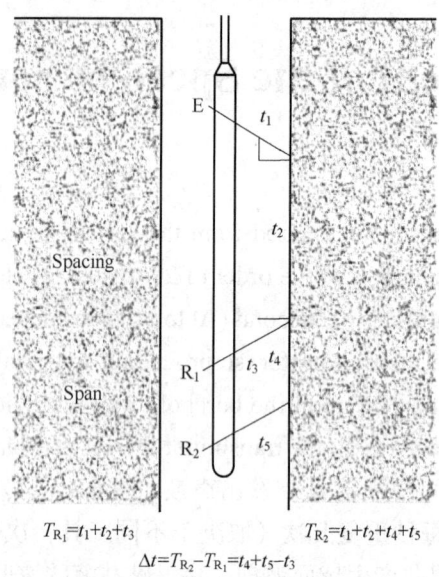

Fig.6.9　Schematic of the principle for measuring the interval transit time
(tool with two receivers) (from Oberto et al., 1984)

图 6.9　测量时差的原理示意图（仪器具有两个接收器）（据 Oberto 等，1984）

The incident or reflected longitudinal waves traveling in the mud are slower than the refracted compressional waves propagated in the formation, since the speed of sound in the ground is greater than that in mud.

由于声波在地面的传播速度大于在钻井液中的传播速度，因此在钻井液中传播的入射纵波或反射纵波要比在地层中传播的折射纵波慢。

Among the refracted longitudinal waves we are particularly interested in those waves refracted at the critical angle, since they propagate along the borehole wall at a speed v_{L_2}.

在折射纵波中，值得注意的是以临界角折射的波，它们沿着井壁以速度 v_{L_2} 传播。

Each point reached by this wave acts as a new source transmitting waves, so creating effectively cones of waves in the mud traveling at a speed v_{L_1}.

这个波所到达的每个点都是一个新的波源，因此可以在钻井液中有效地形成以速度 v_{L_1} 传播的锥形波。

If we place two receivers, R_1 and R_2 at certain distances from the transmitter and along the axes of the tool and of the hole (supposed the same) they are reached by the sound at times T_{R_1} and T_{R_2}, respectively given by:

如果我们放置两个接收器，在距离发射器 R_1、R_2 的位置，沿着测井仪器和井眼的轴线（假定相同），声波会在 T_{R_1}、T_{R_2} 时间后到达被接收，有：

$$T_{R_1} = \frac{\overline{EA}}{v_{L_1}} + \frac{\overline{AB}}{v_{L_2}} + \frac{\overline{BR_1}}{v_{L_1}} \qquad (6.17)$$

$$T_{R_2} = \frac{\overline{EA}}{v_{L_1}} + \frac{\overline{AB}}{v_{L_2}} + \frac{\overline{BC}}{v_{L_2}} + \frac{\overline{CR_2}}{v_{L_1}} \qquad (6.18)$$

We can measure the time T_{R_1}, (or T_{R_2}) taken for the sound wave to reach R_1 (or R_2). This is the method known as the single-receiver time. However, the total time has to be corrected for the time spent crossing and recrossing the mud. This gives:

我们还可以测量声波到达 R_1（或 R_2）所需的时间 T_{R_1}（或 T_{R_2}），这是单接收机方法。然而，总时间必须根据两次穿过钻井液的时间进行校正，则：

$$\frac{\overline{AB}}{v_{L_2}} = T_{R_1} - \frac{\overline{EA}}{v_{L_1}} - \frac{\overline{BR_1}}{v_{L_1}} \qquad (6.19)$$

Knowing $\overline{AB}$ (which is not equal to $\overline{ER_2}$) we can deduce v_{L_2}. However, we need to know the hole diameter, possibly from a caliper log.

在通过井径测井知道井眼直径的条件下已知 $\overline{AB}$（不等于 $\overline{ER_2}$）可以推导出 v_{L_2}。

We can measure the time Δt that elapsed between the wave arrival at R_1 and R_2. This is the two-receiver method. The time Δt known as the transit time is directly proportional to the speed of sound in the formation and the distance between the two receivers R_1 and R_2.

If the tool is at the centre of the hole and the hole is of uniform diameter we have, in effect:

我们可以测量波到达 R_1 和 R_2 之间经过的时间差 Δt，这是双接收器方法。时间差 Δt 被称为传输时间，与地层中声波传播速度及两个接收器之间的距离成正比。

若测井仪位于井眼中心，且井径均一，则有：

$$\Delta t = T_{R_2} - T_{R_1} = \frac{\overline{BC}}{v_{L_2}} \qquad (6.20)$$

As $\qquad \dfrac{\overline{BR_1}}{v_{L_1}} = \dfrac{\overline{CR_2}}{v_{L_1}}; \quad \overline{BC} = \overline{R_1R_2}$

N.B. If the distance $\overline{R_1R_2}$ is one foot the measurement gives transit time for one foot. From this time we can derive velocity using:

$$\Delta t (\mu s/ft) = 10^6/v(ft/s) \qquad (6.21)$$

那么 $\qquad \dfrac{\overline{BR_1}}{v_{L_1}} = \dfrac{\overline{CR_2}}{v_{L_1}}; \quad \overline{BC} = \overline{R_1R_2}$

注意：当距离 $\overline{R_1R_2}$ 为 1 英尺时，则测量得到的是声波在 1 英尺内的传播时间。根据传播时间和式（6.21）可以计算出速度。

The measurement of the first wave arrival relates only to those waves refracted at the critical angle as these are the fastest. In fact: (a) other longitudinal waves refracted into the formation travel at the same speed as the first arrival but due to their path length generally arrive later (see the waves shown in Fig.6.10); and (b) transverse waves refracted into the formation travel more slowly than the longitudinal wave and so give rise to later waves at the receiver. However, as their energy is higher they are easily seen on the oscilloscope and can be detected.

首先测量到的波应当是以临界角折射的波，因为这些波的传播速度是最快的。实际上：（a）在地层中折射的其他纵波与首先到达的波具有相同的传播速度，但是由于它们的传播路径较长，通常到达较晚（见图 6.10）；（b）在地层中折射的横波比纵波传播得慢，因此在接收器处产生的波更晚。然而，由于它们具有较高的能量，因此容易在示波器上看到并被检测到。

N.B. The compressional interval transit time, derived from the difference between the first compressional arrival times at the two receivers, is reasonably accurate since the compressional arrival is easily detected because it arrives first and because at the spacings generally used it stands out against the background noise preceding it.

注意：纵波时差为两个接收器接收到的第一个纵波的时间之差，这一测量的准确性在于纵波首波很容易被检测到，因为它是最先到达的，且在常规的时间间隔内，它明显异常于之前的背景噪声。

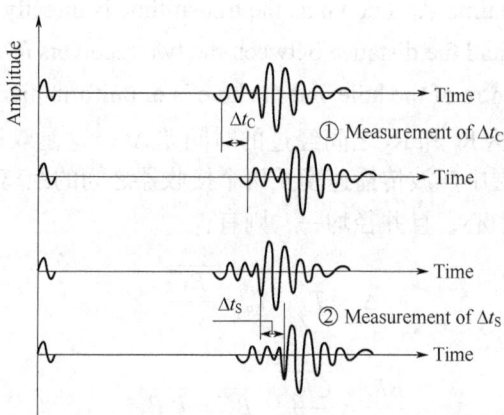

Fig.6.10　Method for measuring the interval transit time of the shear wave
图 6.10　测量横波时差的方法

In any case the arrival of the wave front corresponding to the refracted shear wave could be detected by raising the wave detection threshold to an amplitude level higher than that used to detect compressional arrivals.

一般来说，可通过将探测阈值提高到比检测纵波阈值还高的振幅水平来探测折射横波对应的波前到达。

Indeed, the shear arrivals generally have higher energy and so can be separated from the compressional. This allows us to measure the shear interval transit time.

事实上,横波通常具有较高的能量,因此可以与纵波区分开来。这使我们能够测量横波时差。

This measurement can be obtained from a variable density log (see further for explanation). On Fig.6.11 one can recognize the compressional arrivals which form the first set of bands and which also show practically uniform variations in time delay with changing depth. The shear arrivals can be picked out as a later set of bands, which are generally of higher energy. They again show variations in time delay with depth, but they are different in shape from those of the compressional bands, due to their lower velocity (the angle is higher). The fluid arrivals can be identified in a similar manner. Also handy for identification, the use of the variable density log for shear interval transit time estimation is not reliable because of the lack of time resolution in the display.

纵波层间传播时间的测量可以通过变密度测井实现(参见进一步的解释)。图6.11中,可以识别出第一波段的纵波,并且随着深度的变化,时间延迟的变化趋于一致。其后识别出的波段是横波,这些波通常具有较高的能量。横波同样随深度变化,时间延迟的变化趋于一致,但由于速度较低(角度较高),这一波段的波形与第一波段的纵波的波形有所不同。用类似的方法也能够轻易识别钻井液波,但显示中缺乏时间分辨率参数,所以运用变密度测井估算横波时差是不可靠的。

The shear interval transit time can automatically be obtained by using the Schlumberger Long Spacing Sonic tool (Fig.6.12). The advantages of this new tool are the following:

使用斯伦贝谢长间距声波仪器可以自动获得横波时差(图6.12)。这种新型仪器的优点如下:

Fig.6.11 Use of variable density log for identification of arrivals(from Aron et al., 1978)

图6.11 变密度测井识别波至(据Aron等,1978)

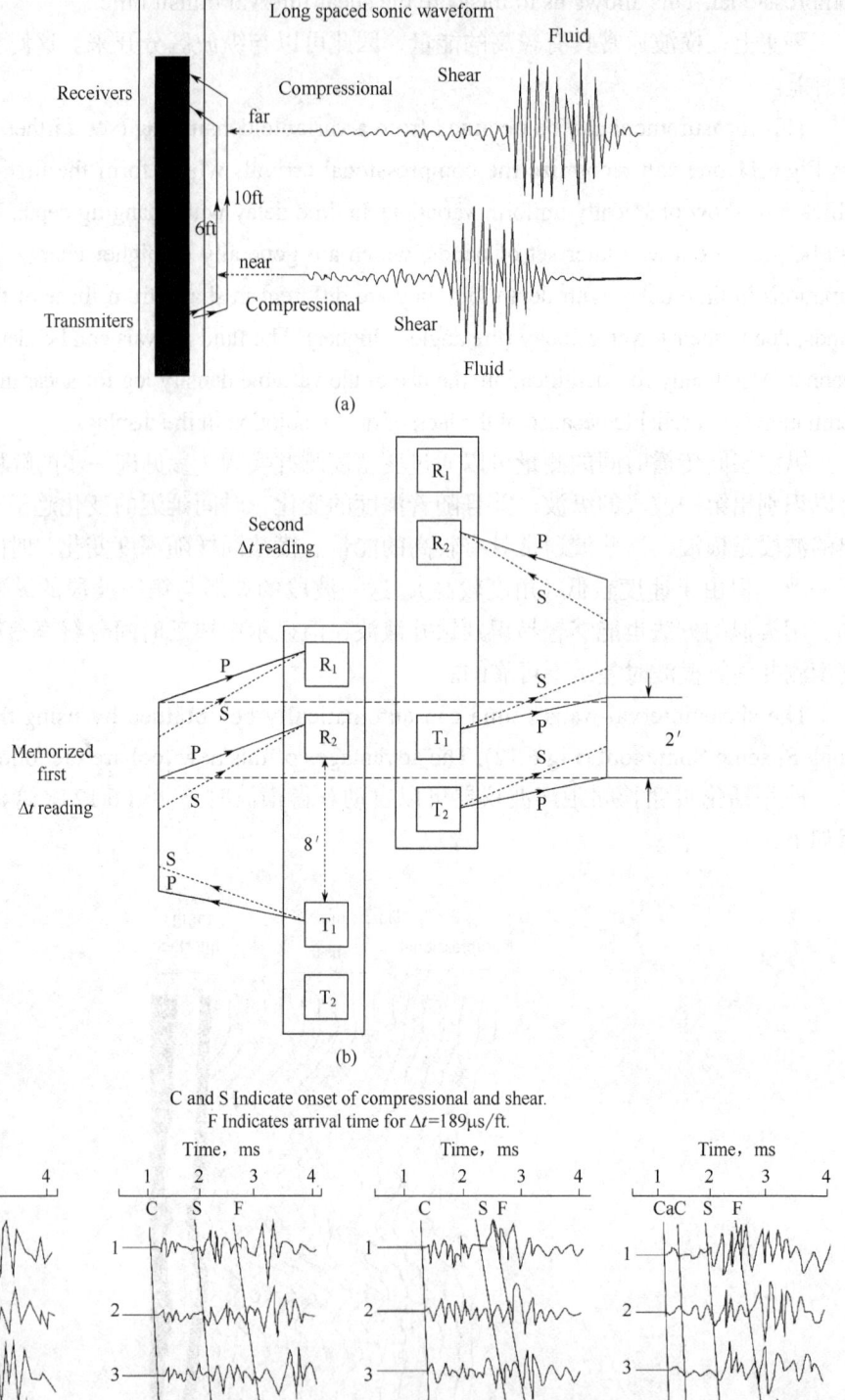

Fig.6.12 The Long Spacing Sonic tool
图 6.12 长间距声波测井仪

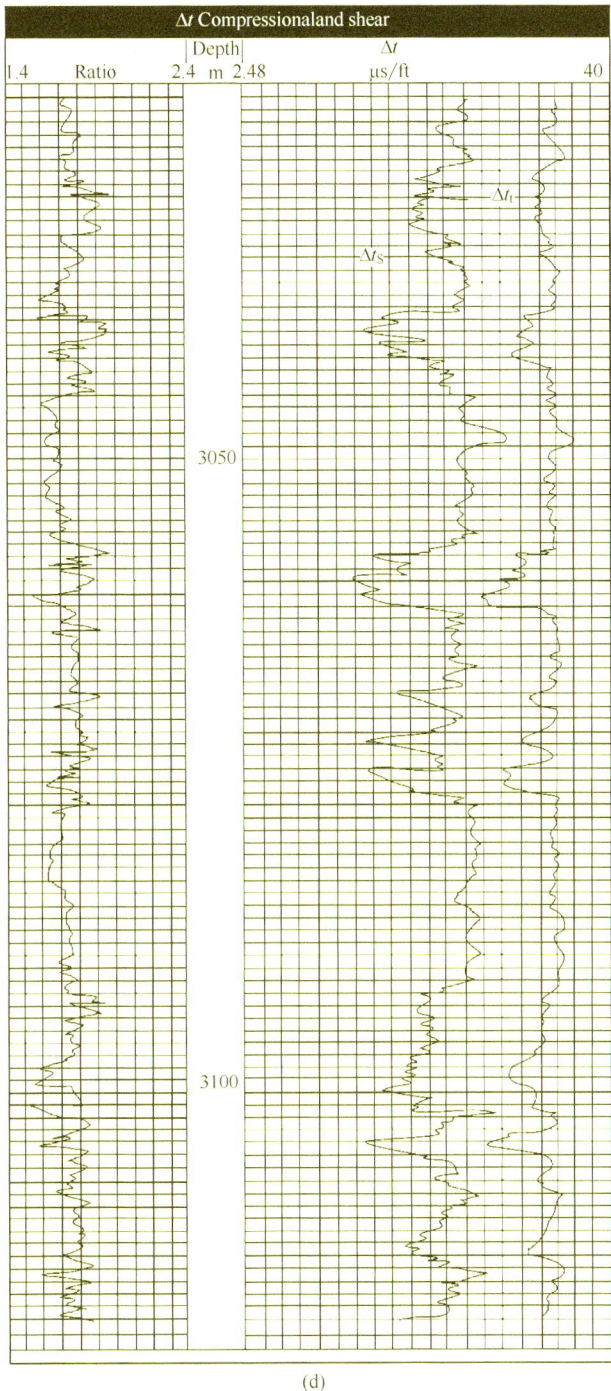

(d)

Fig.6.12 The Long Spacing Sonic tool

(a) The Long Spacing Sonic tool of Schlumberger (courtesy of Schlumberger); (b) Principle of measurement; (c) Feature of the complete signal as recorded by the Long Spacing Sonic tool (courtesy of Schlumberger); (d) Example of Δt compressional and shear (courtesy of Schlumberger).

图 6.12 长间距声波测井仪

（a）长间距声波测井仪（斯伦贝谢提供）；（b）测量原理；（c）长间距声波测井仪记录的完整信号特征（斯伦贝谢提供）；（d）纵波、横波层间传播时间的测量实例（斯伦贝谢提供）

(1) It digitally records the entire received waveform(not the first arrival) from which compressional, shear and fluid arrivals can be separated and studied.

(2) The spacing can be varied; an increase of the spacing between transmitter and receivers allows for adequate time separation between the various arrivals, a good signal-to-noise ratio and a minimum signal distortion.

(3) The frequency used is lower (11 kHz instead of 20 kHz).

（1）它以数字方式记录整个接收的波形（不是首先到达的），从中可以分离和研究纵波、横波和钻井液波。

（2）间距可以变化；增大发射器和接收器之间的间隔距离，可使不同声波波列之间有足够的时间间隔，同时具有良好的信噪比以及最低程度的信号失真。

（3）使用的频率较低（11 kHz，而不是 20kHz）。

This allows a lower attenuation of the signal.

The interest of the shear interval transit time measurement has been shown by Pickett. He has demonstrated that the ratio of the compressional to the shear velocities (v_L/v_T) can be used as a lithology indicator (Fig. 6.13, Fig. 6.14). Further investigations seem to confirm this but to indicate also the textural influence on the measurement.

这可以降低信号的衰减。

皮克特对横波时差的测量很感兴趣。他证明了纵横波速度之比（v_L/v_T）可以用作岩性指标（图 6.13、图 6.14）。通过进一步的研究似乎证实了这一点，但也表明了结构对测量的影响。

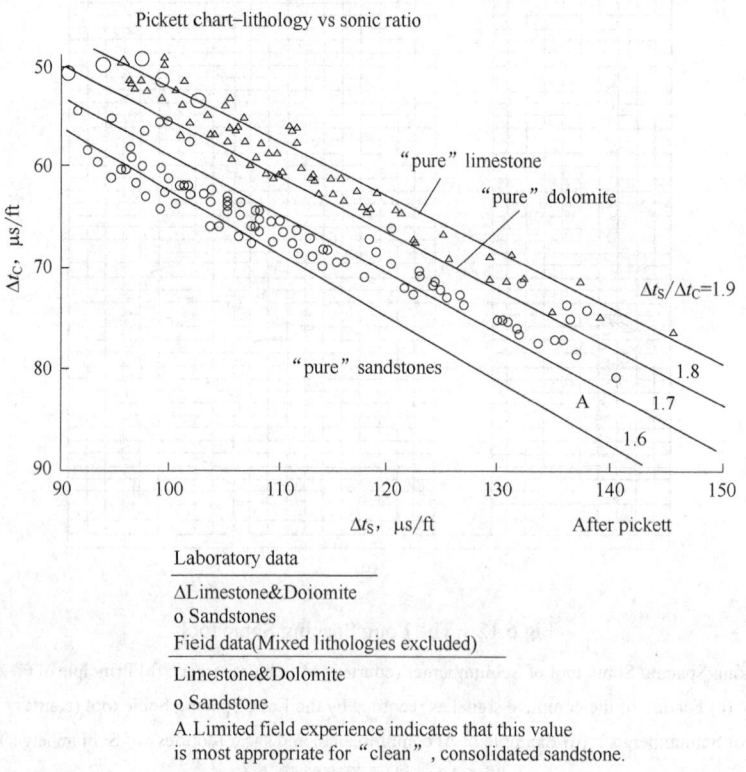

Fig.6.13　Definition of the lithology from the v_L/v_T ratio (from Pickett, 1963)

图 6.13　根据 v_L/v_T 定义岩性（据 Pickett，1963）

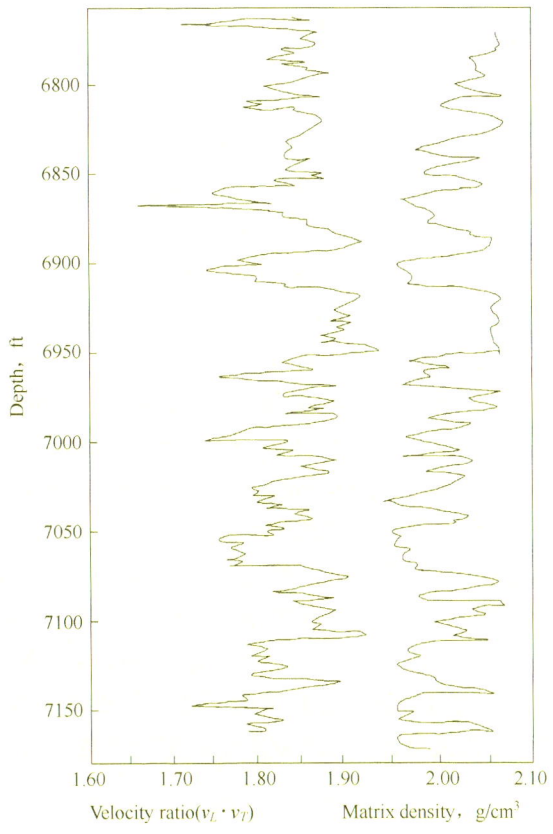

Fig.6.14　Example of v_L/v_T ratio log and comparison with the matrix density measured from cores (from Pickett, 1963)

图 6.14　纵横波速度比测井及与岩心测得的岩石骨架密度的对比（据 Pickett，1963）

6.7　Applications
　　　应用

　　Sonic transit-time is mainly measured to determine the porosity in a reservoir. We have to recognize that, partly through the difficulty of interpretation and factors affecting the measurement and partly because of the introduction of new nuclear devices for porosity measurement, this is no longer as important as before. It is used though both as a safeguard in porosity determination, especially as the measurement is not very sensitive to borehole size, and to compute secondary porosity in carbonate reservoirs.

　　声波时差主要用于确定储层中的孔隙度。我们必须认识到，一方面由于声波测井很难精确解释，且影响测量的因素繁多，另一方面由于引入了新的用于测定孔隙度的核仪器，这项技术已经不像从前那么重要了。它既可以在测量对井眼尺寸不敏感的时候确定孔隙度，也可用于计算碳酸盐岩储层的次生孔隙度。

6.7.1 Determination of Porosity
孔隙度的测定

The Wyllie formula for calculating sonic porosity can be used to determine porosity in consolidated sandstones and carbonates with intergranular porosity (grainstones) or intercrystalline porosity (sucrosic dolomites). However, when sonic porosities of carbonates with vuggy or fracture porosity are calculated by the Wyllie formula, porosity values will be too low. This will happen because the sonic log only records matrix porosity rather than vuggy or fracture secondary porosity. The percentage of vuggy or fracture secondary porosity can be calculated by subtracting sonic porosity from total porosity. Total porosity values are obtained from one of the nuclear logs (i.e. density or neutron). The percentage of secondary porosity called SPI or secondary porosity index, can be a useful mapping parameter in carbonate exploration.

计算声波孔隙度的威利公式可以用来确定固结砂岩和具有粒间孔（粒状灰岩）或晶间孔（糖粒状白云岩）的碳酸盐岩的孔隙度。然而，对于含具有孔洞或裂缝的碳酸盐岩，用威利公式计算声波孔隙度时，计算得到的孔隙度值过低。这是由于声波测井仅记录岩石骨架孔隙度，而不记录孔洞和裂缝的次生孔隙度。将总孔隙度减去声波孔隙度，可以计算出孔洞或裂缝的次生孔隙度所占百分比。总孔隙度可通过核测井（即密度测井或中子测井）得到。次生孔隙度所占百分比又可称为 SPI 或次生孔隙度指数，是碳酸盐岩勘探中重要的成图参数。

$$\phi_{\text{sonic}} = \frac{\Delta t_{\log} - \Delta t_{\text{ma}}}{\Delta t_{\text{f}} - \Delta t_{\text{ma}}} \tag{6.22}$$

Where ϕ_{sonic} ——sonic derived porosity, %;

Δt_{ma} ——interval transit time of the matrix (see Table 6.1), μs/ft;

$\Delta t_{\log}$ ——interval transit time of formation, μs/ft;

Δt_{f} ——interval transit time of the fluid in the well bore (fresh mud = 189; salt mud = 185), μs/ft.

式中 ϕ_{sonic} ——声波孔隙度，%;

Δt_{ma} ——岩石骨架的声波时差（见表 6.1），μs/ft;

$\Delta t_{\log}$ ——地层声波时差，μs/ft;

Δt_{f} ——井筒中流体的声波时差（淡水钻井液=189μs/ft；盐水钻井液=185μs/ft），μs/ft。

Table 6.1 Sonic Velocities and Interval Transit Times for Different Matrixs (from Schlumberger, 1972)

	v_{ma}, ft/s	Δt_{ma}, μs/ft	Δt_{ma}, μs/ft commonly used
Sandstone	18000 to 19500	55.5 to 51.0	55.5 to 51.0
Limestone	21000 to 23000	47.6 to 43.5	47.6
Dolomite	23000 to 26000	43.5 to 38.5	43.5

continued

	v_{ma}, ft/s	Δt_{ma}, μs/ft	Δt_{ma}, μs/ft commonly used
Anhydrite	20000	50.0	50.0
Salt	15000	66.7	67.0
Casing (Iron)	17500	57.0	57.0

N.B. These constants are used in the Sonic Porosity Formula.

表 6.1 不同岩石骨架的声速和声波时差（据斯伦贝谢，1972）

	v_{ma}, ft/s	Δt_{ma}, μs/ft	Δt_{ma}, μs/ft (commonly used)
砂岩	18000～19500	55.5～51.0	55.5～51.0
石灰岩	21000～23000	47.6～43.5	47.6
白云石	23000～26000	43.5～38.5	43.5
硬石膏	20000	50.0	50.0
盐	15000	66.7	67.0
套管（铁）	17500	57.0	57.0

注：表中信息用于声速孔隙度公式。

Where a sonic log is used to determine porosity in unconsolidated sands, an empirical compaction factor or C_p should be added to the Wyllie equation:

当使用声波测井来确定松散砂岩的孔隙度时，应在威利方程中加入经验压实校正系数 C_p：

$$\phi_{sonic} = \left(\frac{\Delta t_{log} - \Delta t_{ma}}{\Delta t_f - \Delta t_{ma}} \right) \times 1/C_p \tag{6.23}$$

Where ϕ_{sonic} ——sonic derived porosity, %;

Δt_{ma} ——interval transit time of the matrix (see Table 6.1), μs/ft;

Δt_{log} ——interval transit time of formation, μs/ft;

Δt_f ——interval transit time of the fluid in the well bore (fresh mud = 189; salt mud = 185), μs/ft.

C_p ——compaction factor.

式中 ϕ_{sonic} ——声波孔隙度，%;

Δt_{ma} ——岩石骨架的声波时差（表 6.1），μs/ft;

Δt_{log} ——由声波时差曲线读出的地层声波时差，μs/ft;

Δt_f ——井筒中流体的声波时差（淡水钻井液 = 189μs/ft；盐水钻井液 = 185μs/ft），μs/ft。

C_p ——压实校正系数。

The compaction factor is obtained from the following formula:

压实校正系数由下式计算：

$$C_p = \frac{\Delta t_{sh} \times C}{100} \tag{6.24}$$

Where　C_p——compaction factor;

　　　　Δt_{sh}——interval transit time for adjacent shale, ms;

　　　　C——a constant which is normally 1.0.

式中　C_p——压实校正系数；

　　　　Δt_{sh}——围岩的声波时差，ms；

　　　　C——常数，一般取值1.0。

The interval transit time (Δt) of a formation is increased due to the presence of hydrocarbons is not corrected, the sonic derived porosity will be too high. Hilchie suggests the following empirical corrections for hydrocarbon effect:

由于油气的存在没有得到校正，地层的声波时差（Δt）会增加，声波孔隙度会过高。谢尔契提出了如下对油气的经验校正公式

$$\phi = \phi_{sonic} \times 0.7 \quad (gas) \tag{6.25}$$

$$\phi = \phi_{sonic} \times 0.9 \quad (oil) \tag{6.26}$$

Track #1—this track includes both the gamma ray and caliper curves. Note that the gamma ray scale reads from 0 to 100 API gamma ray units, increasing from left-to-right in increments of 10 units. The gamma ray scale is represented by a solid line.

第1道对应自然伽马曲线和井径曲线。注意，自然伽马的刻度范围为0~100API（自然伽马单位），从左到右递增10个单位，由实线表示。

The caliper scale ranges from 6 to 16 inches, from left-to-right in one-inch increments, and is represented by a dashed line.

井径的刻度范围为6~16英尺，从左到右每格递增1英尺，由虚线表示。

Tracks #2 and #3—both the interval transit time (Δt) scale and the porosity scale are shown in this track. Sonic log interval transit time (Δt) is represented by a solid line, on a scale ranging from 40 to 80 μs/ft increasing from right-to-left.

第2、第3道对应声波时差（Δt）和孔隙度。声波时差（Δt）由实线表示，刻度范围40~80μs/ft，从右到左递增。

The sonic porosity measurement (limestone matrix) is shown by a dashed line, on a scale ranging from −10% to +30% porosity increasing from right-to-left. At the sane depth used in Fig.6.15 (9,310ft), read a sonic log interval transit time (Δt) value of 63 μs/ft.

声波孔隙度测量（岩石骨架为石灰岩）由虚线表示，孔隙度刻度范围−10%~+30%，从右到左递增。在图6.15（9310英尺）处，由声波测井读取的声波时差（Δt）为63μs/ft。

6.7.2　Determination of Elasticity Parameters Using Logs
测井用于确定弹性参数

If we can record, systematically, the density and the speeds of both the longitudinal and the transverse waves, the elastic moduli of the rock can be determined using the following equations.

如果我们能够系统地记录纵波和横波的密度和速度，岩石的弹性模量可以使由以下几

式确定。

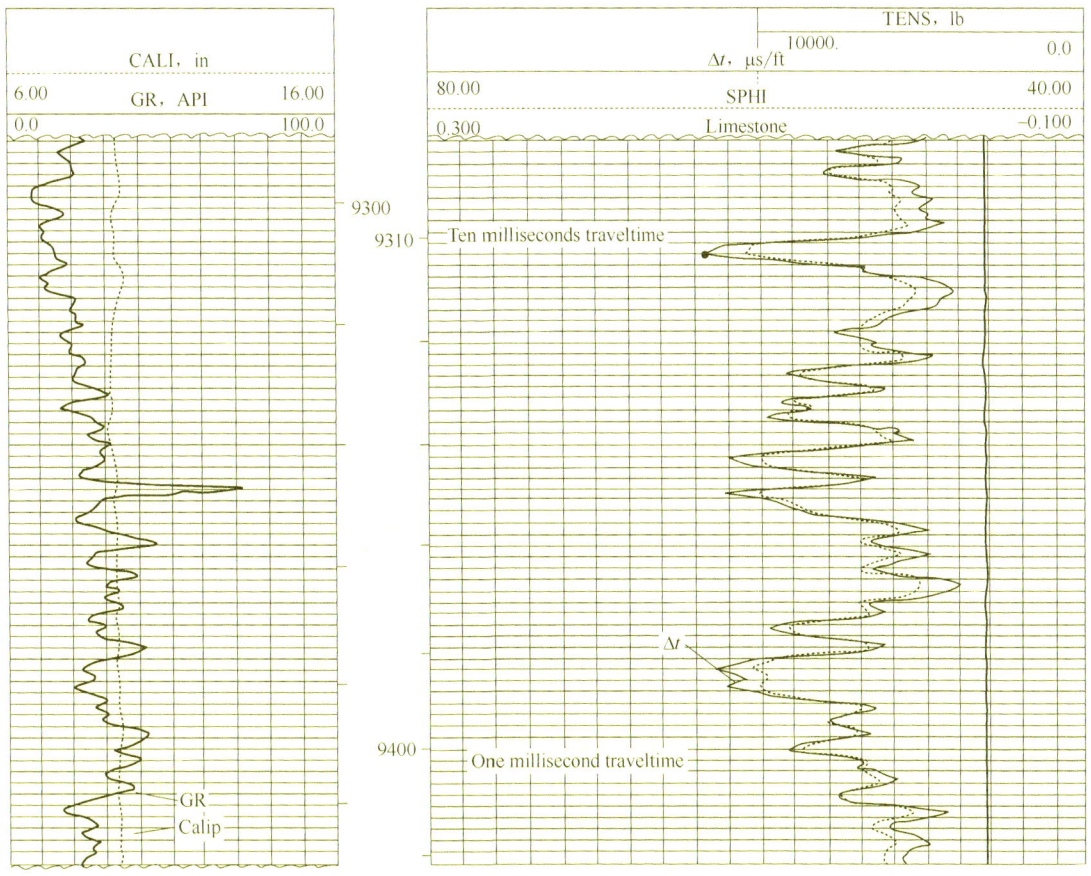

Fig.6.15 Example sonic log with gamma ray log and caliper (from George et al., 1982).
This example is shown to display the scales of a sonic log, and to be used in picking an interval transit time (Δt) value

图 6.15 声波测井结合自然伽马测井和井径测井（据 George 等, 1984）
显示了声波测井用于选取声波时差（Δt）的刻度

Young's modulus, E:
杨氏模量 E 的计算式为：

$$E = \frac{9k\rho v_T^2}{3k + \rho v_T^2} \tag{6.27}$$

Bulk modulus, k:
体积模量 k 的计算式为：

$$k = \rho\left(v_L^2 - \frac{4}{3}v_T^2\right) \tag{6.28}$$

Shear modulus, μ:
剪切模量 μ 的计算式为：

$$\mu = \rho v_T^2 \tag{6.29}$$

Poisson's ratio, σ :

泊松比 σ 的计算式为：

$$\sigma = \frac{1}{2} \frac{\frac{v_L^2}{v_T^2} - 2}{\frac{v_L^2}{v_T^2} - 1} = \frac{1}{2} \frac{\Delta t_T^2 - 2\Delta t_L^2}{\Delta t_T^2 - \Delta t_L^2} \tag{6.30}$$

Exercises
课后练习

6.1 What is P-wave?

6.2 What is S-wave?

6.3 The sonic tool responds to the primary and not the secondary porosity in rocks. True or False?

6.4 Will the presence of gas in an otherwise water saturated formation cause an increase or a decrease of the interval transit time in the sonic (slowness) log?

(A) Increase　　　(B) Decrease

6.5 An interval transit time of 90 μs/ft was measured in a sandstone reservoir. The acoustic velocity of the matrix was 18000 ft/sec.

(a) What is the interval transit time of the matrix?

(b) Assume a fluid transit time of 189 μs/ft. Calculate the porosity in the sandstone reservoir using Wyllie's time average equation.

7 Borehole Compensated Sonic Logging
补偿声波测井

If there are caves in the borehole wall or, where the tool axis is inclined to the hole axis, for some reason, the transit time is in error since the mud travel time is not the same for both receivers.

若存在井壁坍塌，或者由于某些种原因测井仪器相对于井轴倾斜，到达两个接收器的钻井液传输时间不相同，因此传输时间会存在误差。

A way to counteract this is to use a tool that has two transmitters and four receivers arranged in pairs, two to each transmitter. Fig.7.1 and Fig.7.2 show how the cave or tool inclination effect is inverted for the second transmitter-receiver pair. The average of two measurements and one for

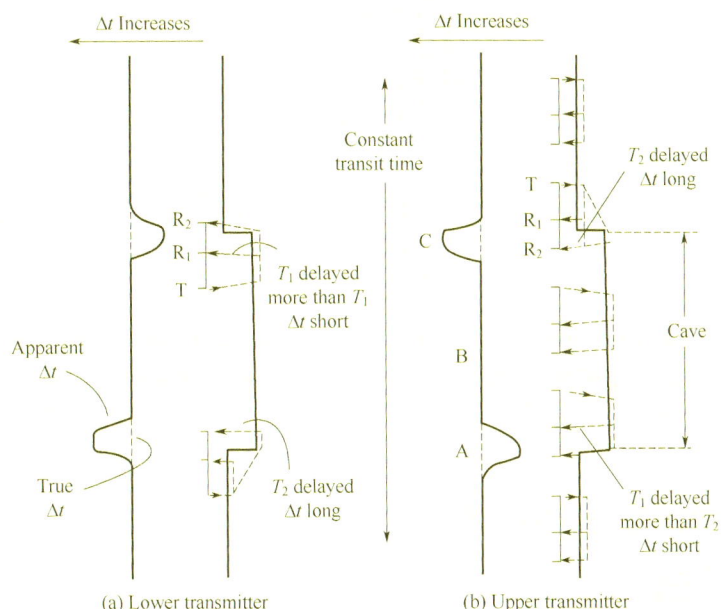

Fig.7.1　Influence of a cave on the Δt measurement (from Kokesh et al., 1969)
(a) Transmitter above receivers; (b) Transmitter below receivers

图 7.1　井壁坍塌对声波时差 Δt 测量结果的影响（据 Kokesh 等，1969）
（a）发射器位于接收器之上；（b）发射器位于接收器之下

each receiver should eliminate the effect. The tool first transmits from E_1, using receiver R_1 and R'_1, and then from E_2 using R_2 and R'_2. The average is taken of the two measurements. It is this average that is recorded.

要解决这一问题，采用了双发射双（对）接收声速测井仪。每个发射器对应两个接收器。图 7.1 和图 7.2 显示了第二对发射器—接收器如何修正井壁坍塌和轴线倾斜造成的影响。采用两次接收器测量的平均值能有效消除这种影响。该工具首先使用 E_1 发出信号，使用 R_1 和 R'_1 接收，然后使用 E_2 发出信号，R_2 和 R'_2 接收信号。记录两次测量的平均值。

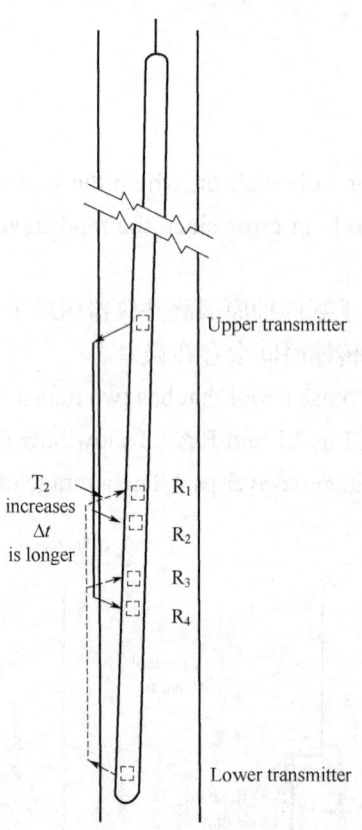

Fig.7.2 Influence of the tool inclination on the Δt measurement (from Kokesh et al., 1964)

图 7.2 仪器倾斜对声波时差 Δt 测量结果的影响（据 Kokesh 等，1964）

7.1 Measuring Point
测量点

In the BHC configuration it corresponds to the middle of the interval between the two outside receivers.

在补偿声波测井仪中，测量点位于两个外接收器中点。

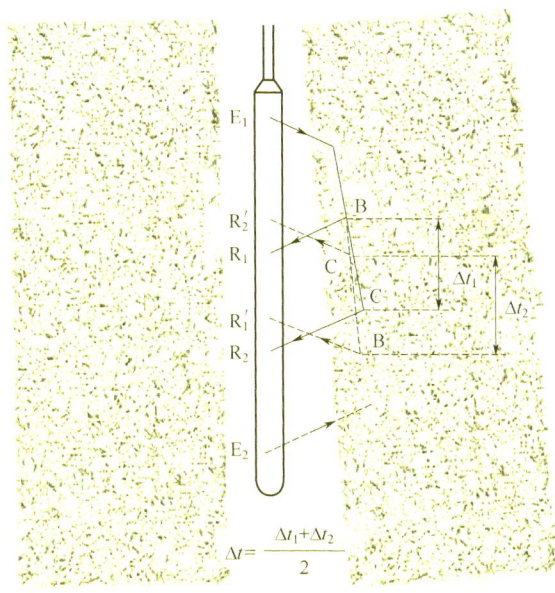

Fig.7.3 Principle of the borehole-compensated sonic logging(from Obert et al., 1984)

图 7.3 井眼补偿声波测井的原理（据 Obert 等，1984）

7.2 Depth of Investigation
探测深度

As we have just seen, in the BHC configuration, the first arrival is detected, that is the fastest and that is linked with the longitudinal waves refracted at the critical angle.

据上文，补偿声波测井仪中最先检测到的是传播速度最快，且以临界角折射的纵波。

Intuitively, in these conditions, the depth of investigation should be of the order of a few centimeters. However, we have to take into account the wave length A. Laboratory experiments show that a thickness of at least 3λ is needed to propagate a pressure wave through several feet of formation.

直观地说，在上述条件下，探测深度应为几厘米左右。然而我们必须考虑波长的影响。实验结果表明，只有层厚超过 3λ 时，纵波才能在几英尺的地层中传播。

Knowing the frequency f and that v ranges between 5000 and 25000 ft/s, λ varies between 8 and 40 cm (for f equal to 20kHz) and from 4 to 20 cm (for f equal to 40 kHz).

已知速度 v 为 5000～25000ft/s 时，若波长 λ 为 8～40cm 时，对应的频率 f 约为 20kHz，若波长 λ 为 4~20cm，对应的频率 f 约为 40kHz。

Hence, the depth of investigation varies between 12 cm and 100 cm. It should be a function of the formation velocity. In fact, when the invaded zone is deep and full of a fluid whose sonic velocity is less than the fluid in the virgin zone, a short spacing will give the speed of sound in the invaded zone and a long spacing that in the virgin formation.

因此，探测深度在 12~100cm 之间，是地层中声速的函数。事实上，当侵入带深度较深且充满其声波传播速度低于原状地层内流体中声波传播速度的流体时，短源距可获得侵入带声波速度，长源距则可获得原状地层声波速度。

This is also the case in formations micro-fractured by drilling (in some shales), hence the interest of long spacing sonic tools in massive shales.

这种情况也适用于钻井产生的（泥页岩）微裂缝地层，因此长源距声波测井在大段泥岩中有较好的应用前景。

Remark. One must take into account that an increase of the spacing implies a decrease of the signal amplitude received at the detector. If the attenuation is too strong, the amplitude of the first arrival can be too low and consequently the first arrival not detected giving a wrong interval transit time measurement. So the long spacing will improve the Δt measurement only if the attenuation of the signal is not too important.

再次强调，源距的增加意味着检测器接收信号幅度的减小。如果信号衰减强烈，则首波到达的振幅可能过低而无法检测到，从而得到错误的时差。因此，只有在信号衰减的影响可以忽略的情况下，长源距才能提高时差 Δt 的测量结果。

By contrast, if the invaded zone is of a depth of 50 cm and has a speed higher than the virgin formation (for example gas reservoirs) it seems that Δt will always be that of the invaded zone.

相比之下，当侵入带深度为 50cm，声速高于原状地层（例如气藏），Δt 反映的总是侵入带的声波时差。

7.3 Vertical Resolution
垂向分辨率

This is about equal to the distance between the receiver pairs, generally 2 feet, but sometimes 1, 3 or 6 feet.

两对接收器之间的距离近似相等，通常为 2 英尺，有时也可以是 1、3 或 6 英尺。

7.4 Units of Measurement
测量单位

The petroleum industry uses microseconds per foot as units for transit time. It is related to the velocity in ft/s. To convert μs/ft to μs/m, multiply by 3.28084; to convert ft/s to m/s, divide by 3.28084.

石油工业中使用微秒/英尺作为声波时差的单位，它与速度（英尺/秒）的关系为：将微秒/英尺乘以 3.28084 可转换为微秒/米；将英尺/秒除以 3.28084 可转换为米/秒。

7.5 Factors Influencing the Measurement
影响测量的因素

7.5.1 The Matrix
岩石骨架

The speed of sound in the formation depends on the kind of minerals making up the rock. The effect of the minerals is determined by their densities and their parameters of elasticity.

声波在地层中的传播速度取决于构成岩石的矿物类型，其由矿物的密度和弹性参数所决定。

These parameters are not always well known. However; the transit time has been measured for a few of the common minerals (Table 7.1).

这些参数并不是全部已知，表7.1介绍了几种常见矿物的声波时差。

In the case of complex lithologies the individual mineral effect is determined by their volume fraction and their individual speed of sound. The way the minerals are distributed is also important.

在复杂岩性的情况下，个别矿物效应由它们的体积分数和个别声速决定。此外，矿物的排列方式也很重要。

(1) Laminations: in this case the rock transit time is given by
（1）层状分布：在这种情况下，岩石的声波时差的计算式为

$$\Delta t_{ma} = v_1 \Delta t_{ma_1} + v_2 \Delta t_{ma_2} + \cdots + v_n \Delta t_{ma_n} \tag{7.1}$$

(2) Dispersed: in this case we need to bring in the concept of a continuous phase (cf. 7.5.4).
（2）分散分布：在这种情况下，我们需要引入连续相的概念（见7.5.4）。

Table 7.1 Interval transit time and speed of compressional wave of the most common minerals and rocks (from Obert et al., 1984)

	Δt, μs/ft		v_L, μs/ft		Bulk modulus K
	Mean value	Extreme values	Mean value	Extreme values	
Hematite		42.9		23.295	
Dolomite	44.0	(40.0~45.0)	22.797	(22.222~25.000)	82
Calcite	46.5	(45.5~47.5)	21.505	(21.053~22.000)	67
Aluminium		48.7		20.539	
Anhydrite		50.0		20.000	54
Granite	50.8	(46.8~53.5)	19.685	(18.691~21.367)	

continue

	Δt, μs/ft		v_L, μs/ft		Bulk modulus K
	Mean value	Extreme values	Mean value	Extreme values	
Steel		50.8	18.231	19.686	
Tight limestone	52.0	(47.7~53.0)		(18.750~21.000)	
Langbeinite		52.0		18.231	
Iron		51.1		18.199	
Gypsum	53.0	(52.5~53.0)	19.047	(18.868~19.047)	40
Quarzite	55.0	(52.5~57.5)	18.182	(17.390~19.030)	
Quartz	55.1	(54.7~55.0)	18.149	(18.000~18.275)	38
Sandstone	57.0	(53.8~100.0)	17.544	(10.000~18.500)	
Casing(steel)		57.1		17.500	
Basalt		57.5		17.391	
Polyhalite		57.5		17.391	
Shale		(60.0~170.0)		(5.882~16.667)	
Aluminium tubing		60.9		16.400	
Trona		65.0		15.400	
Halite		66.7		15.000	23
Sylvite		74.0		12.500	
Carnalite		83.3		12.000	
Concrete	95.0	(83.3~95.1)	9.526	(9.526~12.000)	
Anthracite	105.0	(90.0~120.0)	8.524	(8.333~10.111)	
Bituminous coal	120.0	(100.0~140.0)	8.333	(5.906~10.000)	
Sulphur		122.0		8.200	
Lignite	160.0	(140.0~180.0)	6.250	(3.281~7.143)	
Lead		141.1		7.087	
Water, 200000μg/g NaCl, 15psi		180.5		5.540	
Water, 150000μg/g NaCl, 15psi		186.0		5.375	
Water, 100000μg/g NaCl, 15psi		192.3		5.200	2.752
Water, pure(25℃)		207.0		4.830	2.239
Ice		87.1		10.480	

continue

	Δt, μs/ft		v_L, μs/ft		Bulk modulus K
	Mean value	Extreme values	Mean value	Extreme values	
Neoprene		190.5		5.248	
Kerosene, 15psi		214.5		4.659	
Oil		238.0		4.200	
Methane, 15psi		626.0		1.600	
Air, 15psi		910.00		1.100	

表 7.1 常见矿物和岩石的层内传播时间和压缩波速度（据 Obert 等，1984）

	Δt, μs/ft		v_L, μs/ft		体积模量 K
	平均值	极值	平均值	极值	
赤铁矿		42.9		23.295	
白云石	44.0	(40.0~45.0)	22.797	(22.222~25.000)	82
方解石	46.5	(45.5~47.5)	21.505	(21.053~22.000)	67
铝		48.7		20.539	
无水石膏		50.0		20.000	54
花岗石	50.8	(46.8~53.5)	19.685	(18.691~21.367)	
钢		50.8	18.231	19.686	
轻质石灰石	52.0	(47.7~53.0)		(18.750~21.000)	
无水钾镁矾		52.0		18.231	
铁		51.1		18.199	
石膏	53.0	(52.5~53.0)	19.047	(18.868~19.047)	40
石英岩	55.0	(52.5~57.5)	18.182	(17.390~19.030)	
石英	55.1	(54.7~55.0)	18.149	(18.000~18.275)	38
砂岩	57.0	(53.8~100.0)	17.544	(10.000~18.500)	
钢套管		57.1		17.500	
玄武岩		57.5		17.391	
杂卤石		57.5		17.391	
泥岩		(60.0~170.0)		(5.882~16.667)	
铝管		60.9		16.400	
天然碱		65.0		15.400	
岩盐		66.7		15.000	23

续表

	Δt, μs/ft		v_L, μs/ft		体积模量 K
	平均值	极值	平均值	极值	
钾盐		74.0		12.500	
光卤石		83.3		12.000	
混凝土	95.0	(83.3~95.1)	9.526	(9.526~12.000)	
无烟煤	105.0	(90.0~120.0)	8.524	(8.333~10.111)	
烟煤	120.0	(100.0~140.0)	8.333	(5.906~10.000)	
硫		122.0		8.200	
褐煤	160.0	(140.0~180.0)	6.250	(3.281~7.143)	
铅		141.1		7.087	
水,200.000μg/g 食盐,15psi		180.5		5.540	
水,150.000μg/g 食盐,15psi		186.0		5.375	
水,100.000μg/g 食盐,15psi		192.3		5.200	2.752
纯水 (25℃)		207.0		4.830	2.239
冰		87.1		10.480	
氯丁橡胶		190.5		5.248	
煤油,15psi		214.5		4.659	
油		238.0		4.200	
甲烷,15psi		626.0		1.600	
空气,15psi		910.00		1.100	

7.5.2 Porosity and Fluids
孔隙与流体

The speed of sound also depends on the porosity and the pore space fluids:

(1) Everything else being equal, the higher the porosity the lower the speed.

(2) Generally, if for a constant porosity and matrix we replace water by oil or oil by gas the speed goes down, at least down to a certain depth.

(3) The speed of sound in water depends on the salinity, the higher the salinity, the higher the speed.

声速也取决于孔隙度和孔隙空间中的流体类型：
(1) 其他条件相同时，孔隙度越高，速度越低。

（2）一般来说，如果孔隙度和岩石骨架不变，当孔隙中的流体由水变为油或油变为气时，速度在一定的深度范围内会降低。

（3）声速在液体中的传播速度取决于矿化度，矿化度越高，速度越快。

The chart in Fig.7.4 gives the speed of sound in water at various salinities and also as a function of pressure and temperature. The variation in velocity seems to depend above all on the variation in compressibility, as Fig.7.5 demonstrates.

图 7.4 给出了在不同矿化度流体中声速和压力、温度的函数关系。速度的变化似乎首先取决于压缩率的变化（图 7.5）。

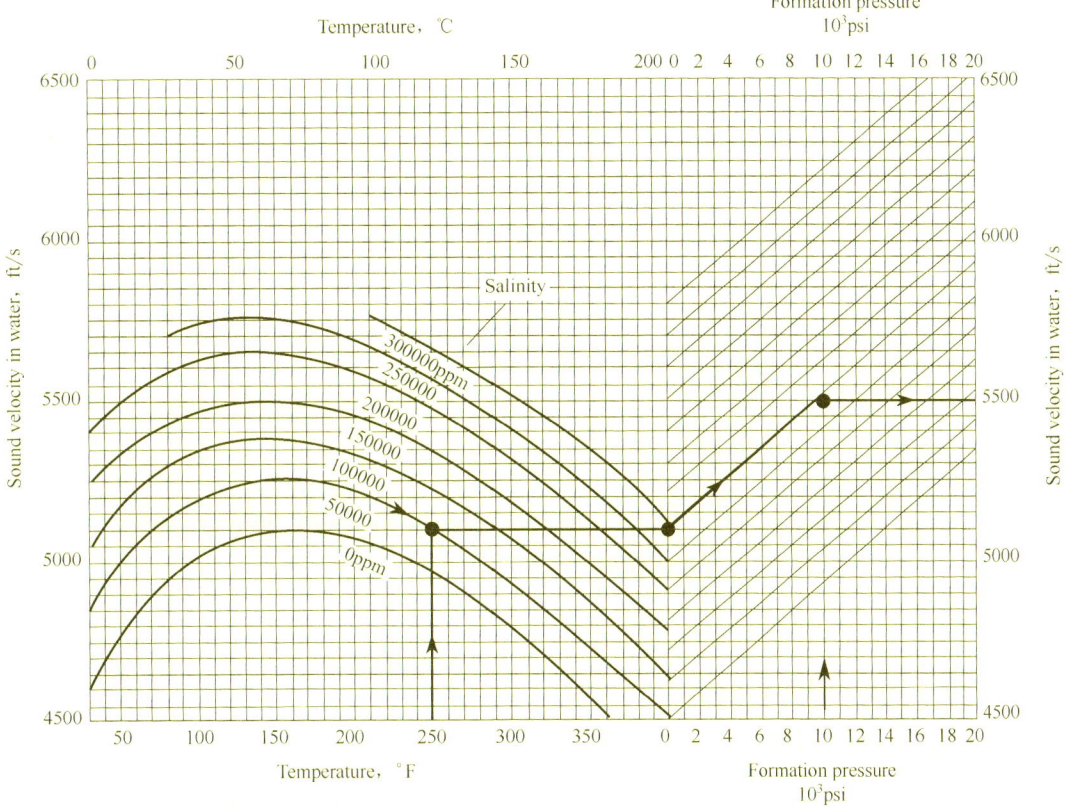

Fig.7.4　Speed of sound in water as a function of its salinity, temperature and pressure (from Obert et al., 1984)

图 7.4　水中声速与其矿化度、温度和压力的函数关系（据 Obert 等, 1984）

N.B. For a water of constant salinity above 150°F the change in velocity due to an increase in temperature is compensated by the pressure effect. The speed goes up as the salinity increases. This is really in some way the effect of density changes, as the increase in salinity implies a density increase.

注：对于温度高于 150°F 且矿化度一定的水，由温度升高引起的速度变化可以通过压力效应补偿。速度随着矿化度的增加而增加。在某种情况下，这其实是密度变化的影响，因为矿化度的增加使密度增大。

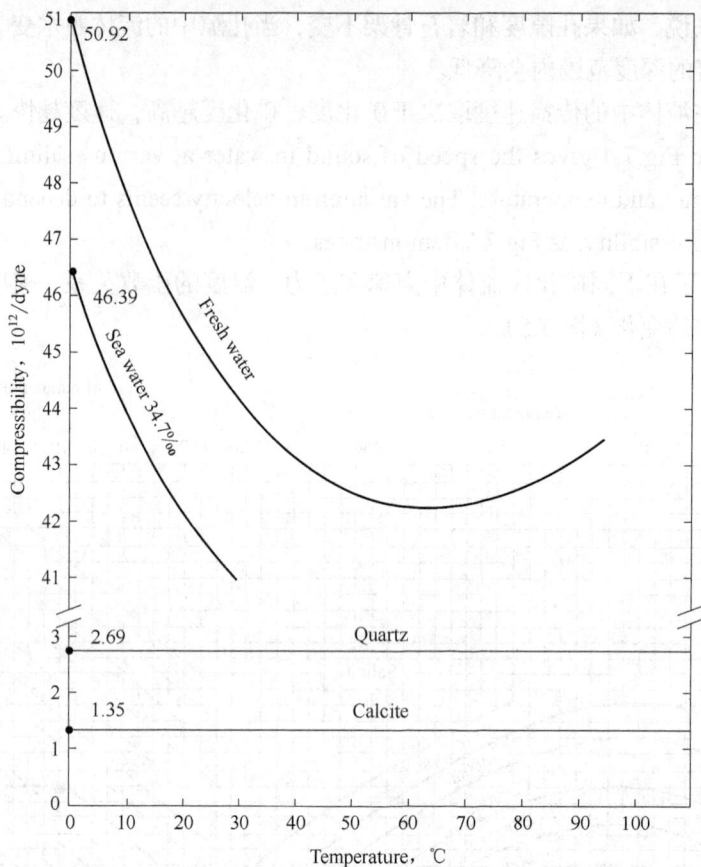

Fig.7.5 Variation of the compressibility with the temperature(from Shumway, 1958)
图 7.5 压缩性与温度的变化关系（据 Shumway，1958）

7.5.3 Temperature and Pressure
温度和压力

As we have seen these have an effect in saline water. This is equally true in gas or oil and also in the matrix itself, as experiments at the French Institute of Petroleum (I.F.P.) seem to show (see Fig.7.6 and Fig.7.7). Examination of Fig.7.7 shows that the speed tends towards a limit, known as the terminal velocity, as the pressure increases.

正如所见，在盐水中这些效应明显，这也同样适用于天然气或石油，或岩石骨架本身，法国石油学会（I.F.P.）的实验似乎证明了这一点（图 7.6，图 7.7）。如图 7.7 所示，随着压力的增加，速度趋于极限，即极限速度。

On the other hand, at constant external pressure, the speed of sound is a monotonic increasing function of the pressure difference Δp (Fig.7.8) between the internal and external pressures.

此外，外部压力恒定时，声速是内外压差 Δp 的单调递增函数（图 7.8）。

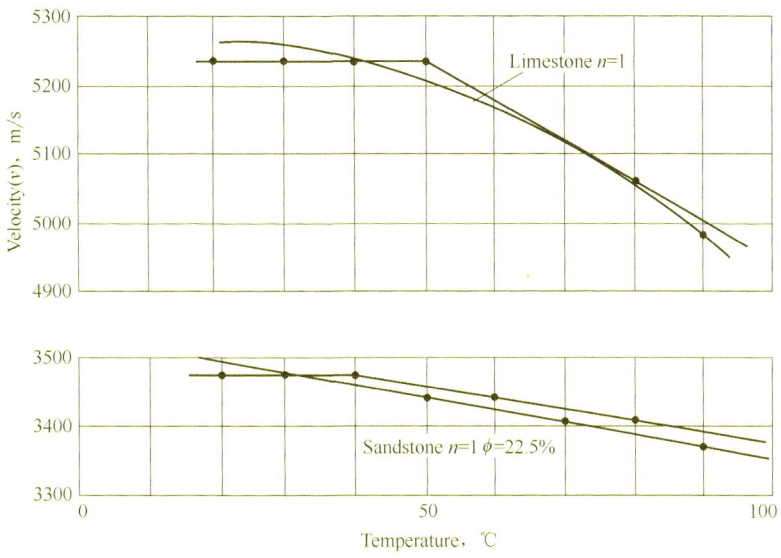

Fig.7.6 Speed of sound of rocks as a function of temperature (from Institut Franpise du Petrole, 1961)

图 7.6 岩石中声速与温度的函数关系（据 Franpise du Petrole 研究所，1961）

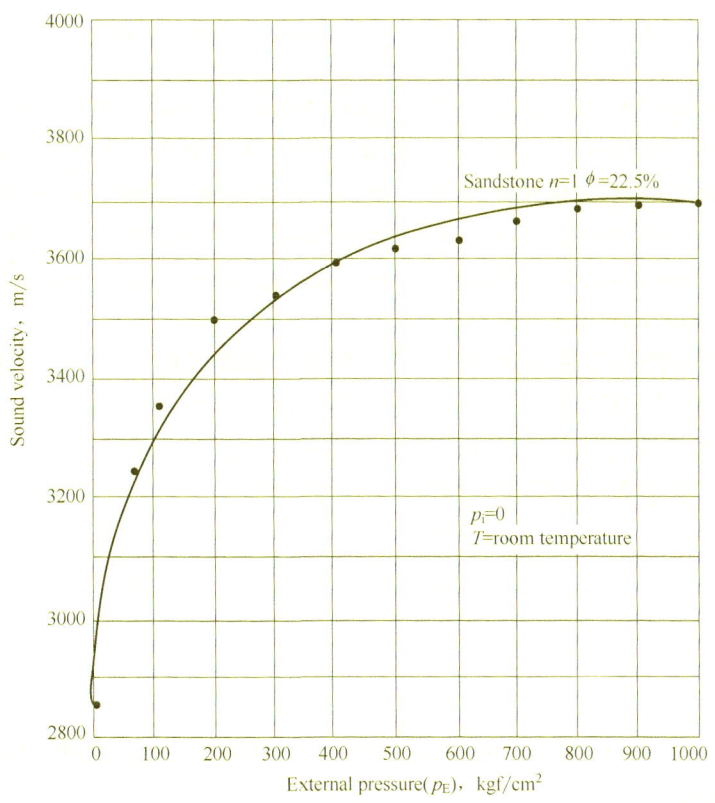

Fig.7.7 Speed of sound of a sandstone as a function of the external pressure (from Institut Franpise du Petrole, 1961)

图 7.7 砂岩中声速与岩石外部压力的函数关系（据 Franpise du Petrole 研究所，1961）

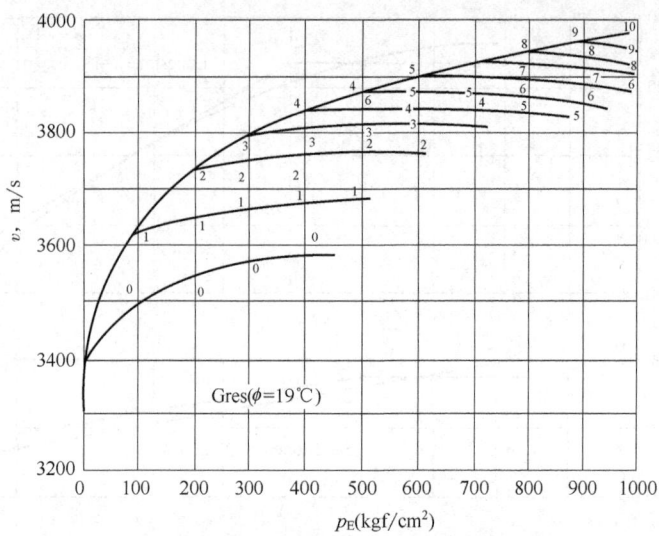

Fig.7.8 Influence of Δ*p* on the speed of sound in a sandstone (from Institute Franpise du Petrole, 1961)

0—Δp=0kg/cm²; 1—Δp=100kg/cm²; 2—Δp=200kg/cm²; 3—Δp=300kg/cm²; 4—Δp=400kg/cm²; 5—Δp=500kg/cm²;
6—Δp=600kg/cm²; 7—Δp=700kg/cm²; 8—Δp=800kg/cm²; 9—Δp=900kg/cm²; 10—Δp=1000kg/cm²;

图 7.8　Δp 对砂岩声速的影响（据 Franpise du Petrole 研究所，1961）

N.B. From the various experiments we can come to no conclusion on the influence of pressure and temperature on the speed of sound in the matrix as the variations in speed observed may be explained by the influences of these factors on the fluid alone. In any case it seems that the matrix speed is affected by pressure and temperature if we refer to the modifications necessary Δt_{ma} for a sand, limestone and dolomite to get sonic porosity values compatible with core data and minor variations in compressibility.

注意：我们无法从各种实验中得出压力和温度能够对岩石骨架的声速造成影响的结论，因为所观察到的声速变化可以用这些因素对流体的影响来解释。如果为了获得与岩心数据相匹配的声波孔隙度值以及更小的压缩率变化，从而参考 Δt_{ma} 对砂岩、石灰岩、白云岩进行必要的修正，我们可以发现，在任何情况下，岩石骨架速度似乎都受到了压力和温度的影响。

7.5.4　Texture
结构

The way in which the grains and the porosity of formation arrange both have an influence on the speed of sound.

颗粒的排列方式和地层孔隙度都对声速有影响。

Sarmiento (1961) has shown that the type, size and distribution of pores (intergranular, vugs and fractures) all have an effect on the speed: "Below a certain size the pores are probably included in the elastic character of rocks, but for large pores, or vugs, it is probable that the sound vibration follows the shortest path in the matrix, thus around the pores rather than across them. The critical size of the pores is directly related to the wave length."

1961 年，Sarmiento 研究发现，孔隙（粒间孔、孔洞和裂缝）的类型、大小和分布都对速度有影响："当孔隙小于某个临界尺寸时，声波受到岩石弹性特征影响，但是对于大孔或孔洞而言，声音通常会沿着最短的路径传播，因此围绕孔隙而不是穿过孔隙。孔隙的临界尺寸与波长直接相关。"

We can also see that for the same porosity the speed will depend on the kind of intergranular contact. These may be of a point (the case of an arrangement of spheres), line (spheroids) or surface type(polyhedra: cubes, dodecahedra, or flakes).

我们还可以了解到，当孔隙度相同时，速度取决于颗粒间的接触类型，例如点接触（球体排列）、线接触（球体）或表面接触（多面体：立方体、十二面体和薄片）。

This leads to the idea of anisotropy in the speed of sound, that is, it is not the same if it is measured parallel to or perpendicular to the grains. From this we see the influence of bed dip on measured speed and it also brings us to the concept of a continuous phase.

这就引出了声速各向异性的概念，也就是说，如果平行或垂直于颗粒测量声速时，它是不一样的。由此，我们可以看到地层倾角对测量速度的影响，也引入了连续相的概念。

(1) In formations with low porosity, which means with pores more or less isolated and randomly distributed, the matrix constitutes the continuous phase and it seems logical that the first arrival wave, and so the fastest, travels in this phase and avoids pores. Consequently, until porosity reaches a certain value(5%~10%) the transit time does not vary significantly from the Δt_{ma}. This is why the sonic log is considered as not "seeing" secondary porosity of a vug type.

（1）孔隙度较低的地层中，孔隙多呈分散的无规律分布，声波在岩石骨架中的传播是连续的。传播速度最快的首波，在传播过程中避开孔隙。因此，在孔隙度达到 5% ~ 10% 前，传输时间与岩石骨架的声波时差 Δt_{ma} 不会发生显著变化。这就是声波测井无法测量溶孔等次生孔隙的原因。

(2) Conversely, if a grain is in suspension in the fluid, as in the case of low compaction shale series and surface sands with high porosity (higher than 48% ~ 50%), the continuous phase is the fluid, and what is measured is the interval transit time of the sound in the fluid. This was confirmed by measurements made on shallow shales subjected to the permafrost.

（2）反之，如果颗粒悬浮在流体中，例如压实作用不强烈的泥岩和高孔隙（48%~50%以上）的砂岩表层，声波在流体中的传播是连续的，测量到的是声波在流体中的时差。在受永久冻土影响的浅层泥岩上所做的实验证实了这一点。

In this case it is the transit time of sound in ice that is measured. This means that transit time in fluid is reached as soon as the porosity is higher than 50%. Consequently in this case it is impossible to measure the interval transit time in the formation, the first arrival being this traveling in the mud. This analysis seems confirmed by investigations made by Raymer et al., 1980.

在这种情况下，测量的是声速在冰中的传播时间。这说明当孔隙率高于 50% 时，流体中的传播时间就会达到此值。因此在这种情况下，无法测出地层中的声波时差，首先到达的是在钻井液中传播的波。这一分析被 Raymer 等人于 1980 年的调查所证实。

Besides, the existence of microfissures, either natural or caused by drilling, will equally reduce the speed of sound by the production of microporosity in the form of planes which the waves have to cross. This is why in some kinds of formation, usually shales and carbonates but rarely sands, there is a discrepancy between seismic and sonic log velocities. It is recommended to measure interval transit times by using long-spacing sonic tools that avoid the area of cracked, altered formation (Fig.7.9).

此外，天然裂缝和人工裂缝（钻井）等微裂缝的存在，都会在裂缝壁上产生微孔，从而使声波必须穿过微孔，导致声速降低。因此在泥岩或碳酸盐岩地层中，地震波和声波的传播速度存在差异。通过使用长源距声波测井仪测量声波时差，能够避免裂缝和地层溶蚀作用造成的影响（图7.9）。

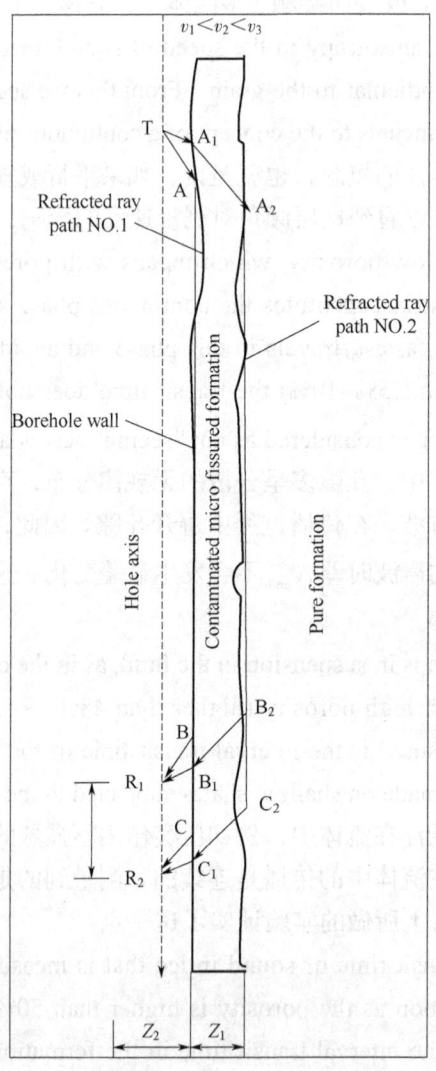

Fig.7.9 Two refracted paths for a step profile of alteration (The use of a long-spacing sonic allows us to measure the interval transit time of the undisturbed formation) (from Obert et al., 1984)

图7.9 两条折射路径（长间距声波测量仪的应用使我们能够测量原状地层的层间传播时间）

（据 Obert 等，1984）

7.6　Interpretation
测井解释

From the factors influencing the measurement, as in the previous sections, we can see that the sonic log can be used as an indicator of lithology and of porosity, both intergranular and intercrystalline.

如前文所述，从影响声波测量的因素中，我们可以发现声波测井可以作为岩石和孔隙度（粒间孔、晶间孔）的指标。

For any given lithology, with the zone of investigation of the tool mainly in the invaded zone containing mud filtrate, the speed of sound (or the interval transit time Δt) is a function of porosity.

对于任一岩性，当声波测井的测量范围主要集中在含钻井液滤液的侵入带时，声速（或声波时差）是孔隙度的函数。

In fact, for rocks that are sufficiently compacted, we can, to a first approximation, accept that the variation of the speed of sound with the depth (temperature and pressure) of the fluid and matrix are negligeable and that a terminal velocity is reached.

实际上，对于压实作用强烈的岩石，我们可以粗略地认为，声速随流体和岩石骨架的深度（温度和压力）的变化是可以忽略不计的，且声速最终可达（岩石中的）极限速度。

Wyllie et al. have proposed an empirical equation based on numerous laboratory experiments on clean formations. This links interval transit time directly with porosity by taking the total interval transit time as equal to the sum of the interval transit times in the grains of the matrix and in the pores (Fig.7.10):

威利等人以纯地层为实验对象，进行大量实验后得到一个经验方程。方程建立了声波时差与孔隙度的相关关系，将总的声波时差等同于孔隙流体中的声波时差与骨架颗粒中的声波时差之和（图7.10）：

$$\Delta t = \frac{t}{L} = \frac{\Sigma(L_\mathrm{f}/L)}{v_\mathrm{f}} + \frac{\Sigma(L_\mathrm{ma}/L)}{v_\mathrm{ma}} \tag{7.2}$$

Which can be written as:
方程可以被改写为：

$$\Delta t = \phi \Delta t_\mathrm{f} + (1-\phi)\Delta t_\mathrm{ma} \tag{7.3}$$

Where we assume a relationship between L_f and ϕ from Eq.7.3 it follows that:
由式（7.3）可知 L_f 和 ϕ 的关系如下式：

$$\phi_\mathrm{s} = \frac{\Delta t - \Delta t_\mathrm{ma}}{\Delta t_\mathrm{f} - \Delta t_\mathrm{ma}} \tag{7.4}$$

N.B. The Wyllie equation establishes a linear relationship between Δt and ϕ which is not really in agreement with previous remarks on rock texture. In any case it is approximately correct in the range of usual porosities encountered, that is from 5% to 25%, and in the case of an arrangement of almost spherical grains. There remains the difficulty of choosing Δt_{ma} and Δt_f for the matrix and the fluid.

注意：威利方程建立 Δt 和 ϕ 之间的线性关系，这与前文分析岩石结构得到的结论并不完全一致。威利方程基本适用于孔隙度在 5%~25% 的范围内，且颗粒为近球形排列的岩石。然而，为岩石骨架的和流体选择合理的声波时差（Δt_{ma} 和 Δt_f）仍存在困难。

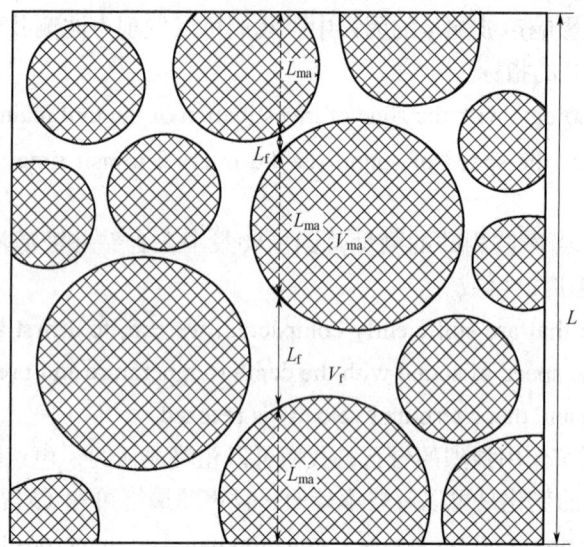

Fig.7.10 Trajectory of the compressional wave in a water saturated sand (from Wyllie et al., 1956)
图 7.10 饱和水砂岩中纵波的运动轨迹（据 Wyllie 等，1956）

Eq.7.4 is represented by the chart in Fig.7.11.
式（7.4）由图 7.11 中的图表示。

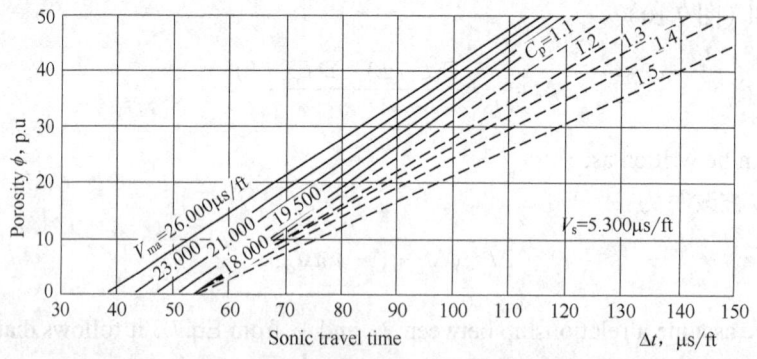

Fig.7.11 Relationship between interval transit time Δt, and porosity ϕ from the Wyllie's EQ
图 7.11 Wyllie 方程中声波时差 Δt 与孔隙度 ϕ 之间的关系

In uncompacted formations, the Wyllie equation gives porosities that are too high. It is therefore not directly applicable. A correction factor is needed, to take into account the effects of temperature and pressure, or in other words that the terminal speed of sound is not reached.

Eq.7.5 is then written:

对于未压实的地层，威利方程计算的孔隙度过高，因此不能直接适用，需要一个校正系数来考虑温度和压力的影响。换句话说，声波不能达到地层中的极限速度，有

$$(\phi_s)_c = \frac{\Delta t - \Delta t_{ma}}{\Delta t_f - \Delta t_{ma}} \cdot \frac{100}{c\Delta t_{sh}} \tag{7.5}$$

And it is given by the chart in Fig.7.11. The best way to compute $c\Delta t_{sh}$ is to compare computed sonic porosities with the true porosity from another source. Where this is possible several approaches can be tried:

如图 7.11 所示，计算 $c\Delta t_{sh}$ 的最佳方法是将计算出的声波孔隙度与其他方法测得的真实孔隙度进行比较。在可能的情况下，可以尝试以下几种方法：

(1) $\rho_b - \Delta t$ cross-plot method (Fig.7.12). ρ_b and Δt are plotted on linear grids for water-bearing clean formations close to the zone of interest. From this a clean formation line is established that can be scaled in porosity units using the density log. Similarly, atheoretical porosity line using Eq.7.5 can be drawn. For any value of porosity a corresponding value of Δt can be found. Using the actual value of Δt and this new value in the chart of Fig.7.12 $c\Delta t_{sh}$ can be determined.

（1）$\rho_b - \Delta t$ 交会图法（图 7.12）。将 ρ_b 和 Δt 绘制在靠近有利区的含水地层的线性网格上，由此得到一条地层线，可以用密度测井进行孔隙度单位的缩放。类似地，利用式（7.5）可以绘制理论孔隙度线。对于任意孔隙度值，都可以找到相对应的 Δt 值。利用 Δt 的真实值和通过该方法取得的值就可以确定 $c\Delta t_{sh}$（图 7.12）。

(2) The neutron method (SNP or CNL). The porosity is obtained from the neutron for water-bearing sands. This value should be about equal to the actual porosity. Hence we have:

（2）中子法（SNP 或 CNL）。含水砂岩的孔隙度由中子数确定，计算得到的值应等于实际的孔隙度。因此：

$$c\Delta t_{sh} = 100\phi_s / \phi_N \tag{7.6}$$

N.B. We can also plot the values of ϕ and Δt (Fig.7.13) to make a statistical evaluation of $c\Delta t_{sh}$. This can also give the value of Δt_{ma}.

注意：将 ϕ 和 Δt 的值绘制在图上，既可以对 $c\Delta t_{sh}$ 进行统计学评估，也可得到 Δt_{ma}（图 7.13）。

(3) The R_0 method. In clean-water-bearing sands we can estimate ϕ from R_{IL}, knowing R_w:

（3）R_0 法。已知 R_w，含水砂岩的孔隙度 ϕ 可通过 R_{IL} 估算得出：

$$F_R = \frac{R_{IL}}{R_w} = \frac{a}{\phi_R^m} \tag{7.7}$$

Then giving $c\Delta t_{sh}$, using ϕ_R:

给出 Δt_{sh} 的值，结合上式 ϕ_R 的计算结果，得到：

$$c\Delta t_{sh} = \frac{100\phi_s}{\phi_R} \tag{7.8}$$

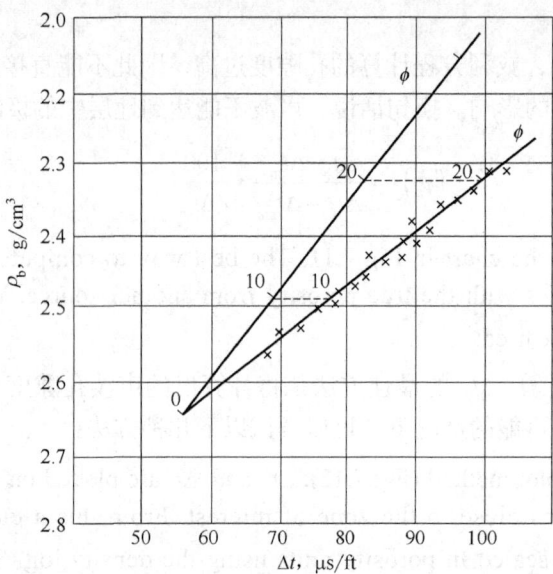

Fig.7.12. ρ_b vs Δt cross-plot to determine $c\Delta t_{ma}$ (from Obert et al., 1984)

图 7.12 ρ_b 和 Δt 交会图确定 $c\Delta t_{ma}$ （据 Obert 等, 1984）

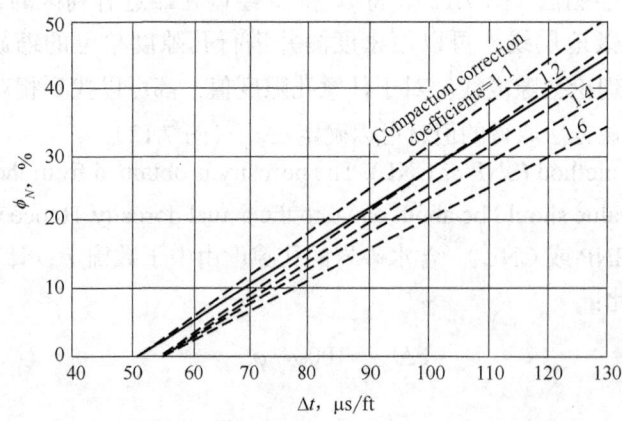

Fig.7.13. ϕ_N vs Δt cross-plot to determine $c\Delta t_{sh}$ (from Obert et al., 1984)

图 7.13 ϕ_N 和 Δt 交会图确定 $c\Delta t_{ma}$ （据 Obert 等, 1984）

From studies, Geerstma (1961) proposed the following equation:

据研究，Geerstma（1961）提出了以下等式：

$$v_L = \left[\left(M + \frac{(1-\beta)^2}{(1-\phi-\beta)c_{ma} + \phi c_f} \right) \frac{1}{\rho_b} \right]^2 \tag{7.9}$$

where: M——elastic modulus (or space modulus);

ρ_b——bulk density.

式中 M——弹性模量（或空间模量）；

ρ_b——体积密度。

$$M = k + \frac{4}{3}\mu = \frac{3}{c_b}\frac{1-\sigma}{1+\sigma} \qquad (7.10)$$

$$M = \frac{\beta}{c_{ma}} + \frac{4}{3}\mu \qquad (7.11)$$

where: σ ——Poisson's coefficient (ratio);

β ——c_{ma}/c_b;

ϕ ——porosity;

c_{ma} ——the compressibility of the matrix;

c_b ——compressibility of the empty matrix;

c_f ——compressibility of the fluids.

式中 σ ——泊松比;

β ——c_{ma}/c_b;

ϕ ——孔隙度;

c_{ma} ——岩石骨架的压缩系数;

c_b ——空岩石骨架的压缩系数;

c_f ——流体的压缩系数。

$$c_f = c_w S_w + (1-S_w)c_h \qquad (7.12)$$

where: c_h ——compressibility of hydrocarbons;

c_w ——compressibility of water.

式中 c_h ——油气压缩系数;

c_w ——水的压缩系数。

$$\rho_b = \phi \rho_w S_w + \phi \rho_h (1-S_w) + (1-\phi)\rho_{ma} \qquad (7.13)$$

where: S_w ——water saturation;

ρ_w ——water density;

ρ_h ——hydrocarbon density;

ρ_{ma} ——matrix density.

式中 S_w ——含水饱和度;

ρ_w ——水的密度;

ρ_h ——油气密度;

ρ_{ma} ——岩石骨架密度。

Eq.7.13 which corresponds to an infinite medium of fluid and matrix may seem complicated. It has the advantage of including all the different factors influencing the speed of sound according to classical theories. Besides, when most of the parameters are known it should be possible to get porosity knowing the saturation, or vice versa. Raymer et al., proposed another transit time-to-porosity transform. This seems more in agreement with observations made. It is illustrated by Fig.7.15 provides superior transit-time-porosity correlation over the entire porosity range. It suggests more consistent matrix velocities for given rock lithology and permits the determination of porosity in unconsolidated low velocity sands without the need to determine a "lack of composition", or similar correction factor.

式（7.13）对应流体和岩石骨架的无限介质，看起来很复杂。根据经典理论，该式的优点是包括了所有影响声速的不同因素，且在多数参数已知时，可通过饱和度求取孔隙度，反之亦然。Raymer 等人提出了一种时差—孔隙度的转化方法，这种方法似乎更符合观测规律。图 7.15 提供了整个孔隙度范围内声波时差与孔隙度的相关关系。该方法表明，对于给定的岩性，声波在岩石骨架中的传播速度是一定的，且可以在不需要确定"缺乏成分"或者相似的修正因子的情况下就可以确定松散低速砂岩的孔隙度。

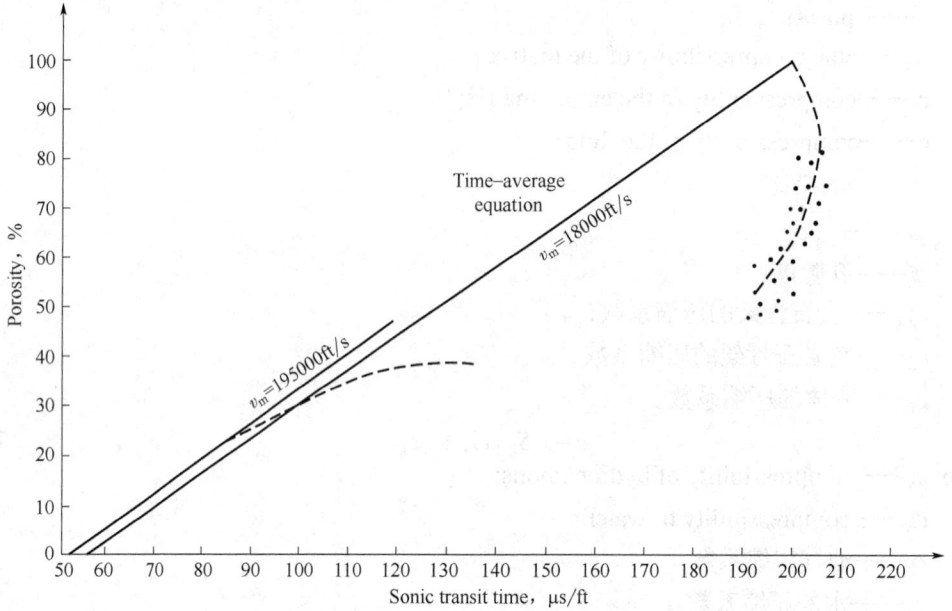

Fig.7.14　Comparison of sonic transit time to core porosity from published data (from Raymer et al., 1980)

图 7.14　声波传播时间与岩心孔隙度的对比公开数据（据 Raymer 等，1980）

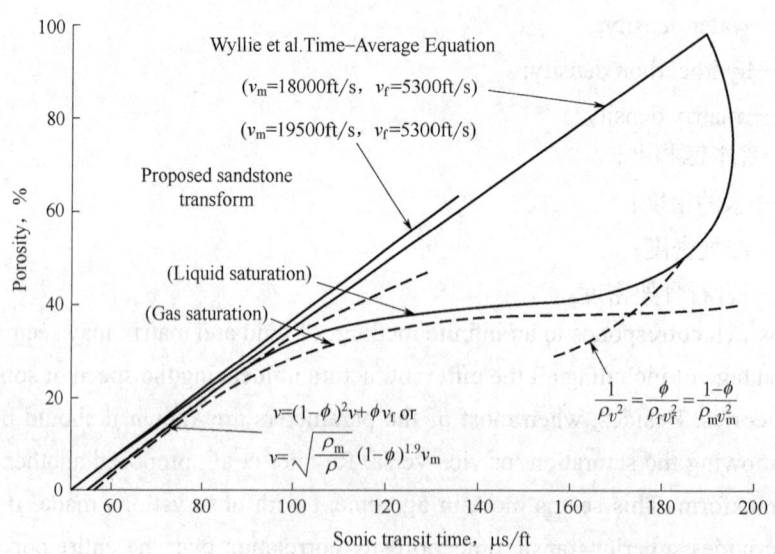

Fig.7.15　The proposed sonic transit time to porosity transform. showing comparison to Wyllie time average equation and to suggested algorithms (from Raymer et al., 1980)

图 7.15　与 Wyllie 时间平均方程对比后提出的声波时差与孔隙度转换的算法（据 Raymer 等，1980）

7.7 Environmental and Other Effects
环境及其他

7.7.1 Transit Time Stretching
声波时差增大

As the sound arriving at the second receiver has a longer path, the signal is generally weaker. As the detector threshold is the same for both receivers, the detection may occur later on the further receiver. This gives a Δt that is too large (Fig.7.16).

由于声音到达第二个接收器的路径较长，信号通常较弱。由于两个接收器的检测器阈值相同，声波应该被较远的接收器接收，因此导致 Δt 增大（图 7.16）。

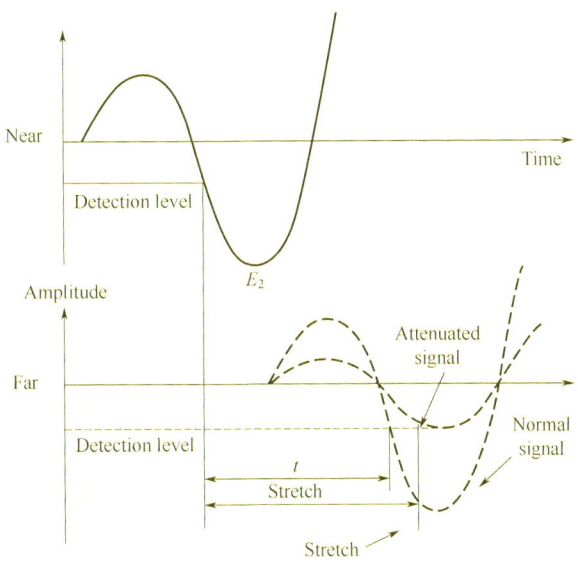

Fig.7.16 Schematic explaining transit time stretching (from Obert et al., 1984)
图 7.16 传播时间延后（据 Obert 等，1984）

7.7.2 Cycle Skipping
周波跳跃

In some cases the signal arriving at the second receiver is too low to trigger the detection on the first arrival. The detection then occurs at the second or third arriving cycle (Fig.7.17). We therefore have missed or skipped cycles. This shows up as sudden and abrupt increases in the interval transit time (Fig.7.18).

在某些情况下，到达第二个接收器的信号幅度太低，无法在首次到达时被检测到，之后信号会在第二个或第三个周期中被检测到（图 7.17）。因此产生了周波跳跃现象，表现为某区间内的传播时间突然增大（图 7.18）。

If cycle skipping appears on only one of the far detectors, the increases in Δt is between 10 and 11.5μs/ft for the second cycle and 20 to 25μs/ft for the third. If cycle skipping occurs on both far receivers the error on Δt is between 20 and 25μs/ft for one cycle missed and 30 to 37.5μs/ft for two.

如果仅在其中一个远端探测器上出现周期跳跃，则第二个周期 Δt 的增加量在 10~11.5μs/ft 之间，第三个周期 Δt 的增加量在 20 ~ 25μs/ft 之间。如果在两个远端接收器上都发生周波跳跃，则一个周期内 Δt 的误差在 20 ~ 25μs/ft 之间，两个周期内 Δt 的误差在 30~37.5μs/ft 之间。

This sudden jump in Δt is often linked to the presence of gas and sometimes oil. It can also happen in fractured zones. This is due to a strong attenuation of the signal.

鉴于探测信号的强烈衰减，Δt 的突然增加通常与油气的出现和裂缝的产生有关。

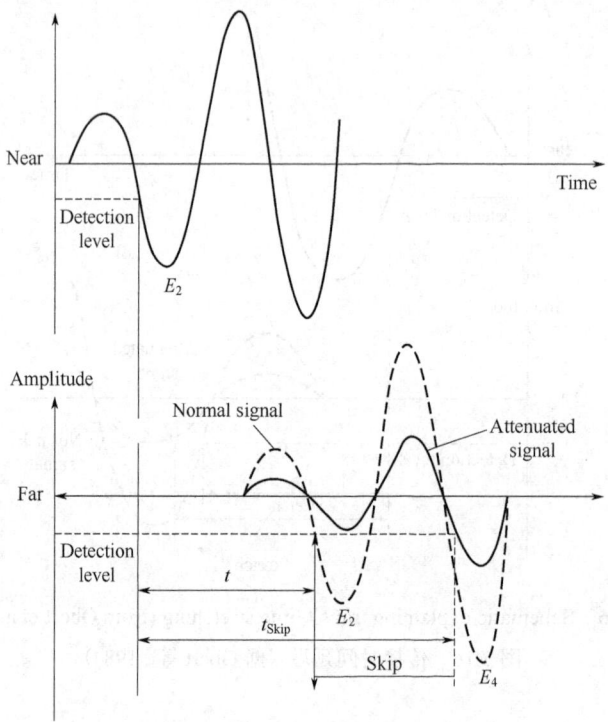

Fig.7.17　Schematic explaining cycle skipping (from Obert et al., 1984)

图 7.17　周波跳跃示意图（据 Obert 等，1984）

7.7.3　Kicks to Smaller Δt
　　　　Δt 减小

This happens when the signal to the first receiver is weaker than that arriving at the second or, where Δt is suddenly diminished by the detection jumping forward from the usual sound arrival to detect on noise appearing before the actual sonic signal.

这种现象通常发生在到达第一个接收器的信号比到达第二个接收器的信号弱的情况下，或由于声信号检测到实际声信号之前的噪声而出现的周波跳跃，导致 Δt 突然减小。

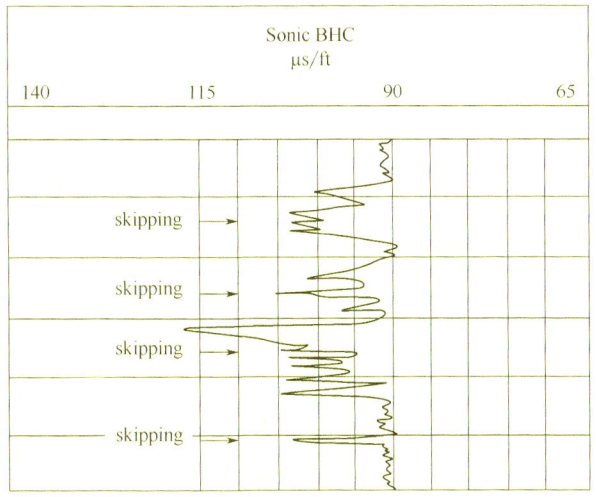

Fig.7.18 Example of cycle skipping (from Obert et al., 1984)
图 7.18 周波跳跃示例（据 Obert 等，1984）

7.7.4 The Borehole
井眼

Holesize, which comes into effect only when the sum of the transit times from emitter to borehole wall, and the wall to the receiver is greater than the distance from the transmitter to the receiver directly. In this case the first arrival is straight through the mud. This only happens in holes larger than about 24 inches for common rocks (Fig.7.19). To eliminate this effect, the sonic tool is run excentralized.

井眼尺寸在声波由发射器到井壁与井壁返回发射器的传输时间值之和大于声波由发射器到接收器的传输时间时，才会对声波传播产生影响。在常规岩层大于 24 英寸的井眼中，声波首先到达钻井液处（图 7.19）。为了消除这种影响，声波工具分开运行。

For the borehole, compensated sonic (BHC) caving has little effect except where the caving is very large.

对于井眼来说，井壁坍塌对补偿性声波测井仪（BHC）几乎没有影响，除非井壁坍塌的程度非常严重。

The drilling mud. If the borehole is air-filled or if the mud is gas-cut, the attenuation of the sonic signal is too high to allow detection on the first arrival. This problem may arise in front of zones that are producing gas into the mud (Fig.7.20).

井筒内钻井液气侵会使声波信号发生较大的衰减，从而不能在首波到达时被检测到（图 7.20）。此类问题在产气侵入钻井液的区域将尤为突出。

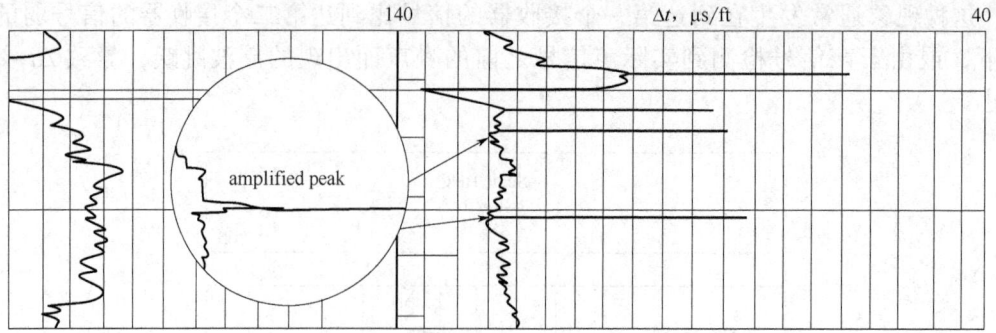

Fig.7.19　Example of kicks of smaller Δt

图 7.19　Δt 减小的例子

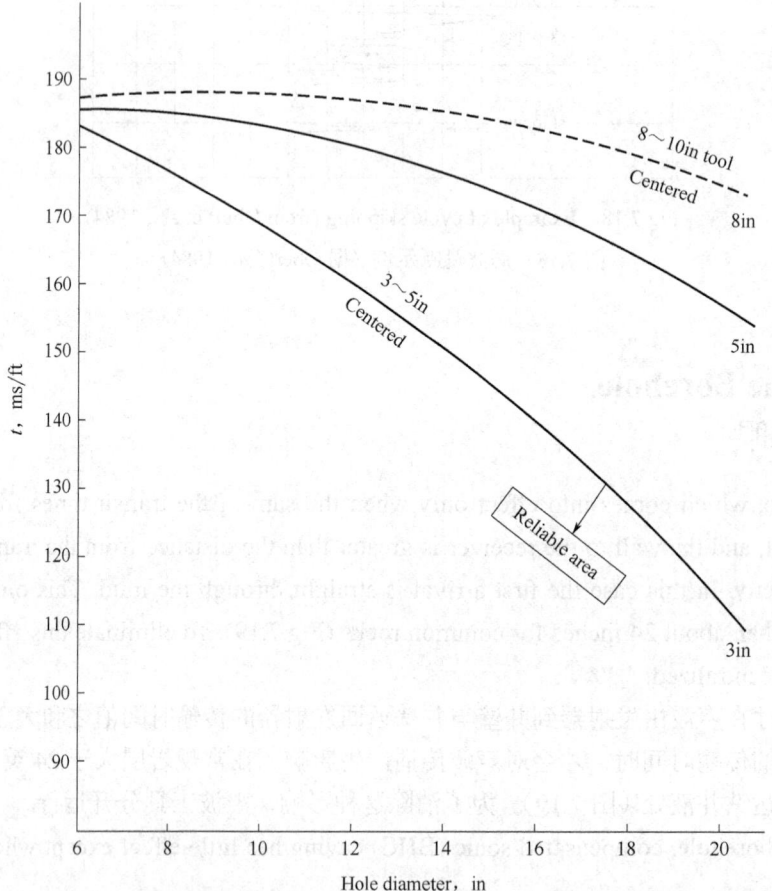

Fig.7.20　Effect of large hole size (from Goetz et al., 1979)

For a given centered sonic tool, the maximum Δt detectable is read at a given hole diameter from the

curve identifying the transmitter–near receiver spacing

图 7.20　大井眼造成的影响（据 Goetz 等，1979）

对于给定的中心声波工具，在表示发射器—最近接收器的曲线上

读取直径一定的井眼的最大可检测值

7.7.5 Invasion
侵入作用

There is little invasion effect in water-bearing zones. However, in gas or oil zones, even with highwater saturations, the interval transit time in the invaded zone may be very different to that in the virgin zone. We can look at several cases.

侵入作用对含水层几乎不造成影响。然而，在含油气层，即使含水饱和度很高，侵入带的声波时差也可能与原状地层的声波时差大不相同。例如：

(1) Deep invasion: the sonic reads only the flushed zone and does not see the gas or oil at all. There is no problem in calculating porosity in this case. The reading may need correction using the Geerstma equation before comparison or use in seismic work.

（1）深度侵入：只能在冲洗带读取到声波，含油气层无法读取声波。在这种情况下，能够计算孔隙度，但在进行对比或用于地震工作之前，需要使用 Geerstma 方程进行修正。

(2) Little or no invasion: the gas or light oil affects the measurement. If the interval transit time is less in the hydrocarbon formation than through the mud, the reading is representative of the virgin formation.

（2）浅度侵入或无侵入：气体或轻质油会影响测量结果，如果含油气地层的声波时差小于钻井液的声波时差，则读数代表着原状地层的声波时差。

However this transit time needs careful interpretation in terms of porosity. If the formation transit time is longer than that in the mud (for example very porous, shallow depths) then of course the sonic just gives the mud transit time. The virgin formation transit time cannot be less. To determine it, we have to use the Geerstma equation but no porosity determination is possible.

然而，这种传播时间需要从孔隙度的角度来仔细解释。如果在地层中的传播时间比在钻井液中的时间更长（例如地层孔隙含量高，深度较浅），那么声波只给出了一个在钻井液中传播的时间。在原状地层的传播时间不会减少。为了确定这一点，我们必须使用 Geerstma 方程，但是孔隙度则无法确定。

(3) No invasion and slight production: in this case bubbling occurs in the mud and cycle skipping occurs due to the strong attenuation.

（3）无侵入或轻微侵入：在这种情况下，钻井液会发生起泡现象，并且声波由于强烈衰减而发生周波跳跃。

It is possible sometimes to see very low sonic velocities or high transit times in formations that are apparently water bearing from other logs. This is generally due to a very small percentage of gas in the form of micro-bubbles in the water, leading to a strong attenuation of the sonic wave. As shown by Domenico, a gas saturation of 15% reduces drastically the velocity with respect to a water saturated formation.

有时可能会发现声波速度非常低或者声波在由其他测井资料确定的含水层中的传播时间很长。这通常是由于水中含有一小部分以微气泡形式存在的气体，从而导致声波的强烈衰减。Domenico 研究表明，相对于水饱和地层，15％的含气饱和度会大大降低声波在饱和水地层中传播的速度。

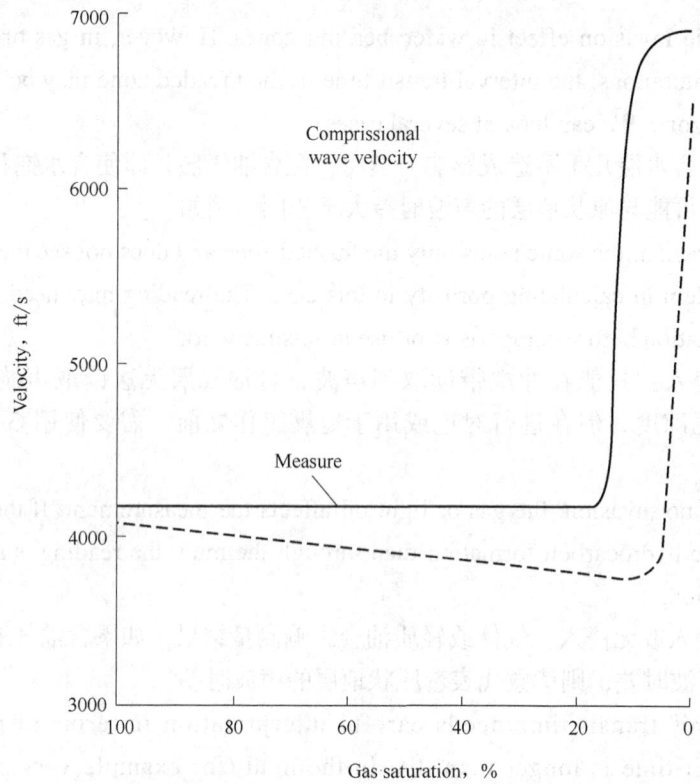

Fig.7.21　Effect of gas saturation on velocity in a shallow Sandstone
(from Domenico, 1976)

图 7.21　含气饱和度对声波在浅层砂岩中传播的影响
（据 Domenico，1976）

7.7.6　Radial Cracking Effects
径向开裂效应

Microfractures in the rock linked with radial cracking caused by drilling leads to an increase in the interval transit time. Rocks liable to this phenomenon (shales, shaly limestone, etc.) — which are also liable to caving caused by particles dropping down from the fracturing or breaking—will show a sonic Δt too large, or a velocity that is too low. To obtain a measurement in the non-fractured formation a long spacing sonic is needed that reads beyond the damaged zone.

岩石中的微裂缝与钻井时引起的径向开裂有关，微裂缝导致声波时差增加。易受这种现象影响的岩石（泥岩、泥质灰岩等），也容易由于颗粒在压裂或破裂过程中掉落而引起崩裂，从而出现 Δt 过大或速度过低的现象。为了获取非裂缝地层的测量数据，需要读取已受损区域外的长源声波读数。

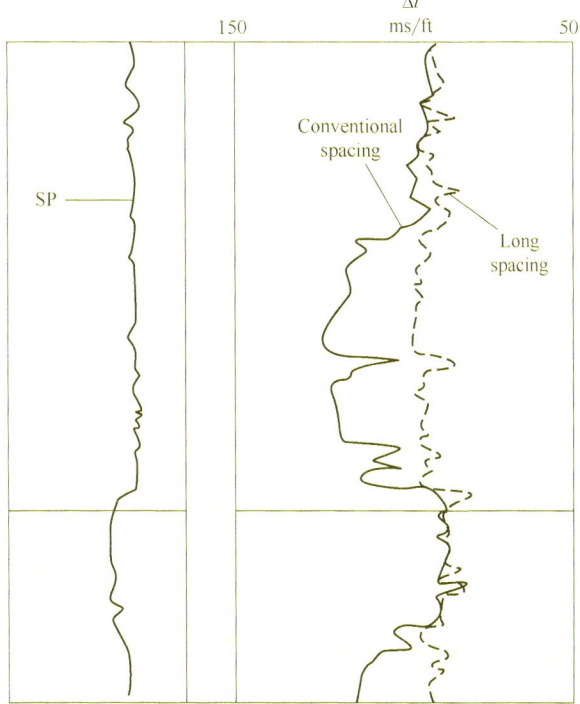

Fig.7.22 Example showing the effect of radial cracking (alteration) on the short-spacing sonic measurement of the interval transit time in the non-altered formation (from Obert et al., 1984)

图 7.22 径向开裂对于未改造地层中短距离声波传播时间的影响（据 Obert 等，1984）

Exercises
课后练习

7.1 State the applications of Sonic Log.

7.2 What is the Cycle Skips?

7.3 Will the presence of gas in an otherwise water saturated formation cause an increase of decrease of the interval transit time in the sonic log?

(A) Increase　　　　(B) Decreases　　　　(C) Remains the same

7.4 The interval transit times (Δt) listed below were measured over various depth intervals in a sandstone reservoir. Calculate the porosity using Wyllie's average equation. The acoustic velocity of the matrix is 18000ft/s. Assume a fluid transit time of 18 μs/ft.

Δt, μs/ft	Porosity
100	
94	

7.5 Choose Δt value at different depths(125,156,204ft) for Δt and then compute prosity using Wyllie time average model ($\Delta t_{ma}=55\mu s/ft$, $\Delta t_{fl}=189\mu s/ft$).

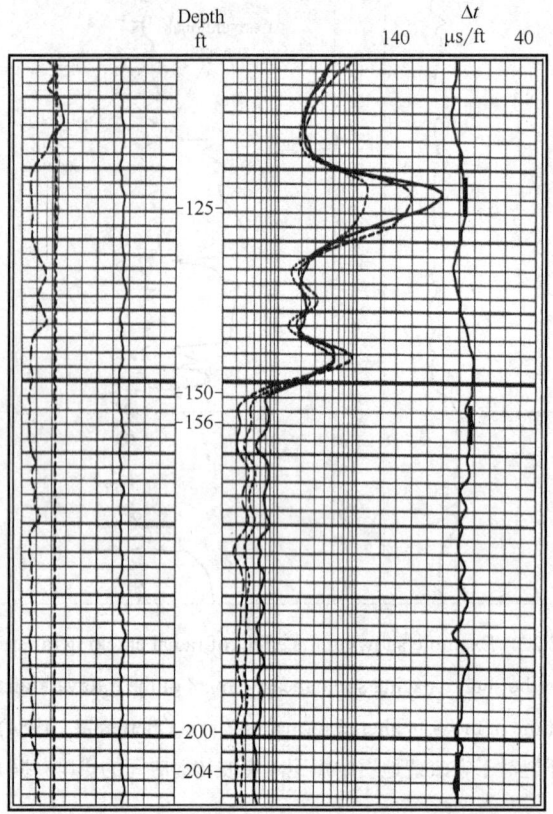

Fig.7.23 Logging curve

8 The Gamma Ray Log
自然伽马测井

8.1 Generalities
概述

The GR log is a measurement of the natural radioactivity of the formation. In sedimentary formations the log normally reflects the shale contents of the formations. This is because the radioactive elements tend to concentrate in clays and shales. Clean formations usually have a very low level of radioactivity, unless radioactive contaminant such as volcanic ash or granite wash is present or the formation waters contain dissolved radioactive salts. The radiation emanates from naturally-occurring uranium, thorium and potassium (see below). The simple gamma ray log gives the radioactivity of the three elements combined, while the spectral gamma ray log shows the amount of each individual element contributing to this radioactivity.

自然伽马测井是一种测量地层自然放射性的测井方法。在沉积地层中，测井通常反映地层的泥质含量，这是因为放射性元素主要在黏土或泥页岩中富集。纯砂岩放射性元素含量很低，除非存在一些放射性杂质，如火山灰、花岗岩冲积物，或地层水中含有溶解的放射性盐类。放射物来自天然产生的铀、钍和钾（见下文）。自然伽马测井只能反映地层中三种放射性核素的总效应，而自然伽马能谱测井则显示了每种放射性核素导致这种放射性的含量。

The geological significance of radioactivity lies in the distribution of these three elements. Most rocks are radioactive to some degree, igneous and metamorphic rocks more so than sediments. However, amongst the sediments, shales have by far the strongest radiation. It is for this reason that the simple gamma ray log has been called the 'shale log', although modern research shows that it is quite insufficient to equate gamma ray emission with shale occurrence. Not all shales are radioactive, and all the radioactive rocks are not necessarily shale (Fig.8.1).

放射性核素的地质意义在于上述三种元素的分布。大多数岩石在某种程度上都具有放射性，火成岩和变质岩比沉积岩的更具放射性。然而，在沉积岩中，泥岩的放射性最为强烈。正是由于这个原因，简单的伽马射线测井被称为"泥岩测井"，但是现代研究表明，将自然伽马放射性与泥岩发育等同起来是远远不够的，并非所有泥岩都具有放射性，而且放射性岩石也不一定都是泥岩，如图 8.1 所示。

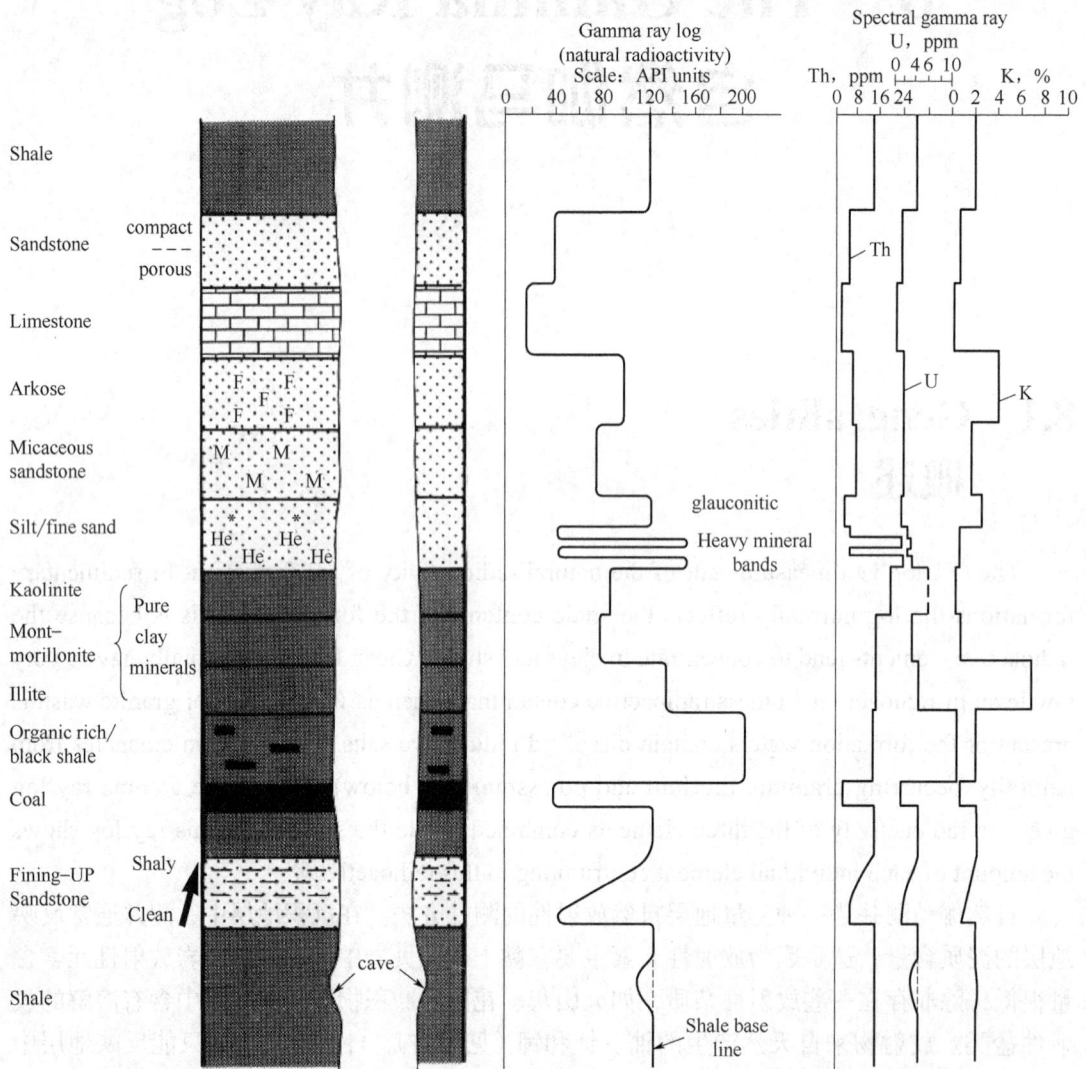

Fig.8.1 The gamma ray log and spectral gamma ray log: some typical responses (from Malcolm Rider, 2002)

The gamma ray log shows natural radioactivity. The spectral gamma ray log gives the abundances of the naturally radioactive elements, thorium (Th) and uranium (U) in parts permillion (ppm) and potassium, K in %. F = feldspar; M = mica; *= glauconite

图 8.1 自然伽马和自然伽马能谱测井曲线典型的测井响应特征（据 Malcolm Rider, 2002）

自然伽马测井反映总的自然放射性，自然伽马能谱测井可以给出铀、钍、钾三种放射性核素含量，铀、钍含量的单位是 ppm，钾含量的单位是 %。F 代表长石；M 代表云母；* 代表海绿石

The gamma ray log is still principally used quantitatively to derive shale volume. Qualitatively, in its simple form, it can be used to correlate, to suggest facies and sequences and, of course, to identify lithology (shaliness). (Table 8.1).

伽马测井主要用于定量计算泥岩含量，也可以以简单形式定性表征沉积相和沉积序列。当然，也可以用于识别岩性（泥质含量），见表 8.1。

Table 8.1 Principal uses of the gamma ray log (from Malcolm Rider, 2002)

	Discipline	Used for	Knowing
Quantitative	Petrophysics	Shale volume (V_{sh})	gamma ray (max) gamma ray (min)
Qualitative	Geology	Shale (shaliness)	gamma ray (max) gamma ray (min)
		Lithology	typical radioactivity values
		Mineral identification	Mineral radioactivity
	Sedimentology	Facies	Clay/grain size relationship
	Sequence Stratigraphy	Parasequence & condensed sequence identification	Clay/grain size & organic matter/radioactivity relationships
	Stratigraphy	correlation	—
		Unconformity identification	—

表 8.1 伽马测井的主要用途（据 Malcolm Rider, 2002）

	学科	用途	数据来源
定量	岩石物理学	泥岩体积（V_{sh}）	自然伽马射线（最大值） 自然伽马射线（最小值）
定性	地质学	泥岩（泥质含量）	自然伽马射线（最大值） 自然伽马射线（最小值）
		岩性	典型岩石的放射性数值
	地质学	识别矿物	矿物的放射性数值
	沉积学	沉积相	黏土/颗粒大小的关系
	层序地层学	识别层序和凝缩段	黏土/颗粒大小和有机质/放射性的关系
	地层学	地层对比	—
		识别不整合面	—

8.2 Principle of Gamma-ray Log
自然伽马放射性测井原理

Natural radiation in rocks comes essentially from three elemental sources: the radioactive elements of the thorium family, the uranium-radium family and the radioactive isotope of potassium ^{40}K.

岩石中的自然放射性主要来自三种元素来源：钍族的放射性元素，铀—镭家族的放射性元素和钾—40 的放射性同位素。

Quantitatively, potassium is by far the most abundant in the three elements (Table 8.2), but its contribution to the overall radioactivity in relation to its weight is small. In reality, the contribution to the overall radioactivity of the three elements is of the same order of magnitude, the abundance seeming to be the inverse of the contribution in energy: a small quantity of uranium has a large effect on the radioactivity, a large quantity of potassium has a small effect.

从数量上说，钾在这三种元素中最为丰富（表 8.2），但是，它对总放射性的贡献相对于它的重量来说，影响很小。实际上，三种元素对整体放射性的贡献是相同数量级的，丰度似乎与放射能量的贡献成反比：少量的铀对放射性有很大的影响，大量的钾对放射性影响很小。

Table 8.2 Abundance and relative radiation activity of the natural radioactive elements (from Serra et al, 1980)

	K	Th	U
Relative abundance in the earth's crust	2.59%	~12μg/g	~3μg/g
Gamma rays per unit weight	1	1300	3600

表 8.2 天然放射性元素的丰度和相对辐射活动（据 Serra et al, 1980）

	K	Th	U
地壳中的相对丰度	2.59%	~12μg/g	~3μg/g
单位重量的伽马射线放射量	1	1300	3600

Each of the three sources emits gamma rays spontaneously. This means that they emit photons with no mass and no charge but great energy (which is the definition of a gamma ray). The energy in the case of uranium, thorium and potassium emissions occurs in the spectrum from 0-3MeV (million electron volts).

三个放射源在地层中都自发地发射伽马射线。也就是说，它们发射的光子没有质量，没有电荷，但能量很大（这就是伽马射线的定义）。在铀，钍和钾发射的情况下，能量发生在 0 ~ 3MeV（百万电子伏特）的光谱中。

The radiation from ^{40}K is distinct, with a single energy value of 1.46MeV (Fig.8.2). Both thorium and uranium emit radiations with a complete range of energies, but with certain peak frequencies. These peaks are especially distinct at the higher energy levels of 2.62MeV for thorium and 1.76 MeV for uranium (Fig.8.2).

其中钾—40 辐射明显，单次能量值 1.46 MeV（图 8.2）。而钍和铀发射能量范围都很广，但具有一定的峰值频率。钍的峰值在 2.62 MeV，铀的峰值在 1.76 MeV（图 8.2）。

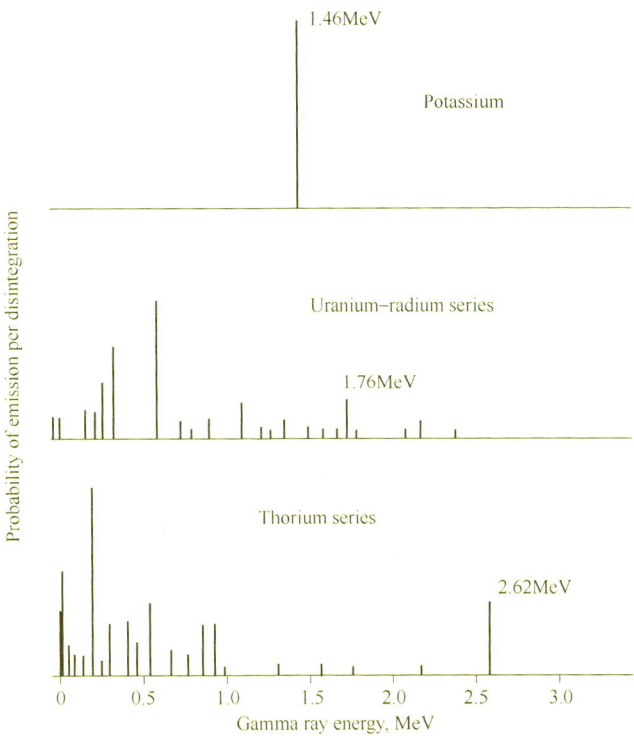

Fig.8.2 The gamma ray emission spectra of naturally radioactive minerals (The principal peaks used to identify each source are indicated) (from Schlumberger, 1972)

图 8.2 天然放射性矿物的伽马射线发射光谱（已标明每个放射源的主峰）（据 Schlumberger, 1972）

The spectra and the energy levels illustrated are those at the point of emission. One of the characteristics of gamma rays is that when they pass through any material, their energy is progressively absorbed. The effect is known as the Compton scattering, and is due to the collision between gamma rays and electrons which produces a degrading (lowering) of energy. The higher the common density through which the gamma rays pass, the more rapid the degradation or loss of energy (in reality it depends on the material's electron density, which is very similar to common density).

上述所示的光谱和能级是发射点的光谱和能级。伽马射线的特征之一是，当它们穿过任何物质时，它们的能量会逐渐被吸收，这种由于伽马射线和电子之间的碰撞导致能量降低的现象称为康普顿散射。伽马射线通过的介质密度越高，能量的降低或损失越快（实际上它取决于物质的电子密度，这与普通密度非常相似）。

In borehole logging, when radiations are observed by the tool, they have already passed through the formation and probably also the drilling mud, both of which cause Compton scattering. Thus, the discrete energy levels at which gamma rays are emitted become degraded, and a continuous spectrum of values is observed (Fig.8.3). When each of the radioactive minerals is present, their radiations become mixed and the resulting spectrum is very complex. However, a glance at the original spectra will show that the final complex, mixed spectrum, even after Compton scattering, will still contain diagnostic peaks, especially in the 1–3 MeV region. The original distinct peaks of potassium at 1.46 MeV, uranium at 1.76 MeV and thorium at 2.62 MeV still exist and can be used to identify the original source of radiations. This is the principle used in the spectral gamma ray tool.

在裸眼井测井中，当仪器测量到辐射时，辐射已经穿过地层，并且可能穿过钻井液，这两者都会引起康普顿散射。因此，射出的伽马射线的离散能级降低，并且观察到连续的光谱值（图 8.3）。当放射性矿物出现时，它们的辐射就会混合，产生的光谱会非常复杂。然而，看一眼原始光谱就会发现，即使经过康普顿散射，最终的复合光谱仍将包含易于识别的光电峰，特别是在 1～3MeV 区域。钾在 1.46 MeV、铀在 1.76MeV 和钍在 2.62MeV 的原始峰值仍然存在，可用于确定原始的辐射源。这就是能谱伽马射线仪器所使用的原理。

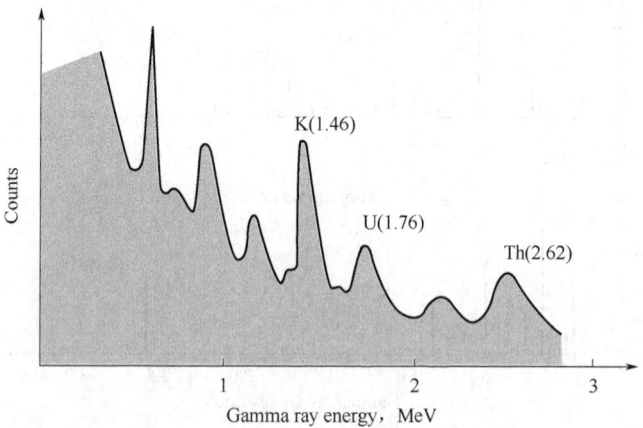

Fig.8.3　Complex spectrum observed from a radioactive source containing potassium, thorium and uranium, after Compton scattering（from Hassan et al., 1976）

图 8.3　钾、钍和铀的放射康普顿散射后的复杂光谱（据 Hassan et al., 1976）

8.3　Simple Gamma Ray Tools
　　　自然伽马测井仪器

The simple gamma ray tool is a sensitive gamma ray detector consisting of a scintillation counter and a photomultiplier (Fig.8.4). The scintillation counter is typically a sodium iodide crystal, 2 cm in diameter and 5 cm long in the simple tool, with minor impurities of Thallium. When gamma rays pass through the crystal, they cause a flash. These are collected by the photo-multiplier and stored in the attached condenser over a set period of time, the time constant. The energy accumulated during the constant time is the detector value at that depth for that time constant. The tool literally 'counts' the gamma rays.

自然伽马射线测井仪器中含有一个灵敏的伽马射线探测器，由一个闪烁计数管（探测器）和一个光电倍增管（放大器）组成（图8.4）。闪烁计数管通常是一个碘化钠晶体，在测井仪中直径 2cm，长 5cm，含有少量铊杂质。当伽马射线穿过晶体时会闪光。在一段时间内，放大器收集闪光数并存储在附设的电容器中，这一设定时间称为时间常数。在时间常数期间累积的能量是探测器在该时间常数下该深度处的值。测井仪器由此来对伽马射线"计数"。

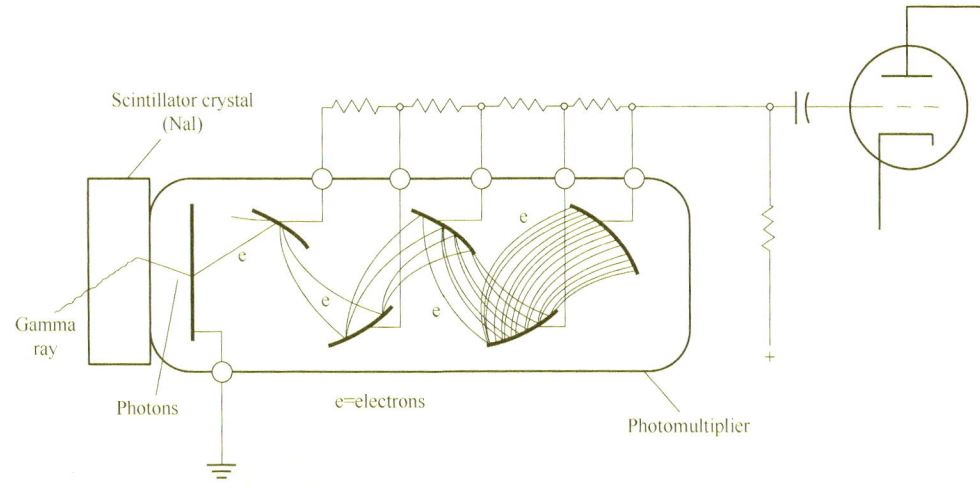

Fig.8.4　Schema of a gamma ray tool (from Serra, 1979)
图 8.4　伽马射线测量仪器的测量模式（据 Serra，1979）

The GR log can be recorded in cased wells, which makes it very useful as a correlation curve in completion and workover operations. It is frequently used to complement the SP log and as a substitute for the SP curve in well drilled with salt mud, air, or oil-based muds. In each case, it is useful for location of shales and nonshaly beds and, most importantly, for general correlation.

GR 测井也用于套管井，这使其在完井和修井作业中成为非常有用的相关对比曲线。在使用盐水钻井液，空气或油基钻井液的井中，它经常被用于补充 SP 测井曲线，并作为 SP 曲线的替代品。在不同情况下，它都有助于泥岩和非泥岩的定位，最重要的是，可用于地层对比。

8.4　Application of Simple Gamma Ray Log
　　　自然伽马射线测井的应用

8.4.1　Quantitative Use
　　　　 定量评价

The gamma ray log may often be used quantitatively, and although the gamma ray value for shales varies enormously, in an arbitrary area or a well, the values for pure shale tend to be constant (Fig.8.5). Thus, if one considers the maximum average gamma ray log value to be pure 100% shale (i.e., shale line, Fig.8.5), and the lowest value to indicate no shale at all (i.e., sand line, Fig.8.5), a scale from 0 to 100% shale can be constructed. If the scale is considered to be linear, any value (GR) of the gamma ray log will give the volume of shale from the simple calculation.

自然伽马射线测井常用于定量评价。虽然泥岩的伽马射线值变化很大，但在任何一个区域或一口井中，纯泥岩的伽马射线值趋于恒定（图 8.5）。因此，如果将自然伽马射线测井平均值的最大值视为纯泥岩（即泥岩线），将并且最低值视为根本没有泥岩（即砂岩线）（如图 8.5 所示），则可以构建 0 ~ 100% 泥岩的伽马取值范围。如果认为比例是线性的，那么自然伽马测井的任何值（GR）都可以通过简单计算得出泥岩体积。

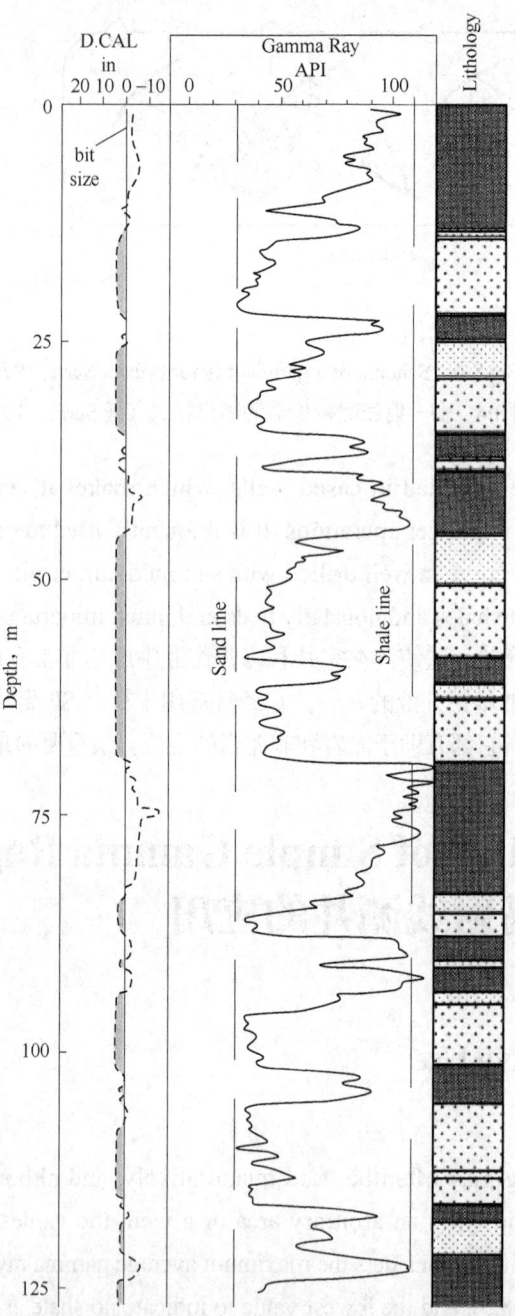

Fig.8.5 Sand line and shale line defined on a gamma ray log (from Malcolm Rider, 2002)

These 'baselines' are for the quantitative use of the log, and may be reasonably constant in any one zone

图 8.5 在自然伽马测井曲线上定义的砂岩线和泥岩线（据 Malcolm Rider, 2002）

这些"基线"用于定量使用测井曲线值，并且在任何一个区域中都可能是相当稳定的

$$\text{Volume of shale \%} = \frac{GRvalue_{\log} - GR_{\min}}{GR_{\max} - GR_{\min}} \tag{8.1}$$

whrer: $GR_{\max}$—— the GR value of 100% shale;

$GR_{\min}$——0% shale (i.e. clean formation).

式中 $GR_{\max}$——纯泥岩伽马值;

$GR_{\min}$——纯砂岩的伽马值。

Generally, the value is not very accurate and tends to give an upper limit to the volume of shale (V_{sh} or V_{clay}). Moreover, there is no scientific basis for assuming that the relationship between gamma ray value and shale volume should be linear. Thus, a modification of the simple linear relationship used above has been proposed as a result of empirical correlation. The relationship changes between younger (unconsolidated) rocks and older (consolidated) rocks (Fig.8.6)。

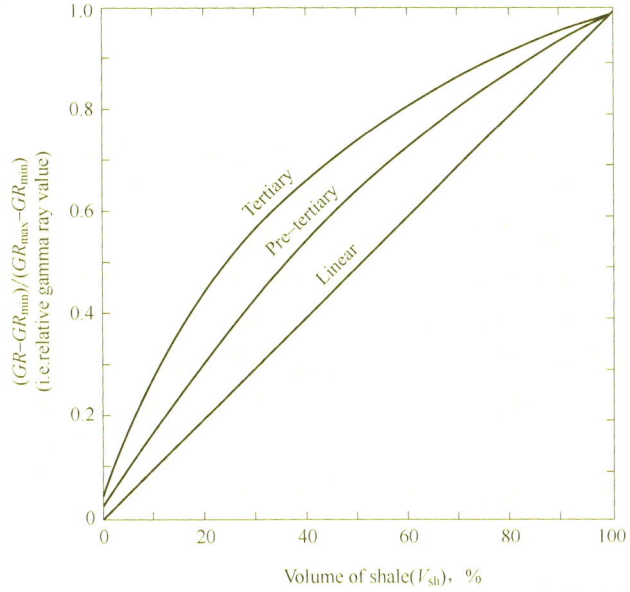

Fig.8.6 Graphical representation of the relationship between relative gamma ray deflection and shale volume (from Dresser Atlas, 1982)

图 8.6 相对伽马射线偏转与泥岩体积之间关系图 (from Dresser Atlas, 1982)

一般来说,该泥岩体积值不是非常准确,往往给出泥岩体积(V_{sh} 或 V_{clay})的上限。此外,伽马射线值与泥岩体积之间的线性关系也没有科学依据。因此,根据经验结果,对上面使用的简单线性关系进行了修正。年轻的岩层(未固结)岩石与老岩层(固结)的关系发生变化(图 8.6)。

$$V_{sh} = \frac{2^{GCUR \cdot V_{sh-1}^*} }{2^{GCUR} - 1} \tag{8.2}$$

Where V_{sh} is shale volume from these formulae (see Fig .8.6) and as shown previously; *GCUR* is Hichie Index, which is related to geological age, and it can be determined according to core analysis data together with the values of natural gamma logging, (for pre-Paleocene (consolidated) rocks, GCUR is 2, for after-Paleocene (unconsolidated) rocks, that is 3.7); V_{sh}^* is Natural Gamma relative value, also known as shale content index.

式中，V_{sh} 为泥岩体积，如图 8.6 所示；GCUR 为希尔奇指数，它与地层地质年代有关，可根据取心资料分析资料与自然伽马测井值进行统计确定［对于古近纪之前（压实）的岩石，GCUR 取 2，对于古近纪之后（未固结）的岩石，取 3.7］；V_{sh}^* 为自然伽马相对值，也称泥质含量指数。

$$V_{sh}^* = \frac{GR - GR_{min}}{GR_{max} - GR_{min}} \tag{8.3}$$

8.4.2　Qualitative Use
定性评价

8.4.2.1　Lithology
岩性

As a first indicator of lithology, the gamma ray log is extremely useful as it suggests where shale may be expected. Moreover, as shown above, the higher the gamma ray value, the higher the percentage of shale. Nevertheless, the log is only a first indicator. The radioactivity of some typical lithologies other than shale is now considered. This shows that any lithology indicated by the simple gamma ray log must be confirmed by other logs.

作为识别岩性的第一个指标，自然伽马测井非常有用，因为它可以显示可能出现泥岩的位置。此外，从上图可以看出，自然伽马射线值越高，泥岩的百分比越高。然而，测井值只是一个指标。还需考虑除泥岩之外还有一些典型岩性具有放射性。这表明，任何由简单的自然伽马测井识别的岩性都必须得到其他测井的验证。

8.4.2.2　Unconformities
不整合面

Unusually high gamma ray values often occur as narrow, isolated peaks. Considering the geochemistry of the radioactive minerals, these peaks are generally associated with uranium concentrations. As discussed, uranium concentrations indicate extreme conditions of deposition. Experience has shown that these conditions frequently occur around unconformities where a long passage of time is represented by little deposition. The minerals associated may be uranium-enriched phosphates or uranium-enriched organic matter.

异常高的自然伽马值通常显示为狭窄的尖峰。考虑到放射性矿物的地球化学特征，这些尖峰通常与铀的富集有关。如前所述，铀的富集常表明极端的沉积条件。经验表明，这些情况经常发生在不整合面附近，这些不整合面为长时间的沉积间断，仅有少量的沉积物。沉积的主要矿物为富含铀的磷酸盐或富含铀的有机物质。

8.4.2.3 Facies and Grain Size
沉积相与颗粒大小

An interesting and fairly comprehensive scheme for facies identification in detrital sediments (sand-shale) has been developed using gamma ray log shapes. The basis for the scheme is the relationship between grain size and shale content. It is shale content that gamma ray log indicates, but it is interpreted in terms of grain size. For example, coarse-grained sand will have very low shale content; a medium-grained sand some shale; and fine-grained sand may be very shaly. The changes in grain size will be represented by changes in gamma ray value.

利用自然伽马测井曲线形态，可以实现相当全面的碎屑沉积物（砂泥岩）沉积相识别。该方法的依据是粒度和泥质含量之间的关系。自然伽马测井反映的是根据粒度大小解释的泥质的含量。例如，粗粒砂岩的泥质含量非常低，中粒砂岩的泥质含量中等，细粒砂岩的泥质含量较高。颗粒大小的变化可由自然伽马值的变化来反映。

This method of indicating facies with the gamma ray log, however, is not straightforward. The relationship between grain size and shale content is very variable, as is the relationship between shale volume and gamma ray value. Empirically, if the gamma ray log shows a typical shape, it can be taken as indicating grain-size changes. However, a lack of changes in curve shape is not evidence for lack of grain-size change since it cannot be interpreted.

然而，这种用伽马射线测井指示沉积相的方法并不是简洁明了的。粒度与泥质含量之间的关系非常多变，泥岩体积与伽马射线值之间的关系也是如此。根据经验，如果自然伽马测井曲线形状典型，则可以将其视为粒度变化的指示。然而，曲线形状没有变化并不能证明粒度没有发生改变，因为它无法被解释。

8.4.2.4 Correlation of Strata
地层对比

The gamma ray log is one of the most frequently-used logs for correlation. It is characteristic, repeatable, while is not affected by depth; it gives some indication of lithology and is simple. Moreover, it is almost always run and the sensitivity scales are always relatively similar.

自然伽马测井是地层对比最常用的测井之一。它具有特征明显、可重复对比、不受深度影响等特点，而且它给出的一些岩性指示也很简单直观。此外，自然伽马测井是必测系列，且对地层的灵敏度相似。

Exercises
课后练习

8.1 What are uses of GR Log?

8.2 State the difference between gamma ray tool and spectral gamma ray tool.

8.3 State the Statistical Issues about gamma ray log.

8.4 What is V_{sh}?

8.5 Which of the following indicate that a rock is permeable? (Circle all that apply).

(A) Low gamma-ray　　　　　(B) SP deflection
(C) Low resistivity　　　　　(D) High porosity

8.6　You are given the Gamma-Ray log on a well which has been drilled through a siliciclastic sequence. The Gamma-Ray reading of clean sand is 20 API units and the shale baseline has a reading of 120 API units. The Gamma-Ray shale Index of a formation is 0.25. The Gamma Ray reading across of this formation is?

(A) 25 API units　　(B) 35 API units　　　(C) 45 API units

8.7　The response of the gamma ray tool is unaffected by the presence of hydrocarbons.

(A) True　　　(B) False　　　　(C) It depends on the depth of invasion

8.8　State the differences between the Gamma Ray log and the Spontaneous Potential log.

8.9　A gamma ray log may be considered

(A) a permeability log　　　(B) a density log

(C) a shale log　　　　　　(D) a caliper log

Indicate which the correct answer is and in no more than two sentences, state why?

8.10　Choose value for GR_{max} and GR_{min} and compute Shale Index in sand "A".

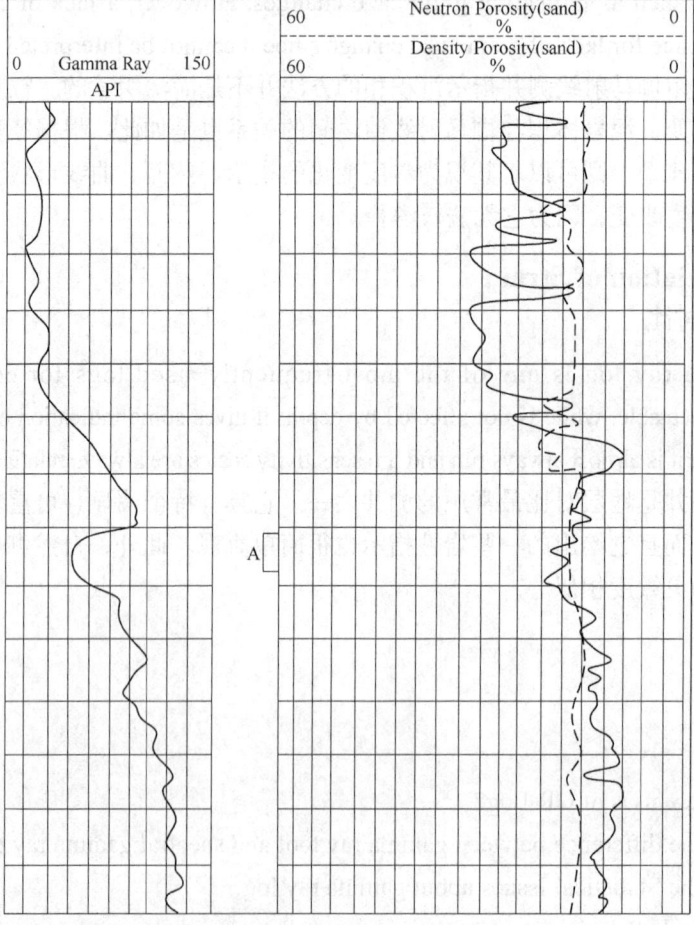

Fig.8.7　GR logging curve

9 The Density Log
密度测井

9.1 Generalities
概述

The density log is a continuous record of a formation's bulk density (Fig.9.1). This is the overall density of a rock including solid matrix and the fluid enclosed in the pores. Geologically, the bulk density is a function of the density of the minerals forming a rock (i.e. matrix) and the volume of free fluids it encloses (i.e. porosity). For example, sandstone with no porosity will have a bulk density of 2.65g/cm^3, the density of pure quartz. At 10% porosity the bulk density is only 2.49g/cm^3, being the sum of 90% quartz grains (density 2.65g/cm^3) and 10% water (density 1.0g/cm^3).

密度测井是对地层体积密度的连续记录（图9.1）。它是包括岩石骨架和饱含流体的孔隙的岩石的总密度。从地质学上讲，体积密度是形成岩石的矿物（岩石骨架）的密度和它所包围的自由流体的体积（即孔隙度）的函数。例如，没有孔隙的砂岩的体积密度为2.65g/cm^3，这是纯石英的密度。孔隙度为10％时，体积密度仅为2.49g/cm^3，这是90％石英颗粒（密度2.65g/cm^3）和10％水（密度1.0g/cm^3）的总和。

Quantitatively, the density log is used to calculate porosity and indirectly, hydrocarbon density. It is also used to calculate acoustic impedance. Qualitatively, it is a useful lithology indicator, can be used to identify certain minerals, can help to assess source rock organic matter content (even quantitatively) and may help to identify overpressure and fracture porosity (Table 9.1).

密度测井可用于定量计算孔隙度、间接计算烃类密度，还能用于计算声阻抗。从定性上讲，它还是一种有用的岩性指标，可用于识别某些矿物，帮助评估烃源岩的有机质含量（甚至是定量），并有助于识别超压和裂缝孔隙度（表9.1）。

Table 9.1　The principal uses of the density log(from Malcolm Rider.,2002)

	Discipline	Used for	Knowing
Quantitative	Petrophysics	Porosity	Matrix density, Fluid density
	Seismic	Acoustic impedance	(Use mw log)

续表

	Discipline	Used for	Knowing
Qualitative and semiquantitative	Geology	General Lithology; Shale textural changes; Mineral identification	Combined with neutron; Average trends; Mineral densities
	Reservoir geology	Overpressure identification; Fracture recognition	Average trends; Sonic porosities
	Geochemistry	Source rock evaluation	Density – OM calibration

表 9.1 密度测井的主要用途（据 Malcolm Rider，2002）

	学科	用途	数据需求
定量	岩石物理学	孔隙度	骨架密度；流体密度
	地震学	声阻抗	原始测井曲线
定性和半定量	地质学	岩性；泥岩结构变化；矿物识别	与中子测井结合；平均走向；矿物密度
	储层地质	超压识别；裂缝识别	平均走向；声波孔隙度
	地球化学	烃源岩评价	密度—OM 校准

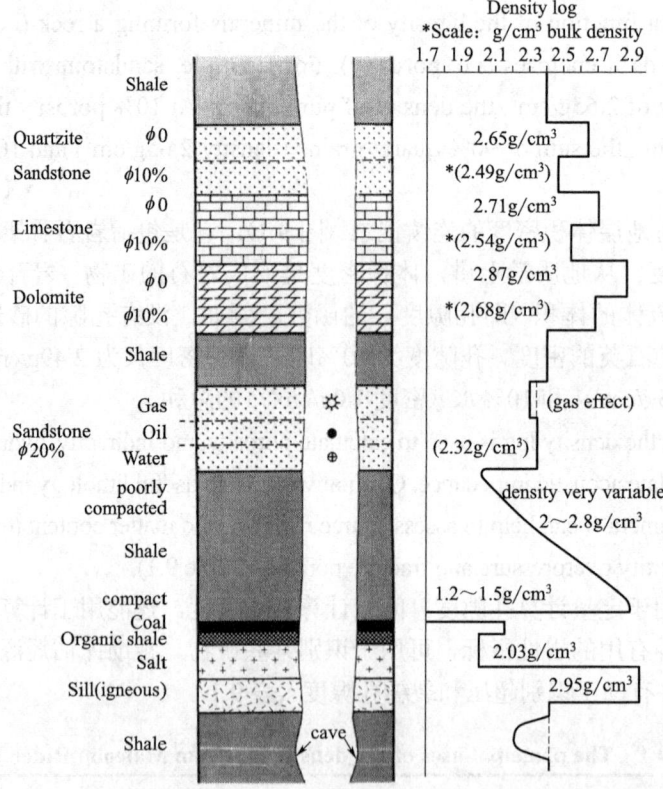

Fig.9.1 The density log: some typical responses. The density log shows bulk density. Density and porosity with fresh formation-water density 1.0g/cm³(from Malcolm Rider, 2002)

图 9.1 密度测井：典型地层的密度测井响应。密度测井显示的是在地层水密度为 1.0g/cm³ 条件下的地层密度和孔隙度（据 Malcolm Rider,2002）

9.2 Principles of Measurement
密度测井原理

The logging technique of the density tool is to subject the formation to a bombardment of medium-high energy (0.2-2.0 MeV) collimated (focused) gamma rays and to measure their attenuation between the tool source and detectors. Such is the physical relationship that the attenuation (Compton scattering) is a function of the number of electrons that the formation contains-its electron density (electrons/cm^3) which in turn is very closely related to its common density (g/cm^3). In dense formations, Compton scattering attenuation is extreme and few detectable gamma rays reach the tool's detectors, while in a lower density the number is much higher. The change in counts with change in density is exponential over the average logging density range from about 2.0-3.0g/cm^3. Detector counts in modem tools are converted directly to bulk density for the log printout. However, although electron density, as detected by the tool, and real density are almost identical, there are differences when water (hydrogen) is involved. For this reason, the actual values presented on the density log are transformed to give actual values of calcite (2.71g/cm^3) and pure water (1.00g/cm^3). (There are still slight differences between log density and real density, especially when chlorine is involved.)

密度测井技术是利用中高能（0.2～2.0MeV）准直（聚焦）伽马射线轰击地层，然后测量伽马射线在仪器源和探测器之间的衰减。它们的物理关系如下：伽马射线在地层中受康普顿散射的影响发生衰减，衰减的程度与地层所包含的电子数量相关，反过来地层的电子密度（电子/cm^3）又与其地层密度（g/cm^3）密切相关。在高密度地层中，康普顿散射衰减现象非常严重，测井仪的探测器只能检测到很少的伽马射线，而在密度较低的地层中，伽马射线数量要大得多。在平均测井密度范围内（约2.0～3.0g/cm^3），测井探测器得到的伽马射线计数随地层密度变化呈指数变化关系。仪器中的检测器计数直接转换为地层体积密度输出。然而，尽管由测井仪器检测到的电子密度和实际密度几乎相同，但是当地层中存在水（氢）时，二者数值会存在差异。因此，需将密度测井的实际值转换为方解石（2.71g/cm^3）和纯水（1.00g/cm^3）的实际值。（测井密度和实际密度之间仍然存在细微差别，尤其是地层中含有氯时。）

9.3 Density Logging Instrument
密度测井仪器

The standard density tools have a collimated gamma ray source (usually radiocaesium which emits gamma rays at 662 keV, but radiocobalt is also used) and two detectors (near and far), which allow compensation for borehole effects when their readings are combined and compared in calculated ratios. The near detector response is essentially due to borehole influences which, when removed from the far detector response enhance the formation effects. The most recent density tools use more efficient scintillation detectors which separate high (hard) and low (soft) gamma ray energy levels. This allows a better evaluation of borehole effects, therefore providing a more accurate density measurement as well as the additional photoelectric factor value. Source and detectors are mounted on a plough-shaped pad which is pressed hard against the borehole wall during logging (Fig.9.2). Density-log readings therefore refer to only one sector on the borehole wall.

标准密度测井仪有一个准直伽马射线源（通常是放射性铯，可发射662keV的伽马射线，也可使用放射性钴）和两个探测器（长源距和短源距），当两个探测器的读数结合并以计算比例进行比较时，可以补偿井眼效应。短源距探测器响应主要受钻孔影响，当将其从长源距探测器响应中去除时，会增强地层效应。最新的密度测井仪器使用了更有效的闪烁探测器，分离高（硬）和低（软）伽马射线能级。这样可以更好地评估井眼效应，从而提供更精确的密度测量以及额外的光电因子值。放射源和探测器安装在楔形的极板上，在测井过程中将其紧贴在井壁上（图9.2）。因此，密度测井数值反映的是井壁上的一个扇形区域。

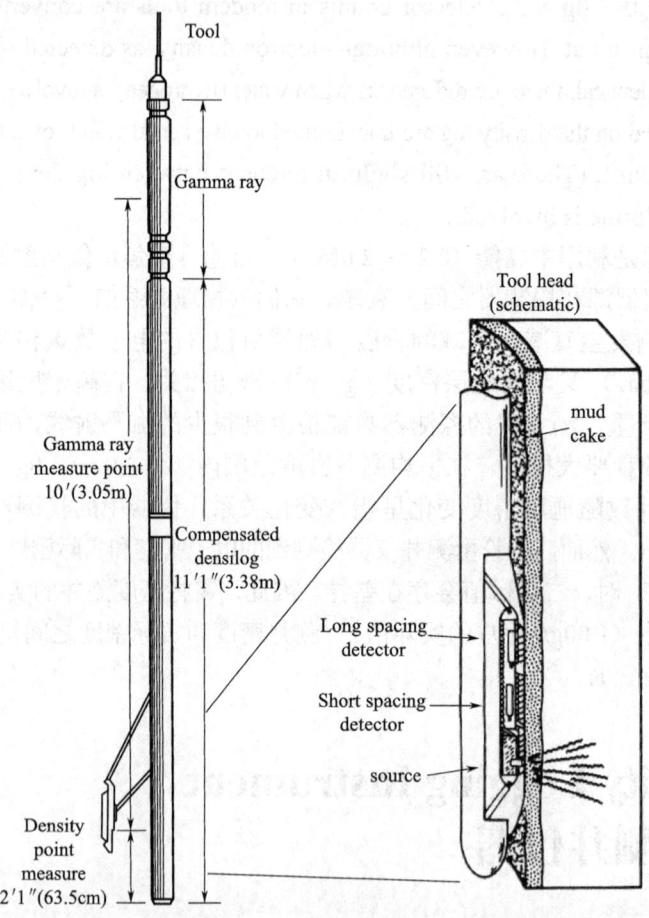

Fig.9.2　A density tool (Densilog from Atlas Wireline) and a tool head
(modified from Dresser Atlas, 1982 and Ellis, 1987)

图9.2　密度测井仪器（阿特拉斯电缆测井的密度测井仪）和探头
（据Atlas，1982；Ellis，1987，有改动）

9.4 Application of Density Log
密度测井应用

9.4.1 Quantitative Uses
定量评价

9.4.1.1 Porosity Calculation
孔隙度计算

The density log is used to calculate porosity and it may also, with difficulty, be used to calculate hydrocarbon density. To calculate porosity from log-derived bulk density it is necessary to know the density of all the individual materials involved. The density tool aquires global (bulk) density, the density both of the grains forming the rock and of the fluids enclosed in the interstitial pores (Fig.9.3).

密度测井用于计算孔隙度，也可用于计算烃类密度，但难度相对较大。要利用测井得到的体积密度计算孔隙度，必须知道岩石所有组分的密度。密度测井可得到体积密度，即形成岩石的骨架颗粒密度和封闭在孔隙中的流体密度（图 9.3）。

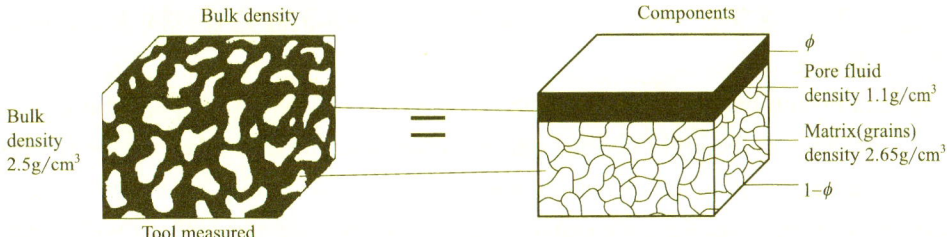

Fig.9.3 Tool measured bulk density and a visualization of the derivation of the porosity component. (The figures are for a sandstone with 10% porosity)(from Malcolm Rider, 2002)

图 9.3 测井测量的体积密度和孔隙度组分的可视化推导（数值为孔隙度为 10% 的砂岩）

（据 Malcolm Rider, 2002）

As an example, if the tool measures a bulk density of 2.5g/cm³ in a salt-water-bearing formation (fluid density 1.1g/cm³, as seen by the tool), we can interpret all of the following based on Table 9.2.

例如，如果密度测井仪器在盐水储层中测量的体积密度为 2.5g/cm³（流体密度为 1.1g/cm³，由仪器测量得到），我们可以据表 9.2 解释以下所有内容。

Table 9.2 Standard rock density model

Lithology	Grain density	Porosity
Sandstone	2.65g/cm³	10%
Limestone	2.71g/cm³	13%
Dolomite	2.87g/cm³	21%

表 9.2 标准岩石密度模型

岩性	颗粒密度	孔隙度
砂岩	2.65g/cm^3	10%
石灰石	2.71g/cm^3	13%
白云石	2.87g/cm^3	21%

If we know the grain (matrix) density and the fluid density we can solve the equation that gives porosity from the summation of fluid and matrix components. For example,

当然，如果我们知道颗粒（岩石骨架）密度和流体密度，我们可以通过流体和岩石骨架的总和得到孔隙度的方程。例如

bulk density (ρ_b)=porosity (ϕ)×fluid density (ρ_f)+(1-ϕ)×matrix density (ρ_{ma})

体积密度 (ρ_b)= 孔隙度 (ϕ)× 流体密度 (ρ_f)+(1-ϕ)× 骨架密度 (ρ_{ma})

When solved for porosity this equation becomes:

当求解孔隙度时，该等式变为：

$$\phi = \frac{\rho_{ma} - \rho_b}{\rho_{ma} - \rho_f} \tag{9.1}$$

Where, ρ_{ma}=matrix (or grain) density, ρ_f=fluid density and ρ_b=bulk density (as measured by the tool and hence includes porosity and grain density).

其中，ρ_{ma} 为骨架（或颗粒）密度，ρ_f 为流体密度，ρ_b 为体积密度（由测井测量，因此包括孔隙度和骨架密度）。

The relationship between the bulk density (as measured by the tool) and porosity can be extremely close when the grain density remains constant. The example shows a reservoir of orthoquartzite composition and a reasonably constant grain density of 2.68g/cm^3 (Fig.9.4). The porosity derived from the bulk density log in this example corresponds well to the core porosity when a matrix density of 2.68g/cm^3 and tool-registered fluid density of 1.1 g/cm^3 are applied.

当骨架密度保持不变时，体积密度（由测井测量）和孔隙度之间的关系是固定的。举例说明，图 9.4 中所示储层由纯石英砂岩组成，颗粒密度为 2.68g/cm^3。当岩石骨架密度为 2.68g/cm^3，测井测量的流体密度为 1.1g/cm^3 时，由密度测井得到的孔隙度与岩心孔隙度吻合良好。

If constant grain-density figures are applied to a formation and the grain density is not constant, the porosity calculated is inaccurate. An error in grain density of 0.01g/cm^3 can cause an error of 0.5%. Such errors occur in the North Sea Jurassic sands, where up to 30% mica can increase the average grain density to 2.84g/cm^3 (mica density is about 2.76-3.1g/cm^3). When too low a grain density is used, the porosity is underestimated by the density log (Fig.9.5).

如果将固定不变的骨架密度数据应用于地层，而实际骨架密度发生变化时，则计算的孔隙度是不准确的。骨架密度 0.01g/cm^3 的误差可引起 0.5%的误差。这种误差出现在北海的侏罗纪储层砂岩中，其中高达 30%的云母可以将平均骨架密度增加到 2.84g/cm^3（云母

密度约为 2.76～3.1g/cm³）。当使用过低的颗粒密度时，用密度测井计算的孔隙度会偏低（图 9.5）。

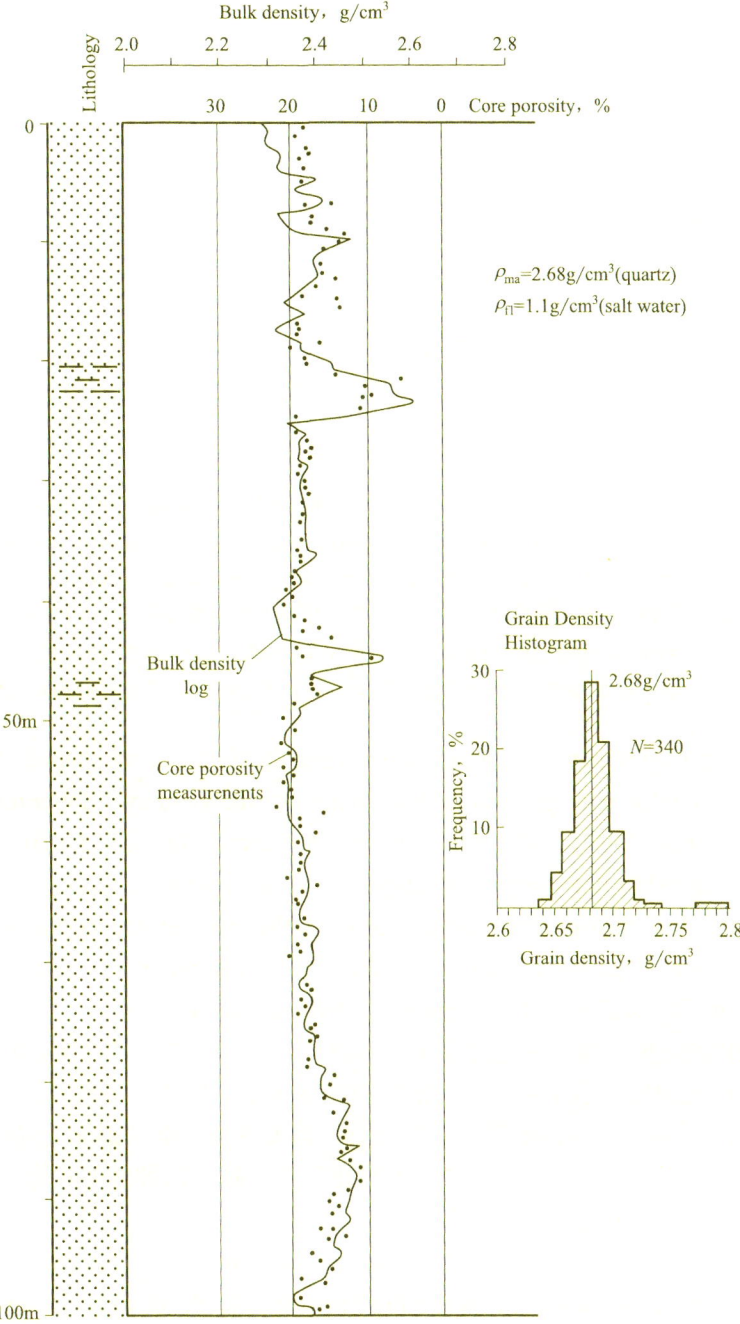

Fig.9.4　Relationship between the bulk density log and core-measured porosity in the quartzite
(from Malcolm Rider, 2002)

The bulk density can be converted to porosity using a matrix density of 2.68g/cm³, as indicated by the inset histogram

图 9.4　在石英砂岩中体积密度测井与岩心测量孔隙度之间的密切对应关系（据 Malcolm Rider，2002）

如插图直方图所示，可以使用 2.68g/cm³ 的骨架密度将体积密度转换成孔隙度

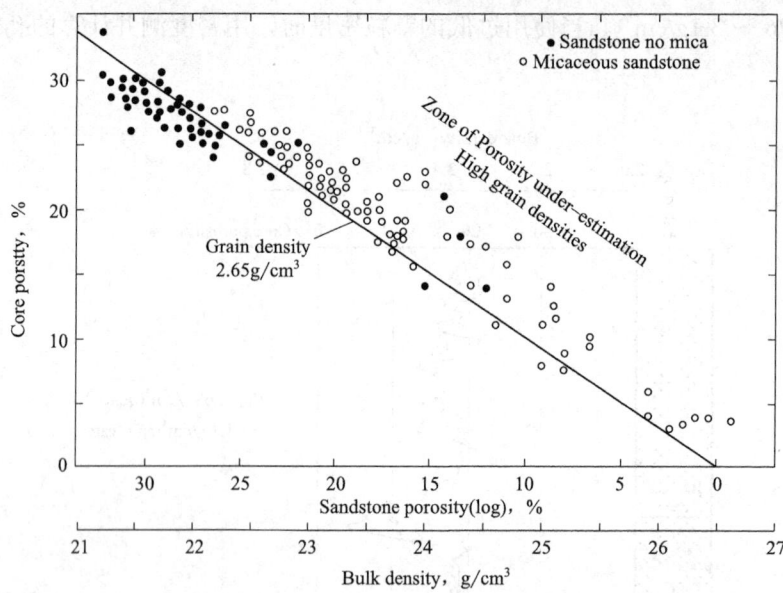

Fig.9.5　The effect of mica on porosity values derived from the bulk density log (Re-drawn from Hodson, 1975)
For the graph a matrix density of 2.65g/cm³ was used (giving the diagonal line). For the micaceous sands, core-measured porosities are consistently higher than those given by the log, because the grain density is too low at 2.65g/cm³. Mica has densities up to 3.10g/cm³

图 9.5　云母对由体积密度测井得到的孔隙度值的影响（据霍德森，1975 年重绘）
对于该图，对角线为使用 2.65g/cm³ 的骨架密度计算的孔隙度。对于含云母砂岩，岩心测量的孔隙度始终高于测井所给出的孔隙度，因为骨架密度给的值太低，为 2.65g/cm³，而云母的密度高达 3.10 g/cm³

　　Erroneous porosities may also be calculated when the fluid density changes. This is the case when a rock is saturated with gaseous hydrocarbons. As shown above, the porosity equation is furnished with a grain density and a fluid density. The latter is 1.0g/cm³ for fresh water and 1.1 g/cm³ for salt water (but may vary with temperature). In the presence of gas (typical density 0.0007g/cm³), the fluid density drops dramatically. As the example shows, the density log gives a high porosity value (Fig.9.6). If the porosity (and water saturation) can be calculated by other means, the density log can be used to calculate the hydrocarbon density.

　　当流体密度改变时，也会引起孔隙度计算错误。当岩石被气态烃饱和时就会出现该情况。如上所示，孔隙度方程中包含骨架密度和流体密度，后者为淡水时为 1.0g/cm³，为盐水时为 1.1g/cm³（但可随温度而变化）。当气体（典型密度 0.0007g/cm³）存在时，流体密度急剧下降。如图 9.6 所示，密度测井给出的孔隙度较高。如果通过其他方法计算孔隙度（水饱和），则密度测井可用于计算烃类密度。

　　When the oil is present, the porosity given by the density log is essentially correct. This is because the density tool investigates the flushed zone (depth of investigation) where only a small volume of oil remains. Moreover, the density of oil is quite close to that of water (0.7g/cm³ v.s. 1.0g/cm³). Gas, however, is more mobile and frequently occurs in the flushed zone where, because of the large density difference with water, it has the effect of diminishing the bulk density as described above.

　　当存在油时，密度测井给出的孔隙度基本上是正确的。这是因为密度测井测量的主要是冲洗带，在那里只有少量的油残留。此外，油的密度（0.7g/cm³）非常接近水的密度（1.0g/cm³）。然而，由于气与水的密度差大，气体更易移动并且经常发生在冲洗带中，它具有如上所述的减小体积密度的效果。

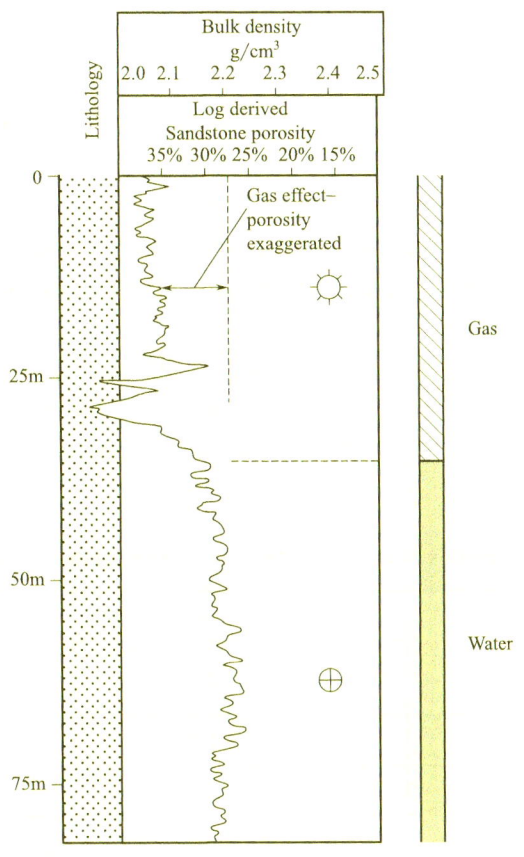

Fig.9.6　The effect of gas on the density log (from Malcolm Rider, 2002)

In this example the gas zone reads about 35% porosity: it should read 27% porosity

图 9.6　气体对密度测井的影响（据 Malcolm Rider，2002）

实例中，含气区域的孔隙度约为 35%，实际孔隙率为 27%

9.4.1.2　Acoustic Impedance
　　　　　计算声阻抗

The density log is used in conjunction with the sonic log to calculate acoustic impedance.
密度测井与声波测井结合使用，以计算声阻抗。

9.4.2　Qualitative Uses
　　　　定性评价

　　The density tool gives a continuous log of the formation's bulk density and it needs no interpretation as the character is given directly. The qualitative use of this log therefore depends on the geological significance of the density of a formation.

密度测井仪器可以连续记录地层的体积密度，因为该信息特征是直接给出的，所以不需要再进行测井解释。因此，密度测井的定性使用取决于地层密度的地质意义。

9.4.2.1 Lithology Identification
岩性识别

The densities of the more common lithologies are rarely diagnostic since there is too much overlap and too much spread caused by differences in composition and texture. Shales, for example, may have densities ranging from 1.8g/cm^3 to 2.7g/cm^3: the density difference between a plastic clay and a compacted shale (Table 9.3). Overall, oilfield densities generally measure between 2.0g/cm^3 and 3.0g/cm^3, the common lithologies spanning the whole of this range (Fig.9.7).

常规地层的岩性很难只通过密度值来确定。不同岩性的地层由于组成和结构的差异，导致密度值发生重叠和扩散。例如，泥岩的密度可能在 1.8g/cm^3 至 2.7g/cm^3 之间，这是塑性黏土和压实泥岩之间的密度差（表 9.3）。总体而言，油田地层密度一般在 2.0g/cm^3 和 3.0g/cm^3 之间，包含所有常见岩性（图 9.7）。

Table 9.3 Densities of common lithologies (from Malcolm Rider, 2002)

Lithology	Range, g/cm^3	Matrix, g/cm^3
Clays—shales	1.8～2.75	Varies (av. 2.65～2.7)
Sandstones	1.9～2.65	2.65
Limestones	2.2～2.71	2.71
Dolomites	2.3～2.87	2.87

表 9.3 见岩性的密度（据 Malcolm Rider，2002）

岩性	范围，g/cm^3	岩石骨架，g/cm^3
黏土—泥岩	1.8～2.75	根据情况而变化（平均 2.65～2.7）
砂岩	1.9～2.65	2.65
石灰岩	2.2～2.71	2.71
白云岩	2.3～2.87	2.87

9.4.2.2 The Density Log in Shales: Compaction, Age and Composition
泥岩的密度测井：压实，地质年代和组成

The compaction of shales with burial is a well-known phenomenon and it can be followed on the density log. Shale compaction involves a series of textural and compositional changes, resulting in a progressive increase in density. For example, shall uncompacted clays have densities around 2.0g/cm^3, while at depth, this figure commonly rises to 2.6g/cm^3.

泥岩埋藏压实是常见现象，在密度测井中可以进行跟踪。泥岩压实包括一系列结构和成分变化，导致密度逐渐增加。例如，未压实黏土的密度应为 2.0g/cm³ 左右，而被埋藏时，这个数字通常会升至 2.6g/cm³。

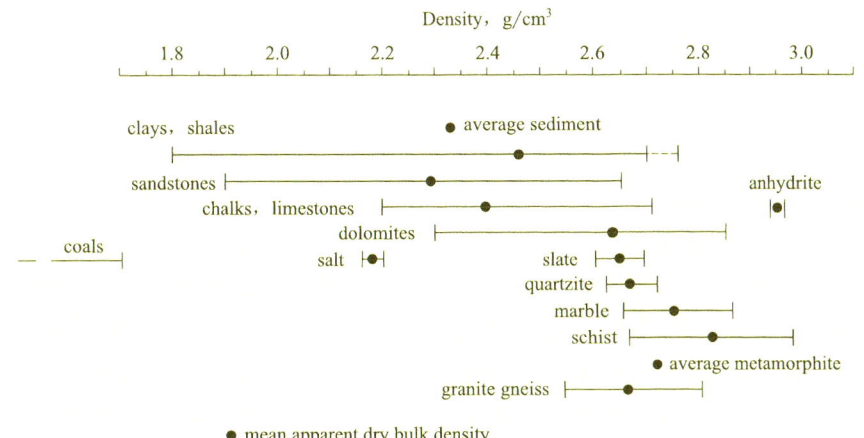

Fig.9.7　Density ranges of some common lithologies (modified from Jackson and Talbot, 1986)
Note the similar ranges of clay/shale, sandstone and limestone
图 9.7　一些常见岩性的密度范围（据 Jackson 和 Talbot，1986，有修改）
注意黏土/页岩、砂岩和石灰岩的相似范围

Although it is by no means diagnostic, shale density is often indicative of age. In general, older shales are denser. Palaeozoic clays are rare, as are Tertiary shales. The increase in shale density during compaction, although essentially due to a decrease in porosity, is accompanied by irreversible diagenetic changes. This means that in the subsurface, a change in compaction trends will indicate a change in age, in other words an unconformity. Besides, if general compaction curves for a region can be established, the maximum depth of burial of a formation can be estimated. However, for compaction studies the density log must be used carefully.

虽然不是绝对确定的，但泥岩密度通常能够指示地质年代。一般来说，较老的泥岩密度更大。古生代黏土很少见，新生代泥岩也是如此。压实过程中泥岩密度的增加，虽然主要是由于孔隙度的降低，但同时也伴随着不可逆的成岩变化。这意味着在地层中，压实趋势的变化将表明岩层地质年代的变化，换句话说，即不整合接触。除此之外，如果可以确定一个区域的总压实线，就可以估算出地层的最大埋藏深度。但是，对于压实研究，必须仔细使用密度测井。

9.4.2.3　The Density Log in Sandstones – Composition and Diagenesis
砂岩的密度测井：成分和成岩作用

Bulk density variations in sandstone generally indicate porosity changes. However, as explained above, this is not true when there are changes in grain density. Pure quartz sands are considered to have a grain density of 2.65g/cm³, but in reality such sands are rare. Overall grain density will change depending on the non-quartz constituents. Sands are commonly mixed with feldspars (density 2.52～2.63g/cm³), micas (2.65～3.1g/cm³) lignite fragments (0.5～1.8g/cm³) and rock fragments (variable density). Heavy minerals may also be a constituent (2.7 ~ 5.0g/cm^3). The well-known mica sands of the North Sea Jurassic reservoirs (as already discussed) contain up to 30% muscovite. The density of muscovite (2.76 ~ 3.10g/cm^3) increases the average grain density from 2.65g/cm^3 to 2.82g/cm^3 and it varies with the mica content. In sands without shale, therefore, grain density can give some idea of sand composition.

砂岩中的体积密度变化通常表明孔隙度的变化。但是，如上所述，当骨架密度发生变化时，情况并非如此。一般认为纯石英砂岩的骨架密度是2.65g/cm^3，但实际上这种砂岩很少见。总的骨架密度将根据非石英成分而变化。砂中通常混有长石（密度2.52 ~ 2.63g/cm^3）、云母（2.65 ~ 3.1g/cm^3）、褐煤碎片（0.5 ~ 1.8g/cm^3）和岩石碎屑（密度不定），重矿物也可能包括（2.7 ~ 5.0 g/cm^3）。北海侏罗系储层中著名的云母砂（如前所述）含有高达30%的白云母，白云母的密度（2.76 ~ 3.10g/cm^3）使平均骨架密度从2.65g/cm^{3}增加到2.82g/cm^3，并随云母含量的变化而变化。因此，在不含泥岩的砂中，骨架密度可以反映砂质组成。

Changes in grain density in sands are generally gradual and of a moderate order. Abrupt changes, especially in otherwise homogeneous beds, often indicate diagenetic or secondary changes. The example shows a sand with zones of secondary carbonate cement (Fig.9.8). In cores these zones are shown to have very abrupt limits. A similar phenomenon may also occur with secondary pyrite cement.

砂岩中骨架密度的变化通常是渐进和适度的。突然的变化，特别是在一些均质储层中，往往表明发生了成岩或次生变化。图9.8所示为具有钙质胶结的砂岩。在岩心中，这些区域突变明显。类似现象也可能发生在次生黄铁矿胶结中。

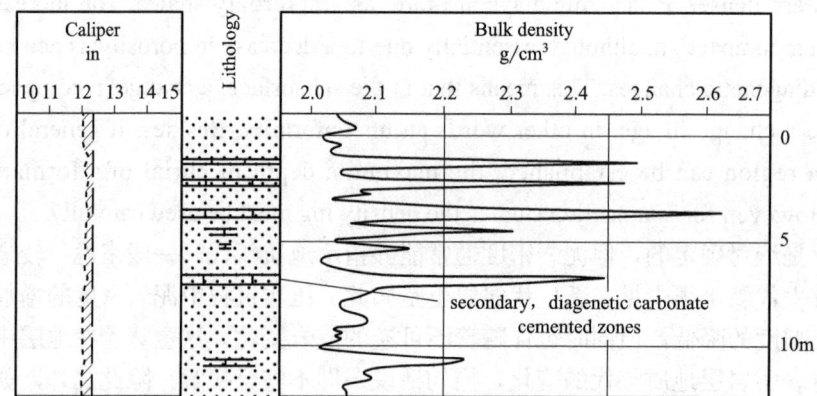

Fig.9.8 Secondary calcareous cementation in sandstone (from Malcolm Rider, 2002)

The density log shows thin, cemented intervals which have little or no porosity while the reservoir generally has 30% ~ 35% porosity

图9.8 砂岩中的次生钙质胶结（据 Malcolm Rider, 2002）

密度测井显示了薄的胶结层段，孔隙很少或没有，而储层孔隙度通常为30%~35%

9.4.2.4 Overpressure Identification
超压实区域识别

The general increase in shale density with depth of burial was described under the heading of compaction. The principal cause for this gradual increase is a diminution in shale porosity with increasing overburden. However, porosity may increase with depth and when it occurs there is overpressure. The general decrease in shale porosity is accompanied by an expulsion of both pore-water and interstitial water. The fluids are gradually squeezed out during burial. If the fluids cannot escape, once trapped they inevitably become over pressured: they begin to support some of the overburden pressure. This has the effect of preserving porosity. It is this preservation which causes a break in the compaction trend which is registered by the density log. The density break therefore identifies zones of abnormal pressure.

在压实作用下泥岩的密度随埋藏深度的增加而逐渐增加。这种逐渐增加的主要原因是泥岩孔隙度随上覆地层的增加而减小。然而，当存在超压作用时，孔隙度还可能随着深度的增加而增加。泥岩孔隙度的普遍降低伴随着孔隙水和间隙水的排出。流体在埋藏过程中逐渐被挤出。如果流体无法渗流，一旦被困，它们就不可避免地压力过大：它们开始支撑一些上覆压力，这具有保持孔隙度的效果。正是这种保存导致了密度测井记录到的压实趋势中断。因此，密度中断可识别出异常压力区域。

9.4.2.5 Fracture Recognition
裂缝识别

Numerous methods have been proposed for the identification of fractures. One of these involves the comparison of density-log porosity with sonic-log porosity. The density tool records bulk density, and as such will include both intergranular porosity and fracture porosity. For the sonic measurement, however, the sound waves will take the quickest path from emitter to receiver. This path should avoid the fractures. The sonic velocity will therefore give only intergranular porosity. When the density derived porosity is much more than the sonic porosity, the difference is due to the fracture porosity.

裂缝的识别方法很多，其中之一就是密度测井孔隙度与声波测井孔隙度的比较。密度测井记录的是体积密度，其中包括了粒间孔隙度和裂缝孔隙度。然而对于声波测井，声波将通过最快的路径从发射器到接收器，这条路径一般会避开裂缝。因此，声速只能体现粒间孔隙度。当密度孔隙度远大于声波孔隙度时，其差异是由裂缝孔隙度造成的。

9.4.2.6 Source Rock Evaluation
烃源岩评价

The presence of organic matters in shales lowers their density. The normal average matrix density of a mixture of clay minerals is around $2.7 g/cm^3$, while organic matter has densities between $0.50-1.80 g/cm^3$. The presence of organic matter therefore has a significant effect on the overall shale bulk density.

泥岩中有机质的存在降低了它们的密度。黏土矿物混合物的正常平均基质密度约为 $2.7 g/cm^3$，而有机质的密度为 $0.50\sim 1.80 g/cm^3$ 之间。因此，有机物质的存在对整个泥岩体积密度影响显著。

This effect of the organic matter on the density log can be quantified, as was very early recognized, so that the log can be used to evaluate source rocks. Traditionally, to do this the relationship between organic matter content and the density log is normalized using sample analyses (Fig.9.9). The normalized density log can then be used to interpolate between analyzed points. More importantly, in the same basin, a normalized log can also be used in wells where no analyses are available. Difficulties arise when the organic matter is mixed with a high density mineral such as pyrite (density 4.8–5.17g/cm^3) since the high density of the pyrite masks the effect of the low density organic matter. Compaction must also be taken into account. This has led some workers to abandon the density log for source rock studies.

有机物质对密度测井的这种影响是可以量化的，这一点很早就被认识到，因此可以用密度测井评价烃源岩。为了做到这一点，习惯使用样品实验测量数据将有机质含量和密度测井之间的关系进行标准化（图 9.9），然后使用归一化的密度测井数据在分析点之间进行插值。更重要的是，在同一个盆地，标准化测井也可用于没有样品实验分析的井中。但当有机质与高密度矿物如黄铁矿（密度 4.8～5.17g/cm^3）混合时，就会很难分辨，因为黄铁矿的高密度掩盖了低密度有机物的作用。压实作用也必须考虑在内。这使得一些研究人员放弃使用密度测井研究烃源岩。

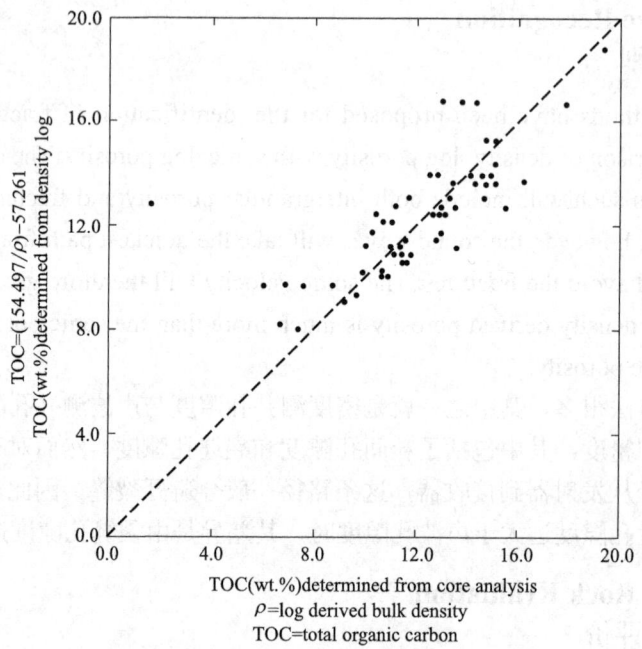

Fig.9.9　Comparison of the organic content derived from the density logs and from core analysis (Re-drawn from Schmoker and Hester, 1983)

Bakken Formation, Williston Basin. Dashed line shows ideal agreement

图 9.9　密度测井与岩心分析的有机物含量比较（据 Schmoker 和 Hester，1983，重绘）

Bakken 地层，威利斯顿盆地。虚线表示了二者相等

Exercises
课后练习

9.1　What are uses of density log?

9.2 What is the bulk density?

9.3 State density log principle.

9.4 What is Compton Effect?

9.5 What is Photoeletric Effect?

9.6 State factors affecting density log response.

9.7 The porosity which the density tool responds to is total formation porosity not effective porosity. Ture of False?

9.8 If you are to conclusively determine whether a formation is sandstone of limestone and you can use only one well log survey, which would be more appropriate?

(A) Density　　　(B) PEF　　　(C) GR

9.9 The density porosity tool responds to the total formation porosity not effective porosity.

(A) True　　　(B) False　　　(C) It Depends on the depth of invasion

9.10 You are analyzing a well log and have determined the PEF of a particular formation to be 5.1 b/e and the bulk density to be less than 2.75 gm/cc. Assuming that the formation is a simple lithology(not a mixed lithology), the formation is most likely?

9.11 The following Pe and ρ_b values were recorded at various depths in a well drilled with fresh mud. Determine the lithology and the porosity for each set of figures.

Pe, b/e	ρ_b, gm/cc	Lithology	Porosity
3.0	2.40		
1.8	2.36		
4.6	2.48		
5.0	2.65		

9.12 The volumetric concentration of a particular formation of interest averages 40%, 20% calcite, and 15% potassium feldspar (2.52 gm/cc). The irreducible oil saturation is 30% with the oil having an in situ density of 0.7 gm/cc. The mud-filtrate has a density of 1.0 gm/cc. What is the bulk density of the formation? What would you expect the density porosity log to read in this formation in sandstone porosity units?

10 The Neutron Log
中子测井

10.1 Generalities
概述

The neutron log provides a continuous record of a formation's reaction to fast neutron bombardment. It is quoted in terms of neutron porosity units, which are related to a formation's hydrogen index, an indication of its richness in hydrogen.

中子测井提供地层被快中子轰击反应后的连续记录。本章引用了中子孔隙度单位，其与地层的氢指数有关，表明地层中氢的丰富程度。

Formations adsorb neutrons rapidly when they contain abundant hydrogen nuclei, which in the geological context are supplied by water (H_2O). The log is therefore principally a measure of a formation's water content, be it bound water, water of crystallization or free pore-water. This hydrogen richness is called the hydrogen index (HI) which is defined as the weight % hydrogen in the formation/weight % hydrogen in water, where $HI_{water}=1$. However, the oilfield interest in water is as a pore fluid filler and porosity indicator so that the neutron log response is given directly in neutron porosity units. Neutron porosity is real porosity in clean limestones, but other lithologies require conversion factors. Since it is calibrated to limestones, the log is sometimes called the Limestone Curve (Fig.10.1).

当地层含有丰富的氢原子核时，它们会迅速吸收中子，这些氢原子核在地质背景下由水（H_2O）提供。因此，中子测井主要测量地层含水量，无论是束缚水、结晶水还是自由孔隙水。这种氢丰度被称为氢指数（HI），定义为地层中氢质量百分比（%）/水中氢的质量百分比（%），其中 $HI_{水}=1$。然而，油田对水的兴趣在于将水作为孔隙流体填充物和孔隙度指标，因此中子测井响应直接以中子孔隙度单位给出。在纯净的石灰岩中，中子孔隙度是地层真实孔隙度，但其他岩性需要进行转换。由于该测井曲线以石灰岩为基准，因此有时也被称为石灰岩曲线（图 10.1）。

Quantitatively, the neutron log is used to measure porosity. Qualitatively, it is an excellent discriminator between gas and oil. It can be used geologically to identify gross lithology, especially evaporites, hydrated minerals and volcanic rocks. When combined with the density log on compatible scales, it is one of the best subsurface lithology indicators available (Table 10.1).

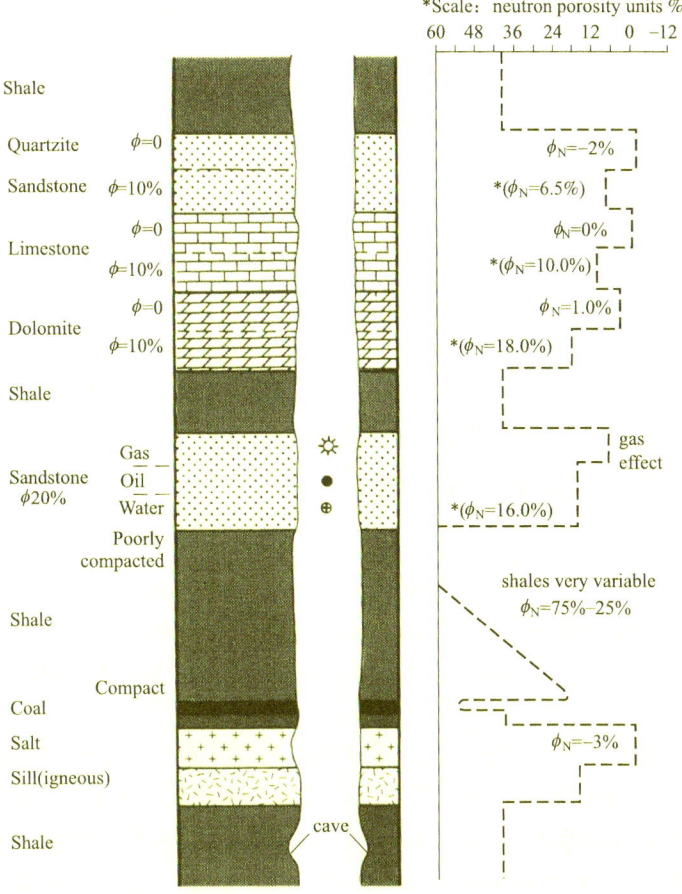

Fig.10.1 The neutron log: some typical responses (from Malcolm Rider, 2002)

The neutron log shows hydrogen index which is converted to neutron porosity units

图 10.1 中子测井：一些典型的响应（据 Malcolm Rider, 2002）

中子测井显示氢指数，氢指数转换为中子孔隙度单位

中子测井可定量测量孔隙度，精确定性鉴别天然气和石油。在地质上还可以用于识别岩性，特别是蒸发岩，水合矿物和火山岩。当中子测井与相同比例尺的密度测井结合使用时，是现有的最佳地下岩性指示工具之一（表 10.1）。

Table 10.1 The principal uses of the neutron log

	Discipline	Used for	Knowing
Quantitative	Petrophysics	Porosity	Matrix, Hydrogen index
Qualitatively	Petrophysics	Identification of gas	Lithology
	Geology	Lithology –Shales, Evaporites	Gross Lithology, Neutron evaporite values
		Hydrated minerals, Volcanic and intrusive rocks, General lithology	Calibration Combined with density

N. B. Using neutron loss combined with density log on compatible scales.

表 10.1 中子测井的主要用途

学科		用途	已知
定量	岩石物理学	孔隙度估算	岩石骨架 氢指数
定性	岩石物理学	气体识别	岩性
	地质学	岩性识别：泥岩；蒸发岩	总体岩性 蒸发岩中子测井值
		水合矿物； 火山岩与侵入岩； 其他一般岩性	与密度测井相结合

注：与相同比例尺的密度测井结合使用。

10.2 Principles of Measurement 中子测井测量原理

Neutrons are subatomic particles which have no electrical charge but whose mass is essentially equivalent to that of a hydrogen nucleus. They interact with matters in two principal ways, by collision and absorption; collisions are mainly at higher energy states, absorption occurs at lower energy.

中子是不带电荷的亚原子粒子，但其质量基本上相当于一个氢核的质量。它们通过碰撞和吸收两种主要方式与物质相互作用：碰撞主要发生在高能态，吸收主要发生在低能态。

The energy loss from fast neutron energy levels through epithermic to the limit of thermic energy, is generally treated as a loss of velocity which occurs especially through elastic scattering, that is collisions with particles having the same mass as neutrons. For logging purposes, this is mainly hydrogen nuclei. Collision with other heavier particles, called inelastic scattering, does not result in significant energy loss. These two moderating reactions are considered to cause the velocity loss over a certain trajectory called the slowing-down length. The slowing down length is proportional to the root mean-square distance from the point of emission of high energy neutrons to the point at which they reach the lower limit of epithermal energy levels.

高能快中子降为低能热中子是一种速度损失，特别是当中子与具有与相同质量的粒子发生碰撞时，即弹性散射时，极易发生。在中子测井中减速过程主要发生在与氢核作用时。当中子与其他较重粒子发生碰撞，称为非弹性散射，不会导致显著的能量损失。这两种减速反应会导致中子在特定的轨迹上的速度损失，这个轨迹称为减速长度。减速长度与从高能中子发射点到它们达到超热能量水平下限的点的均方根距离成比例。

Most logging tools use a chemical source producing fast neutrons. These have an initial energy of around 4 MeV(see Tools), which means that they have an initial velocity of approximately 2800cm/μs. With this energy and velocity, the neutrons have considerable penetration capabilities but after a few microseconds and successive collisions (100 or so), the original fast neutrons have slowed down through epithermic to thermic levels with about 0.25eV of energy and a velocity of around 0.22cm/μs. Expressed in another way, elastic collision with hydrogen can take all a neutron's energy but in non-elastic collisions with heavier elements, the energy reduction is typically around 10% to 25%: the effect of hydrogen is seen as dominant.

大多数测井仪使用能够产生快中子的化学源，它们的初始能量约为 4MeV，这意味着它们的初始速度约为 2800cm/μm。在这样的能量和速度下，中子具有相当大的穿透能力，但经过几微秒和连续碰撞（大约 100 次）后，原始快中子减速变为热中子，能量约为 0.25eV，速度约为 0.22cm/μm。换句话说，与氢核的弹性碰撞可以消耗中子的全部能量，但是在与更重元素的非弹性碰撞中，能量的减少通常在 10%至 25%左右：氢的影响是决定性的。

At the lower thermic energy, the neutron is thought of as diffusing, rather than having a velocity. For example, in a vacuum, a thermal neutron will diffuse randomly for 13 minutes, but in earth materials the time varies: 5μs in rock salt, 450μs in a limestone without porosity and 900μs in a quartzite. The period of diffusion comes to an end as the neutrons undergo absorption interactions. That is, they are captured by other nuclei which then change energy state and, mostly, become unstable. For example, some nuclei, on capturing a neutron, spontaneously de-excite and emit gamma rays of capture, the so-called n-γ capture radiation (an effect used in pulsed neutron logging). The rapidity of neutron absorption depends on the capture cross-section of the absorbing nuclei of the formation, which is a measure of how effective it is at capturing neutrons.

在较低的能量条件下，热中子主要进行扩散运动，而不具有速度。例如，在真空中，热中子将随机扩散 13min，但在不同地层中，时间将会不同：岩盐中为 5μs，无孔隙的石灰岩中为 450μs，石英岩中为 900μs。扩散期在中子发生吸收相互作用时结束。也就是说，它们被其他原子核捕获，然后改变能量状态，并且大多数变得不稳定。例如，一些原子核在捕获中子时，自发地去激发并发射捕获的伽马射线，即所谓的 n—γ 俘获辐射（脉冲中子测井中使用的一种效应）。中子吸收的速度取决于捕获地层吸收核的横截面，这是衡量其捕获中子效率的一个指标。

As far as logging is concerned, the dominant effect on neutrons during the collision and scattering phase, is the mass of the (formation) nuclei, hydrogen dominating; the dominant effect during the absorption phase is the capture cross-section of the thermal neutron absorbers, the effect of hydrogen being much less marked.

就测井而言，在碰撞和散射阶段对中子的主要影响因素是（形成）原子核的质量，氢占主导地位；吸收阶段的主要影响因素是热中子吸收的捕获截面，氢的影响要小得多。

10.3 Neutron Logging Tools 中子测井仪器

The neutron tool today generally consists of a fast neutron source and two detectors (Fig.10.2). The source bombards the formation with neutrons and the detectors measure their loss of energy as they pass through it.

目前中子测井仪一般由快中子源和两个探测器组成（图 10.2）。放射源用中子轰击地层，探测器测量中子穿过地层时的能量损失。

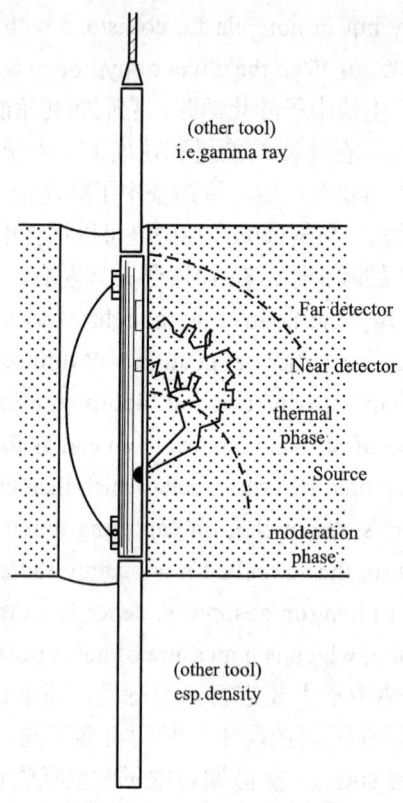

Fig.10.2　A compensated neutron tool- schematic (from Malcolm Rider, 2002)

The source and detectors are held pressed against the borehole wall

图 10.2　补偿中子测井仪原理图（据 Malcolm Rider, 2002）

中子源和探测器被压在井壁上

Tool sources are mostly chemical, such as plutonium-beryllium (PuBe) or americium-beryllium (AmBe), which produce fast neutrons with a peak energy level around 4 Mev. These are the most common cases. Infrequently, high energy neutrons at up to 14 MeV are produced using accelerometers, in which the neutrons are created by bombarding a target with charged particles.

测井仪器的放射源主要是化学物质，常见的如钚铍（PuBe）中子源或镅铍（AmBe）中子源，它们产生峰值能量约为 4MeV 的快中子。少数情况可使用加速度计产生高达 14 MeV 的高能中子，这种方法是用带电粒子轰击目标来产生中子。

Historically, the first neutron tools consisted of a source and just a single detector but these were quite affected by borehole environment and most tools now have two detectors, a near and far (Fig.10.2). Neutron detection is not simple and consists of a two-step process. First, the neutrons react with a material to produce charged, energetic particles; these, in turn, are detected through their ionizing ability. Thus a detector will consist of a target material and a proportional counter. The most common tool detectors are based on the ^{3}He n, p (n-p) reaction in which ^{3}He is used as both a target and proportional gas in a counter.

历史上第一个中子测井仪器是由一个中子源和一个探测器组成，但这种仪器受到井眼环境的影响很大，因此目前大多数仪器都使用两个探测器，一个近探测器和一个远探测器

(图 10.2)。仪器检测中子包括两步过程，首先，中子与物质发生反应，产生带电高能粒子；之后，通过它们的电离能力来检测它们。因此，检测器由靶点和计数器组成。最常见的仪器基于 ^{3}He 反应，其中 ^{3}He 既是目标，也是计数器内成比例的气体。

The efficiency of these counters varies inversely with the square root of the neutron energy. They therefore respond primarily to thermal neutrons (lower energy). If epithermal neutrons are to be sensed the same detectors can be used but covered by a cadmium sheath which effectively absorbs the thermal neutrons, leaving only the epithermal neutrons to pass. The most commonly used tools now use thermal-epithermal neutron detection but tools also exist for epithermal detection or even gamma rays of capture.

这些计数器的计数率与中子能量的平方根成反比。因此，它们主要响应热中子（能量较低）。如果要检测到超热中子，可以使用相同的探测器，但是要用镉鞘进行覆盖，才能有效地吸收热中子，仅留下超热中子通过。目前常用的测井仪器主要使用热—超热中子探测，但也有用于超热探测甚至伽马射线捕获的探测仪。

In the tool, both source and detectors are placed on a skid pressed against the borehole wall (Fig.10.2). The two detectors are placed along the skid, away from the source, at a distance calculated from the slowing down length so that they are mainly in the area of thermal neutron energy in typical formations. The tool results are given by a ratio of the near detector/far detector counts, thereby eliminating borehole effects as much as possible. This is because the far detector readings, which contain both hole and formation effects, are 'corrected' by the near detector readings which have mainly hole effects, leaving only the effects of the formation. The ratio results are presented on the log as neutron porosity units after empirical calibration.

在该仪器中，中子源和探测器都固定在井壁上的滑道上（图 10.2）。两个探测器沿着滑道远离中子源放置，其距离由减速长度计算，因此它们主要位于典型地层中的热中子能量区域。仪器测量结果由短源距探测器/长源距探测器计数的比值来表示，从而尽可能地消除井眼影响。这是因为包含井眼效应和地层效应的长源距探测器读数可以由主要包含井眼效应的短源距探测器读数"校正"，仅留下地层的影响。在经验校正之后，比值结果以中子孔隙度单位显示在测井曲线上。

10.4 Application of Neutron Log
中子测井的用途

10.4.1 Quantitative Uses
定量评价

10.4.1.1 Porosity
孔隙度

The neutron log is used to derive porosity. The tool, as indicated above, measures hydrogen abundance or hydrogen index. In clean, water-bearing formations, the only hydrogen present is in the formation water (H$_2$O). The neutron tool therefore responds to the volume of water filled pore space, and gives a measure of the porosity. Expressed mathematically,

中子测井被用于计算孔隙度。如上所述，该测井仪器测量地层的含氢丰度或氢指数。在纯水层中，唯一的氢存在于地层水（H$_2$O）中。因此，当中子测井对充满水的孔隙空间体积进行测量响应时，便可给出孔隙度的量度。以数学方式表达为

$$\log_{10}\phi = aN + B \tag{10.1}$$

where ϕ is the true porosity, a, B are constants, and N is the neutron-tool reading.
其中，ϕ 为真实孔隙度；a、B 为常数；N 为中子测井的读数。

However, calibration is necessary for the above calculation as matrix materials have differing effects on the neutron log which change with porosity. A water-filled sandstone with 20% porosity gives a different neutron log reading to water-filled limestone with 20% porosity (Fig.10.3). Alternatively, if very accurate results are required, for example in a field study, the neutron log porosities can be compared to measured core porosities (Fig.10.4). The empirical calibration allows zones not cored to be accurately and confidently interpreted.

然而，上述计算必须进行必要的校准，因为岩石骨架对中子测井具有不同的影响，而中子测井随孔隙度的变化而变化。孔隙度为 20% 的饱和水砂岩与孔隙度为 20% 的饱和水石灰岩的中子测井读数不同（图 10.3）。另外，如果需要非常精确的结果，例如在现场研究中，可以将中子测井孔隙度与实测岩心孔隙度进行比较（图 10.4），校准后的结果用于没有岩心数据区域的测井解释。

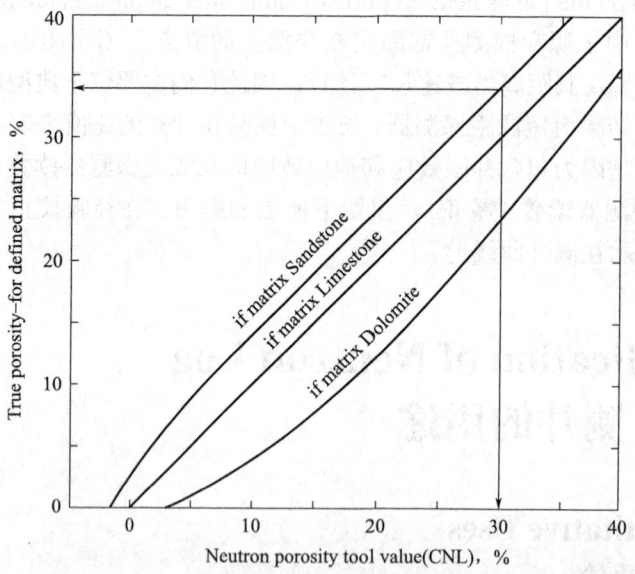

Fig.10.3 Graph for deriving the true porosity from a Schlumberger CNL tool values for defined sandstone, limestone and dolomite matrices (from Schlumberger, 1972)

Note that only the limestone matrix gives a 1/1 relationship. Example: tool neutron porosity =30%, true porosity for sandstone matrix =34%

图 10.3 用于定义砂岩、石灰岩和白云岩基质的斯伦贝谢 CNL 仪器值的真实孔隙度图（斯伦贝谢，1972）

只有石灰岩关系为 1/1。例如：测井中子孔隙度 = 30%，砂岩的真实孔隙度 = 34%

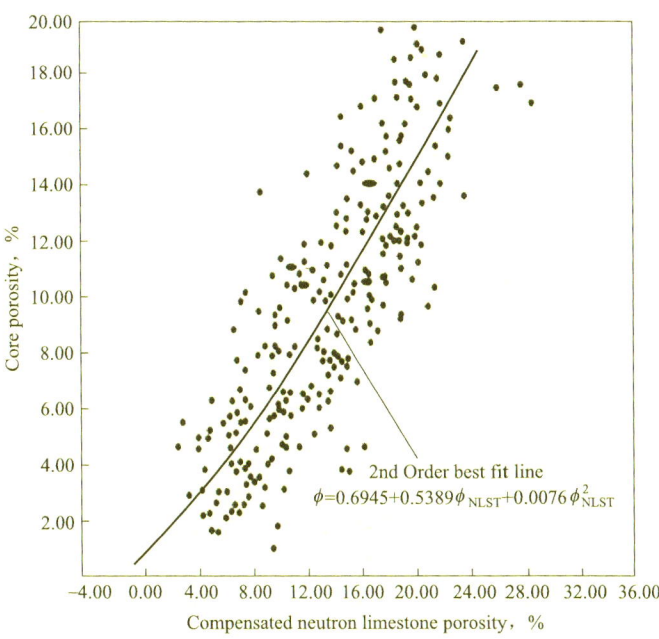

Fig.10.4　Compensated neutron log values plotted against core porosity values (points with grain densities between 2.84 – 2.88g/cm³) (from McFadzean, 1983)

图 10.4　针对岩心孔隙度值绘制的补偿中子测井值（颗粒密度 2.84～2.88g/cm³ 的点）

（据 McFadzean，1983）

10.4.1.2　Shale Effects on Neutron Porosity
泥岩对中子孔隙度的影响

Since the neutron log is sensitive to all hydrogen nuclei, it is sensitive to both free and bound water. The former is formation water, the latter occurs in clays either within the molecule or adsorbed between clay mineral layers.

由于中子测井对所有氢核都敏感，因此它对自由水和束缚水都敏感。前者是地层水，后者存在于黏土分子内或吸附在黏土矿物层之间。

Slight admixtures of shale with reservoir matrix material therefore disrupt neutron porosity values, and the true porosity cannot be calculated without corrections. The example (Fig.10.5) shows that the neutron porosity stays constant while the true porosity varies considerably.

因此，泥岩与储层岩石骨架的轻微混合会破坏中子孔隙度值，因此，如果没有校正，就无法计算出真实孔隙度。示例（图 10.5）表明，中子孔隙度保持不变，而真实孔隙度变化很大。

A study of shaly sandstones showed that in quartz-clay mixtures the hydrogen indexes of wet clay and formation water are very similar. In other words, the neutron log is incapable of separating wet clay from water. Cross-plotting gamma ray values (as a clay indicator) against neutron log values illustrates this. The gamma ray log shows diminishing clay volume and the neutron maintains a constant value (Fig.10.6). The neutron-derived porosity is therefore erroneous and the neutron cannot be used to derive a clay volume. In shaly sandstones, therefore, the neutron porosity value should not be used.

对泥质砂岩的研究表明，在石英-黏土混合物中，湿黏土和地层水的氢指数非常相似。换句话说，中子测井不能将湿黏土从水中分离出来。交叉绘制伽马射线值（作为黏土指示器）与中子测井值说明了这一点。伽马射线测井显示黏土体积逐渐减小，中子孔隙度保持恒定值（图10.6）。因此，中子孔隙度是错误的，中子不能用于得出黏土体积。因此，在泥质砂岩中，不应使用中子孔隙度值。

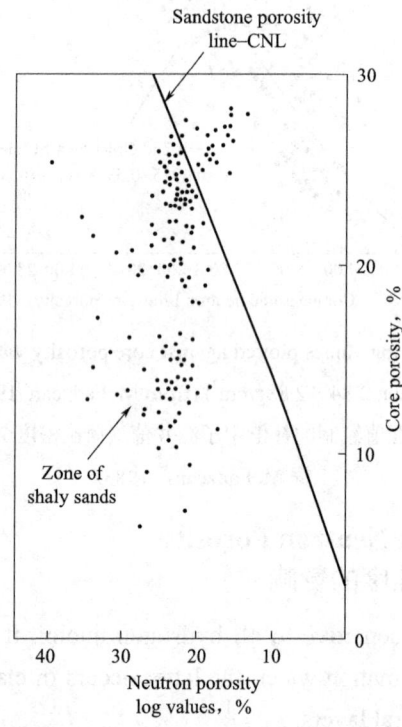

Fig.10.5　The effect of shale on neutron porosity values (from Malcolm Rider, 2002)

The neutron log registers shale as porosity (water). The true porosities should fall along the diagonal line (compare Figure 10. 6)

图10.5　泥岩对中子孔隙度值的影响（据 Malcolm Rider,2002）

中子测井将泥岩记录为孔隙度（水），真正的孔隙应沿对角线下降（比较图10.6）

10.4.2　Qualitative Uses
定性评价

10.4.2.1　Lithology Identification
岩性识别

The use of the neutron log to identify lithologies depends on an understanding of the distribution of the hydrogen index in natural materials.

使用中子测井来识别岩性取决于对不同岩石中氢指数分布的理解。

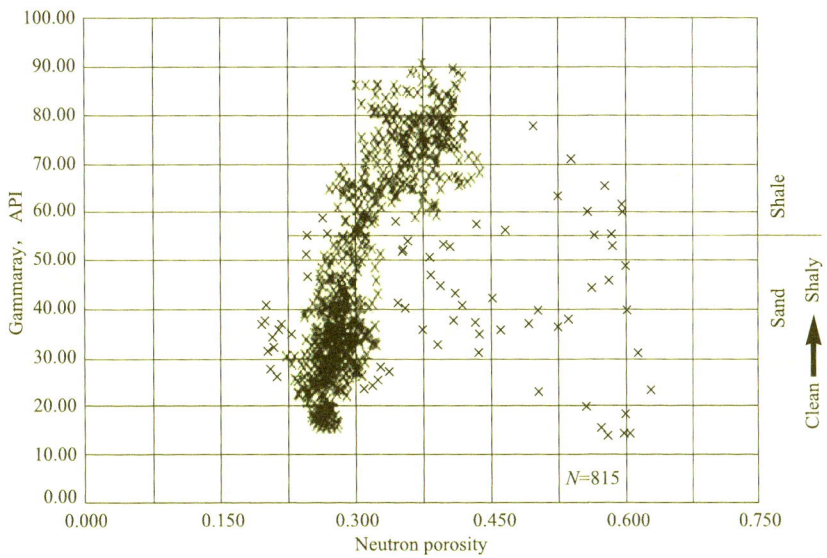

Fig.10.6 Neutron log values cross-plotted with gamma ray values in a shaly sand formation

(from Malcolm Rider, 2002)

The neutron log indicates the same porosity in shaly sands, with gamma ray values between 40-55 API, as in the clean sands with gamma ray values below 40 API. This is not the case, porosities are lower in the shaly sands (compare with Fig.10.5)

图 10.6 中子测井值与泥质砂层中的伽马射线值交叉绘制（据 Malcolm Rider,2002）

中子测井表明在泥质砂岩中具有相同的孔隙度，伽马射线值在 40 ～ 55 API 之间，如在纯净的砂岩中，伽马射线值低于 40 API。事实并非如此，泥质砂岩中的孔隙度较低（与图 10.5 相比）

The hydrogen detected by the neutron tool occurs in two principal chemical combinations, one between hydrogen and carbon (the hydrocarbons), and one between hydrogen and oxygen (simply water). Hydrocarbons occur as gases (methane, etc.), as liquids (oil, bitumen, etc.) or as solids (coal, organic matter). Water occurs as free water (in pores), as adsorbed ions (as in clay interlayer zones), as water of crystallization (as in evaporites), or as combined water (as in igneous rocks).

由中子测井检测到的氢主要存在于两种化学组合中，一种在氢和碳（碳氢化合物）中，一种在氢和氧（简单地说就是水）中。碳氢化合物以气体（甲烷等）、液体（石油、沥青等）或固体（煤、有机物）的形式存在。水以游离水（在孔隙中）、吸附离子（如在黏土层间带中）、结晶水（如在蒸发物中）或结合水（如在火成岩中）的形式存在。

The lithologies in which these various forms of combined hydrogen are found have hydrogen indexes which cover almost the entire scale between 1 and 0. (Table 10.2) Probably only pure water can be recognized categorically by its hydrogen index, which is 1. However, the neutron log gives an extremely sensitive reflection of lithological characteristics and changes, and combined with other log responses the hydrogen index becomes diagnostic.

这些各种形式的组合氢的岩性中，氢指数几乎涵盖了 1 到 0 之间的整个范围（表 10.2）。可能只有氢指数为 1 的纯水才能被直接识别。然而，中子测井能够非常敏感地反映岩性特征和变化，结合其他测井响应，氢指数具有诊断意义。

Table 10.2 Neutron log values of some common lithologies
(from Serra, 1979; Edmundson and Raymer, 1979)

	Limestone porosity units CNL	Hydrogen index
Water, (fresh)	100	1.00
Water, (salt)	60⁺	0.90
Quartz	−2	0.01
Sandstones*	−2 to 25	
Calcite	−1	—
Limestones*	−1 to 30	
Dolomite	1	—
Dolomites*	1 to 30	
Shales	25 to 75	0.09 to 0.37
Coal (lignite)	52	0.66
Coal (anthracite)	38	0.40
Methane	(20 to 50)	0.49

N. B. *Approximate ranges up to 30% porosity; ⁺200°F, 7000 psi.

表 10.2 一些常见岩性的中子测井值（据 Serra，1979; Edmundson 和 Raymer，1979）

	石灰岩孔隙度单位 CNL	氢指数
淡水	100	1.00
盐水	60⁺	0.90
石英	−2	0.01
砂岩*	−2～25	
方解石	−1	—
石灰岩*	−1～30	
白云石	1	—
白云岩*	1～30	
页岩	25～75	0.09～0.37
褐煤	52	0.66
无烟煤	38	0.40
甲烷	(20～50)	0.49

注：*代表孔隙度大约为 30%；⁺200°F，7000 psi。

Table 10.3 Combined water in clay (from Weaver et al, 1973; Serma, 1979)

Clay type	S_w(av.), %	Hydrogen index	Neutron porosity, %
Elite	8	0.06	30
Kaolinite	13	0.37	37
Chlorite	14	0.32	52
Smectite	18–22	0.17	44

表 10.3 黏土中的结合水（据 Weaver 等，1973；Serma，1979）

黏土类型	平均含水率, %	氢指数	中子孔隙度, %
伊犁石	8	0.06	30
高岭石	13	0.37	37
亚氯酸岩	14	0.32	52
蒙脱石	18～22	0.17	44

10.4.3 Neutron-density Combination: Lithology Identification
中子密度组合：岩性识别

10.4.3.1 Clean Formations
纯地层

By themselves, both the neutron and the density log are difficult to use for gross lithology identification. However, once combined, they become probably the best available indicator for the reasons given below.

中子和密度测井本身都难以用于总体岩性识别。但是，一旦组合起来，它们可能成为最佳岩性识别指标，原因如下。

Both the neutron log and the density log should be showing the same formation parameter - porosity. Plotted on compatible porosity scales, they should give identical values and it should be possible to superimpose the two logs (Fig.10.7). In practice, this is only the case in clean, water-filled limestones, which give almost perfectly superimposable logs, as shown in Fig.10.7.

中子测井和密度测井都能反映相同的地层参数——孔隙度。在相同的孔隙度尺度上绘制，将两个测井值进行叠合对比，它们应该给出相同的值（图 10.7）。在实际中，这种情况只发生在纯净的、充满水的石灰岩中，如图 10.7 所示，两种测井值几乎完全叠合。

The explanations can be taken in two stages. Firstly, the scales of the two logs are made compatible (normally) on a clean-limestone scale. A neutron-log value of zero (no porosity, 100% matrix) corresponds to a bulk density of 2.70 g/cm^3 (the density of pure calcite is 2.71g/cm^3), and so on to a neutron value of 100 (100% fluid) and a density of 1.0 g/cm^3 (the density of fresh water) (Fig.10.8). A cross-plot of density-log values against neutron-log values will show a straight-line relationship, a point on the line corresponding to a particular porosity (Fig.10.8). This is the 'clean-limestone line'.

解释可以分两步进行。首先，两种测井在纯净的石灰岩上的尺度（通常）是重叠的。中子测井值为零（无孔隙度，100％岩石骨架）时，对应的体积密度是2.70g/cm³（纯方解石的密度为2.71g/cm³）。以此类推，中子值为100（100％流体）时，对应的密度为1.0g/cm³（即淡水的密度）（图10.8）。密度—中子测井交汇图将显示一条直线关系，该线上的每个点都对应于特定的孔隙度（图10.8），这就是"纯净的石灰岩线"。

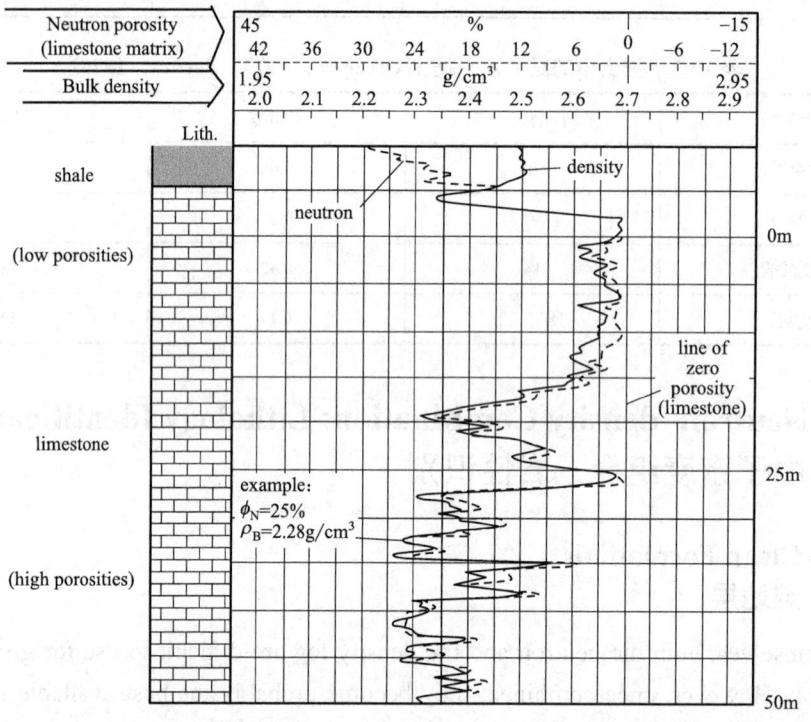

Fig.10.7 Neutron porosity log and bulk density log plotted on compatible scales(from Malcolm Rider, 2002)
The neutron porosity is displayed with a scale for a limestone matrix: the density for a matrix of 2.70g/cm³ (= zero porosity). The two logs follow each other closely over the limestone interval. Example: ϕ_N=25%. Bulk density =2.28g/cm³.
See Figure 10-8 for cross-plot position

图 10.7 在相同尺度上绘制的中子孔隙度测井和体积密度测井（据 Malcolm Rider,2002）
中子孔隙度用石灰石基质的比例显示：基质的密度为2.70g/cm³（孔隙度为0）。这两个测井在石灰岩层段上紧密相连。示例：
ϕ_N=25％。ρ_B（体积密度）=2.28g/cm³。有关交会图的位置，请参见图 10.8

The second stage of the explanation is that the straight-line relationship only holds good for clean limestone because matrix material has variable effects on both logs. A sandstone is seen differently from a limestone by the density log because of a different matrix density and by the neutron log because of the different matrix effect (Fig.10.8). On the cross-plot of density-log values against neutron-log values, the clean sandstone line plots as shown on Fig.10.8. Again, a point on this line corresponds to a clean sandstone with a particular porosity. In the same way a 'clean-dolomite line' may also be constructed (Fig.10.8).

解释的第二阶段是，直线关系仅适用于纯净的石灰岩，因为岩石骨架对两种测井都有不同程度的影响。在密度测井和中子测井中，砂岩和灰岩的差异由于岩石骨架密度的不同，具有不同的效应（图 10.8）。在密度—中子测井交会图上，纯净的砂岩线如图 10.8 所示。同样，该线上的每一点都对应具有特定孔隙度的纯净砂岩。用同样的方式也可以构建"纯净白云岩线"（图 10.8）。

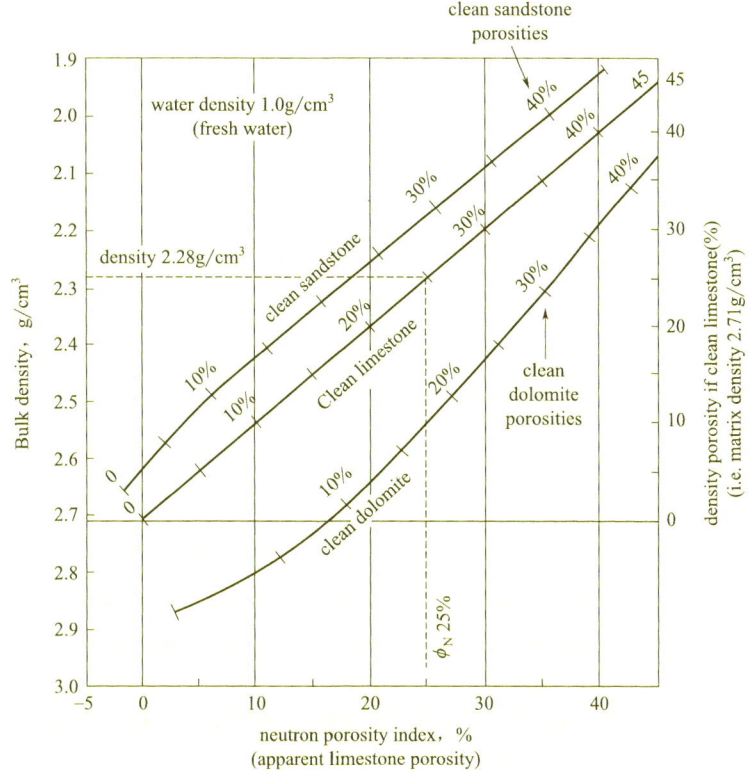

Fig.10.8　Cross-plot for Schlumberger FDC-CNL logs in fresh water-filled sandstone (from Schlumberger, 1979)

The plot is necessary to find real, clean formation porosities because of the differing effects of matrix type on the two logs. Example: density 2.28g/cm³, ϕ_N=25%: real porosity 25%, lithology clean limestone (cf. Fig.10.7)

图 10.8　FDC-CNL 测井在淡水饱和砂岩中的交会图（据 Schlumberger，1979）

由于基质类型对两种测井的不同影响，该图必须要首先找到纯地层的孔隙度。例如：密度 2.28g/cm³、ϕ_N=25%为真实孔隙度25%、岩性纯净的石灰岩（参见图 10.7）

For logs plotted on compatible scales, the variations in matrix are translated into a separation of the curves and this is used for lithology identification. A clean limestone shows no separation, while for a clean sandstone the separation is slightly negative and for a clean dolomite moderately positive (Fig.10.9). For a constant matrix the absolute values will change with variations in porosity, but the separation will remain more or less constant (e.g. Fig.10.7).

对于在相同尺度上绘制的测井曲线，岩石骨架的变化转换为曲线的分离，用于岩性识别。纯净的石灰岩没有分离，而纯净的砂岩有轻微的负分离，纯净的白云岩则有中度的正分离（图 10.9）。对于保持不变的岩石骨架，测井曲线读值将随孔隙度的变化而变化，但将保持或多或少恒定的曲线分离（如图 10.7）。

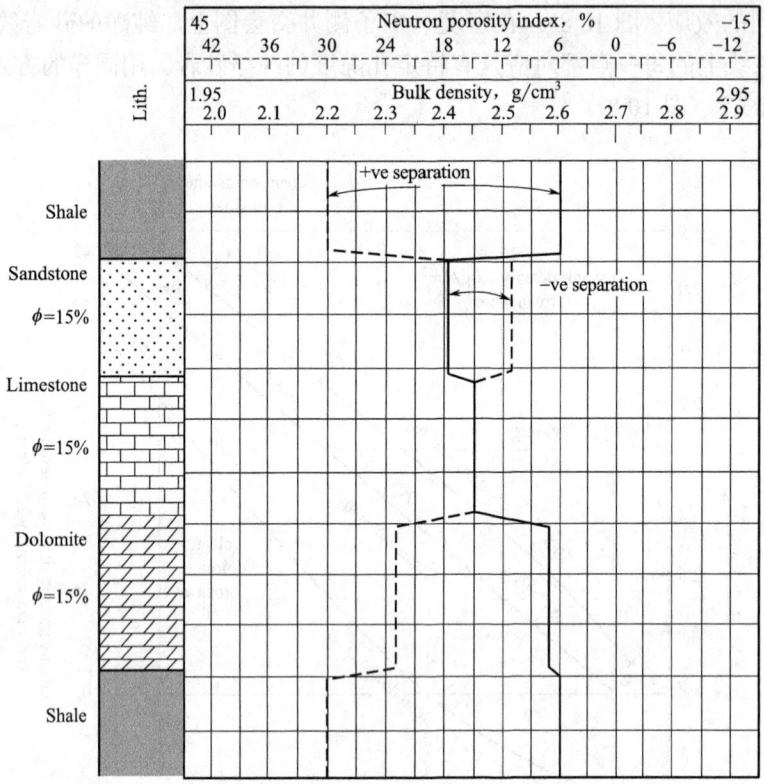

Fig.10.9 Idealized neutron-density log combination responses (from Malcolm Rider, 2002)

The figure shows clean sandstone, limestone and dolomite, all with 15% water-filled porosity

图 10.9 理想化的中子密度测井组合响应（据 Malcolm Rider, 2002）

该图显示了纯净的砂岩、石灰岩和白云石，都具有 15% 的饱和水孔隙度

10.4.3.2 Shale and Shaly Formations
页岩和泥质地层

Clean formations and the ideal reactions described above are only the minority of cases. Shale is usually present. Pure shale is recognized on the neutron-density combination when the neutron value is high relative to the density value. It gives a large positive separation to the logs, the neutron well to the left of the density. This separation is typical and diagnostic (Fig.10.9) and is due to the high hydrogen index of shale matrix material.

纯净的地层和上述理想的测井响应只是少数情况。泥岩总是存在的。当中子值相对于密度值高时，在中子密度组合上可以识别出纯泥岩。测井曲线正幅度差明显，即中子测井值在密度值的左边。泥岩氢指数较高，因此这种幅度差是典型泥岩的识别标志（图 10.9）。

If shale becomes diluted by matrix grains such as quartz or calcite with low hydrogen indexes, the neutron-log value decreases rapidly. Such a change is not seen markedly on the density log since the matrix density of shales (2.65–2.7g/cm^3) is similar to that of quartz and calcite (2.65–2.71g/cm^3). On the log combination, the result is a decrease in the neutron-log value and a decrease in the log separation. The decreases continue until clean formation values are reached.

如果泥岩混有低氢指数的石英或方解石岩石骨架颗粒，则中子测井值会迅速下降。由于泥岩（2.65～2.7g/cm³）的岩石骨架密度与石英和方解石的岩石骨架密度（2.65～2.71g/cm³）相似，因此在密度测井中没有明显的变化。反映在测井组合中，是中子测井值的减少以及曲线幅度差的降低。这种变化持续下降，直至达到纯净地层。

Ideally, the changes from pure shale to clean formation are progressive on both logs as the volume of shale decreases. The relationship can be considered as roughly linear. A 50% shale mixture should thus show 50% of the change from pure shale to clean formation. Qualitatively large or small separations can be considered to indicate more or less shale. In practice, small separations and slightly shaly formations tend to be related to low neutron values, while pure shales show large positive separation and high neutron values.

理想情况下，随着泥岩体积的减少，两种测井曲线从纯泥岩到纯地层的变化都是渐进的。这种关系可以被认为是近似线性的。因此，50%的泥岩混合物应显示了从纯泥岩到纯地层的50%的变化。定性地讲，幅度差的大小可被认为是泥岩多少的标志。实际上，较小幅度差和含微量泥质的地层往往与低中子值有关，而纯泥岩则表现出较大的正幅度差和高中子值。

If used properly, the neutron-density combination is the best log indicator of shale. It allows a more reliable indication than the gamma ray log and, at least qualitatively, can be used to evaluate the degree of shaliness. Therefore, as a shale indicator and with typical known separations in clean formations, the neutron-density combination can give a good idea of lithology in almost all normal formations.

如果使用得当，中子密度组合是泥岩的最佳测井指标。它比伽马射线测井更可靠，至少可以定性地用于估算泥质含量。因此，作为泥岩指示物，并且在纯净地层中具有典型的幅度差，中子密度组合可以在几乎所有正常地层中提供岩性的识别。

10.4.3.3　Distinctive lithologies and Minerals
特殊岩性和矿物

Certain minerals and some less common lithologies have very distinctive neutron and density values and show unusual neutron-density separations. Some of these are shown graphically on the neutron-density cross-plot grid (Fig.10.10). This figure shows clearly that on log plots some of these responses will be very distinctive and can be diagnostic. Coals, for example, are easily recognized from their very distinctive neutron-density response of unusually low density combined with unusually high neutron values. Pyrite, hematite and to some extent siderite, are recognized by having very high density values with zero neutron response.

某些矿物和一些不太常见的岩性具有非常独特的中子和密度值，并显示出不寻常的中子密度幅度差。其中一些在中子密度交会图网格上以图形方式显示（图10.10）。这张图清楚地表明，在测井对比图中，这些特殊的响应是可以作为岩性识别标志的。例如，很容易从非常独特的中子密度响应中识别出煤层，即异常低的密度值和异常高的中子值。黄铁矿、赤铁矿和某些情况下的菱铁矿具有非常高的密度值，且中子响应为零。

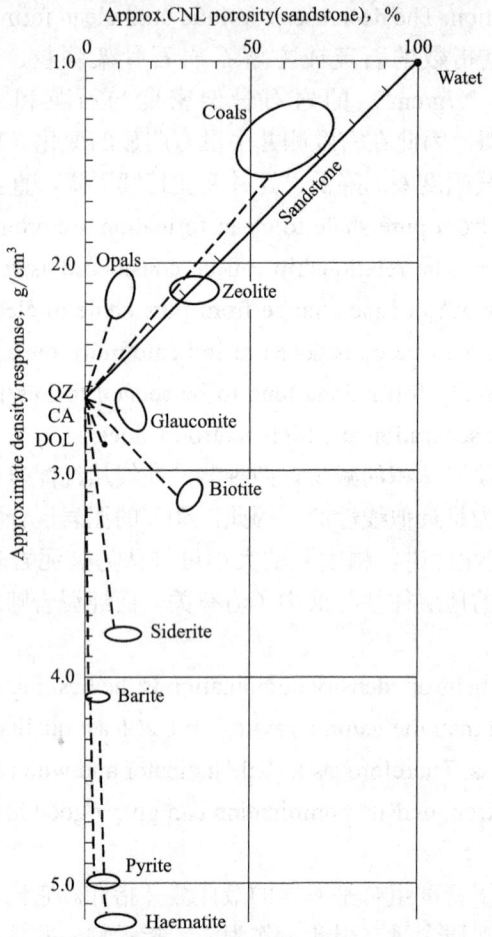

Fig.10.10 Neutron-density cross-plot with tentative locations of some zero-porosity, non-quartz materials (modified from Ransom, 1977)

图 10.10 中子密度交叉图（包含一些零孔隙度、非石英材料的暂定位置）（据 Ransom，1977，有修改）

A further, interesting example underlines the use of the combined neutron-density response in identifying unusual lithologies and minerals. On log plots, both the density and the neutron-log generally 'move together', a higher density corresponding to a lower neutron-log value. When a very high density value corresponds to an even higher neutron-log value, a simple lithological explanation is not possible.

下一个例子强调了中子密度交互响应在识别异常岩性和矿物中的应用。在测井图中，密度和中子测井通常"一起移动"，较高的密度值对应于较低的中子测井值。当非常高的密度值对应于更高的中子测井值时，不能进行简单的岩性解释。

The neutron-density combination is the best lithology indicator for most formations. Shales and shaliness and evaporites can be identified; clean formations and even matrix type can be suggested; and unusual minerals with the possibility of identification can be located.

中子密度组合是大多数地层的最佳岩性指标。不仅可以识别泥岩及泥质含量以及蒸发岩，还可以识别纯地层乃至岩石骨架类型，并且能识别部分特殊矿物。

Exercises
课后练习

10.1 What are uses of Neutron ?

10.2 State Neutron tool principle.

10.3 State gas effects on Neutron log.

10.4 State shale effects on Neutron log.

10.5 Which of the following is correct with respect to the effect of the presence of shale and gas on the Compensated Neutron tool?

(A) They have the similar effects, each causing the tool to read high porosities.

(B) They have similar effects, each causing the tool to read low porosities.

(C) They have opposite effects, shale causing the tool to read high and gas causing it to read low porosities.

10.6 When gas replaces oil in a clean sandstone, Density-Neutron log separation :

(A) increase   (B) decreases   (C) remains the same

10.7 A neutron log shows a neutron porosity of 20 percent limestone porosity. What would the porosity be in sandstone porosity units?

10.8 Indicate whether the following statement is True or False

Gas and Shale have opposing effects on the response of Neutron logs

(A) True   (B) False

10.9 Indicate whether the following statement is True or False

The density porosity tool is unable to differentiate between the primary and secondary porosity of a rock formation

(A) True   (B) False

10.10 You are working with porosity logs the header indicates that the logs are recorded on a "limestone matrix" and fluid density is 1.0 g/cc. The density porosity reading is 15% and the neutron pososity reading is 29%. What is the most likely lithology of the formation? The only choices are:

(A) Sandstone   (B) Limestone   (C) Dolemite

10.11 The table below shows the porosity values in limestone porosity units which were obtained across two formations. Determine the lithology and the effective porosity of each formation. Compute the effective porosity and as the average of the density and neutron porosities after they have been corrected to the correct rock matrix or lithology.

Formation	Density Porosity, %	Neutron Porosity, %
A	12	27
B	22	15

11 The Nuclear Magnetic Resonance Log
核磁共振测井

11.1 Generalities
概述

Magnetic resonance imaging (MRI) is one of the most valuable clinical diagnostic tools in health care today. These same nuclear magnetic resonance (NMR) principles, used to diagnose anomalies in the human body can be used to analyze the fluids held in the pore spaces of reservoir rocks. And, just as physicians do not need to be NMR experts to use MRI technology for effective medical diagnosis, neither do geologists, geophysicists, petroleum engineers, nor reservoir engineers need to be NMR experts to use MRI logging technology for reliable formation evaluation.

核磁共振成像（MRI）是当今医疗保健中最有效的临床诊断方法之一。利用与诊断人体异常相同的核磁共振原理，也可以对赋存在储层岩石孔隙中的流体进行分析。而且，就像医生不需要成为核磁共振专家就可以进行有效的医学诊断一样，地质学家、地球物理学家、石油工程师和油藏工程师也不需要成为核磁共振专家就可以利用核磁共振测井方法进行正确的地层评价。

11.2 Principle of NMR Physics
核磁共振的原理

Nuclear magnetic resonance (NMR) refers to the response of atomic nuclei to magnetic fields. Many nuclei have a net magnetic moment and angular momentum or spin. In the presence of an external magnetic field, an atomic nucleus processes around the direction of the external field in much the same way a gyroscope processes around the earth's gravitational field. When these spinning magnetic nuclei interact with the external magnetic fields, measurable signals can be produced.

核磁共振（NMR）是指原子核对磁场的响应。许多原子核都有净磁矩和角动量或自旋。当外部磁场存在时，原子核围绕着外部磁场的方向进动，就像陀螺仪绕着地球的重力场运动一样。当这些自旋的磁核与外部磁场相互作用时，就可以产生可测量的信号。

The nucleus of the hydrogen atom is a proton, which is a small, positively charged particle with an associated angular momentum or spin. The spinning proton represents a current loop that generates a magnetic field (or magnetic moment) with two poles (north and south) aligned with the spin axis. Therefore, the hydrogen nucleus can be considered as a bar magnet whose magnetic axis is aligned with the spin axis of the nucleus, as illustrated in Fig.11.1(left). When many hydrogen atoms are present and no external magnetic field exists, the hydrogen nuclear spin axes are randomly aligned, as seen in Fig.11.1(right).

氢原子核是质子。质子是一种带正电荷的小粒子，具有相应的角动量或自旋。自旋质子代表一个电流环，它产生一个磁场（或磁矩）。两极（北极和南极）与自旋轴对齐。因此，可以将氢核视为一个条形磁铁，其磁轴与原子核的自旋轴对齐，如图 11.1 左所示。当存在许多氢原子且无外部磁场存在时，氢核的自旋轴随机排列，如图 11.1 右所示。

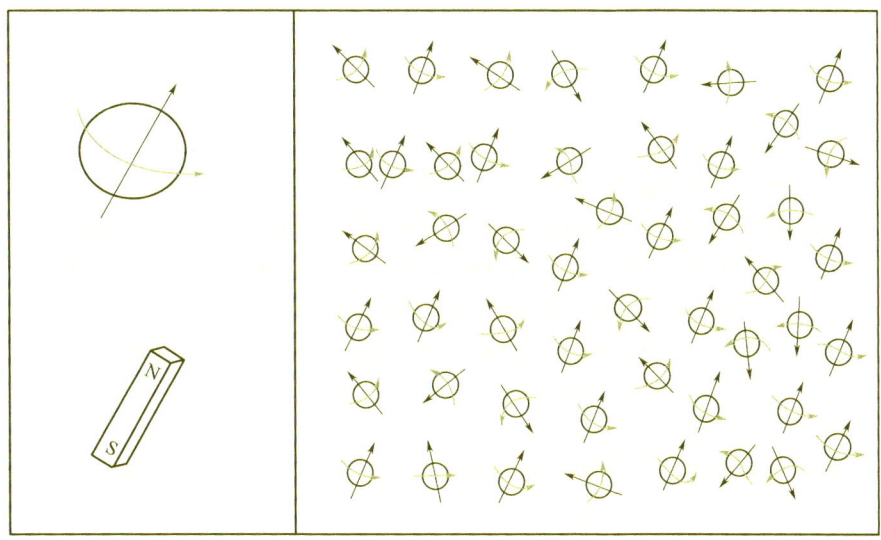

Fig.11.1　The spin of hydrogen atom (from George R. Coates, 1999)

Because of their inherent nuclear magnetism, hydrogen nuclei (left) behave as though they are tiny bar magnets aligned with the spin axes of the nuclei. In the absence of an external magnetic field, the nuclear magnetic axes (right) are randomly aligned

图 11.1　氢原子核的自旋（据 George R. Coates，1999）

由于其固有的核磁特性，氢原子核（左）自旋，犹如一个小磁轴。没有外部磁场时，单个核磁矩随机取向

The first step in making an NMR measurement is to align magnetic nuclei with a static magnetic field, B_0. When B_0 is applied to a magnetic nucleus, B_0 exerts a torque on the nucleus that acts to align the nuclear spin axis with B_0. When a torque is applied to a spinning object, the axis of the object moves perpendicular to the torque in a motion called precession, as illustrated in Fig.11.2(left). Thus, when B_0 is applied to a magnetic nucleus, the nucleus will precess around B_0. When a proton is subjected to an external magnetic field, the proton is forced into one of two energy states as indicated in Fig.11.2(right). After the protons are aligned in the static magnetic field, they are said to be polarized. Polarization does not occur immediately but rather grows with a time constant, which is the longitudinal relaxation time T_1.

核磁共振测量的第一步是将磁核与静磁场 B_0 对齐。当 B_0 作用于磁核时，B_0 对原子核施加一个力矩，使原子核的自旋轴与 B_0 对齐。当对旋转物体施加力矩时，该物体的轴垂直于力矩运动，称为进动，如图 11.2 左所示。因此，当 B_0 作用于一个磁性原子核时，该原子核将绕 B_0 进动。当质子受到外部磁场作用时，质子被强迫进入如图 11.2 右所示的两种能量状态之一。质子在外加静磁场中排列，被称为极化。极化不是即时完成的，而是随着时间常数，即纵向弛豫时间 T_1 而增长。

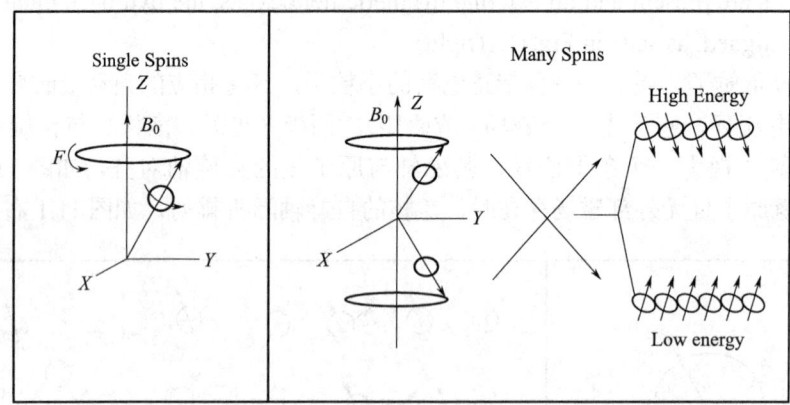

Fig.11.2　In an external magnetic field (left), the processional frequency of a nucleus depends on the gyromagnetic ratio of the nucleus and the strength of the external field. The alignment of the processional axis of the nucleus with respect to the direction of the external field (right) determines the energy state of the nucleus（from George R. Coates,1999）

图 11.2　在外部磁场中（左），原子核的进动频率与核的旋磁比以及外部磁场的强度有关，原子核的进动轴与外部磁场的方向决定着原子核的能级（据 George R. Coates,1999）

The second step in the NMR measurement cycle is to tip the magnetization from the longitudinal direction to a transverse plane. This tipping is accomplished by applying an oscillating magnetic field (B_1) perpendicular to B_0, the static magnetic field. For effective tipping, the frequency of B_1 must equal the Larmor frequency of the protons relative to B_0.

An oscillating magnetic field interacting with protons is illustrated in Fig.11.3. From the quantum mechanics point of view, if a proton is at the low-energy state, it may absorb energy provided by B_1 and jump to the high-energy state. The application of B_1 also causes the protons to precess in phase with one another. This change in energy state and in-phase precession caused by B_1 is called nuclear magnetic resonance.

核磁共振测量的第二步就是将磁化矢量从纵向扳转到横向平面。扳转是通过施加一个垂直于静态磁场 B_0 的交变磁场 B_1 来完成的。为了达到有效的扳转，B_1 的频率必须等于质子相对于 B_0 的拉莫尔频率。

交变磁场和质子的相互作用如图 11.3 所示。从量子力学的角度来看，如果质子处于低能态，它就会吸收由 B_1 提供的能量而跃迁到高能态。使用 B_1 还会使质子彼此同相进动。这种由 B_1 引起的能级的变化和同相进动就称为核磁共振。

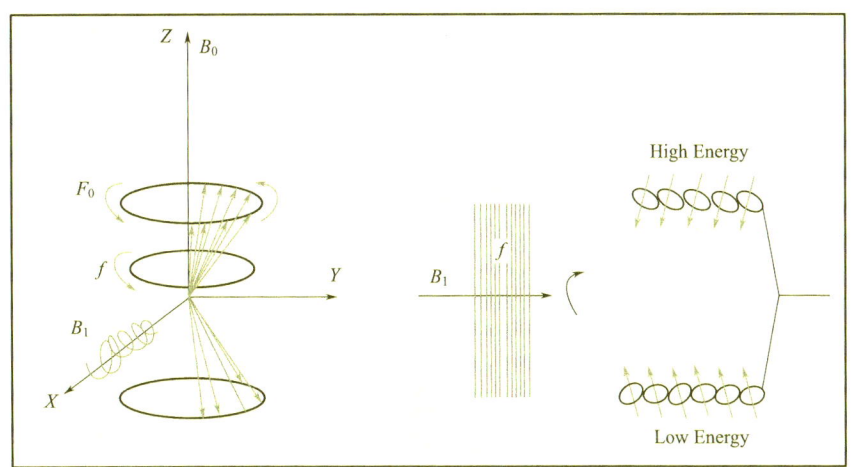

Fig.11.3 For effective interaction with protons (left), the oscillating magnetic field B_1 must have a substantial component perpendicular to the static field B_0 and must have frequency f equal to the proton's Larmor frequency f_0 in the static field. In this case (right), the protons will precess in phase with one another and may absorb energy from the oscillating field and change to the high-energy state. Nuclear magnetic resonance thus occurs

(from George R. Coates,1999)

图 11.3 为了产生对质子的有效作用（左），交变磁场 B_1 必须具有与静磁场 B_0 正交的实分量，而且其频率 f 必须等于质子在静磁场中的拉莫尔频率 f_0。在此情况下（右），质子相互之间将同相进动，从交变磁场吸收能量变为高能态（据 George R. Coates,1999）

11.3 Logging Tools of NMR
核磁共振测井仪

The basic structure of an MRIL instrument includes a probe short section (4½in, 4⅞in or 6in in diameter), an electronic circuit short section, and one or two capacitive short sections, as shown in Fig.11.4. Fluid excluders, centralizers, and isolators are optional, but are recommended to be selected according to the size of the wellbore.

MRIL 的基本结构包括探头短节，（直径 4½in，4⅞in 或 6in）、电子线路短节、一个或两个电容短节，如图 11.4 所示。流体排除器、扶正器和隔离器是可选项，但建议按照井眼尺寸进行选择。

The use of a fluid eliminator can reduce the loading effect of drilling fluid and increase the signal-to-noise ratio. Both the centralizer and the isolator are used to center the instrument in the wellbore. In addition, the isolator is also used to separate the fiberglass body from the casing and the well wall, thereby protecting the instrument.

使用流体排除器可以减少钻井液的负载影响，并增加信噪比。扶正器和隔离器用于保证仪器在井眼居中。另外，隔离器还用于将玻璃纤维体与套管和井壁分离，从而保护仪器。

The MRIL instrument is fully compatible with Halliburton's other naked-eye instruments, such as high-resolution array induction (HRAI), resistivity scanning (EMI), and per well acoustic scanning (CAST-V).

MRIL 与哈里伯顿公司的其他裸眼仪器完全兼容，如高分辨率阵列感应仪（HRAI）、电阻率扫描仪（EMI）和井周声波扫描仪（CAST-V）。

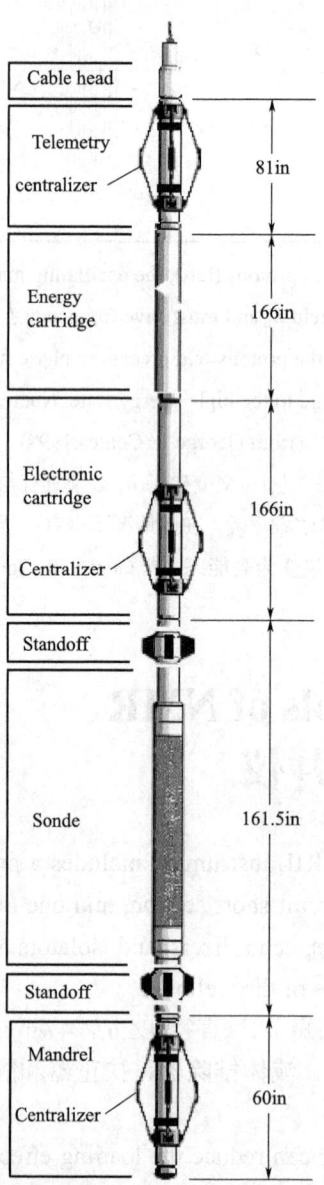

Fig.11.4 In its basic configuration, the MRIL tool consists of a magnetic mandrel, an electronics cartridge, and one or two energy-storage cartridges(from George R. Coates, 1999)

图 11.4 MRIL 仪器的基本结构包括探头短节、电子线路短节和 1～2 个电容短节

（据 George R. Coates, 1999）

11.4 Qualitative Uses of NMR
核磁共振测井的定量评价

11.4.1 Pore Size Distribution
孔径分布

When a water-wet rock is fully saturated with water, the T_2 value of a single pore is proportional to the surface-to-volume ratio of the pore, which is a measure of the size of the pore. Thus, the observed T_2 distribution of all the pores in the rock represents the pore-size distribution of the rock. Fig.11.5 compares the T_2 distribution of a brine saturated rock with the pore throat size distribution of the rock obtained from mercury injection data. The information from the mercury porosimetry incremental injection curve is difficult to quantify exactly, but it is essentially pore throat sizes weighted by the pore volumes to which the pore throats control access. As seen in the left of the Fig.11.5, when a shift is applied to account for factors such as surface relaxivity, the T_2 distribution shows a remarkable correlation with the pore throat size distribution. Although distributions from NMR and mercury can often be shifted to closely overlay each other, the distributions represent somewhat different rock properties. This good quantitative agreement is due to the correlations often seen among some properties of sedimentary rocks.

如前所述，当亲水岩石完全被水饱和时，单一孔隙的 T_2 值与孔隙的比表面（岩石中孔隙表面积与孔隙体积之比）成正比，这是衡量孔隙大小的指标。因此，观测到的岩石中所有孔隙的 T_2 分布代表了岩石的孔径分布。图 11.5 是饱和盐水岩石的 T_2 分布与压汞实验得到的岩石孔喉尺寸分布的对比。压汞曲线的信息通常难以准确量化，但它本质上是由孔喉控制进入的孔体积加权的孔喉大小。如图 11.5 左图所示，当考虑表面弛豫度等因子时，将曲线进行合理的移动，T_2 分布与孔喉尺寸分布有很好的相关性。尽管通过这种平移，核磁共振 T_2 谱与压汞曲线能够较好地重合在一起，但实际上两者反映的是岩石不同方面的性质。这种良好的定量一致性是由于沉积岩中某些性质之间具有相关性。

11.4.2 Estimating BVI
BVI 的分布确定

Estimating BVI, the bulk volume of irreducible water in a formation, is one of the earliest and still one of the most widely used applications of NMR logging. Currently, two methods are available for BVI determination. The first method, cutoff BVI (CBVI), is based on a fixed T_2 value ($T_{2cutoff}$) that divides the T_2 distribution into two components, one consisting of pore sizes containing bound water and the other consisting of pore sizes containing free fluids. The second method for BVI determination, called spectral BVI (SBVI), is based on the recognition that a given pore can contain both free and bound fluids.

估算 BVI，即地层中束缚水体积，是核磁共振测井最早的用途之一，也是目前应用最广泛的应用之一。目前有两种方法可用于测定 BVI。第一种方法是 BVI 截止值法（CBVI），是基于一个固定的 T_2 值（$T_{2cutoff}$，即 T_2 截止值），将 T_2 分布分为两部分，一部分表示包含束缚水的孔径，另一部分表示包含可动流体的孔径。第二种测定 BVI 的方法为 BVI 波谱法（SBVI），是基于对给定的、既含有束缚流体又含有可动流体的孔隙的认识来建立的。

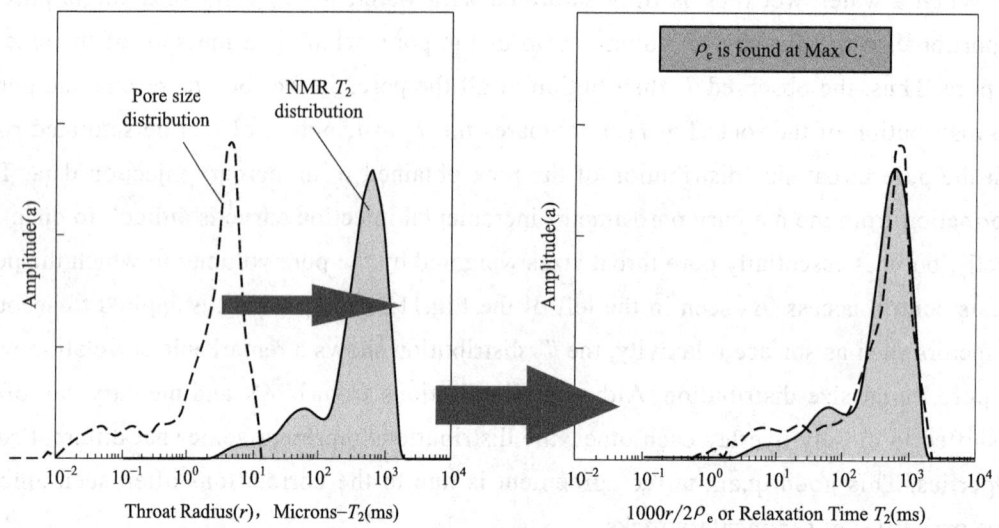

Fig.11.5　When shifted by the effective surface relaxivity, the pore-size distribution from mercury injection data nearly overlays the NMR T_2 distribution (from George R. Coates, 1999)

图 11.5　以有效表面弛豫为因子作适当移动，压汞曲线和核磁共振 T_2 分布基本重合

（据 George R. Coates,1999）

Fig.11.6 shows the CBVI concept. The NMR estimate of BVI is based on the assumption that bound fluids reside in small pores and producible fluids reside in large pores. This assumption is based on the fact that pore throat size and pore body size are often related. Because T_2 values can be related to pore body size, a T_2 value can be selected below which the corresponding fluids are expected to reside in small pores and are thus immobile, and above which the corresponding fluids are expected to reside in larger pores and thus can move freely. This T_2 value is called the $T_{2\,cutoff}$ ($T_{2\,cutoff}$). Through its partitioning of the T_2 distribution, the T_2 cutoff divides MPHI into two parts, BVI and FFI, as shown in Fig.11.6. The BVI portion is referred to as the CBVI.

图 11.6 解释了 CBVI 的概念。以这种方法估算 BVI 基于以下假设：束缚流体存在于小孔隙之中，而可动流体则存在于在大孔隙之中。这一假设是基于以下事实：孔隙喉道尺寸与孔隙尺寸相关。由于 T_2 值与孔隙尺寸相关，因此可以选择一个 T_2 值，小于此值，对应的流体驻留在小孔隙中，因此不可流动；大于此值，对应的流体则驻留在较大的孔隙

中，因此可自由流动。这个 T_2 值称为 $T_{2cutoff}$（T_2 截止值）。通过对 T_2 分布划分，$T_{2cutoff}$ 将 MPHI 分为两个部分，即 BVI 和 FFI，BVI 部分即 CBVI，如图 11-6 所示。

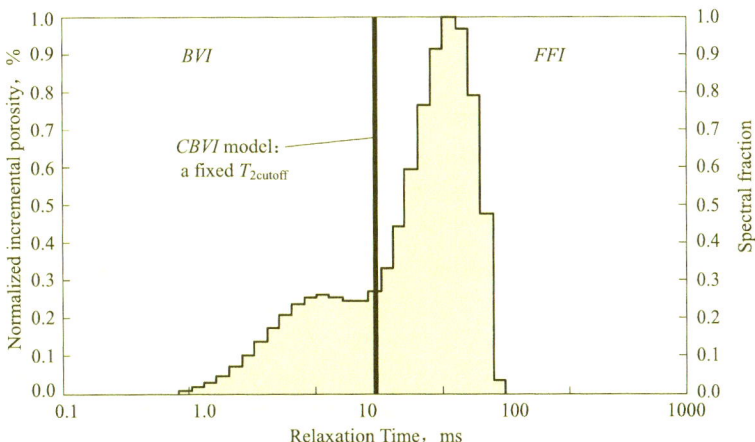

Fig.11.6 When a CBVI model is used for NMR log interpretation, a fixed $T_{2cutoff}$ is selected to calculate C (from George R. Coates, 1999)

图 11.6 当 CBVI 模型用作核磁共振测井解释时选择一个固定 $T_{2cutoff}$ 计算 BVI

（据 George R. Coates, 1999）

Instead of assuming a relaxation-time cutoff, a $T_{2cutoff}$ can be determined in the laboratory with NMR measurements on core samples. Core samples are analyzed for NMR characteristics at two saturation conditions, S_w=100% and (after establishing the appropriate value of saturation from a capillary-pressure curve, or directly desaturating the sample to the appropriate capillary pressure) S_w=irreducible. A centrifuge technique or a porous-plate technique at a specified capillary pressure is used to achieve the latter condition. The T_2 distributions are compared as illustrated in Fig.11.7. The two T_2 distributions are displayed in two ways: incremental porosity and cumulative porosity. The cumulative porosity at a particular T_2, say $T_{2,U}$, is the integral of the incremental porosity for all T_2 values less than or equal to $T_{2,U}$. The cumulative curves are used to determine $T_{2cutoff}$. To determine $T_{2cutoff}$ from a plot of T_2 vs. cumulative porosity, enter the plot from the cumulative porosity axis at the porosity at which the sample is at irreducible condition. Project horizontally to the cumulative porosity curve for S_w=100%. Upon intersecting this curve, project down to the T_2 axis. The T_2 value of the intersection of this projection with the T_2 axis is the $T_{2cutoff}$.

与假设弛豫时间截止值不同，$T_{2cutoff}$ 可以通过在实验室进行岩心样品的核磁共振测量来确定。岩心样品在两种饱和条件下进行核磁共振特征分析，即 S_w=100% 和 S_w= 束缚水饱和度（在根据毛管压力曲线确立适当的饱和度值后，或者直接将岩样脱干到适当的毛管压力之后）。为达到第二种饱和条件，可采用离心技术或在指定毛管压力下的隔板技术。T_2 的分布比较如图 11-7 所示。用两种方式显示这两个 T_2 分布，即孔隙度分量和孔隙度累加。在特定 T_2 的孔隙度累加称为 $T_{2,U}$，它是所有小于或等于 $T_{2,U}$ 的孔隙度分量的积分。可通过 T_2—孔隙度累加图来确定 $T_{2cutoff}$。要从 T_2 分布和孔隙度累加图上求 $T_{2cutoff}$ 时,需在岩样处于束缚水饱和度条件时在图中确定孔隙度累加,并作一条直线,该直线与 S_w=100% 条件下孔隙度累加曲线有一个交点,经过该交点投影于 T_2 轴,交点对应的 T_2 值就是 $T_{2cutoff}$。

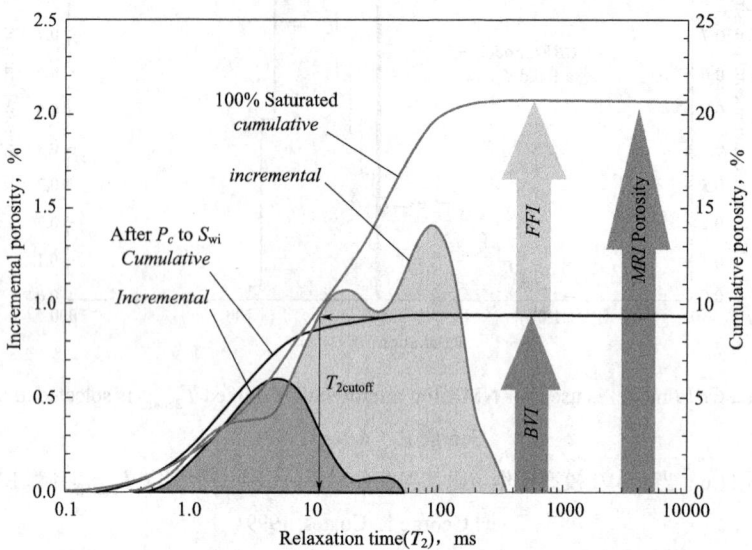

Fig.11.7　NMR measurements on fully saturated (S_w=100%) core samples and on samples at irreducible saturation (S_{wi}) can be used to establish a $T_{2cutoff}$ for use in a CBVI model (from George R. Coates, 1999)

图 11.7　对于完全饱和水 (S_{wi}=100%) 和束缚饱和水 (S_{wi}) 的岩样的核磁共振测量,可以确定 T_{2off},用于 CBVI 模型 (据 George R. Coates,1999)

11.4.3　Permeability Model
　　　　渗透率模型

　　In one expression, the Free Fluid (or Coates) model, the size parameter enters implicitly through $T_{2cutoff}$, which determines the ratio of FFI to BVI, where FFI is the free fluid volume and $FFI=\phi-BVI$. In the other expression, the Mean T_2 (or SDR) model, the size parameter enters through the geometrical mean of the relaxation spectra, T_{2gm}. The use of these particular size parameters in the respective expressions is based on empirical considerations. Other size measures have also been used.

　　表达式一采用自由流体模型或 Coates 模型,孔隙尺寸参数是通过决定了 FFI 与 BVI 比值的 T_{2off} 隐含输入的,其中 FFI 是可动流体体积,$FFI=\phi-BVI$。另一种表达式是采用平均 T_2 模型或 SDR 模型,孔隙尺寸的输入参数是驰豫时间 T_2 的几何平均值,T_{2gm}。在这些表达式中使用这些特定的尺寸参数是基于经验的考虑,还使用了其他尺寸测量方法。

11.4.4 The Free Fluid Model
自由流体模型

In the Free Fluid (or Coates) model, in its simplest form the permeability K is given by MPHI (MRIL porosity) is usually used for ϕ, and BVI is obtained through the CBVI or SBVI method. The coefficient C is a variable that is dependent on the processes that created the formation and can be different for each formation.

在自由流体模型中或 Coates 模型最简单的形式中,渗透率(K)由 MPHI(MRIL 孔隙度,通常记为 ϕ)给出。BVI 通过 CBVI 或 SBVI 方法得到,系数 C 是一个变量,它取决于地层的沉积过程,每个地层都可能不同。

$$K = \left[\left(\frac{\phi}{C}\right)^2 \left(\frac{FFI}{BVI}\right)\right]^2 \tag{11.1}$$

Experience has shown that the Coates model is more flexible than the Mean T_2 model. Through careful core calibration, the Coates model has been customized for successful use in different formations and reservoirs.

经验表明,Coates 模型比平均 T_2 模型更灵活。通过仔细的岩心标定,Coates 模型已经在不同地层和油藏中成功应用。

11.4.5 The Mean T_2 Model
平均 T_2 模型

The Mean T_2 (or SDR) model is given by
平均 T_2(或 SDR)模型由下式给出

$$K = a T_{2gm}^2 \phi^4 \tag{11.2}$$

NMR effective porosity is substituted for ϕ. As before, T_{2gm} is the geometric mean of the T_2 distribution. As with the Coates model, the value a is a coefficient that depends on the formation type. Experience has shown that the Mean T_2 model works very well in zones containing only water.

用核磁共振有效孔隙度代替 ϕ。如前所述,T_{2gm} 是 T_2 分布的几何平均值。与 Coates 模型一样,a 是一个取决于地层类型的系数。经验表明,平均 T_2 模型只在含水地层中应用良好。

11.4.6 Porosity Model
核磁孔隙度模型

The initial amplitude of the NMR spin-echo train, or the area under the T_2 distribution curve, is proportional to the number of hydrogen protons that are contained in the pore fluids within the sensitive volume. Thus, this amplitude can be calibrated to give a porosity value.

Fig.11.8 shows the NMR porosity model for a water-wet formation. The upper part of the figure is a typical volumetric model of the virgin zone, which consists of matrix and dry clay, clay bound water, capillary-bound water, movable water, oil, and gas. The middle part of the figure is the corresponding volumetric model for the invaded zone, which is the region in which MRIL measurements are made; all model elements remain the same as in the virgin zone except that the mud filtrate now displaces some of the movable water, oil, and gas. The bottom part of the figure illustrates the MRIL response to porosity elements. Note that MFFI refers to the same quantity as FFI, and MPHI does not include the contribution from some of the water that is associated with clay porosity and perhaps other materials with clay-size pores.

核磁共振自旋回波串的初始振幅，或 T_2 分布曲线围成的面积，与灵敏范围内孔隙流体中的氢核数量成正比。因此，可以对振幅进行校准，以给出孔隙度值。图 11.8 是亲水地层的核磁共振孔隙度模型。图的上半部分是典型的原状地层的体积模型，由岩石骨架和干黏土、黏土束缚水、毛管束缚水、可动水、油和气组成。该图的中间部分是侵入带对应的体积模型，是 MRIL 的测量范围。除了钻井液代替了部分可动水、油和气之外，所有模型元素都与原状地层模型相同。该图的下部是 MRIL 对各孔隙度分量的响应。注意 MFFI 与 FFI 数量相同，而 MPHI 不含与黏土孔隙度有关的水的贡献，也不包括具有黏土尺寸的其他物质。

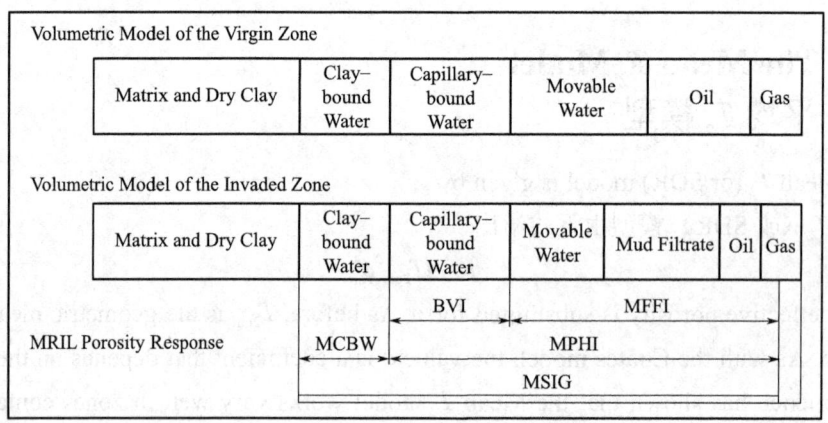

Fig.11.8　MRIL tools respond to the flushed zone (bottom volumetric model), in which mud filtrate has displaced some of the free fluids that were present in the virgin zone (top volumetric model). MRIL responses (bottom) are sensitive to fluids but not to matrix materials and dry clay. MRIL porosity is affected by hydrogen index (HI), polarization time (T_W), and inter-echo spacing (T_E) (from George R. Coates,1999)

图 11.8　MRIL 仪器对冲洗带的响应（底部模型）。在冲洗带，钻井液滤液已经置换了部分原存在于原状地层（顶部模型）中的自由流体。MRIL 响应（底部）对流体是灵敏的，但对骨架物质和干黏土不灵敏。MRIL 孔隙度受 HI、极化时间（T_W）和回波间隔（T_E）的影响（据 George R. Coates,1999）

Fig.11.8 shows sharp divisions between the porosity elements associated with MFFI, BVI, and MCBW. These sharp divisions in porosity elements do necessarily correspond to sharp divisions in the T_2 spectra. For BVI, this has already been discussed in detail. In the case of clays, the water associated with clays has a range of decay times that can overlap decay times for capillary-bound water; thus, a sharp division may not exist between MCBW and BVI in the T_2 spectra.

图 11.8 显示了与 MFFI、BVI 和 MCBW 相关的孔隙度分量之间的明显差异。这些孔隙度分量的明显划分必然对应 T_2 谱的明显划分。前文已经详细讨论过 BVI。在含黏土的情况下，黏土水具有一定的衰减时间，可能与毛管水重叠。因此，MCBW 和 BVI 在 T_2 谱上差异不明显。

Both matrix minerals and dry clay can contain hydrogen atoms in the form of hydroxyl groups (OH). Because the T_1 relaxation times of these nuclei are too long to be polarized by a moving MRIL tool, and their T_2 relaxation times are too short to be recorded, hydrogen in OH groups and in water of hydration is invisible to the MRIL tool. The hydrogen nuclei of clay-bound water are adsorbed on the surfaces of clay grains. These hydrogen protons in clay-bound water can be polarized by the MRIL tool and can be recorded as long as a sufficiently short T_E is used. The clay-bound water is measured by an MRIL CPMG sequence with T_E = 0.6 ms and with polarization time T_W set for partial or full recovery. The measurement yields the component of porosity referred to as MCBW, which provides an estimate of clay-bound water. Similarly, hydrogen protons exist in capillary-bound water and movable fluids, such as movable water, mud filtrates, oil, and gas. These hydrogen protons are measured using a standard T_2-logging CPMG sequence with T_E = 1.2ms and with T_W set for full polarization. This measurement yields MPHI.

岩石骨架矿物和干黏土都含有以羟基（OH）形式存在的氢原子。由于这些核的 T_1 弛豫时间太长，以致移动的测井仪不能使其极化，而且其 T_2 弛豫时间太短，以至于无法被记录，因此，MRIL 仪器无法识别羟基和化合水中的氢。黏土束缚水的氢核被吸附在黏土颗粒的表面，只要使用一个足够短的 T_E，这些束缚水中的氢核就可以由 MRIL 仪器极化并被记录下来。通过 MPIL 的 CPMG 序列测量黏土束缚水，T_E 为 0.6ms，极化时间 T_W 设置为部分或全部极化。测量得到的孔隙度分量称为 MCBW，它可以估算黏土束缚水。类似地，氢核存在于毛管束缚水、可动流体之中，如可动水、钻井液滤液、油和气。使用标准 T_2 测井 CPMG 脉冲序列测量这些氢原子，T_E 为 1.2ms，T_W 设置为全部极化。测量得到的是 MPHI。

Exercises
课后练习

11.1　State the principle of NMR log.

11.2　Examine the log display below.

(a) Give two reasons to predict zones A, B and C are permeable.

(b) Do zone A likely have the same fluid as in Zone C, Give one reason.

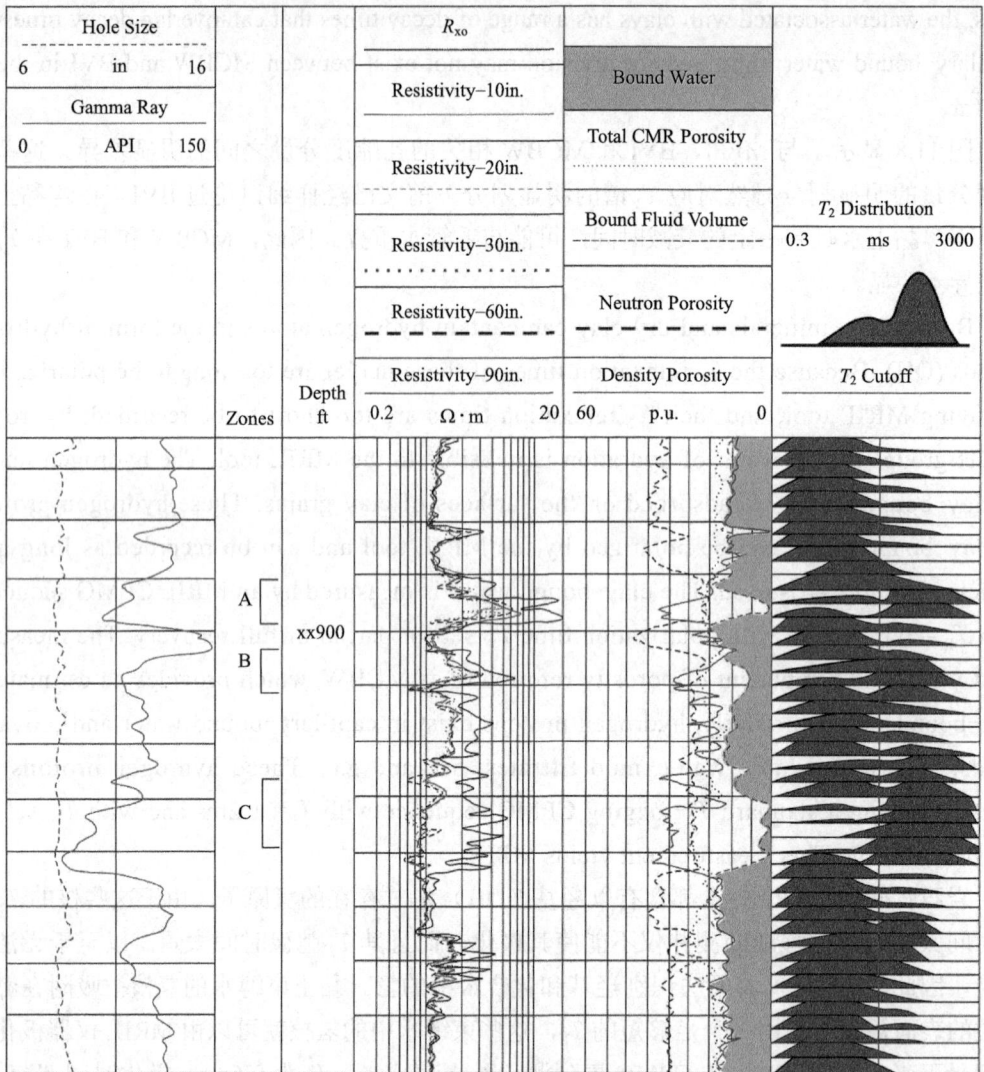

Fig.11.9 Logging curve

12 The Electrical Imaging Log
电成像测井

12.1 Generalities
概述

The electrical imaging tools use the detailed electrical response of a formation to create their images. These tools evolved from dip meter technology and now consist of a device with four or more pads similar to the dip meter. However, instead of one electrode per pad, there is a large array of very small electrode button. The fine resistivity responses of all of the electrodes are processed together, as a matrix, into an image. Necessarily, the electrical images are only measured immediately in front of each pad: a gap is in between the pads. The present electrical imaging tools give excellent, high resolution images while the gaps between pads remain.

电成像测井利用地层详细的电响应来实现其成像。电成像测井是从倾角测井技术发展而来的，一般由具有四个或更多类似于倾角仪的极板装置组成。一个极板并非仅一个电极，而是由大量的非常小的纽扣状小电极（电扣）组成。所有电扣的精细电阻率响应作为一个阵列一起处理，形成电阻率图像。由于极板只有接触地层才能测量得到电阻率，而且每个极板之间存在一定的间隙，因此电成像测井仪可提供高分辨率图像，但存在极板之间的成像间隙。

The standard presentation for image logs is the 'unwrapped borehole' format. The cylindrical borehole surface image is unzipped at the north azimuth and unrolled to a fiat strip (Fig.12.1). The compass points form the horizontal, X coordinates, the vertical Y axis, refer depth. In this way, a continuous representation can be made of the borehole either on a screen or as a hard copy log plot. Generally, 3-D formats exist only for on-screen display while the unwrapped borehole presentation has become the standard.

电成像测井的标准图像是圆柱面展开图。将圆柱形井眼图像在北方位拉开，展开成平坦条带图像（图12.1）。罗经点构成水平的X坐标，垂直向的Y轴代表深度。通过这种方式，便可以在屏幕上得到能连续展示井眼的数据图像或得到硬拷贝图。一般来说，3D格式仅用于屏幕显示，而展开的井眼平面图是成像测井的标准图像。

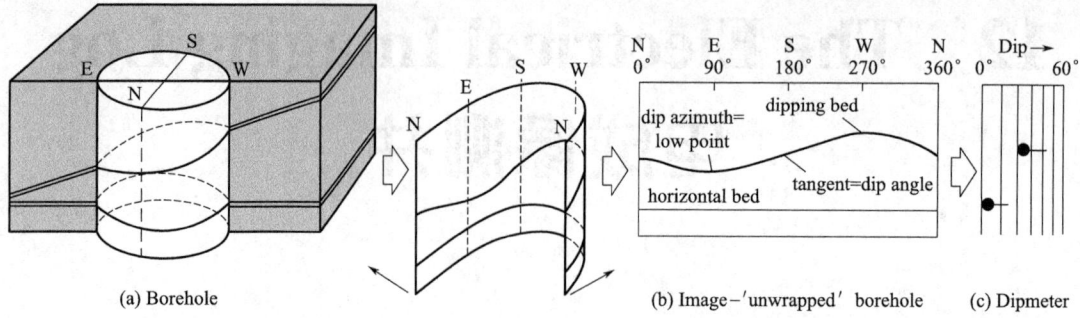

Fig.12.1　Representation of borehole wall images on a flat surface (from Malcolm Rider,2002)

The images derived from the cylindrical borehole (a) are presented on a flat surface (screen or hard copy log plot) by 'unwrapping' onto a vertical depth grid and horizontal grid of compass bearings. In this format (b) , horizontal and vertical surfaces are unchanged but dipping surfaces become represented by a sinusoid. Such dip and azimuth may be represented on a dipmeter tadpole plot (c)

图 12.1　平面上井眼壁图像展示（据 Malcolm Rider,2002）

这些图像来自圆柱形井眼（a）沿垂直的深度和水平的地层方向平面"展开"（即屏幕上的数据图像或硬拷贝图）。在这种格式中（b），水平和垂直表面不变，但倾斜的曲面由正弦曲线表示。倾角和方位角可以用倾角蝌蚪图（c）表示

12.2　Electrical Imaging Tools
　　　电成像测井仪

At present electrical imaging is dominated by Schlumberger, although new tools are being actively introduced by the other service companies. In the mid-1980s, Schlumberger introduced their first electrical imaging tool, the Formation Micro Scanner (FMS), as an evolution of their SHDT dipmeter. The first tools only provided an image of 20% of an 8.5in borehole, using just two pads. Since then there has been steady progress in borehole coverage and tool technology. The present tool, the Full bore Formation Micro Imager (FMI) provides nearly 80% coverage in an 8.5 in diameter borehole of high quality images. Since this is the most recent Schlumberger tool it will be used for description.

尽管其他测井公司也在积极推出新的成像测井仪，但目前斯伦贝谢公司仍然在成像测井方面全球领先。在 20 世纪 80 年代中期，斯伦贝谢在 SHDT 地层倾角仪的基础上开发出第一代电成像测井仪，即地层微电阻率扫描成像测井仪（FMS）。第一代只使用了两个极板，因此只能提供 8.5in 钻孔 20％的图像。从那时起，全井眼覆盖和测井技术一直在稳步发展。目前的全井眼地层微电阻率成像仪（FMI）能够在 8.5 英寸直径的井眼中提供近 80％覆盖率的高质量图像。由于其是斯伦贝谢最新的测井仪，因此将详细介绍。

The Schlumberger FMI consists of four pads on two orthogonal arms like the dipmeter (Fig.12.2), but in the imaging tool, the four pads each have a hinged flap so as to extend the area of electrical contact (Fig.12.3). Pad faces are curved to match borehole curvature. In order that the pads and flaps maintain contact with the formation, they are free to tilt independently of the tool body. Thus, when the tool is not parallel to the borehole wall, as frequently occurs in horizontal and highly deviated wells, the pads still remain in contact. In addition, the tool uses hydraulic self-centreing to improve pad contact, especially in horizontal wells, where the usual pad leaf springs are not adequate.

斯伦贝谢FMI像倾角仪一样,由两个正交臂上的四个类极板组成(图12.2),但在成像测井仪中,四个极板上各有一个铰链阀,以扩大电接触面积(图12.3)。极板是弯曲的,以匹配井眼形状。为了使极板与铰链阀与地层保持接触,每个臂可以独立于测井仪主体自由倾斜。因此,当测井仪与井壁不平行时,在水平和大斜度井中经常发生,极板仍然能保持与井眼地层接触。此外,该仪器还采用液压自定心技术来改善极板接触,特别是在常规极板弹框不足的水平井中。

As well as the tool circuitry, the body of the FMI tool houses the inclinometry (as in the dipmeter), and a digital telemetry sub (Fig.12.2). The upper part of the tool is insulated from the lower part and acts as a return electrode (see below). A gamma ray sonde can be added into the string and the entire tool may be nearly 15 m (50ft) long.

除了仪器电路外,FMI仪器的主体还包含倾角测量仪(如倾角仪)和数字遥测短节(图12.2)。仪器的上部与下部绝缘,并充当回路电极(见下文)。可以在仪器中加入一个伽马射线探测短节,整个仪器长约15米(50英尺)。

The unique design elements of the FMI are the pad and flap and electrode array. Pad and flap are both conductive and have inset, 24 individually insulated button electrodes,arranged in two rows of 12 (Fig.12.3). Individual buttons are 0.5cm (0.2in) apart and the two rows are separated by 0.75cm (0.3in) (Fig.12.3). The buttons of one row are offset 0.25 cm (0.1in) vertically compared to the other. The top row of buttons on the pad is 14.5 cm (5.7in) above the top row of buttons on the flap. When the tool is used with the flaps, 192 (8×24) button samples are recorded at every depth sample point around the borehole. The tool may also be run in four-pad mode when 96 (4×24) button samples will be recorded.

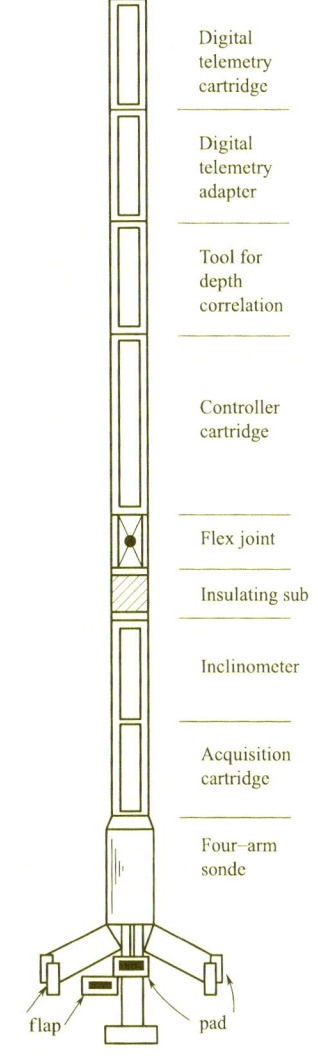

Fig.12.2 The FMI (Fullbore Formation Micro Imager) tool of Schlumberger (from Schlumberger, 1994)

图 12.2 斯伦贝谢的 FMI(全井眼地层微电阻率成像仪)设备(据 Schlumberger, 1994)

FMI的独特设计就是极板、铰链以及阵列电极。极板和铰链都是导电的,并嵌入24个单独绝缘的电扣,排成两排,每排12个(图12.3)。各个电扣间隔0.5cm(0.2in),两排之间间隔 0.75cm（0.3in）（图 12.3）。一排电扣与另一排相比垂直偏移 0.25cm（0.1in）。极板电扣的顶行比铰链电扣的顶行高 14.5cm（5.7in）。当测井仪与铰链一同使用时，井眼周围的每个深度采样点可记录 192 个（8×24）电扣测量数据。测井仪也可以在四极板模式下测量，记录 96 个（4×24）电扣测量数据。

  Button electrodes are 0.4cm (0.16in) in diameter but with surrounding insulation this increases to 0.6cm (0.24in) (Fig.12.3). With this arrangement, it is considered that the electrodes have a resolution of 0.5cm (0.2in). However, because the electrodes are offset vertically, the formation is sampled horizontally across the electrode array at half this distance, that is every 0.25 cm (0.1in) (Fig.12.3). At logging speeds of 1800 ft/h button currents are sampled vertically every 0.25 cm (0.1in). The tool, therefore, acquires a data matrix of 0.1in both vertically and horizontally in front of the pads and flaps (calipers, magnetometers and accelerometers are sampled every 3.8cm (1.5in).

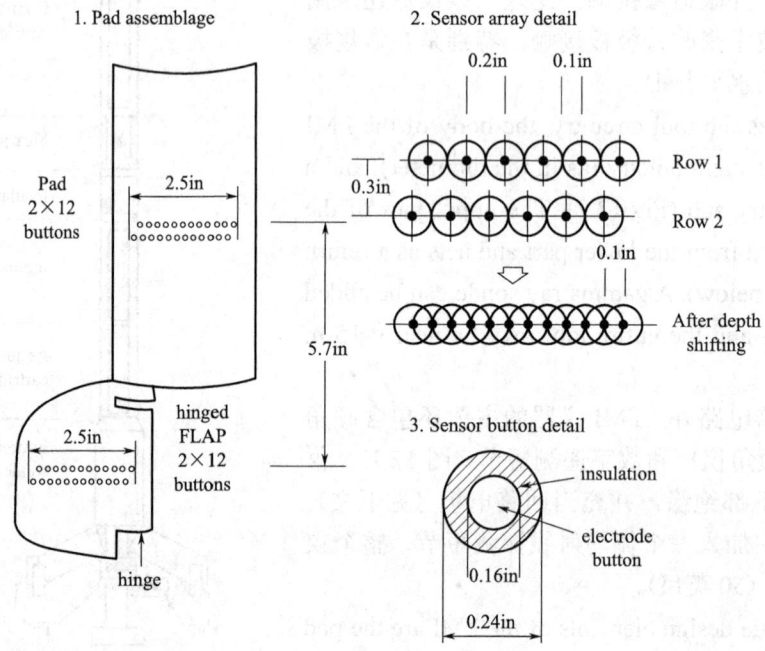

Fig.12.3 Pad assemblage and sensor detail from the Schlumberger FMI tool (from Schlumberger, 1994)
图 12.3 Schlumberger FMI 工具的极板组成和传感器细节（据 Schlumberger, 1994）

  电扣直径 0.4cm（0.16in），但周围绝缘，增加到 0.6cm（0.24in）（图 12.3）。通过这种设计，电极具有 0.5cm（0.2in）的分辨率。然而，由于电极是垂直偏移的，因此阵列电极以该距离的一半进行水平采样，即 0.25cm（0.1in）（图 12.3）。在 1800ft/h 的测井速度下，每 0.25cm（0.1in）垂直采集电扣电流。因此，该仪器在极板和铰链的垂直和水平方向上都获得 0.1 英寸的矩阵数据［卡尺，磁力计和加速度计每 3.8cm（1.5in）采样一次］。

  In terms of electrical circuitry, the imaging tools are similar to the dipmeter tool in that a slowly varying, 'low frequency' EMEX signal, which is modulated for formation resistivity changes, is used to focus a rapidly changing, 'high frequency' signal from the pads themselves

(Fig.12.4). In practice, each conductive pad face is an equipotential surface, held at a constant potential relative to the return electrode, which is the upper section of the tool. The pad injects current into the formation and the current density across the pad is sampled by the button array (Fig.12.4). Changes in current density across the pads are caused by local formation resistivity variations.

在电路方面，成像工具类似于倾角仪，利用缓慢变化的"低频"EMEX 信号（根据地层电阻率变化进行调制）聚焦来自极板本身的快速变化的"高频"信号（图 12.4）。实际上，每个导电极板都是等电位体，相对于仪器上部的回路电极保持恒定电位。电扣电流注入地层，通过该电扣阵列对该极板的电流密度进行采样（图 12.4）。电流密度的变化是由局部地层电阻率的变化引起的。

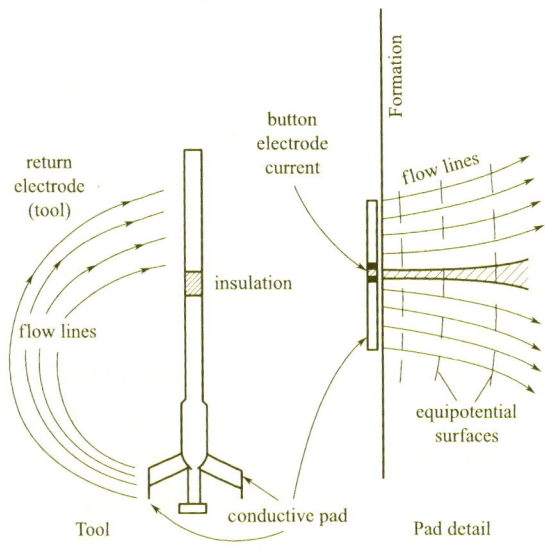

Fig.12.4　Electrical flow characteristics of an electrical imaging tool (based on the FMI of Schlumberger)
(from Schlumberger, 1994)
图 12.4　电成像仪器的电流特性（基于斯伦贝谢 FMI）（据 Schlumberger, 1994）

12.3　Electrical Image Sedimentary Interpretation
　　　电成像测井沉积解释

From a sedimentary and sedimentological point of view, electrical images are used to identify sedimentary structures and features, measure sedimentary orientation and give detailed information on lithology, texture and sedimentary facies and sequences.

从沉积学的角度来看，电成像主要用于识别沉积结构和特征、判断沉积地层的倾向，并提供有关岩性、结构和沉积相和沉积序列的详细信息。

The sedimentary interpretation of electrical image logs tends to follow routines similar to those used in a purely sedimentological analysis, building up through lithology, texture and sedimentary structures to facies and eventually sequences. With the image logs this tends to consist of: feature identification (dip and azimuth measurement with classification) and refinements to lithological interpretations (recognition of image facies and sequences). These aspects are broadly described below.

电成像测井的沉积解释与常规沉积学分析中使用的方法类似，通过岩相、结构和沉积构造建立沉积相和最终的沉积序列。对于成像测井，这往往包括：特征识别（倾角和方位角的分类测量）和岩性解释细化（识别图像相和序列）。具体分析如下：

12.3.1 Feature Identification and Dip and Azimuth Measurement
沉积特征识别和倾角和方位角的测量

In sedimentary image log interpretation, some images are instantly identifiable, some require additional log information and some require calibration with core to be recognized (Table 12.1). For example, foresets can usually be recognized from image characteristics alone, they show fine but faint lamination and variable dip angles (Fig.12.5). The internal structures of ripples, however, are generally beyond the resolution of the tool but ripple bedded facies once calibrated to core, may be recognized outside cored intervals. Finally, without cores it has been found impossible to differentiate between pebbles, mud clasts, concretions and bioturbations. Core calibration is an important aspect of feature identification.

在成像测井解释中，有的图像可立即识别，有的图像需要结合其他测井信息，有的图像需要岩心标定才能识别（表 12.1）。例如，仅从图像特征就可识别出前积层，它们显示出细微的层叠和变化的倾角（图 12.5）。然而，纹层的内部结构通常超出仪器的分辨率，但是一旦利用岩心进行校正，就可以在岩心层段之外被识别出来。最后，如果没有岩心标定，就无法区分砾岩、泥质碎屑、结核和生物扰动构造。因此，岩心标定是沉积特征识别的一个重要方面。

Table 12.1 Grades of image in interpretation (modified from Serra, 1989; Salimulla and Stow, 1992)

	Tectonic	Sedimentary	Diagenetic
Grade 1 Self evident	structural dip, fractures, Folds	bedding surfaces, laminations, cross-bedding, grading, erosional surfaces, deformation features, lithology changes	stylolites (high amplitude peaks)
Grade 2 ambiguous	faults	cobbles, pebbles, breccia, detrital shale, ripples, bioturbation, grain size	nodular concretions, chert, vugs, sulphide/sulphate crystals
Grade 3 Needs core	small fractures, horizontal fractures	bioturbation, thin lamination; limestone textures	stylolites (low amplitude peaks)

表 12.1 解释图像的等级（据 Serra，1989；Salimulla 和 Stow，1992 有修改）

	构造	沉积	成岩
一级 不证自明的	构造倾角； 裂缝； 褶皱	层理面， 纹层， 交错层理， 粒序层理， 侵蚀面， 变形特征， 岩性变化	缝合面 （高振幅峰值）
二级 有歧义的	断层	砾岩，角砾岩，碎屑泥岩，波纹，生物扰动，粒度大小	结节性结核，燧石条带，孔洞，硫化物/硫酸盐晶体
三级需岩心标定的	微裂缝； 水平裂缝	生物扰动， 薄纹层， 石灰岩结构	缝合面 （低振幅峰值）

Beyond simple identification, the image logs allow the measurement of sedimentary structure orientation using the workstation. For these dip and azimuth data to be of most use, the feature measured must be identified as foreset, sand bed, shale lamina, concretion, and so on. The classification will be used for subsequent filtering and, for example, foresets will be extracted to provide palaeocurrent directions. The identification of the causal features is, of course, subject to the difficulties outlined in the previous paragraph, so that any classification must be sufficiently robust to account for surfaces positively recognized, such as foresets, to those vaguely recognized such as ripple bedding and also unrecognized features. A numerical quality rating may be included from certain to doubtful.

除了简单的图像识别外，成像测井还可用工作站识别沉积构造方位。要使倾角和方位角数据发挥最大作用，必须将测量的特征识别为前积层、砂岩层理、泥质纹层、结核等。该分类将用于后续的解释，例如前积层可以指示古水流方向。当然，这些沉积特征的识别受到前期建立的解释模型的影响，因此任何分类解释模型必须足够稳健，以解释如前积层那般能明确识别的表象，以及如波痕层理那般模糊识别甚至是无法识别特征的表象。数值预测质量评价范围可以从确定到难以预测。

As work progresses on an image log, so a more and more detailed picture is built up. For example, orientation data may allow an interval to be identified as deposited in lateral accretion surfaces: mottled images identified as debris flows and so on.

随着成像测井技术的不断发展，图像解释方法也越来越精细。例如，方位数据中存在的间隔可以认为是侧向加积的表面，斑状图像被识别为碎屑流等。

12.3.2 Lithology
岩性

Lithological information will be needed at an early stage of image interpretation outside cored intervals. Many sedimentary features have lithological associations and electrical logs are not primary lithology indicators. Lithological information must come from other sources, such as the neutron-density, gamma ray logs and drill cuttings. However, the image logs provide very detailed textural information, can show thin beds and give accurate bed boundaries and so can be used to refine a routine lithological interpretation. For example, a sand interval may be recognized on the standard logs. Using the images a basal erosion surface can be identified and the fact that the upper interval is interbedded sands and shales rather than gradational (Fig.12.6).

对取心段之外层段进行早期成像解释时，需要岩性信息。许多沉积特征与岩性相关，而电测井不提示主要的岩性指标。岩性信息必须由来自其他数据源，例如中子密度、伽马测井和岩屑资料等。然而，成像测井可以提供非常详细的结构信息，可以显示薄层并给出准确的层边界，因此可用于常规岩性解释的补充和改进。例如，可以利用常规测井曲线识别出砂层。利用这些图像，可以识别出基底冲刷面，以及其上的砂泥岩互层（图 12.6）。

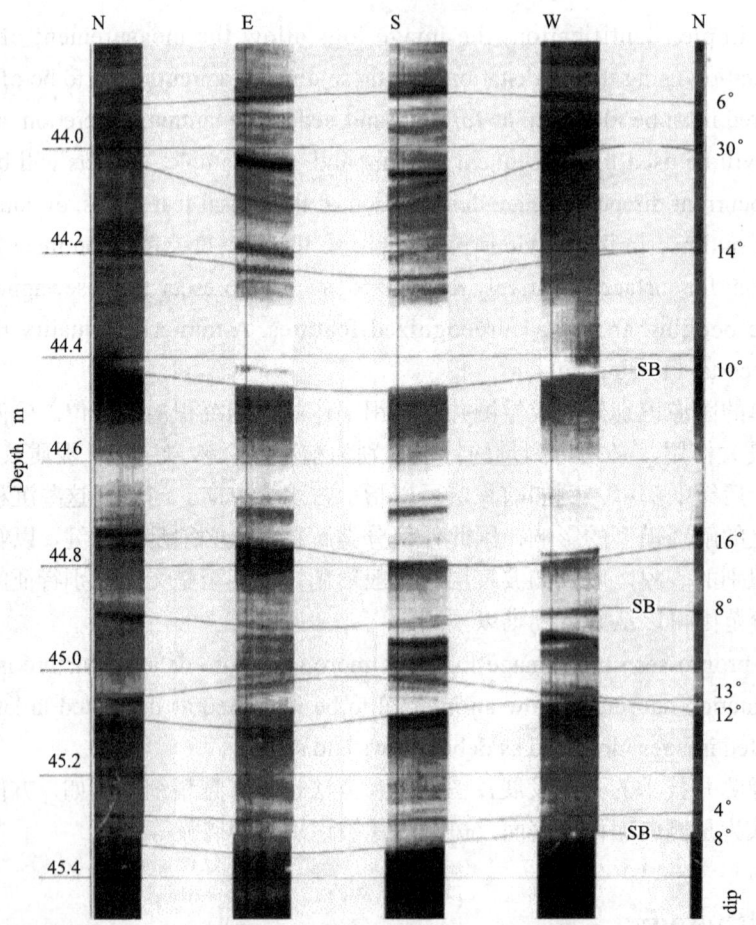

Fig.12.5　Cross-bedding in electrical images (from Schlumberger, 1994)

Good, slightly irregular bedding with moderate dip angles (15°～35°) in sandstone are typical.

SB = set boundary (high resistivity is dark, Schlumberger FMS tool)

图 12.5　成像测井图像中的交错层理（据 Schlumberger, 1994）

在砂岩中具有一定倾角（15°～35°），略微不规则的层理是典型特征。SB 为设定边界

（暗色为低电阻率，Schlumberger FMS 仪器）

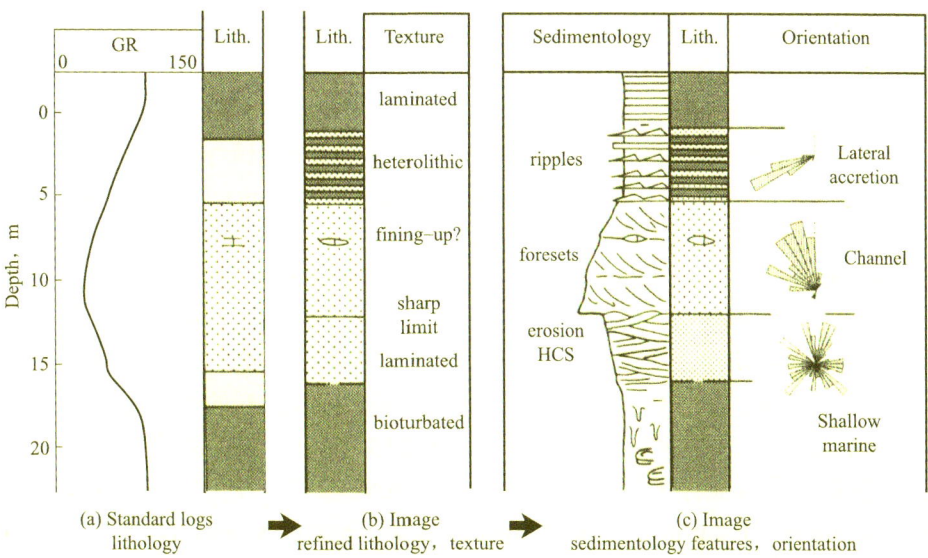

Fig.12.6　Technique for interpreting an image derived grain size, sedimentology and orientation using both the standard logs and the electrical image logs (from Malcolm Rider, 2002)

(a) Lithology interpreted from the standard logs. (b) Lithological boundaries and thin beds refined using the images. (c) Sedimentary structures interpreted from the image characteristics; notional grain size interpreted from the standard logs refined using the images; orientations from image picking

图 12.6　使用常规测井和成像测井图像联合解释地层粒度，沉积特征和方位（据 Malcolm Rider, 2002 ）
(a) 从常规测井解释岩性。(b) 用成像测井分辨岩性边界和薄层。
（c）从图像特征解释沉积构造，利用图像结合常规测井解释粒度、构造方位

The ability of the image logs to detect much thinner beds than the standard logs is a very significant contribution to lithological analysis. For work on lithology, statically normalized images can be used along with the standard open hole logs (and core). The image information can be extracted and transferred to a standard log scale, say 1 ∶ 200, or a standard log plot for reservoir description at a 1 ∶ 50 scale.

成像测井能够识别常规测井无法识别的薄层，这对岩性分析而言是一个非常重要的贡献。在岩性解释工作中，静态标准化图像可以与标准裸眼井测井（和岩心）组合使用。图像信息可以提取并对应到 1 ∶ 200 的标准测井图件或 1 ∶ 50 的标准储层解释成果图上。

12.3.3　Orientation Data, Output and Hardcopy Plots
方位数据，输出和硬拷贝图

The dip and azimuth data that are created from the image log analysis are normally extracted and treated simply as directional data in the same way as for dipmeter measurements. Image log data may be treated in exactly the same manner, but the quality of the information is much better.

从成像测井分析中得到的倾角和方位角数据通常被提取并简单地作为方位数据处理，其方式与倾角测井仪测量相同。可以以完全相同的方式处理成像测井数据，但信息的质量要好得多。

In a final interpretation, the huge amount of data produced by the image logs must be reduced and synthesized for use in routine work by non-image specialists. The basic output is typically a hard copy colour plot at 1 : 5 or 1 : 10 vertical scale, the chosen sine wave measurements being annotated with the dip and azimuth figures and the interpreted or observed causal features noted (Fig.12.5). A 1 : 5 scale log may be made approximately 1 : 1, by choosing the correct plot width (it varies with hole size), but since there is geometric distortion in the type of projection used, a 1 : 1 scale for hard copy is not always necessary.

在最终成像测井解释中，必须对成像测井产生的巨大数据进行筛减和组合，以供非图像专家在日常工作中使用。基本输出通常是垂直比例为 1 : 5 或 1 : 10 的硬拷贝彩图，所选正弦波测量值用倾角和方位角加以注释，并注明解释或观察到的地质特征（图 12.5）。通过选择正确的绘图宽度（随井眼尺寸而变化），深度比例为 1 : 5 的测井图像大约为 1 : 1，但由于所使用的投影类型存在几何失真，对于硬拷贝来说，1 : 1 的比例并不总是必要的。

Beyond the detailed print-out, a summary log of the data is essential, at 1 : 200 scale or the same scale as is used to display reservoir detail. Image interpretation and recognition is impossible at this scale but if a statically normalized image log is used, annotated with both a lithology column and a sedimentary structure column, the document is usable by non specialists and can include most of the features interpreted including sedimentary orientation.

除了详细的测井输出外，以 1 : 200 或与显示储层详细信息相同的比例的成像测井的汇总数据是必不可少的。在这种规模下，图像解释和识别是不可能的，但如果使用静态标准化成像测井，并使用岩性剖面和沉积构造剖面进行注释，其结果就可以被非图像专家使用，并且可以用于解释沉积等大多数特征。

12.4 Electrical Image Structural Interpretation
电成像测井构造解释

The first, simple, basic objective in the structural analysis of images is to recognize and measure an accurate structural dip and recognize unconformities, even disconformities. But objectives normally go far beyond this and the recognition and measurement of fractures, faults and eventually slumps are attempted.

图像构造分析的第一个简单基本目标就是识别和测量准确的地层沉积构造的倾角，及识别不整合面，甚至是假整合面。但目标通常远不止于此，还能用于识别和测量裂缝、断层，甚至是滑塌构造。

12.4.1 Structural Dip and Unconformities
构造倾角和不整合面

Measurement of dip from image logs tends to give values which are very variable and influenced by sedimentary features. Not every possible feature will be measured but an interpreter will take quite a high density of readings especially where values vary. This will favour sedimentary dips and features such as concretions, which stand out electrically but do not give a structural dip and azimuth values.

受沉积特征影响，成像测井测量的倾角值往往变化很大。不是每一个可能的构造特征都能被测量到，但是解释人员会对倾角值变化的层段选择高密度读数，这将有利于沉积倾角和结核等特征的解释，其电性特征往往是突变的，而且无法给出倾角和方位角值。

To find a structural dip, orientation data are extracted from the image interpretation and zoned in the same way as for dipmeter data. However, because of the dominant sedimentary influence, the data will show a very wide spread and often high dip angles (Fig.12.7). To reduce this, the image information must be filtered: only shale dips should be used for structural dip. However, such is the accuracy of the image dip and azimuth measurement that thin shale sections should be avoided as even these show a wide scatter, often as a result of dips from concretions and cemented layers. If thick shale intervals are chosen, a good structural dip can be obtained.

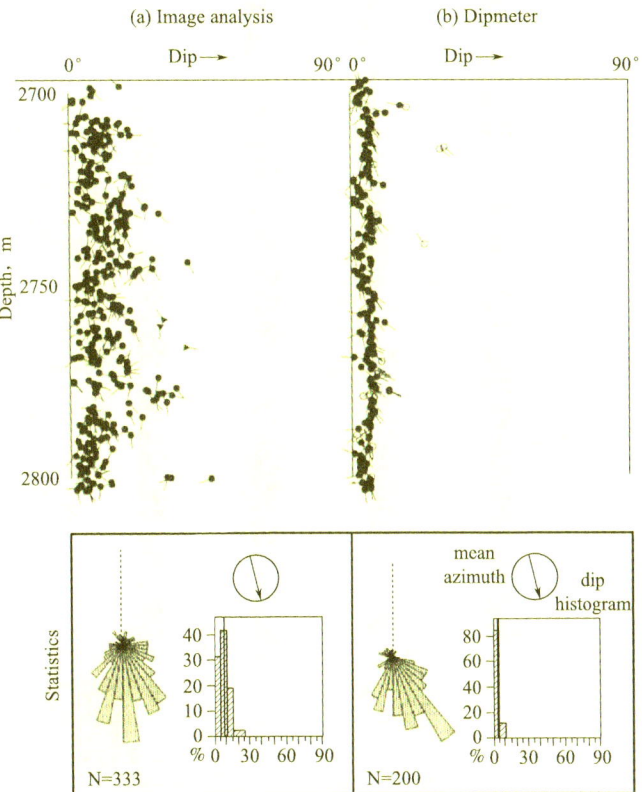

Fig.12.7 Comparison of the orientation data derived from image interpretation (a) and a standard dipmeter processing (b) (from Malcolm Rider, 2002)

The image data show a wider spread reflecting greater detection of sedimentary features. Dipmeter processing parameters: 1.0m correlation interval, step 0.5m, search angle 60°. The dipmeter processing is used for structural analysis

图 12.7 从图像解释（a）和标准倾角测井处理（b）得到的方向数据的比较（据 Malcolm Rider, 2002）

图像数据显示更分散的范围，反映了更多的沉积特征检测。Dipmeter 处理参数：1.0m 相关间隔，步长 0.5m，搜索角 60°。倾角测井处理用于构造分析为了找到构造倾角，在图像解释中提取方位数据，并以与倾角测量数据相同的方式进行展示。然而，由于沉积特征的影响，数据非常离散且往往显示出高倾角（图12.7）。为了减少这种情况，必须过滤图像信息：只有页岩倾角才能用于构造倾角分析。然而，由于图像倾角和方位角测量的准确性，应该避免薄层页岩段，这可能是因为结核和胶结层的倾斜，即使是薄层页岩段，也显示出广泛的分散。如果选择厚页岩层段，则可以获得较好的构造倾角。

A unique element of the interpretation for unconformities and disconformities with the image logs, is that the surface itself can be examined. The actual level of an unconformity can be examined for diagenetic effects, abrupt changes in image facies and biological activity as well as the angular change (Fig.12.8). Such details are also helpful in sequence stratigraphic analysis, as image features around important stratigraphic surfaces are often very distinctive.

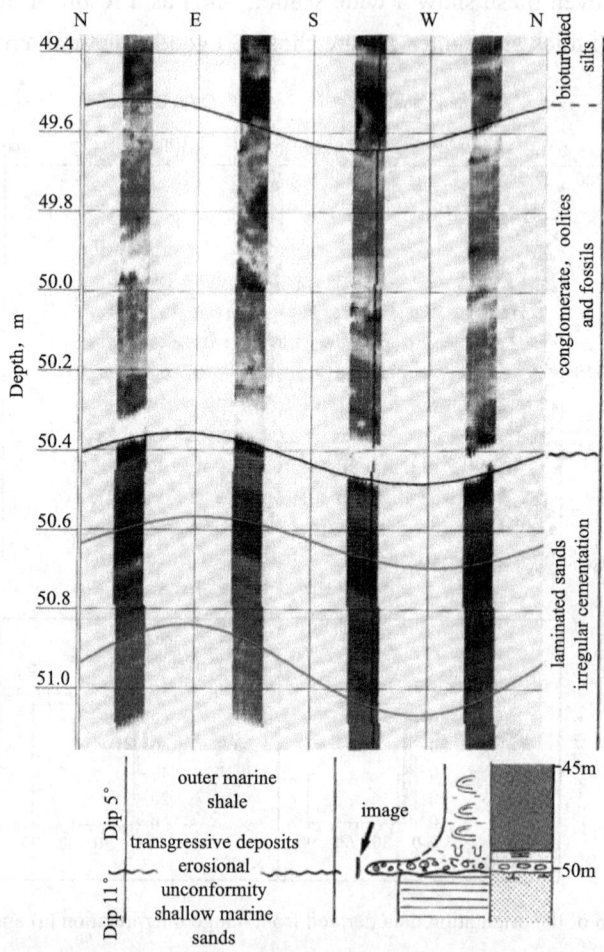

Fig.12.8　Electrical image of an unconformity and covering transgressive lag. (from Schlumberger, 1994)
The unconformity is seen as a sharp surface on the image with cementation below. The transgressive lag gives a speckled image although permeability is suggested by the color (cored interval, high resistivity is dark, Schlumberger FMS tool)

图 12.8　不整合面的电成像图像和覆盖的海进滞留沉积（据 Schlumberger，1994）
不整合面被视为图像上的高亮度层面，下面是胶结物沉积。海进滞留沉积显示为斑点图像，渗透率可以由颜色暗示得到（取心井段，高电阻率为暗的，Schlumberger FMS 仪器）

用成像测井解释不整合和假整合的一个独特要素是，层面本身就是可识别的。不整合面的实际特征可以通过成岩作用、像相突变、生物活动以及地层角度变化来解释（图 12.8）。这些细节也有助于层序地层分析，因为重要地层表面周围的图像特征通常非常独特。

12.4.2 Fractures and Faults
裂缝和断层

The detection of fractures and eventually faults is a fundamental objective of the image logs, traditionally more so for the acoustic images than for the electrical images. Fractures are never satisfactorily cored so that to be able to see them in situ using the image logs, and to measure their attitude accurately. However, frequently there is difficulty in recognizing fractures and certainly in recognizing faults (Table 12.2). The difficulty with fractures depends very much on the sequence and lithology. For example, in sand-shale sequences, sedimentary responses tend to dominate while in carbonates, fractures are often more easily identified.

裂缝和断层的识别是成像测井的基本目标，传统上声波成像比电成像更重要。由于裂缝取心困难，因此使用成像测井在地层原位观察，并准确分析裂缝的形态。但是，在实际情况中裂缝和断层常常难以识别（表 12.2）。识别裂缝的困难在很大程度上取决于地层层序和岩性。例如，在砂泥岩层序中，沉积响应往往占主导地位，而在碳酸盐岩中，裂缝往往更容易识别。

Table 12.2 Some simple test parameters for fracture identification

Surface characteristics	Image characteristics
Sharp surface at an angle to the sedimentary bedding	Images different on either side of surface, visible shift of bedding across surface
Irregular, discontinuous surface at an angle to sedimentary bedding	Images continuous or slightly displaced across the surface
Bedding parallel surface	Images different on either side of surface, visible shift of bedding across surface(maybe a structural change or sedimentary)
Natural fractures	Drilling induced fractures
Cementation evident	Parallel to borehole axis
Shift in bedding	Parallel to axis in deviated hole
Same geometry in core and image	-One side of borehole only -Strike normal to breakouts Sh_{min}, parallel to Sh_{max}

表 12.2 一些简单的裂缝识别测试参数

表面特性	图像特征
平整的层面与沉积层有一定角度	表面两侧的图像不同，在层理表面有偏移
不规则、不连续的层面与沉积层成一定角度	图像表面连续或有略微偏移
与层理表面平行	表面两侧的图像不同，层间可见的层理偏移（可能是结构变化或沉积）

续表

天然裂缝	人工裂缝
胶结明显	平行于井眼轴线
层理位移	平行于斜井轴线
图像和中心的几何形状相同	仅位于钻孔一侧 走向穿过 Sh_{min} 平行于 Sh_{max}

To be seen on the images, fractures must show some form of electrical contrast, that is be open and filled with mud (Fig.12.9), be cemented, or have associated displacement. Closed fractures will not be seen. Or show some geometrical relationship such as high dip in a sequence with low structural dip. Clearly, measured fractures need to be classified: as cemented, induced and so on, so that they can be separated in subsequent orientation analysis. Most interpreters will provide themselves with a conscious or unconscious flow path for fracture recognition. As always, it is necessary to begin with cored intervals and fractures seen on cores may be explored on the images (Fig.12.10). However, drilling induced fractures are common in cores and although they have typical characteristics, separating them from natural fractures is not always easy. Beyond cores, a series of test parameters may be applied to identify fractures (Table 12.2) but care must be taken to account for the physical effects that drilling has on them.

为了在图像上看到裂缝，必须显示出某种形式的电性特征对比，即裂缝张开并充满钻井液（图12.9）、裂缝胶结或发生相应的位移，闭合的裂缝一般识别不到。或者显示出某种几何关系，如低倾角地层中的高角度裂缝。显然，需要对测量的裂缝进行分类，如胶结裂缝、诱导裂缝等，以便在后续的定向分析中进行区分。大多数解释人员会为裂缝识别提供有意识或无意识的分析路径。通常是从取心段开始，在成像测井图像上分析岩心上看到的裂缝（图12.10）。然而，钻井引起的裂缝在岩心中很常见，虽然它们具有典型特征，但将它们与天然裂缝分开并不容易。除岩心外，还可以应用一系列测试参数来识别裂缝（表12.2），但必须考虑钻井对其产生的物理影响。

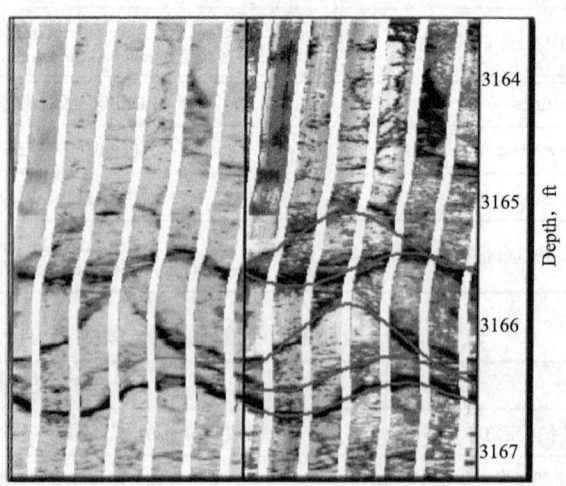

Fig.12.9　Electrical image of a open fracture in a carbonate gainstone (Baker Hughes STAR tool)
图 12.9　碳酸盐岩张开裂缝的电成像图像（贝克休斯 STAR 仪器）

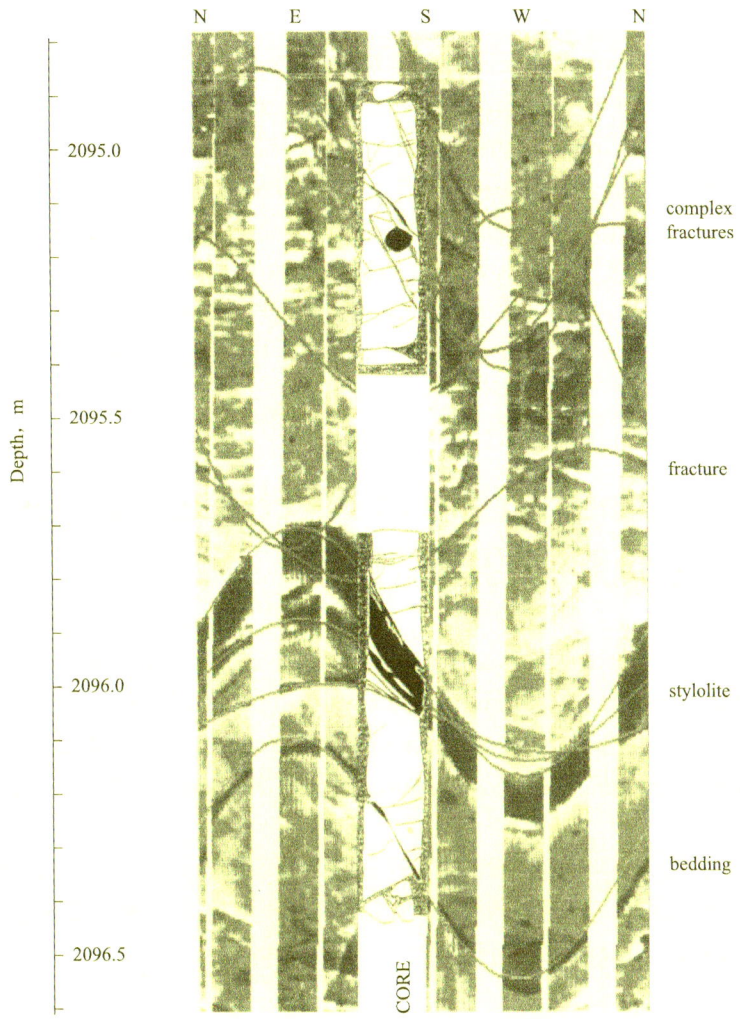

Fig.12.10 Electrical image of extensively fractured chalk with stylolites (cored section, high resistivity light colours, Schlumberger FMI tool, two passes) (from Malcolm Rider, 2002)

图 12.10 带有缝合线的白垩系破碎地层的电成像测井图像（取心井段，高电阻率浅色，斯伦贝谢 FMI 工具，两次通过）（据 Malcolm Rider,2002 ）

Image logs are generally too detailed to allow the identification of faults on images alone, although cases do exist. Examination of any outcrop will soon show that actual fault planes are more chaotic the closer you get. Stand away from a fault and it is obvious: stand close to and order disappears. For fault identification, a dipmeter processed to bring out structural information is necessary. This will allow intervals where faulting is possible to be identified. These intervals may then be examined with the detail of the image log.

成像测井通常信息量过于详细，无法单独识别断层，尽管确实存在这种情况。通过对任何露头断层的观察就会很快发现，你离得越近，断层面的发现就越困难。当远离断层面时，断层面会很明显，当接近时又消失了。对于断层识别，必须使用地层倾角测量仪分析地层结构信息，从而够识别出现断层的层段，然后再用成像测井的图像细节分析这些层段。

Details in fault zones are quite variable. Certain faults are associated with an increase in fracture intensity but frequently there is a change in texture. Within faults with considerable throw, these textures tend towards shear fabrics or chaotic breccias. Image logs tend to be very difficult to interpret in such zones especially if several lithologies are involved. Moreover, there is a tendency for fault zones to cave so that images are of poor quality.

断层带的细节变化很大。某些断层与断裂强度的增加有关，但经常与结构变化有关。在具有大位移的断层中，这些结构倾向于剪切位移或断层角砾岩。在这些区域，成像测井往往很难解释断层，特别是如果涉及多种岩性时。此外，当存在断层带破裂时，一般测得图像质量都很差。

12.5 Quantitative Uses of Electrical Images
电成像测井的定量评价

Much of the interpretation on image logs is qualitative. But there is a need and the possibility for quantitative methods. The quantitative analysis of images should use the two dimensional aspects of the logs and not simply be modifications of the one dimensional, standard log analysis. Some of the more interesting methods proposed so far with some rather limited examples are given below.

成像测井的大部分解释都是定性的，但也有定量解释的必要和可行性。图像的定量分析应该基于测井的二维信息，而不是简单地完善一维标准测井分析。下面给出了迄今为止提出的一些有效的方法和极少数的例子。

12.5.1 Bed Thickness
地层厚度

Electrical images can be used to quantify thin beds. The fine resolution of the electrical images (see resolution) allows beds down to at least 5cm (2in) to be accurately evaluated. Beds down to 1.0cm (0.4in) can be detected but from about 2.5cm (1in), bed thickness is apparently exaggerated. However, this evaluation is simply in terms of sand/shale and similar to the standard thin bed analysis using dipmeter curves. It is a one dimensional analysis albeit at a scale finer than for the standard logs and images lend themselves to two dimensional analysis.

电成像图像可用于量化薄层厚度。电成像图像的精细分辨率（实际分辨率）可以准确地识别并计算至少5cm（2in）的地层。1.0cm（0.4in）到2.5cm（1in）的地层被识别检测到，但是地层厚度明显被夸大了。然而，这个预测和计算仅仅针对砂泥岩，类似于使用倾角测量仪曲线的标准薄层分析。该方法是一种一维分析，尽管其尺度比标准测井和图像更适合二维分析。

12.5.2 Porosity and Permeability
孔隙度和渗透性计算

A quantitative, two dimensional approach is used by Schlumberger in the analysis of carbonate textures. Carbonate textures lend themselves to electrical image analysis because pores and vugs can be large and have large electrical contrast to the matrix. The method proposed by Schlumberger is based on an analysis of the images themselves, either leading to new images of selected features or new summary data.

斯伦贝谢使用定量二维方法分析碳酸盐岩结构。碳酸盐结构中的孔洞可用于电成像图像分析，因为孔隙和孔洞可能很大，与岩石骨架有很大的电性对比度。斯伦贝谢提出的方法可以基于图像本身分析，也可以基于所选图像与其他数据得到新图像的分析。

Without descending into details, images are analyzed to identify individual vugs, to define their size and their shape from which a porosity can be inferred. That is, the large scale reservoir behavior is built up by adding together individually observed features. The method may be used in cases where conductivity differences are large, such as in some conglomerates (the inverse case to vugs). This method of analysis is the antithesis of standard log analysis where elements are 'bulked' or an overall effect is analyzed, not the individual contributions. The success of this form of image analysis method depends on formation characteristics and the size of the individual features. However, two dimensional analysis leading to predictions in three dimensions is the direction image quantification should take.

在不深入细节的情况下，通过分析图像可以识别地层的各个孔洞，确定它们的尺寸和形状，并而推断孔隙度。也就是说，通过将单独观察到的图像特征累加在一起，建立了大规模的储层特征。该方法可用于电导率差异较大的情况，例如在一些大型砾岩中（与孔洞相反）。这种分析方法与标准测井分析相反，其强调的是因素"聚集"或整体效应分析，而不是个体分析。这种形式的图像分析方法的成功与否取决于地层总体特征和个体特征的大小。然而，二维分析导致三维预测是图像量化发展的方向。

Permeability has yet to be derived quantitatively from images. However, empirical comparisons may be made in two ways and quantification may be possible. The first is by using the mini-permeameter. If sufficient mini-permeameter readings are taken, images can be produced of permeability distribution across core slabs. These can then be compared directly to the electrical images having relatively similar sampling densities. A different method of comparison is to use electrical images of core slabs. These images can be effectively explored under laboratory conditions.

渗透率尚难以通过图像分析定量得出。然而，可以用两种经验对比的方式进行量化。第一种是使用小型渗透率仪。如果获得足够多的小型渗透率读数，则可以得到岩心的渗透率分布图像。然后可以直接将这些图像与具有相对相似采样密度的电成像图像进行比较。另一种比较方法是直接使用岩心的电成像图像，可以在实验室条件下有效分析和对比。

12.5.3 Fractures
裂缝

Fracture porosity and aperture have been evaluated quantitatively using the FMS by Schlumberger. The technique used was to model the FMS tool response to open fractures, that is open apertures filled with conductive mud, taking account of mud and formation conditions. Conductive anomalies were then statistically extracted from the image log and compared to the model to provide the fracture width. Output can be provided as an azimuthal plot (like the images themselves) with color coded widths, a maximum fracture width and a fracture porosity (/inch or /feet). By comparison with other methods and with core analysis, the calculations showed some success.

使用斯伦贝谢的 FMS 仪器图像可以定量评估裂缝孔隙度和孔径。该技术用于模拟 FMS 仪器对张开裂缝充填泥质、钻井液和地层条件等情况下的响应特征。然后从成像测井图像中统计提取导电异常，并与模型进行比较，以提供裂缝宽度。输出结果可以是带有颜色编码宽度、最大裂缝宽度和裂缝孔隙度（每英寸或每英尺）的方位图（如成像测井图像本身）。通过与其他方法和岩心分析的比较，表明该方法是成功的。

Exercises
课后练习

12.1 Try to use FMI images to analyze sedimentary features.

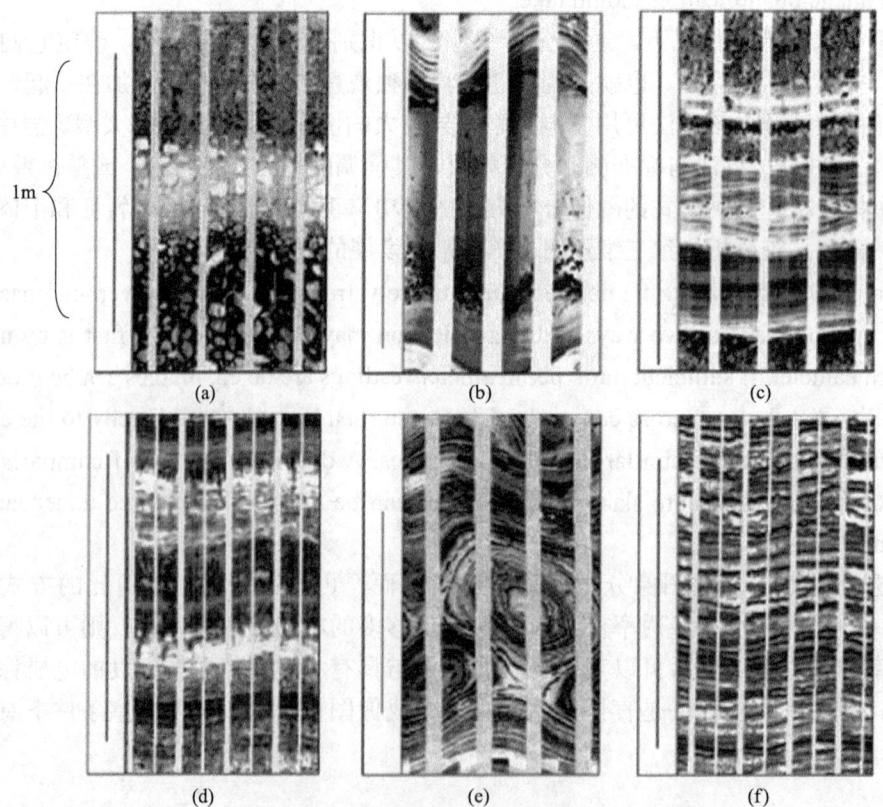

12.2 Try to use FMI images to analyze fracture types.

References/ 参考文献

Adams J et al. ,1989. Advances in log interpretation in oil-base mud. Oilfield Rev. , 1(2):22-38.

Adamson A W, 1979. A textbook of physical chemistry. 2nd ed. New York: Academic Press: 291.

Aguilera M S, Aguilera R, 2003. Improved models for petrophysical analysis of dual porosity reservoirs. Petrophysics, 44(1):21-35.

Alpin L M, 1939.The method of the electric logging in the borehole with casing. U.S.S.R. Patent No 56026PROBLEMS 147.

Anderson B, Chang S K, 1982. Synthetic induction logs by the finite element method. The Log Analyst, 23(6):17-26.

Anderson B, Chang S K, 1983. Synthetic deep propagation tool: response by finite element method. Trans SPWLA 24th Annual Logging Symposium, paper T.

Anderson B, 1986. The analysis of some unsolved induction interpretation problems using computer modeling. The Log Analyst, 27(5):60-73.

Anderson B, Barber T D, 1997. Induction logging. Houston: Schlumberger.

Anderson B, 2001. Modeling and inversion methods for the interpretation of resistivity logging tool response. Delft: DUP Science.

Arps J J, 1967. Inductive resistivity guard logging apparatus including toroidal coils mounted in a conductive stem. US patent No 3,305,771.

Archie G E, 1942. The electrical resistivity log as an aid in determining some reservoir characteristics. Pet. Trans. AIME, 146:54-62.

Asquith G B, Gibson C R, 1982. Basic well log analysis for geologists. Tulsa: AAPG.

Asquith G B, Krygowski D, Gibson C R, 2004. Basic well log analysis. Tulsa: American Association of Petroleum Geologists.

Barber T, Anderson B, Mowatt G, 1995. Using inductions to identify magnetic formations and to determine relative magnetic susceptibility and dielectric constant. The Log Analyst, 36(4):16-26.

Barber T, Vandermeer W, Flanagan W, 1989. Method for determining induction sonde error. US Patent No 4,800,496.

Benimeli D, Levesque C, Rouault G, et al. , 2002. A new technique for faster resistivity measurements in cased holes. Trans SPWLA 43rd Annual Logging Symposium, paper K.

Beguin P, Benimeli D, Boyd A, et al. , 2000. Recent progress on formation resistivity measurement through casing. Trans SPWLA 41st Annual Logging Symposium, paper CC.

Berg C R, 1996. Effective-medium resistivity models for calculating water saturation in shaly sands. The Log Analyst, 37 (3):16-28.

Bonner S, Bagersh A, Clark B, et al. , 1994. A new generation of electrode resistivity measurements for formation evaluation while drilling. Trans SPWLA 35th Annual Logging Symposium, paper OO.

Bussian A E, 1983. Electrical conductance in a porous medium. Geophysics, 48(9):1258-1268.

Clavier C, Coates G, Dumanoir J, 1984. Theoretical and experimental basis for the dual water model for interpretation of shaly sands. SPE J. , April:153-168.

Chemali R, Gianzero S, Strickland R, 1983. The shoulder bed effect on the dual laterolog and its variation with the resistivity of the borehole fluid. Trans SPWLA 24th Annual Logging Symposium, paper UU.

Chemali R, Gianzero S, Su S M, 1987. The effect of shale anisotropy on focused resistivity devices. Trans SPWLA Annual Logging Symposium, paper H.

Cheung P, et al. , 2002. A clear picture in oil-base muds. Oilfield Rev. , winter 2001/2002:2-27.

Crary S, Smith D, 1990. The use of electromagnetic modeling to validate environmental corrections for the dual laterolog. Trans SPWLA 31st Annual Logging Symposium, paper C.

Coates G R, Xiao L, Prammer M G, 1999. NMR logging: principles and applications. Houston: Haliburton Energy Services.

Davies D H, Faivre O, Gounot M T, et al. , 1992. Azimuthal resistivity imaging: a new generation laterolog. SPE, 24676.

Darling T, 2005. Well logging and formation evaluation. New York: Elsevier.

Dewan J T, 1983. Essentials of modern open-hole log interpretation. Tulsa: PennWell Publishing.

de Kuijper A, Sandor R K J, Hofman J P, et al. , 1995. Electrical conductivities in oil-bearing shaly sand accurately described with the SATORI saturation model. Trans SPWLA 36th Annual Logging Symposium, paper M.

Doll H G, 1949. Introduction to induction logging and application to wells drilled with oil base mud. Pet. Trans. AIME,1(6):148-162.

Doll H G, 1955. Electrical resistivity well logging method and apparatus. US Patent No 2712627.

Doveton J H, 1986. Log analysis of subsurface geology, concepts and computer methods. New York: Wiley.

Dresser Atlas, 1982. Well logging and interpretation techniques: the course for home study. Houston: Dresser Atlas Publication.

Eisenmann P, Gounot M T, Juchereau B, et al. , 1994. Improved R_{xo} measurements through semi-active focusing. The 69th SPE Annual Technical Conference and Exhibition, paper SPE 28437.

Ekstrom M P, Dahan C A, Chen M Y, et al. , 1986. Formation imaging with microelectrical scanning arrays. Trans SPWLA 27th AnnualLogging Symposium, paper BB.

Ellis D Y, 1987. Well logging for earth scientists. New York: Elsevier: 532p.

Ellis D Y, Singer J M, 2008. Well Logging for Earth Scientists, New York: Springer.

Evans H B, Brooks A G, Meisner J E, et al. , 1987. A focused current resistivity logging system for MWD. The 62nd SPE Annual Conference and Exhibition, Dallas, paper 16757.

Griffiths R, Smits J W, Faivre O, et al. , 1999. Better saturation from new array laterolog. Trans SPWLA 40th Annual Logging Symposium, paper DDD.

Gianzero S, Anderson B, 1982. A new look at skin effect. The Log Analyst, 23(1):20-34.

Gianzero S, Chemali R, Lin Y, et al. , 1985. A new resistivity tool for measurement while drilling. Trans SPWLA 26th Annual Logging Symposium, paper A.

Guyod H, 1944. Fundamental data for the interpretation of electric logs. Oil Weekly, 115(38): 21-27.

Hassan, M, Hossin, A, Combaz, A, 1976. Fundamentals of the differential gamma raylog interpretation technique. SPWLA 17th Ann. Symp. Trans. paper H:1-18.

Herrick D C, Kennedy W D, 1996. Electrical properties of rocks: effects of secondary porosity, laminations and thin beds. Trans SPWLA 37th Annual Logging Symposium, paper C.

Herrick D C, Kennedy W D, 1993. Electrical efficiency: a pore geometric model for the electrical properties of rocks. Trans SPWLA 34th Annual Logging Symposium, paper HH.

Hearst J R, Nelson P, 1985. Well logging for physical properties. New York: McGraw-Hill.

Hill H J, Milburn J D, 1956. Effect of clay and water salinity on electro-chemical behavior of reservoir rocks. Pet. Trans. AIME, 207:65-72.

Hodson G M, 1975. Some aspects of the geology of the middle Jurassic in the northern North Sea with particular reference to electro-physical logs.NPF Jurassic Northern N. Sea Symp. , Stavanger. Paper 16 :1-39.

Itskovitch G B, Mezzatesta A, Strack K M, Tabarovsky L, 1998. High-definition lateral log resistivity device: basic physics and resolution. Trans SPWLA 39th Annual Logging Symposium, paper V.

Jakosky J J, 1940. Exploration geophysics. Los Angeles: Times-Mirror Press.

Jackson M P A, Talbot C J, 1986. External shapes, strain rates and dynamics of salt structures. BGSA, 97:305-323.

Jorden J R, Campbell F L, 1984. Well logging II - electrical and acoustic logging. Dallas: SPE.

Keller G V, Frischknecht F C, 1966. Electrical methods in geophysical prospecting. Oxford: Pergamon Press.

Kennedy W D, Herrick D C, 2004. Conductivity anisotropy in shale-free sandstone. Petrophysics, 45(1):38-38.

Khokhar R W, Johnson W M, 1989. A deep laterolog for ultrathin formation evaluation.Trans SPWLA 30th Annual Logging Symposium, paper SS.

Leverett M C, 1939. Flow of oil-water mixtures through unconsolidated sands. Pet. Trans. AIME, 132:149-171.

Lest A M, 1982. Introduction to physical chemistry. New Jersey: Prentice-Hall.

Li Q, Rasmus J, Cannon D, 1999. A novel inversion method for the interpretation of a focused multisensor LWD laterolog resistivity tool. Trans SPWLA 40th Annual Logging Symposium, paper AAA.

Lofts J, Evans M, Pavlovic M, Dymmock S, 2003. New microresistivity imaging device for use in non-conductive and oil-based muds. Petrophysics, 44(5):317-327.

Luthi S, 2001. Geological well logs: their use in reservoir modeling. Berlin: Springer.

Lynch E J, 1962. Formation evaluation. New York: Harper & Row.

Martin M, Murray G H, Gillingham W J, 1938.Determination of the potential productivity of oil-bearing formations by resistivity measurements. Geophysics, 3:258-272.

Maurer H M, Hunziker J, 2000. Early results of through casing resistivity field tests. Trans SPWLA 41st Annual Logging Symposium, paper DD.

Maute R E, Lyle W D, Sprunt E S, 1992. Improved data-analysis method determines Archie parameters from core data. J. Pet. Tech. , January:103-107.

McFadzean, T B, 1973. Cross-plotting, a neglected technique in log analysis.SPWLA 14 Ann. Symp. Trans. paperY, 1-18.

Moran J H, 1982. Induction logging - geometrical factors with skin effect. The Log Analyst, 23(6):4-10.

Moran J H, Kunz K S, 1962. Basic theory of induction logging and application to study of two-coil sondes. Geophysics, 27(6): 829-858.

Owen J E, 1952. The resistivity of a fluid-filled porous body. Pet. Trans. AIME, 195:169-174.

Passey Q R, Creaney, S Kulla, et al. , 1990. A practical model for organic richness from porosity and resistivity logs. Bull. Am. Assoc. Petrol Geol. 74 (12), 1777-1794.

Pirson S J, 1977. Geologic well log analysis. Houston: Gulf Publishing.

Ransom, R.c, 1977. Methods based on density and neutron well logging responses to distinguish characteristics of shaly sandstone reservoir rock. Log Analyst, 18 (3): 47-63.

Revil A, Leroy P, 2004. Constitutive equations for ionic transport in porous shales. J. Geophys. Res. , 109(B3):B03208.

Revil A, Pezard P A, Darot M, 1997. Electrical conductivity, spontaneous potential and ionic diffusion in porous media. // Lovell M A, Harvey P K, Developments in petrophysics. London: Geological Society: 253-275.

Sen P N, Scala C, Cohen M H, 1981. A self-similar model for sedimentary rocks with application to the dielectric constant of fused glass beads. Geophysics, 46(5):781-795.

Serra O, 1984. Fundamentals of well-log interpretation. Amsterdam: Elsevier.

Serra O, 1985. Sedimentary environments from wireline logs. New York: Schlumberger.

Schmoker J W, Hester T C, 1983. Organic carbon in Bakken formation, United States portion of Williston Basin. Bull. Am. Assoc. Petrol Geol, 67(12); 2165-2174.

Schwartz L M, Kimminau S, 1987. Analysis of electrical conduction in the grain consolidation model. Geophysics, 52(10):1402-1411PROBLEMS 87.

Schlumberger, 1972. The Essentials of Log interpretation Practice. Houston: Schlumberger .

Schlumberger, 2005. Log interpretation charts. Houston: Schlumberger.

Schlumberger, 1970. Fundamentals of dipmeter interpretation. New York: Schlumberger.

Schlumberger, 1989. Log interpretation principles/applications. Houston: Schlumberger.

Schlumberger, 1994. FMI fullbore formation Microimager. Houston: Schlumberger Educational Services.

Serra O, 1989. Formation micro scanner image interpretation. Houston: Schlumberger Educational Services.

Smits J W, Benimeli D, Dubourg I, et al. , 1995. High resolution from a new laterolog with azimuthal imaging. The 70th SPE Annual Technical Conference and Exhibition, paper SPE 30584.

Smits J W, Dubourg I, Luling M G, et al. , 1998. Improved resistivity interpretation utilizing a new array laterolog tool and associated inversion processing. The 73rd SPE Annual Technical Conference and Exhibition, paper SPE 49328.

Smythe W R, 1950. Static and dynamic electricity. New York: McGraw-Hill.

Souhaite P, Misk A, Poupon A, 1975. R_t determination in the eastern hemisphere. Trans SPWLA 16th Annual Logging Symposium, paper LL.

Suau J, Grimaldi P, Poupon A, Souhaite P, 1972. The dual laterolog-R_{ox} tool. Presented at the 47th SPE Annual Technical Conference and Exhibition, paper SPE 4018122.

Sweeney S S, Jennings H Y, 1960. The electrical resistivity of preferentially water wet and preferentially oil wet carbonate rock. Prod. Mont. , 24(7): 29-32.

Tabanou J R, Rouault G F, Glowinski R, 1987. SP deconvolution and quantitative interpretation in shaly sands. Trans SPWLA 28th Annual Logging Symposium, paper SS.

Taherian M R, Habashy T M, Schroeder R J, et al. , 1995. Laboratory study of the spontaneous potential – experimental and modeling results. The Log Analyst, 36(5):34-48.

Tittman J, 1986. Geophysical well logging. Orlando: Academic Press.

Tixier, M P, 1967. Log evaluation of non-metallic mineral deposits. SPWLA 8th Ann. Symp. Trans. paper R: 1-22.

Trouiller J C, Dubourg I, 1994. A better deep laterolog compensated for Groningen and reference effects. Trans SPWLA 35th Annual Logging Symposium, paper VV.

Waxman M H, Smits L J M, 1968. Electrical conductivities in oil-bearing shaly sands. paper 1863-A.

Wong P Z, Koplik J, Tomanic J P. Conductivity and permeability of rocks. Phys. Rev. B., 30(11):6606-6614.

Winsauer W O, Shearin H M, Masson P H, et al., 1952. Resistivity of brine saturated sands in relation to pore geometry. AAPG Bull., 36:253-277.

Wyllie M R J, Rose W D, 1950. Some theoretical considerations related to the quantitative evaluation of the physical characteristics of reservoir rock from electrical log data. Pet. Trans. AIME, 189:105-118.

Zienkiewicz O C, 1971. The finite element method in engineering sciences. New York: McGraw-Hill.